KT-472-581

Java™ Network Programming

THE JAVA™ SERIES

Exploring Java™

Java™ Threads

Java™ Network Programming

Java™ Virtual Machine

Java™ AWT Reference

Java™ Language Reference

Java™ Fundamental Classes Reference

Database Programming with JDBC™ and Java™

Java™ Distributed Computing

Developing Java Beans™

Also from O'Reilly

Java™ in a Nutshell

Java™ in a Nutshell, Deluxe Edition

Java™ Examples in a Nutshell

Netscape IFC in a Nutshell

Java Network Programming

Elliotte Rusty Harold

O'REILLY™

Beijing · Cambridge · Köln · Paris · Sebastopol · Taipei · Tokyo

Java™ Network Programming
by Elliotte Rusty Harold

Copyright © 1997 O'Reilly & Associates, Inc. All rights reserved.
Printed in the United States of America.

Cover photo copyright © 1996 O'Reilly & Associates, Inc. All rights reserved.

Published by O'Reilly & Associates, Inc., 101 Morris Street, Sebastopol, CA 95472.

Editor: Mike Loukides

Production Editor: Nancy Wolfe Kotary

Printing History:

February 1997:   First Edition.

Nutshell Handbook, the Nutshell Handbook logo, and the O'Reilly logo are registered trademarks and The Java™ Series is a trademark of O'Reilly & Associates, Inc. Java™ and all Java-based trademarks and logos are trademarks or registered trademarks of Sun Microsystems, Inc., in the United States and other countries. O'Reilly & Associates, Inc., is independent of Sun Microsystems.

Many of the designations used by manufacturers and sellers to distinguish their products are claimed as trademarks. Where those designations appear in this book, and O'Reilly & Associates, Inc. was aware of a trademark claim, the designations have been printed in caps or initial caps.

While every precaution has been taken in the preparation of this book, the publisher assumes no responsibility for errors or omissions, or for damages resulting from the use of the information contained herein.

This book is printed on acid-free paper with 85% recycled content, 15% post-consumer waste. O'Reilly & Associates is committed to using paper with the highest recycled content available consistent with high quality.

ISBN: 1-56592-227-1   [4/99]

Table of Contents

Preface

Java as a Platform for Network Programs

Java's growth over the last couple of years has been nothing short of phenomenal. The only similar examples of such rapid growth are the Internet itself and the World Wide Web. Given Java's rapid rise to prominence, and the general interest in networking, it's a little surprising that network programming in Java™ is still so mysterious to many. But little exists in writing about network programming in Java. A few books cover some of the basics. Most of them get the advanced topics wrong, if indeed they cover advanced topics at all.

Network programming in Java does not need to be mysterious. In fact, writing network programs in Java is quite simple, as this book will show. Readers with previous experience in network programming in a UNIX, Winsock, or MacTCP environment should be pleasantly surprised at how much easier it is to write equivalent programs in Java. Because Java is a full general-purpose programming language, and comes with class libraries that incorporate well-thought-out interfaces to most network features, there is virtually nothing you can write in C that you can't write in Java. The biggest difference is that developing the program in Java will be much less work.

Unfortunately, all too many people think of Java as a language for writing cute web page animations; all too few have looked into Java's potential for developing new kinds of network applications. In this book, my goal is to enable you to push the borders of what's possible: to get you started investigating Java's capabilities as a platform for serious network programming. To do so, this book provides a general background in network fundamentals, as well as detailed discussions of Java's facilities for writing network programs. You'll learn how to write Java applets and applications that share data across the Internet for games, collaboration, updates, and more. You'll also get a behind-the-scenes look at HTTP, CGI, TCP/IP, and the other protocols which enable the Internet. When you finish this book you'll have the knowledge and the tools to create applications and applets that take full advantage of the Internet.

Organization of the Book

This book can be divided into five sections of three chapters each.

1. Chapters 1 through 3 review basic network concepts and the World Wide Web from the perspective of a programmer and a developer.

2. Chapters 4 through 6 explore Java's high-level classes for network access: InetAddress, URL, and Applet.

3. Chapters 7 through 9 discuss Java's low-level socket classes for network access: Socket, ServerSocket, DatagramPacket, and DatagramSocket.

4. Chapters 10 through 12 cover protocol and content handlers, concepts unique to Java that make it possible to write dynamically extensible software that automatically understands new protocols and new kinds of content.

5. Chapters 13 through 15 discuss things to come: multicast sockets, remote method invocation, and servlets.

Readers with no prior experience in network programming should begin with the first section. Readers who have written network programs, particularly web clients or servers, may begin in section 2, though you may find Chapters 2 and 3 useful for reference. All readers should read sections 2 and 3 more or less in order, as each chapter in these sections builds on the previous ones. Once you feel comfortable with the material in the first three sections, you may attack section 4 on content and protocol handlers, or any of the remaining chapters.

Who You Are

This book assumes you have a basic familiarity with the Java language and programming environment, in addition to object-oriented programming in general. This book does not attempt to be a basic language tutorial; if you need one, look at my earlier book, *Java Developer's Resource* (Prentice Hall), David Flanagan's *Java in a Nutshell* (O'Reilly), or Pat Niemeyer and Josh Peck's *Exploring Java* (O'Reilly). You should be thoroughly familiar with the syntax of the language. You should have written simple applications and applets. You should also be comfortable with the AWT, particularly Events, Components, Containers and Graphics. When you encounter a topic that requires a deeper understanding for network programming than is customary, for instance, Strings, StringBuffers, and Streams, we'll cover that topic as well, at least briefly.

You should also be an accomplished user of the Internet. I will assume you know how to ftp files and visit web sites. You should know what a URL is and how you locate one. You should know how to write simple HTML and be able to publish a home page that includes Java applets, though you do not need to be a super web designer. If you need to know more about HTML, look at *HTML: The Definitive Guide* by Chuck Musciano and Bill Kennedy (O'Reilly).

However, this book doesn't assume that you have prior experience with network programming. You should find that it's a good and complete introduction to networking concepts and network application development. I don't assume that you have a few thousand networking acronyms (TCP, UDP, SMTP, . . .) at the tip of your tongue. You'll learn what you need to know about these here. It's certainly possible that you could use this book as a general introduction to network programming with a socket-like interface, and then go on to learn WSA (the Windows Socket Architecture), and figure out how to write network applications in C++. But it's not clear why you would want to: as I said earlier, Java lets you write very sophisticated applications with ease.

Java Versions

I developed this book using release 1.0.2 of Java. The first documentation for Java 1.1 started appearing when I was close to finishing, and it looks like the final release of 1.1 will happen shortly after this book appears in stores. However, I have covered a number of 1.1 topics, including:

- Changes to the Socket classes. The differences between 1.0.2 and 1.1 are relatively few, and easy to understand. I don't tell you how to write a SocketImpl, but I do tell you how to set socket options, and use other new features of the Socket classes.

- Multicasting. Multicasting was actually available in Java 1.0; the most significant change in 1.1 is that the MulticastSocket class moves from the sun.net packages to java.net, where it belongs.

- Remote Method Invocation (RMI). Alpha versions of RMI have been kicking around since late spring of 1996. Version 1.1 will integrate RMI into Java's core classes. Because the alpha versions have been available for so long, it's unlikely that they will change much in the 1.1 release.

- Server API and servlets. This is probably my biggest stretch. An alpha release of the Server API occurred in August 1996. It has changed several times since then, and looks like it is still fluid. However, the ideas in this area are very interesting; I thought it was worth going out on a limb somewhat to expose you to some of the newest developments.

In short, this book covers the state of the art for network programming in Java 1.1. For non-network programming such as is involved in basic I/O and the AWT, I have chosen to stay slightly further back from the bleeding edge. Explaining new topics like the 1.1 event model could only distract readers from the networking concepts I am covering. I also expect many readers will still need to use Java 1.0, at least for a while. Therefore, I have chosen to use 1.0 idioms and deprecated features in preference to the 1.1 counterparts. For example, I use `DataInput-Stream.readLine()` instead of `BufferedReader.readLine()`. The 1.0 idioms should be supported for some time still, while the 1.1 idioms will not be universally available for a number of months. I will incorporate changes and additions to Java 1.1 in future printings and new editions. However, with the exception of the Server API, things seem fairly stable. You shouldn't have any trouble using this book after 1.1 is released; any discrepancies between the final specification and what I have discussed here should be minor.

About the Examples

Almost every method and field described in this book is illustrated with at least one complete working program, simple though it may be. In my experience, a complete working program is essential to showing the proper use of a method. Without a program, it is too easy to drop into jargon or to gloss over points about which the author may be unclear. The Java API documentation itself often suffers from terse descriptions of the method calls. In this book I have tried to err by providing too much explication rather than too little. If a point is obvious to you, feel free to skip over it. You do not need to type in and run every example in this book, but if a particular method does give you trouble, you are guaranteed to have at least one working example.

The end of each chapter includes at least one (and often several) more complex programs that demonstrate the classes and methods of that chapter in a more realistic setting. These often rely on Java features not discussed in this book. Indeed, in many of the programs, the networking components are only a small fraction of the source code and often the least difficult parts. Nonetheless, none of these programs could be written as easily in languages that didn't give networking the central position it occupies in Java. The apparent simplicity of the networked sections of the code reflects the extent to which networking has been made a core feature of Java, and not any triviality of the program itself.

All example programs presented in this book are available online, often with sub-stantial corrections and additions. These are available through ORA's web site at *ftp://ftp.ora.com/published/oreilly/java/java.netprog.* You can also check out my Java FAQ, Cafe Au Lait, at *http://sunsite.unc.edu/javafaq/* for the latest information.

My discussion assumes you are using Sun's Java Developer's Kit, preferably on Solaris. All the examples given here *should* work on other platforms and with other compilers and virtual machines. In reality, networking is the area least supported by most implementations. *Every* implementation of Java I have tested has had non-trivial bugs in networking. The Sun Solaris JDK does seem to have the fewest bugs. This situation should improve with time.

Java Idioms

There are several common Java idioms which will be used again and again in the examples. Since none of these is specific to network programming, I have elected to discuss them here.

The complete examples are normally applications, not applets.[*] Therefore, they have main() methods. Many of them receive an indefinite number of arguments on the command line. The main() method of these programs just loops through these arguments and passes each one to another method for processing.

```
public static void main (String args[]) {

  for (int i = 0; i < args.length; i++) {
    doTheWork(args[i]);
  }
}/* end main */
```

The doTheWork() method is called repeatedly with each command-line argument. This allows applications to be tested on many different inputs very quickly.

There is one snag in this approach. Static methods (such as main()) cannot call non-static methods of the same class. The above code will cause a compile-time error if doTheWork() is not itself static. To call non-static methods from main() (or any other static method) you first have to instantiate an instance of your class. For example:

```
public class lookup {

  public static void main (String args[]) {

    lookup lkp = new lookup();
    for (int i = 0; i < args.length; i++) {
```

---

[*] Unfortunately, the most popular browsers limit what applets can do over the network.

```
        lkp.doTheWork(args[i]);
      }

    }// end main

  public void doTheWork(String s) {

    ...

    } // end doTheWork

  }// end lookup
```

Exactly how and where the constructor is called depends on the program. In some programs you may create a new object for each command-line argument like this:

```
public static void main (String args[]) {
    for (int i = 0; i < args.length; i++) {
      lookup lkp = new lookup(args[i]);
      lkp.doTheWork();
    }

  }// end main
```

This style is common when the class extends Thread. Each command-line argument spawns a new thread. Thus, main() often takes the form:

```
public static void main (String args[]) {
    for (int i = 0; i < args.length; i++) {
      myThread mt = new myThread(args[i]);
      mt.start();
    }

  }// end main
```

Instantiating the class in the main() method is a common technique in programs that need to be both applets and applications. First, the main() method instantiates the applet by calling its constructor. Often, the only constructor for the applet is the default constructor, which takes no arguments; most applets don't have explicit constructors. Next, the main() method constructs a Frame to display the applet, adds the applet to the Frame, and then sizes, moves, and shows the Frame. Finally, main() calls the applet's init() and start() methods. For example:

```
import java.awt.Frame;
import java.applet.Applet;

public class myApplet extends Applet {

  public static void main(String args[]) {

    myApplet ma = new myApplet();
```

```
    Frame myFrame = new Frame("My Applet Window");
    myFrame.resize(250, 250);
    myFrame.move(300,200);
    myFrame.add("Center", ma);
    myFrame.show();

    ma.init();
    ma.start();

  }


}
```

If the applet is loaded into a web browser or an applet viewer, the main() method is never called.

When an applet like this runs as a free-standing application, it does not have access to an AppletContext or an AppletStub, both of which are normally provided by the applet viewer or web browser. You'll learn more about these in Chapter 6, *The Network Methods of java.applet.Applet*. For now, this means that NullPointerExceptions will be thrown if you call any of the following methods of the applet:

```
public boolean isActive()
public URL getDocumentBase()
public URL getCodeBase()
public String getParameter(String name)
public AppletContext getAppletContext()
public void showStatus(String msg)
public Image getImage(URL url)
public Image getImage(URL url, String name)
public AudioClip getAudioClip(URL url)
public AudioClip getAudioClip(URL url, String name)
public void play(URL url)
public void play(URL url, String name)
```

Therefore, if you plan to use an applet with a main() method, make sure you watch out for NullPointerExceptions thrown by these methods. You can make up for some of these missing methods by using methods of the Toolkit class; to get a Toolkit to work with, call the static method Toolkit.getDefaultToolkit(). In particular, the Toolkit class gives you equivalent methods for working with images, but not with audio. (If you really need audio, check out the sun.audio classes; using these may cause portability problems.) Of course, when the program runs as a normal applet, the browser or viewer will provide an AppletContext and an AppletStub, and you won't need these workarounds.

Conventions Used in This Book

This book uses the following conventions:

A `constant width` font is used for:

- Anything that might appear in a Java program, including keywords, operators, datatypes, method names, variable names, class names, and interface names.

- Command lines and options that should be typed verbatim on the screen (bold is used only in situations where it is important to distinguish between the command itself and output from that command).

- Tags that might appear in an HTML document.

An *italic* font is used for:

- New terms where they are defined.

- Path names, file names, and program names (however, if the program name is also the name of a Java class, it is given in constant width, like other class names).

- Internet addresses, such as domain names and URLs.

When code is presented as fragments, rather than complete programs, the existence of the appropriate import statements should be inferred. For example, in the following code fragment you may assume that `java.awt.Frame` was imported.

```
Frame myFrame = new Frame("My Applet Window");
```

Request for Comments

I enjoy hearing from readers, whether with general comments about how this could be a better book, specific corrections, or other topics you would like to see covered. You can reach me by sending email to *bookquestions@ora.com*. Please realize, however, that I receive several hundred pieces of email a day and cannot personally respond to each one.

Acknowledgments

Many people were involved in the production of this book. My editor, Mike Loukides, got this book rolling, and provided many helpful comments that substantially improved the book. My agent, David Rogelberg, convinced me it was possible to make a living writing books like this rather than working in an office. All these people deserve much thanks and credit.

Thanks also to the staff at O'Reilly & Associates for guiding this book through the stages of production. Nancy Wolfe Kotary was the production editor and project manager; Erik Ray, Ellen Siever, and Lenny Muellner provided technical support and conversion services; Chris Reilley created the technical diagrams and figures; Madeleine Newell and Ellie Fountain Maden made edits to the book in various stages of production; Peter Fell served as copyeditor; Clairemarie Fisher O'Leary and Sheryl Avruch provided quality control; and Seth Maislin created the index. Edie Freedman designed the cover, and Nancy Priest designed the inside layout.

Finally I'd like to save my largest thanks for my wife, Beth, without whose support and assistance this book would never have happened.

Elliotte Rusty Harold
elharo@sunsite.unc.edu
January 15, 1997

1

Why Networked Java?

Java is the first programming language designed from the ground up with networking in mind. As the global Internet continues to grow, Java is uniquely suited to build the next generation of network applications. Java provides solutions to a number of problems—platform independence, security, and international character sets being the most important—that are crucial to Internet applications, yet difficult to address in other languages. Together, these and other Java features let web surfers quickly download and execute untrusted programs from a web site without worrying that the program may spread a virus, steal their data, or crash their systems. Indeed, the level of safety you have with a Java applet is far greater than you get with shrink-wrapped software.

One of the biggest secrets about Java is that it makes writing network programs easy. In fact, it is far easier to write network programs in Java than in almost any other language. This book shows you dozens of complete programs that take advantage of the Internet. Some are simple textbook examples, while others are completely functional applications. One thing you'll note in the fully functional applications is just how little code is devoted to networking. Even in network-intensive programs like web servers and clients, almost all the code handles data manipulation or the user interface. The part of the program that deals with the network is almost always the shortest and simplest.

In short, it is easy for Java applications to send and receive data across the Internet. It is also possible for applets to communicate across the Internet, though they are limited by security restrictions. In this chapter you'll learn about a few of the network-centric applets and applications that can be written in Java. In later chapters you'll develop the tools you need to write these programs.

What Can a Network Program Do?

Networking adds a lot of power to simple programs. With networks, one program can retrieve information stored in millions of computers located anywhere in the world. You can communicate with tens of millions of people. You can harness the powers of many computers to work on one problem.

But that sounds like a Microsoft advertisement, not the start of a technical book. Let's talk more precisely about what network programs do. Network applications generally take one of several forms. The distinction you hear about most is between clients and servers. In the simplest case, clients retrieve and display data. More complex clients repeatedly retrieve changing data, send data to other people and computers, and interact with peers in real time for chat, multiplayer games, or collaboration. Servers respond to requests for data. Simple servers merely look up some file and return it to the client, but more complex servers often do a lot of processing on the data before answering an involved question. Beyond clients and servers, the next generation of Internet applications will almost certainly include intelligent agents that move from server to server, searching the web for some information and dragging their findings home. And that's only the beginning. Let's look a little more closely at the possibilities you open up when you add networking to your programs.

Retrieve and Display Data

At the most basic level, a network client retrieves data from a server and shows it to a user. Of course, many programs did just this long before Java came along; after all, that's exactly what a web browser does. However, web browsers are limited. They can only talk to certain kinds of servers (generally web, FTP, Gopher, and perhaps mail and news servers). They can only understand and display certain kinds of data (generally text, HTML, and a couple of standard image formats). If you want to go further, you're in trouble; for example, a web browser cannot send SQL commands to a database server to perform interactive queries. Java programs can do this and a lot more. Even better, a Java program embedded in an HTML page (an applet) can give a Java-enabled web browser capabilities the browser didn't have to begin with.

Java programs are flexible because Java is a general programming language, unlike HTML. Java programs see network connections as streams of data which can be interpreted and responded to in any way that's necessary. Web browsers see only certain kinds of data streams and can interpret them only in certain ways. If a browser sees a data stream that it's not familiar with (for example, a binary response to an SQL query), its behavior is unpredictable.

Thus, a Java program can connect to a network time server to synchronize itself with an atomic clock. A web browser cannot. A Java program can display the local time using the local machine's clock. A web browser cannot. A Java program can connect to an Oracle database to ask for the salespeople in the midwest region whose sales exceeded their quotas by more than 50%. A web browser cannot. Finally, a Java program can use the full power of a modern graphical user interface to show this data to the user. Although web browsers can create very fancy displays, they can only work with HTML.

Connecting to servers is easy. Java includes built-in classes that connect to other Internet hosts, using the TCP and UDP protocols of the TCP/IP family. You just tell Java what IP address and port you want, and Java handles the low-level details. Java does not currently understand Netware, AppleTalk, or other non-IP-based network protocols; but this will cease to be an issue as TCP/IP becomes the *lingua franca* of networked applications. Furthermore, release 1.1 of Sun's JDK (Java Development Kit) allows you to extend Java's network classes to support other protocol families. Doing so is beyond the bounds of this book, but I'll at least show you where Java is headed.

Once you've connected to a server, it is your responsibility to communicate properly with the remote server and interpret the data the server sends you. In almost all cases, packaging data to send to a server and unpacking the data you get back is harder than simply making the connection. Java includes classes that help you communicate with certain types of servers, notably web servers; it also includes classes to process some kinds of data, such as text, GIF images, and JPEG images. However, not all servers are HTTP servers, and not all data are GIFs. Therefore, Java lets you write protocol handlers that communicate with different kinds of servers and content handlers that understand and display different kinds of data. By the time you read this, probably at least one web browser will be available that can automatically download and install the protocol and content handlers needed by a web site it visits. When the protocol or content handler is no longer needed, Java will automatically dispose of it so it doesn't waste memory or disk space. Protocol and content handlers perform a task similar to Netscape plug-ins, but they are much more convenient—they don't require user intervention to download and install the software, and they don't waste memory or disk space when not in use.

Repeatedly Retrieve Data

Web browsers retrieve data on demand; the user asks for a page at a URL and the web browser gets it. This model is fine as long as you only need the information once, and the information doesn't change often. However, continuous access to information that's changing constantly is a problem. There have been a few attempts to solve this problem with extensions to HTML and HTTP. For example, server push and client pull are fairly awkward ways of keeping a client up to date. There are even services that send email to alert you that a page you're interested in has changed.[*]

A Java client, however, can repeatedly connect to a server to keep an updated picture of the data. If the data changes very frequently, like a stock price, a Java application can keep a connection to the server open at all times, and display a running graph of the stock price on the desktop. A Java program can even respond in real time to changes in the data. For example, a stock ticker applet might ring a bell if IBM's stock price goes over $100 so you know to call your broker and sell. A more complex program could even perform the sale without human intervention. It is easy to imagine considerably more complicated combinations of data that a client can monitor—data you'd be unlikely to find on any single web site. For example, you could get the stock price of a company from one server, the poll standings of candidates they've contributed to from another, and correlate that data to decide whether to buy or sell the company's stock. A stock broker would certainly not implement this scheme for the average small investor.

As long as the data is available through the Internet, a Java program can track it. Data available on the Internet ranges from weather conditions in Tulsa to the temperature of soft drink machines in Pittsburgh to the stock price of Sun Microsystems. Any or all of these can be integrated into your programs in real time.

Send Data

Web browsers are optimized for retrieving data. They send only limited amounts of data back to the server, mostly through forms. Java programs have no such limitations. Once a connection between two machines is established, Java programs can send data across that connection just as easily as they can receive from it. This opens up many possibilities:

File storage

Applet authors often want to store data between runs of the applet. For example, you might want to store the level a player has reached in a game. Applets aren't allowed to write files on local disks, but they can store data on a cooperating server. The applet just opens a network connection to its host and sends the data to it. The host may accept the data through CGI (the Common Gateway Interface), through FTP, or through a custom server (or servlet).

---

[*] See, for example the URL-minder at *http://www.netmind.com/URL-minder/URL-minder.html.*

Massively parallel computing

Since Java applets are secure, you can safely offer the use of your CPU cycles to scientific projects that require massively parallel machines. When your part of the calculation is complete, the program makes a network connection to the originating host, and adds your results to the collected data. This wouldn't work without secure execution of code, two-way network communication, and platform independence.

Smart forms

Java's AWT (Abstract Window Toolkit) has all the user interface components available in HTML forms, including textboxes, checkboxes, radio buttons, pop-up lists, buttons, and a few more besides. Thus, with Java, you can create forms with all the power of a regular HTML form. These forms can even use network connections to send the data back to the server exactly as a web browser does.

However, because Java applets are real programs instead of mere displayed data, these forms can be truly interactive and respond immediately to user input. For instance, an order form can keep a running total including sales tax and shipping charges. Every time the user checks off another item to buy, the applet can update the total price. A regular HTML form would need to send the data back to the server, which would calculate the total price and send an updated version of the form—a process that's both slower and more work for the server.

Furthermore, a Java applet can verify input. For example, an applet can warn the user that he can't order 1.5 cases of jelly beans, that only whole cases are sent. When the user has filled out the form, the applet sends the data to the server over a new network connection. This applet can talk to the same CGI program that would process input from an HTML form, or it can talk to a more efficient custom server.

Peer-to-Peer Interaction

The above examples all follow a client-server model. However, Java applications can also talk to each other across the Internet, opening up many new possibilities for group applications. There is no fundamental reason why Java applets can't talk directly to each other as well, but this is not always allowed by the `AppletSecuri-tyManager` and is not possible at all in Netscape. (You can get around this limitation by writing a custom server that forwards information from one applet to others; again, Java makes the job relatively easy.)

Games

Combine the easy ability to include networking in your programs with Java's powerful graphics and you have the recipe for truly awesome multiplayer games. Some that have already been written include poker, backgammon, Battleship, Othello, Go, mah jongg, Pong, charades, and bridge.

Chat

Java lets you set up private or public chat rooms. Text that is typed in one applet can be echoed to other applets around the world. More interestingly, if you add a Canvas with basic drawing ability to the applet, you can share a whiteboard between multiple locations. And as soon as a sound input facility is added to Java (probably in the first half of 1997), writing a network phone application or adding one to an existing applet will become trivial. Other applications of this type include custom clients for MUDs (multiuser dungeons), which could easily use Java's graphic capabilities to incorporate the pictures people have been imagining for years.

Collaboration

Peer-to-peer networked Java programs can allow many people to collaborate on a document at one time. Imagine a Java word processor that two people, perhaps in different countries, can both pull up and edit simultaneously. Imagine the interaction that's possible when you attach an Internet phone. For example, two astronomers could work on a paper while one is in New Mexico and the other is in Moscow. The Russian could say, "I think you dropped the superscript in equation 3.9," and then type the corrected equation so that it appears on both people's displays simultaneously. Then the astronomer in New Mexico might say, "I see, but doesn't that mean we have to revise Figure 3.2 like this?" and then use a drawing tool to make the change immediately. This sort of interaction isn't particularly hard to implement in Java (a word processor with a decent user interface for equations is probably the hardest part of the problem), but it does need to be built into the word processor from the start. It cannot be retrofitted onto a word processor that did not have networking in mind when it was designed.

Servers

Java applications can listen for network connections and respond to them. This makes it possible to implement servers in Java. A number of people have already written simple web servers in Java. Both Sun Microsystems and the World Wide Web Consortium have written web servers in Java designed to be as fully functional and fast as the common ones like Apache, Netscape, and Microsoft's Internet Information server. There is nothing to stop you from writing servers for other protocols as well, like FTP or POP (Post Office Protocol).

More interestingly, you can write custom servers that fill your specific needs. For example, you might write a server that stored state for your game applet and had exactly the functionality needed to let the players save and restore their games, and no more. Or, since applets can normally only communicate with the host from which they were downloaded, a custom server could mediate between two or more applets that need to communicate for a networked game. Such a server could be very simple, perhaps just echoing what one applet sent to all other connected applets.

As well as classical servers that listen for and accept socket connections, Java provides several higher level abstractions for client-server communication. Remote method invocation allows objects located on a server to have their methods called by clients. Servers that incorporate Java (like Sun's Java server, Jeeves) can load extensions called servlets that give them new capabilities. The easiest way to build your multiplayer game server might be to write a servlet, rather than writing an entire server. In the future, it may be possible for clients to upload servlets, subject to the constraints of a SecurityManager object; this is the reverse of applets being downloaded from a server to a client to be run on the client.

Applications of the Future

Java makes it possible to write many kinds of applications that have been imagined for years, but that would have required too much processing power because they were server-based. Java moves the processing to the client, where it belongs. Other application types (like intelligent agents) require extreme portability, and some guarantee that the application can't do anything hostile to its host. While Java's security model has been criticized (and yes, some bugs have been found), it's a quantum leap beyond anything that has been attempted in the past, and an absolute necessity for the software we will want to write in the future.

Shopping carts

Shopping carts (pages that keep track of where users have been and what they have chosen) are at the outer limits of what's possible with HTML and forms. Building a server-based shopping cart is difficult, requires lots of CGI and database work, and puts a huge CPU load on the server.

Java can move all this work to the client. Applets can store state as the user moves from page to page, making shopping carts much easier to build. In future browsers, applets will even be able to store the state of a shopping cart between visits to a web site, further expanding the convenience of online shopping.

Three-dimensional worlds

Virtual Reality Modeling Language (VRML) lets you create three-dimensional environments you can move through, but those environments have a limited range of behavior. For example, it's not really possible in VRML to set up a world in which pushing a button makes a jack-in-the-box pop up. You can create a button and you can create a jack-in-the-box, but you can't connect the two. Java provides the logical glue you need to add behavior and connections to the otherwise static worlds of VRML. In the future, Java will have a 3D API (Application Programming Interface, a fancy term for a class library) that will make visual environments even more interactive and exciting.

Spiders

Java programs can wander through the web, looking for crucial information. These sorts of programs are called *spiders*. Spiders crawl the web by following the links they find on pages. Generally a spider does something with each page it sees, ranging from indexing it in a database to performing linguistic analysis to hunting for specific information. This is more or less what services like Altavista do to build their indices. Building your own spider to search the Internet is a bad idea because Altavista and similar services have already done the work, and a few million private spiders would soon bring the Net to its knees. However, this doesn't mean that you shouldn't write spiders to index your own local intranet. In a company that uses the Web to store and access internal information, building a local index service might be very useful. You can use Java to build a program that indexes all your local servers, and interacts with another server program (or acts as its own server) to let users query the index. Example 5–13 is a simple spider that restricts itself to a single site. More general spiders can crawl from site to site.

It is easy to write a spider in Java, but there are some caveats. As mentioned previously, uncontrolled proliferation of spiders could quickly make the Internet unusable. If you write a spider, keep a list of the URLs you've already visited so you don't visit a page twice just because it's linked from two other pages. When visiting a site, check for a *robots.txt* file, and respect any restrictions you find there. If you are writing a spider for a local network, make sure it doesn't "escape" by following links to the outside world. When you're testing a spider, put a restriction on the depth or breadth to which the spider will search. Finally, don't run your spider at the maximum speed it can handle. Slow it down. Restrict the number of requests the spider will make per minute.

Intelligent Agents

Intelligent agents are programs that can move from host to host on their own, performing some action (like researching a stock price, or soliciting quotations for a purchase), and eventually returning with data, possibly even a completed contract for some goods or service. People have been talking about intelligent agents for some time, but until now, practical agent technology has been rather boring. It hasn't come close to achieving the levels envisioned years ago in various science fiction novels, most notably John Brunner's *Shockwave Rider* and William Gibson's *Neuromancer*. The primary reason for this is that agents have been restricted to running on a single system—and that's neither useful nor exciting. It's like a personal shopper that can call up different stores on the telephone to find out who has what you need, but can't actually go to the different stores to buy it. In fact, until 1996, there's been only one widely successful (to use the term very loosely) true agent that ran on multiple systems, the Morris Internet worm of 1989.

The Internet worm demonstrates one reason why developers haven't been willing to let agents go beyond a single host. It was destructive; after breaking into a system through one of several known bugs, it proceeded to overload the system, rendering it useless. In order for an agent to do something useful, it must be powerful enough to do some damage—and that's a risk most network managers haven't been willing to take. Java mitigates the security problem by providing a controlled environment for the execution of agents. This environment has a SecurityManager that can ensure that, unlike the Morris worm, the agents won't do anything nasty. This allows different systems to open their doors to these agents.

The second problem with agents has been portability. Agents aren't very interesting if they can only run on one kind of computer. That's sort of like having a credit card for Niemann-Marcus; it's a little bit useful and exotic, but won't help as much as a Visa card if you want to buy something at Macy's. Java provides a platform independent environment in which agents can run; the agent doesn't care if it's visiting a Sun workstation, a Macintosh, or a Windows machine.

The spider application discussed above could be implemented in Java as an intelligent agent. Instead of downloading pages from servers to the client, and building the index there, the spider could travel to each server, build the index locally, and send much less data across the network. Another kind of agent could move through a local network to inventory hardware, check software versions, update software, perform backups, and take care of other necessary tasks. Commercially oriented agents might let you check different record stores to find the best price for a CD, see if opera tickets are available on a given evening, and more. The same security features that allow clients to run untrusted applications downloaded from a server lets servers run untrusted applications uploaded from a client.

Electronic commerce

Ever since the Internet's popularity exploded, people have been talking about electronic commerce. Unfortunately, this explosion happened so quickly that people haven't given much thought to the details. Although many sites accept credit cards through HTML forms, the mechanism is clunky. It is inconvenient to fill out a form with your name, address, billing address, credit card number, and expiration date every time you want to pay $0.50 to read today's *Daily Planet*. Furthermore, many sites trying to sell something don't address security.

Imagine how easy it would be to implement this kind of transaction in Java. The user clicks on a link to some information. The server downloads an applet that pops up a dialog box saying, "Access to the information at *http://www.greedy.com/* costs $2.00. Do you wish to pay this?" The user can then click buttons that say "Yes" or "No." If the user clicks "No," then they don't get into the site. Now let's imagine what happens if the user clicks "Yes."

When the applet is downloaded from the server, it contains a small amount of information: the price, the URL, and the seller. If the client agrees to the transaction, the applet adds the buyer's information to the transaction, perhaps a name and an account number, and signs the information with the buyer's private key. Then the applet sends the data back to the applet host over the network. The applet host grants the user access to the requested information using the standard HTTP security model. Then it signs the transaction with its private key and forwards the data to a central clearinghouse. Sellers can offer money-back guarantees or delayed purchase plans (No money down! Pay nothing until July!) by agreeing not to forward the transaction to the clearinghouse until a certain amount of time has elapsed.

The clearinghouse verifies each transaction with the buyer's and seller's public keys, and enters the transaction in its database. The clearinghouse can use credit cards, checks, or electronic fund transfers to move money from the buyer to the seller. Most likely, the clearinghouse won't move the money until the accumulated total for a buyer or seller reaches a certain minimum threshold, keeping the transaction costs low.

Every part of this can be written in Java. An applet is used to request the user's permission. The `java.security` package authenticates and encrypts the transaction. The data can be sent from the client to the applet using sockets, URLs and CGI programs, servlets, or remote method invocation. These can also be used for the host to talk to the central clearinghouse. The web server itself can be written in Java, as can the database and billing systems at the central clearinghouse; or JDBC (Java Database API) can be used to talk to a traditional database like Informix or Oracle.

The hard part of this is setting up a clearinghouse, and getting users and sites to subscribe. First Virtual (*http://www.fv.com/*) and the major credit card companies have a head start, though none of them yet uses the scheme described here. In an ideal world, you'd like the buyer and the seller to be able to use different banks or clearinghouses. However, this is a human problem, not a technological one, and it is solvable. You can deposit a check from any American bank at any other American bank where you have an account. The two parties to a transaction do not need to bank in the same place.

At present, this is a little on the speculative side, so the details are likely to change. Nonetheless, all the technical pieces needed to make this happen should be in place by the time you read this. The Java Electronic Commerce Framework (JECF) should make it easier to tie the different pieces into an easily managed package.

But Wait. There's More!

Most of this book describes the fairly low-level APIs needed to write the kinds of programs discussed above. Some of these programs have already been written. Others are still only possibilities. Many of the low-level details will be encapsulated in high-level APIs in the future. This year promises to be a watershed, as Sun releases Java APIs for cryptography, advanced multimedia, commerce, telephony, and many other crucial areas. At present, you'll frequently hear the lament, "This would be possible if such-and-such a feature were available." Over the next year, this complaint should become much less frequent.

This chapter has just scratched the surface of what you can do when you make your Java programs network-aware. The real advantage of a Java-powered web site is that anything you can imagine is now possible. You're going to come up with ideas others would never think of. For the first time, you're not limited by the capabilities that other companies build into their browsers. You can give your users both the data you want them to see and the code they need to see that data at the same time. If you can imagine it, you can code it.

2

Basic Network Concepts

This chapter covers the terminology you need to understand before writing networked programs in Java (or, for that matter, in any language). Moving from the most general to the most specific, it explains what you need to know about networks in general, IP and TCP/IP-based networks in particular, and the Internet. This chapter doesn't try to teach you how to wire a network or configure a router, but you will learn what you need to know to write applications that communicate across the Internet. Topics covered in this chapter include: the definition of "network," the layered model used to discuss networks, the IP, TCP, and UDP protocols, firewalls and proxy servers, the Internet, and the Internet standardization process. Experienced network gurus may safely skip this chapter.

Network

A *network* is a collection of computers and other devices that can send data to and receive data from each other, more or less in real time. A network is normally connected by wires, and the bits of data are turned into electrons that move through the wires. However, wireless networks that transmit data through infrared light or microwaves are beginning to appear, and many long-distance transmissions are now carried over fiber optic cables that send visible light through glass filaments. There's nothing sacred about any particular physical medium for the transmission of data. Theoretically, data could be transmitted by coal-powered computers that sent smoke signals to each other. The response time (and environmental impact) of such a network would be rather poor!

Each machine on a network is called a *node*. Most nodes are computers, but printers, routers, bridges, gateways, dumb terminals, and Coca-Cola machines can also be nodes. You might use Java to interface with a Coke machine (in the future, one major application for Java might be embedded systems), but otherwise you'll mostly talk to other computers. Nodes that are fully functional computers are also called *hosts*. We will use the word *node* to refer to any device on the network, and *host* to mean that subset of devices which are general-purpose computers.

Every network node has an *address*: a series of bytes that uniquely identify it. You can think of this group of bytes as a number, but, in general, it is not guaranteed that the number of bytes in an address, the ordering of those bytes (big endian or little endian), or the number of bytes matches any primitive numeric datatype in Java. The more bytes in each address, the more addresses there are available and the more devices can be connected to the network simultaneously.

Addresses are assigned differently on different kinds of networks. AppleTalk addresses are chosen randomly at startup by each host. The host then checks to see if any other machine on the network is using that address. If another machine is using that address, the host randomly chooses another, checks to see if that address is already in use, and so on until it gets one that isn't being used. Ethernet addresses are attached to the physical Ethernet hardware. Manufacturers of Ethernet hardware use preassigned manufacturer codes to make sure there are no conflicts between the addresses in their hardware and the addresses of other manufacturers' hardware. Each manufacturer is responsible for making sure it doesn't ship two Ethernet cards with the same address. Internet addresses are normally assigned to a computer by the organization that is responsible for it. However, the addresses that an organization is allowed to choose for its computers are given out by an organization called the InterNIC.

On some kinds of networks, nodes also have names that help human beings identify them. At a set moment in time, a particular name normally refers to exactly one address. However, names are not locked to addresses. Names can change while addresses stay the same or addresses can change while the names stay the same. It is not uncommon for one address to have several names, and it is possible, though somewhat less common, for one name to refer to several different addresses.

All modern computer networks are *packet-switched* networks. This means that data traveling on the network is broken into chunks called packets, and each packet is handled separately. Therefore, each packet contains information about who sent it and where it's going. The most important advantage of breaking data into individually addressed packets is that you can dump packets from many ongoing exchanges onto one wire. This makes it much cheaper to build a network—many computers can share the same wire without interference. (In contrast, when you make a telephone call, you have essentially reserved a wire from your phone to the callee's.) Another advantage is that you can use checksums to detect whether or not a packet was damaged in transit.

We're still missing one important piece: some notion of what computers need to say to pass data back and forth. A *protocol* is a precise set of rules defining how computers communicate—how addresses work, how data is split into packets, etc. There are many different kinds of protocols defining different aspects of network communication. For example, HTTP defines how web browsers and servers communicate; at the other end of the spectrum, a protocol might define how black a puff of smoke needs to be to constitute a "1". Open, published protocol standards allow software and equipment from different vendors to communicate with each other; your web browser doesn't care whether any given site is using a UNIX machine, a Windows machine, or a Macintosh to run its server because the server and the browser both speak the HTTP protocol.

The Layers of a Network

There are different *layers* of communication on a network. Each layer represents a different level of abstraction between the physical hardware (wires and electrons) and the information being transmitted. In theory, each layer only talks to the layers immediately above and immediately below it.

There are several different layer models, each organized to fit the needs of a particular kind of network. This book uses a simplified four-layer model appropriate for the Internet,[*] shown in Figure 2–1. Separating the network into layers lets you modify or even replace one layer without affecting the others, as long as the interfaces between the layers stay the same. Thus, applications talk only to the transport layer. The transport layer talks only to the application layer and the Internet layer. The Internet layer in turn talks only to the host-to-network layer and the transport layer, never directly to the application layer. The host-to-network layer moves the data across the wires, fiber-optic cables or other medium to the host-to-network layer on the remote system.

As you can guess, the real details are much more elaborate. The host-to-network layer is by far the most complex, and a lot has been deliberately hidden. However, 90% of the time you'll be working in the application layer and will need to talk only to the transport layer. The other 10% of the time you'll be in the transport layer and talking to the application layer or the Internet layer. The complexity of the host-to-network layer is hidden from you; that's the point of the layer model.

---

[*] Network engineers usually use a seven-layer model, called the OSI model. If you only want to write network programs in Java, the OSI model is overkill. The biggest difference between the OSI model and the model I use in this book is that the OSI model splits the host-to-network layer into several other layers, and adds two layers between the transport layer and the application layer.

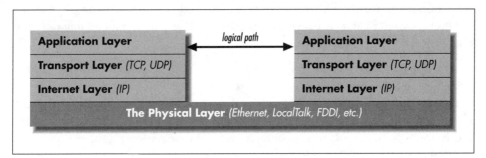

Figure 2–1: The layers of a network

Once data is transmitted across the host-to-network layer, it bubbles up through the layers on the receiving end. It appears, to the application layer, that it is talking directly to the application layer on the other system; the network creates a logical path between the two application layers. It's easy to understand the logical path if you think about an Internet chat session. Most people would say that they're talking to another person. If you really push them, they might say that they're talking to the computer (really the application layer) which is talking to the other person's computer which is talking to the other person. Everything more than one layer deeper is effectively invisible, and that is exactly the way it should be. Let's consider each layer in more detail.

The host-to-network layer

As a Java programmer, you're fairly high up in the network's food chain. A lot happens below your location; in the standard reference model for IP-based internets (the only kind of network Java really understands) the hidden parts of the network belong to the host-to-network layer. The host-to-network layer is an amalgamation of two other layers, the physical layer and the data link layer.

The actual wires, fiber optic cables, or smoke signals used to connect different computers make up the physical layer of the network. As a Java programmer, you don't need to worry about this layer unless something goes wrong with it—the plug falls out of the back of your computer, or someone drops a backhoe through the T1 line between you and the rest of the world. In other words, Java never sees the physical layer.

For computers to communicate with each other, it isn't sufficient to run wires between them and send electrical signals back and forth. The computers have to agree on certain standards for how those signals are interpreted. The first step is to determine how the packets of electricity (or light or smoke) map into bits and bytes of data. Since the physical layer is analog, and bits and bytes are digital, this involves a digital-to-analog conversion on the sending end and an analog-to-digital conversion on the receiving end.

Since all real analog systems have noise, error correction and redundancy need to be built into the way data is translated into electricity. This is done in the data link layer. The most common data link layer is Ethernet. Other popular data link layers include TokenRing and LocalTalk. A specific data link layer requires specialized hardware. Ethernet cards won't communicate on a TokenRing network, for example. Special devices called bridges are used to convert information from one type of data link layer like Ethernet to another like LocalTalk. As a Java programmer, you don't need to worry about the data link layer.

The Internet layer

The next layer of the network, and the first that you need to concern yourself with, is the internet layer. In the internet layer, a protocol defines how bits and bytes of data are organized into larger groups called *packets*, and the addressing scheme by which different machines find each other. The Internet Protocol (IP) is the most popular protocol in the world, and the only internet layer protocol Java understands. IP is almost exclusively the focus of this book. IPX is the second most popular protocol in the world, and is used mostly by machines on Netware networks. AppleTalk is a protocol used mostly by Macintoshes. The protocol is hardware-independent. AppleTalk, IP, and IPX can run across Ethernet, Token Ring, and LocalTalk networks, each of which can themselves run across different kinds of wire.

Data is sent across the Internet layer in packets called *datagrams*. On IP networks, each IP datagram contains a header of between twenty and sixty bytes and a payload that contains up to 65,515 bytes of data. The header of each packet contains the version number of the protocol being used, various other numbers, and, most importantly, the address of the host from which the packet came, and the address of the host to which it's going.

The transport layer

Raw datagrams have some drawbacks. Most notably, there's no guarantee that they will be delivered. Furthermore, even if they are delivered, they do not necessarily arrive in the order in which they were sent. The transport layer is responsible for ensuring that packets are received in the order they were sent and making sure that no data is lost. If a packet is lost, the transport layer can ask the sender to retransmit the packet. IP networks implement this by adding an additional header to each datagram that contains more information. There are two primary protocols at this level. The first, the Transmission Control Protocol (TCP), is a high-overhead protocol that allows for retransmission of lost data, and delivery of bytes in the order they were sent. The second protocol, the User Datagram Protocol (UDP), does not guarantee that packets are delivered in the correct order (or at all), but is often much faster. TCP is called a *reliable* protocol; UDP is an *unreliable* protocol. Later we'll see that unreliable protocols are much more useful than they sound.

The application layer

The layer that delivers data to the user is the application layer. The three lower layers all work together to define how data is transferred from one computer to another. The application layer decides what to do with that data when it's transferred; for example, an application protocol like HTTP (for the World Wide Web) makes sure that your Web browser knows to display a graphic image as a picture, not a long stream of numbers. The application layer is where most of the network parts of your programs spend their time. There is an entire alphabet soup of application layer protocols. Besides HTTP for the web, there are SMTP and POP for email, FTP for file transfer, NNTP for news transfer, and many more. In addition, your programs can define their own application layer protocols as necessary.

The way the application, transport, internet, and host-to-network layers work together is called *encapsulation*. The application produces some data, adds a header to it that tells the receiving application how to handle it, and hands the result off to the transport layer. The transport layer adds another header, and hands the result off to the internet layer. As Figure 2–2 shows, it's like putting a letter in an envelope, putting that envelope in a bigger envelope, and so on. On the receiving end, the network software unpacks the envelopes, one layer at a time, until it hands the original data to the receiving application.

IP, TCP, and UDP

IP, the Internet Protocol, has a number of advantages over other competing protocols like AppleTalk and IPX, most stemming from its history. It was developed with military sponsorship during the Cold War, and ended up with a lot of features that the military was interested in. First, it had to be robust. The entire network couldn't stop functioning if the Soviets nuked a router in Cleveland; all messages still had to get through to their intended destinations (except those going to Cleveland, of course). Therefore IP was designed to allow multiple routes between any two points, and to route packets of data around damaged routers.

Second, the military had many different kinds of computers, and they had to be able to talk to each other. Therefore, the protocol had to be open and platform-

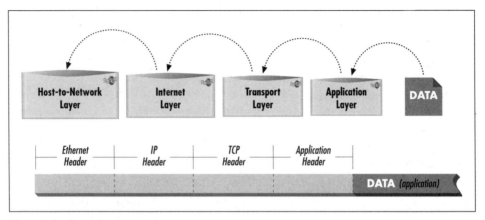

Figure 2–2: Protocol encapsulation

independent. It wasn't good enough to have one protocol for IBM mainframes and another for PDP-11s. The IBM mainframes needed to talk to the PDP-11s and any other strange computers that might be around.

Since there are multiple routes between two points, and since the shortest path between two points may change over time as a function of network traffic and other factors (like the existence of Cleveland), the packets that make up a particular data stream may not all take the same route. Furthermore, they may not arrive in the order they were sent, if they even arrive at all. To improve on the basic scheme, TCP was added to give each end of a connection the ability to acknowledge receipt of IP packets and request retransmission of lost packets. Moreover, TCP allows the packets to be put back together on the receiving end in the same order they were sent on the sending end.

However, TCP carries a fair amount of overhead. Therefore, if the order of the data isn't particularly important, and if the loss of individual packets won't completely corrupt the data stream, packets are sometimes sent without the guarantees that TCP provides. This is accomplished through the use of the UDP protocol. UDP is an unreliable protocol that does not guarantee that packets will arrive at their destination, or that they will arrive in the same order they were sent. Although this would be a problem for some uses like file transfer, it is perfectly acceptable for applications where the loss of some data would go unnoticed by the end user. For example, losing a few bits from a video or audio signal won't cause much degradation; it would be a bigger problem if you had to wait for a protocol like TCP to request a retransmission of missing data. Furthermore, error correcting codes can be built into UDP data streams at the application level to account for missing data.

As a Java programmer, you don't need to worry about the inner workings of IP, but you do need to know about addressing. Every computer on an IP network is identified by a four-byte number. This is normally written in the format 199.1.32.90, where each of the four numbers is one unsigned byte ranging in value from 0 to 255. Every computer attached to an IP network has a unique four-byte address. When data is transmitted across the network, the packet's header includes the address of the machine for which the packet is intended (the destination address), and the address of the machine that sent the packet (the source address). Routers along the way choose the best route by which to send the packet by inspecting the destination address. The source address is included so the recipient will know where to send the reply.

Although computers are very comfortable with numbers, human beings aren't very good at remembering them. Therefore the Domain Name System (DNS) was developed to translate hostnames that humans can remember (like *www.ora.com*) into numeric Internet addresses (like 198.112.208.23). When Java programs access the network, they need to process both these numeric addresses and their corresponding hostnames. There are a series of methods for doing this in the `InetAddress` class, which is discussed in Chapter 4, *Processing Internet Addresses.*

Ports

Addresses would be all you needed if each computer did no more than one thing at a time. However, modern computers do many different things at once. Email needs to be separated from FTP requests, which need to be separated from web traffic. This is accomplished through *ports*. Each computer with an IP address has several thousand logical ports (65,535 to be precise). These are purely abstractions in the computer's memory, and do not represent anything physical like a serial or parallel port. Each port is identified by a number between 1 and 65535. Each port can be allocated to a particular service.

For example, the HTTP service, which is used by the Web, generally runs on port 80—we say that a Web server listens on port 80 for incoming connections. SMTP or email servers run on port 25. When data is sent to a Web server on a particular machine at a particular IP address, it is also sent to a particular port (usually port 80) on that machine. The receiver checks each packet for both the address and the port. If the address matches, the data is sent to the program interested in data sent to that port. This is how different types of traffic are sorted out.

Port numbers between 1 and 1023 are reserved for well-known services like finger, FTP, HTTP, and email. On UNIX systems, you must be "root" to receive data on one of these ports, but you may still send data to them. On Windows (including

Windows NT) and the Mac, any user may use these ports without special privileges. Table 2–1 shows the well-known ports for the protocols that are discussed in this book. These assignments are not absolutely guaranteed; in particular, Web servers often run on ports other than 80, either because multiple servers need to run on the same machine, or because the person who installed the server doesn't have the root privileges needed to run it on port 80. On UNIX machines, a fairly complete listing of assigned ports is stored in the file */etc/services*.

Table 2–1: Well-Known Port Assignments

Protocol	Port	Encoding	Purpose
echo	7	tcp/udp	Echo is a test protocol used to verify that two machines are able to connect by having one echo back the other's input.
discard	9	tcp/udp	Discard is a less useful test protocol that ignores all data received by the server.
daytime	13	tcp/udp	Daytime provides an ASCII representation of the current time on the server.
ftp-data	20	tcp	FTP uses two well-known ports. This port is used to transfer files.
ftp	21	tcp	This port is used to send ftp commands like "put" and "get."
telnet	23	tcp	Telnet is a protocol used for interactive, remote command-line sessions.
smtp	25	tcp	The "Simple Mail Transfer Protocol" is used to send email between machines.
time	37	tcp/udp	A time server returns the number of seconds that have elapsed on the host machine since midnight, January 1, 1900, as a four-byte, signed, big-endian integer.
whois	43	tcp	Whois is a simple directory service for Internet network administrators.
finger	79	tcp	Finger gets information about a user or users.
http	80	tcp	HyperText Transfer Protocol is the underlying protocol of the World Wide Web.
pop3	110	tcp	Post Office Protocol Version 3 is a protocol for the transfer of accumulated email from the host to sporadically connected clients.
nntp	119	tcp	This is the Usenet news transfer, more formally known as the "Network News Transfer Protocol."

Table 2–1: Well-Known Port Assignments (continued)

Protocol	Port	Encoding	Purpose
RMI Registry	1099	tcp	The Remote Method Invocation (RMI) Registry is a registry service for Java remote objects, and is discussed in Chapter 14, *Remote Method Invocation*.
Jeeves	8080	tcp	Jeeves, discussed in Chapter 15, *The Java Server API and Servlets*, is a web server from Sun that runs on port 8080 by default, not port 80. This non-standard port is used because Jeeves is still experimental software.

The Internet

The *Internet* is the world's largest IP-based network. It is an amorphous group of computers in many different countries on all seven continents (and that includes Antarctica) that talk to each other using the IP protocol. Each computer on the Internet has at least one unique IP address by which it can be identified. Most of them also have at least one name that maps to that IP address. The Internet is not owned by anyone, though pieces of it are. It is not governed by anyone, which is not to say that some governments don't try. It is simply a very large collection of computers that talk to each other in a standard way.

The Internet is not the only IP-based network, but it is the largest one. Other IP networks are called *internets* with a little *i*; for example, a corporate IP network that is not connected to the Internet. *Intranet* is a current buzzword that loosely describes corporate practices of putting lots of data on internal web servers. Since web browsers use IP, most intranets do too (though some tunnel it through existing AppleTalk or IPX installations).

Almost certainly the internet that you'll be using is the Internet. To make sure that hosts on different networks on the Internet can communicate with each other, a few rules that don't apply to purely internal internets need to be followed. The most important rules deal with the assignment of addresses to different organizations, companies, and individuals. If everyone randomly picked the Internet addresses they wanted, conflicts would arise when different computers showed up on the Internet with the same address.

Internet Address Classes

To avoid this problem, Internet addresses are assigned to different organizations by the Internet Network Information Center (InterNIC), generally acting through intermediaries called Internet Service Providers (ISPs). When a company or an organization wants to set up an IP-based network, they are assigned a block of addresses by the InterNIC. Currently, these blocks are available in two sizes called Class B and Class C. A Class C address block specifies the first three bytes of the address, for example, 199.1.32. This allows room for 254 individual addresses (from 199.1.32.1 to 199.1.32.254).* A Class B address block only specifies the first two bytes of the addresses an organization may use, for instance, 167.1. Thus a Class B address has room for roughly 65,000 different hosts (in the block 167.1, the hosts would have addresses from 167.1.0.1 to 167.1.255.254).

Addressing becomes important when you want to restrict access to your site. For instance, you may want to prevent a competing company from having access to your web site. In this case you would find out your competitor's address block and throw away all requests that come from there. More commonly, you might want to make sure that only people within your organization can access your internal web server. In this case you would deny access to all requests except those that come from within your own address block.

There's no available block of addresses with a size between a Class B block and a Class C block. This has become a problem because there are many organizations with more than 254 and less than 65,000 computers connected to the Internet. If each of these organizations is given a Class B address, a lot of IP addresses are wasted. This is a problem since the number of addresses is limited to about 4.2 billion. That sounds like a lot, but it gets crowded quickly when you waste fifty or sixty thousand addresses at a shot. The temporary solution is to assign multiple Class C addresses to these organizations, inconvenient though this is for packet filtering and routing.

Several address blocks and patterns are special. All Internet addresses beginning with 10. and 192. are deliberately unassigned. They can be used on internal networks, but no host using addresses in these blocks is allowed onto the global Internet. These *non-routable* addresses are useful for building private networks that can't be seen from the rest of the Internet, or for building a large network when you've only been assigned a class C address block. Addresses beginning with 127 (most commonly 127.0.0.1) always mean the *local loopback address*. That is, these addresses always point to the local computer, no matter which computer you're running on. The hostname for this address is generally *localhost*. The address 0.0.0.0 always refers to the originating host, but may only be used as a source address, not a

---

* Addresses with the last byte either .0 or .255 are reserved and should never be assigned to hosts.

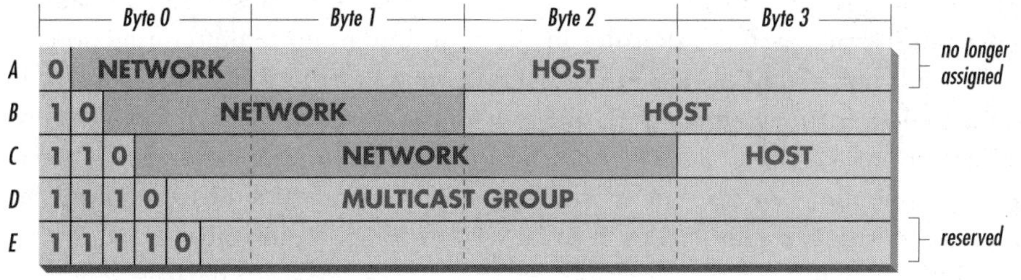

Figure 2–3: Internet address class

What About Class A Addresses?

When the Internet was originally designed, there was also room for 126 Class A addresses that specified only the first byte and allowed over sixteen million different hosts within one organization. However almost no single organization needs this many addresses, and a large part of any Class A address tends to go unused. Since Internet addresses are a finite quantity, the InterNIC stopped giving out Class A addresses a long time ago; and in 1995 they recycled the last two Class A addresses still in use, MIT's and Stanford's.

There are also Class D and E addresses. Class D addresses are used for IP multicast groups, and will be discussed at length in Chapter 13, *Multicast Sockets*. Class D addresses all begin with the 4 bits 1110. Class E addresses begin with the five bits 11110 and are reserved for future extensions to the Internet. Figure 2–3 summarizes all the Internet address classes.

destination. Similarly, any address that begins with 0.0 is assumed to refer to a host on the same local network.

Firewalls

There are some naughty people on the Internet! To keep them out, it's often helpful to set up one point of access to a local network and check all traffic into or out of that access point. The hardware and software that sits between the Internet and the local network, checking all the data that comes in or out, to make sure it's kosher, is called a *firewall*.

The most basic firewall is a packet filter that inspects each packet coming into or out of a network, and uses a set of rules to determine whether or not that traffic is allowed. Filtering is usually based on network addresses and ports. For example, all traffic coming from network 193.28.25 may be rejected, because you had bad experiences with crackers from that net in the past. Outgoing telnet connections may be allowed, but incoming telnet connections may not be. Incoming connections on port 80 (web) may be allowed, but only to the corporate web server. The exact configuration of a firewall—which packets of data are and are not allowed to pass through—depends on the security needs of an individual site. Java doesn't have much to do with firewalls except in so far as they often get in your way.

Proxy Servers

Proxy servers are related to firewalls. If a firewall prevents hosts on a network from making direct connections to the outside world, a proxy server can act as a go-between. Therefore, a machine that is prevented from connecting to the external network by a firewall would make a request for a web page from the local proxy server, instead of requesting the web page directly from the remote web server. The proxy server would then request the page from the web server, and forward the response back to the original requestor. Proxies can also be used for FTP and other services. One of the security advantages of using a proxy server is that external hosts only find out about the proxy server. They do not learn the names and IP addresses of the internal machines, making it more difficult to break into internal systems.

While firewalls generally operate at the level of the transport or internet layer, proxy servers operate at the application layer. A proxy server has detailed understanding of some application level protocols, like HTTP and FTP. Packets that pass through the proxy server can be examined to ensure that they contain data appropriate for their type. For instance, FTP packets that seem to contain telnet data can be rejected.

Since all access to the Internet is forwarded through the proxy server, access can be tightly controlled. For instance, a company might choose to block access to *www.playboy.com* but allow access to *www.microsoft.com*. Some companies allow incoming FTP but disallow outgoing FTP so that confidential data cannot be easily smuggled out of the company. Some companies have begun using proxy servers to track their employees' web usage so they can see who's using the Internet to get tech support, and who's using it to check out the Playmate of the Month. Such monitoring of employee behavior is controversial and is not exactly an indicator of enlightened management techniques.

Proxy servers can also be used to implement local caching. When a file is requested from a web server, the proxy server will first check to see if the file is in its cache. If the file is in the cache, the proxy will serve the file from the cache rather than from the Internet. If the file is not in the cache, the proxy server will retrieve it, forward it to the requester, and store it in the cache for the next time it is requested. This scheme can significantly reduce load on an Internet connection, and greatly improve response time. America Online runs one of the largest farms of proxy servers in the world to speed the transfer of data to its users. If you look at a web server logfile, you'll probably find some hits from clients with names like *www-d1.proxy.aol.com*, but not as many as you'd expect given the six million users on AOL. That's because AOL only requests pages they don't already have in their cache. Most other online services do the same.

The biggest problem with proxy servers is their inability to cope with all but a few protocols. Generally established protocols like HTTP, FTP, and SMTP are allowed to pass through, while newer protocols like RealAudio are not. In the rapidly changing world of the Internet, this is a significant disadvantage. It's a particular disadvantage for Java programmers because it limits the effectiveness of custom protocols. In Java, it's easy and often useful, to create a new protocol that is optimized for your application. However, no proxy server will ever understand these one-of-a-kind protocols.

The Client-Server Model

Client-server is one of the hottest buzzwords in business computing today, almost as hot as Java. Most modern network programming is based on a client-server model (see Figure 2–4). A client-server application typically stores large quantities of data on an expensive, high-powered server, while most of the program logic and the user-interface is handled by client software running on relatively cheap personal computers. In most cases, a server primarily sends data, while a client primarily receives it, but it is rare for one program to send or receive exclusively. A more reliable distinction is that a client initiates a conversation, while a server waits for clients to start conversations with it. In some cases, the same program may be both a client and a server.

Some servers process and analyze the data before sending the results to the client. Such servers are often referred to as "application servers," to distinguish them from the more common file servers and database servers. The latter exist only to send out chunks of information, but don't do anything with that information. In contrast, an application server might look at an order entry database, and give the clients reports about monthly sales trends. An application server is not a server that serves files which happen to be applications.

You are already familiar with many examples of client-server systems. In 1997, the most popular client server system is the World Wide Web. Web servers like Apache

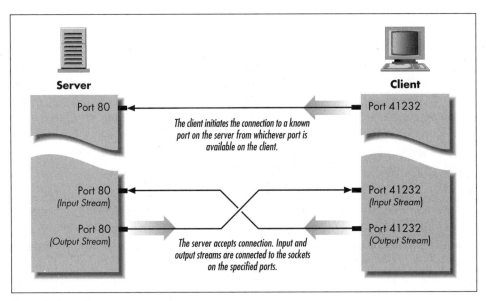

Figure 2–4: A client-server connection

respond to requests from web clients like Netscape Navigator. Data is stored on the web server and is then sent out to the clients that request it. Aside from the initial request for a page, almost all data is transferred from the server to the client, not from the client to the server. Web servers that use CGI programs double as application and file servers. An older service that fits the client-server model is FTP. FTP uses different application protocols and different software, but they are still split into FTP servers that send files and FTP clients that receive them. People often use FTP to upload files from the client to the server, so it's harder to say that the data transfer is primarily in one direction, but it is still true that an FTP client initiates the connection, and the FTP server responds to it.

Java makes it easy to write servers of all sorts, but it really shines when you start writing clients. Java is a powerful environment in which to write GUI programs that access many different kinds of servers. In 1997, the preeminent example of a client program written in Java is HotJava, the web browser from Sun, which is a general purpose web client.

Peer-to-Peer Applications

Not all applications fit easily into a client-server model. For instance, in networked games, both players will send data back and forth roughly equally (at least in a fair game). These sorts of connections are called "peer-to-peer." The telephone system is the classic example of a peer-to-peer network. Each phone can call, or be called by, another phone. You don't have to buy one phone to send calls and another to receive them.

Java does not have explicit peer-to-peer communication in its networking API. However applications can easily implement peer-to-peer communications in several ways, most commonly by acting as both a server and a client.

Internet Standards: RFCs

This book will discuss several application-level Internet Protocols, most notably HTTP. However, this is not a book about those protocols, and it tries not to say more than the minimum you need to know. If you need detailed information about any protocol, the definitive source is the collection of Internet drafts and requests for comments (RFCs). RFCs and Internet drafts range from informational documents of general interest to detailed specifications of standard Internet protocols like NNTP. RFCs that document a standard or a proposed standard are published only with the approval of the Internet Engineering Steering Group (IESG) of the Internet Engineering Taskforce (IETF). All Internet standards are RFCs, but not all RFCs are Internet standards. RFCs are available from many locations on the Internet, including:

http://ds.internic.net/std/
   Standards

http://ds.internic.net/rfc/
   Proposed Standards and Informational Material

http://ds.internic.net/internet-drafts/
   Working Group Drafts

For the most part, RFCs, particularly standards-oriented RFCs, are very technical, turgid and near-incomprehensible. Nonetheless, they are often the only current and reliable source of information.

How Standards are Developed

Most proposals for a standard begin when a person or group gets an idea and builds a prototype. The prototype is incredibly important. Before something can become an Internet standard, it must actually exist and work. This requirement ensures that Internet standards are at least feasible, unlike the standards promulgated by some other organizations.

If the prototype becomes popular outside its original developers, and other organizations begin implementing their own versions of the protocol, a Working Group may be formed under the auspices of the IETF. This working group attempts to document the protocol in an *Internet Draft*. Internet Drafts are working documents, and change frequently to reflect experience with the protocol. The experimental implementations and the Internet Draft evolve in rough synchronization, until eventually the working group agrees that the protocol is ready to become a formal standard. At this point, the proposed specification is submitted to the IESG.

For some time after the proposal is submitted, it is considered *experimental*. Being in an experimental stage does not imply that the protocol is not solid or that it is not widely used; unfortunately, the process usually lags behind *de facto* acceptance of the standard. Protocols in the experimental stage in early 1996 included the digest format for messages and Internet Relay Chat (IRC). By early 1996, HTTP had not even reached the experimental stage. It was still an Internet draft! If the IESG likes the experimental standard or it is in widespread use, it will assign it an RFC number, and publish it as an experimental RFC, generally after some changes.

If the experimental standard holds up well in further real-world testing, the IESG may advance it to the status of *proposed standard*. A proposed standard is fairly loose, and is based on the experimental work of possibly as little as one organization. Changes may still be made to a protocol in this stage.

Once the bugs appear to have been worked out of a proposed standard, and there are at least two independent implementations, the IESG may recommend that a proposed standard be promoted to a *draft standard*. A draft standard will probably not change too much before eventual standardization, unless major flaws are found. The primary purpose of a draft standard is to clean up the RFC that documents the standard document, and make sure the documentation conforms to actual practice, rather than to change the standard itself.

When a protocol completes this process, it is assigned an STD number and becomes an STD in addition to an RFC. The absolute minimum time for a standard to be approved as such is 10 months, but in practice, the process almost always takes much longer. The commercial success of the Internet hasn't helped, since standards must now be worked out in the presence of marketeers, venture capitalists, and others with vested interests in seeing particular technologies succeed or fail. Therefore, many of the "standards" that this book references are in either the experimental, proposed, or draft stage. As of publication, there are over 2,000 RFCs. Less than one hundred of these have become STDs, and some of those that have are obsolete. RFCs relevant to this book are detailed in Table 2–2.

In addition to a protocol's development status, a protocol has a requirement level. The possible requirement levels are:

- Required: must be implemented by all Internet hosts. There are very few required protocols. IP itself is one (RFC791), but even protocols as important as TCP or UDP are only recommended. A standard is required only if it is absolutely essential to the functioning of a host on the Internet.

- Recommended: should be implemented by Internet hosts that don't have a specific reason not to implement it. Most protocols that you are familiar with (like TCP and UDP, SMTP for email, Telnet for remote login, etc.) are recommended.

- Elective: can be implemented by anyone who wants to use the protocol. For example RFC1521, MIME (Mechanisms for Specifying and Describing the Format of Internet Message Bodies), is a Draft Elective Standard. Given the importance of MIME these days, this protocol should probably be promoted to "recommended."

- Limited Use: may have to be implemented in certain unusual situations but won't be needed by most hosts.

- Not Recommended: should not be implemented by anyone.

- Historic: A nice term for obsolete. RFCs that have been classified "historic" have been made obsolete by better protocols or changing technology.

- Informational: Two kinds of RFCs are considered informational. The first group defines protocols that are widely used but weren't developed within the normal Internet standards track, and haven't been through the formal standardization process. For example, the Network File System (NFS), originally developed by Sun, is described in the informational RFC1813. The second group of RFCs provides useful information (like users' guides), but doesn't document a protocol. For example, RFC1635 is an informational RFC.

Table 2–2 lists the RFCs and STDs that provide formal documentation for the protocols discussed in this book. In addition, a few important RFCs are included.

Table 2–2: Selected Internet RFCs

RFC	Title	Subject	Status
RFC1920	Internet Official Protocol Standards	Describes the standardization process and the current status of the different Internet Protocols.	Standards Track

Table 2–2: Selected Internet RFCs (continued)

RFC	Title	Subject	Status
RFC1700	Assigned Numbers	This megalith of a document contains all of the information maintained by the Internet Assigned Numbers Authority including: MIME types and subtypes, port numbers for different services, the meanings of various numbers in IP headers, and more. As RFCs go, this one is rather unusual but absolutely essential.	Standards Track
	Hypertext Markup Language 3.2	HTML 3.2	Internet Draft
RFC1866	Hypertext Markup Language 2.0	HTML 2.0	Proposed Elective Standard
RFC1288	Finger Protocol	The finger protocol requests information about a user at the local or a remote site. It can be a security risk.	Elective Draft Standard
RFC821, STD 10	Simple Mail Transfer Protocol	The process by which one host transfers email to users on another host. This standard doesn't say anything about email user interfaces; it covers the mechanism for passing email from one computer to another.	Recommended Standard
RFC822, STD 11	Format of Electronic Mail Messages	This is the basic syntax for ASCII text email messages. MIME is designed to extend this to support binary data, while insuring that the messages transferred still conform to this standard.	Recommended Standard
RFC1049	Content Type Header Field	The Content Type header field allows mail reading systems to identify the kind of data contained in the body of an email message, and display it appropriately. The message must still conform to STD11.	Recommended Standard

Table 2–2: Selected Internet RFCs (continued)

RFC	Title	Subject	Status
RFC2045, RFC2046, RFC2047, RFC2048, RFC2049	Multipurpose Internet Mail Extensions (MIME)	Encoding different types of binary data for transmission through Internet email and other ASCII-oriented protocols.	Draft Elective Standard
RFC1034, RFC1035, STD 13	Domain Name System	The Domain Name System is the collection of distributed software that translates names, which people can remember, such as *www.ora.com*, into numbers computers can understand. This STD defines how domain name servers on different hosts communicate with each other.	Recommended Standard
RFC862, STD 20	Echo Protocol	Echo is a useful debugging tool that echoes back all the data it receives.	Recommended Standard
RFC863, STD 21	Discard Protocol	Discard is another useful debugging tool that receives packets of data, but sends no response to the client.	Elective Standard
RFC864, STD 22	Character Generator Protocol	The Character Generator Protocol is a useful debugging tool that sends an indefinite sequence of ASCII characters to any client that connects.	Elective Standard
RFC865, STD 23	Quote of the Day	The Quote of the Day protocol returns a quotation to any user who connects and then closes the connection.	Elective Standard
RFC1112, STD 5	Host Extensions for IP Multicasting	This document defines the means by which conforming systems can direct a single packet of data to multiple hosts. This is called multicasting; Java's support for it is discussed in Chapter 13.	Recommended Standard

Table 2–2: Selected Internet RFCs (continued)

RFC	Title	Subject	Status
RFC867, STD 25	Daytime Protocol	The Daytime protocol sends an ASCII string that people can read indicating the current date and time at the server to any client that connects. This contrasts with the various NTP and Time Server protocols that do not return easily readable data.	Elective Standard
RFC868, STD 26	Time Server Protocol	This time protocol sends the time in seconds since midnight, January 1, 1900 to the connecting client. The time is sent as a machine readable, 32-bit signed integer. The standard is incomplete in that it does not specify how the integer is encoded in 32 bits In practice, however, a two's complement, big-endian integer is used.	Elective Standard
RFC2068	HTTP/1.1	This is the first version of the Hypertext Transfer Protocol to become a standards track RFC.	Proposed Standard
RFC1945	HTTP/1.0	The version of the hypertext transfer protocol used by most web browsers and servers as of early 1997.	Informational

3

Basic Web Concepts

By the time you finish this book, I hope you realize that Java can do a lot more than create flashy web pages. Nonetheless, many of your programs will be applets on web pages, or will need to talk to web servers to retrieve files or post data. Therefore, it's important to have a solid understanding of the interaction between web servers and web browsers.

The Hypertext Transfer Protocol (HTTP) is a standard that defines how a web client talks to a server, and how data is transferred from the server back to the client. HTTP relies heavily on two other standards: the Multipurpose Internet Mail Extensions (MIME), and the Hypertext Markup Language (HTML). MIME is a way to encode different kinds of data, such as sound and text, to be transmitted over a 7-bit ASCII connection; it also lets the recipient know what kind of data has been sent, so it can be displayed properly. As its name implies, MIME was originally designed to facilitate multimedia email, and to provide an encoding that could get binary data past the most brain-damaged mail transfer programs. However, it is now used much more broadly. HTML is a simple standard for describing the semantic value of textual data. This means that you can say "this is a header," "this is a list item," "this deserves emphasis," and so on, but you can't (at least in the current version) specify how headers, lists, and other items are formatted; formatting is up to the browser. HTML is a *hypertext* markup language because it includes a way to specify links to other documents identified by URLs (Uniform Resource Locators). A URL is a way to unambiguously identify the location of a file on the Internet. To understand network programming you'll need to understand links, HTML, MIME, and HTTP in somewhat more detail than the average web page designer.

URLs, URIs, and URNs

A Uniform Resource Identifier (URI) is a means of unambiguously locating a *resource* on the Internet. The resource is commonly a file, but it may also be an email address, a news message, a CGI program, or something else. There are two types of URIs: Uniform Resource Locators (URLs), and Uniform Resource Names (URNs). A URL is a pointer to a particular resource on the Internet at a particular location. For example, *http://www.ora.com/* and *ftp://sunsite.unc.edu/pub/javafaq/* are both URLs. A URN is a pointer to a particular resource but without reference to a particular location. The idea behind URNs is that they can conveniently handle resources that are mirrored in many different locations or that have moved from one site to another; they identify the resource itself, not the place where the resource lies. For instance, when given a URN to a file on an FTP site, an FTP program should get the file from the nearest mirror site. A web browser should be able to find a particular web page from its URN even if the page has moved from *http://www.onehost.com/books.html* to *http://www.anotherhost.com/books.html*. URLs are a proposed Internet standard specified in RFC1738 and RFC1808, and are fairly well understood and defined. Unfortunately, URNs are still an area of active research, and are not used by any current software. The rest of this book will use URLs exclusively.

A URL specifies the protocol used to access a server (e.g., ftp, http), the name of the server, and the location of a file on that server. A typical URL looks like *http://sunsite.unc.edu/javafaq/javatutorial.html*. This specifies that there is a file called *javatutorial.html* in a directory called *javafaq* on the server *sunsite.unc.edu*, and that this file can be accessed via the HTTP protocol. The syntax of a URL is:

```
protocol://hostname[:port]/path/filename#section
```

The protocol, also sometimes called the scheme, is one of the following:

file a file on your local disk

ftp an FTP server

http
   a World Wide Web server

gopher
   a Gopher server

news
   a Usenet newsgroup

telnet

   a connection to a Telnet-based service

WAIS

   a WAIS server

The *hostname* part of a URL is the name of the server that provides the resource, like *www.ora.com* or *shock.njit.edu.* It can also be the server's IP address, like 204.29.207.217 or 128.235.252.184. In the case of a news URL, the hostname is a newsgroup rather than an Internet server name.

The *port* number is optional. It's not necessary if the service is running on its default port (port 80 for HTTP servers).

The *path* points to a particular directory on the specified server. The path is relative to the document root of the server, not necessarily to the root of the file system on the server. As a rule, servers that are open to the public do not show their entire file system to clients. Rather, they only show the contents of a specified directory. This directory is called the document root, and all paths and filenames are relative to it. Thus, on a UNIX workstation all files that are available to the public may be in */var/public/html,* but to somebody connecting from a remote machine this directory looks like the root of the file system.

The *filename* points to a particular file in the directory specified by the *path.* It is often omitted, in which case it is left to the server's discretion what file, if any, to send. Many servers send an index file for that directory, often called *index.html* or *Welcome.html.* Others send a list of the files in the directory. Others may send an error message.

Section is used to reference a named anchor in an HTML document. Some documents refer to the section part of the URL as a "fragment"; Java documents rather unaccountably refer to the section as a "Ref." A named anchor is created in HTML document with a tag like this:

```
<A NAME="xtocid1902914">Comments</A>
```

This tag identifies a particular point in a document. To refer to this point, a URL includes not only the document's filename, but also the named anchor separated from the rest of the URL by the pound sign (#):

```
http://sunsite.unc.edu/javafaq/javafaq.html#xtocid1902914
```

Relative URLs

A URL tells the web browser a lot about a document: the protocol used to retrieve the document, the name of the host where the document lives, and the path to that document on the host. Most of this information is likely to be the same for other URLs that are referenced in the document. Therefore, rather than requiring each URL to be specified in its entirety, a URL may inherit the protocol, host-name, and path of its parent document (i.e., the document in which it appears). URLs that aren't complete but inherit pieces from their parent are called *relative* URLs; in contrast, a completely specified URL is called an *absolute* URL. In a rela-tive URL, any pieces that are missing are assumed to be the same as the corre-sponding pieces from the URL of the document in which the URL is found. For example, suppose while browsing *http://sunsite.unc.edu/javafaq/oldnews.html* you click on this hyperlink:

```
<a href="javafaq.html">
```

Your browser cuts *oldnews.html* off *http://sunsite.unc.edu/javafaq/oldnews.html* to get *http://sunsite.unc.edu/javafaq/*. Then it attaches *javafaq.html* onto the end of *http://sunsite.unc.edu/javafaq/* to get *http://sunsite.unc.edu/javafaq/javafaq.html*.

If the relative link begins with a slash (/), then it is relative to the document root instead of relative to the current file. Thus if you click on the following link while browsing *http://sunsite.unc.edu/javafaq/oldnews.html*:

```
<a href="/boutell/faq/www_faq.html">
```

your browser would throw away */javafaq/oldnews.html* and attach */boutell/faq/ www_faq.html* to the end of *http://sunsite.unc.edu* to get *http://sunsite.unc.edu/boutell/ faq/www_faq.html*.

Relative URLs have a number of advantages. First, they save a little typing. Second, and more important, relative URLs allow entire trees of HTML documents to be moved or copied from one site to another without breaking all the internal links.

HTML and SGML

HTML is the format used for writing documents on the Web; they are the primary means by which users interact with web sites. As mentioned earlier, HTML is a sim-ple standard for describing the semantic content of textual data. The idea of describing a text's semantics rather than its appearance comes from an older stan-dard called the Standard Generalized Markup Language (SGML). Standard HTML is an instance of SGML. SGML was created in the early 1970s by the U.S.

Department of Defense to try to bring some order to the multitude of file formats they had to deal with, even then. SGML is now a standard of the International Standards Organization (ISO) standard, ISO 8879:1986.

SGML and, by inheritance, HTML, are based on the notion of design by meaning rather than design by appearance. You don't say that you want some text printed in 18-point type; you say that it is a top-level heading (<H1> in HTML); likewise, you don't say that a word should be placed in italics. Rather, you say it should be emphasized (<EM> in HTML). It is left to the browser to determine how best to display headings or emphasized text.

The tags used to mark up the text are case-insensitive. Thus <STRONG>, <strong>, <Strong>, and <StrONg> are all the same.[*] Some tags have a matching closing tag to define a region of text. A closing tag is the same as the opening tag except that the opening angle bracket is followed by a slash. For example: <STRONG>this text is strong</STRONG>; <EM>this text is emphasized</EM>.

Tags may nest, but they may not overlap. The first line below is standard conforming. The second line is not, though many browsers accept it nonetheless.

```
<STRONG><EM>Jack and Jill went up the hill</EM></STRONG>
<STRONG><EM>to fetch a pail of water</STRONG></EM>
```

Some tags have additional parameters. The <H1> tag and most other paragraph level tags may have an ALIGN parameter that says whether the header should be centered, left-aligned, or right-aligned. For example:

```
<H1 ALIGN=CENTER> This is a centered H1 heading </H1>
```

The value of a parameter may be enclosed in double quotation marks like this:

```
<H1 ALIGN="CENTER"> This is a centered H1 heading </H1>
```

Quotation marks are required only if the value contains embedded spaces. When processing HTML, you need to be prepared for parameter values that do and don't have quotes.

HTML continues to evolve rapidly. The original version (now called HTML 1.0, originally just called HTML) included tags for headers, various kinds of lists, preformatted text, strong and emphasized text, quotations, and few other kinds of content. HTML 1.0 is a de facto standard that is fairly well implemented by most web browsers, but it is not, and never has been, an official standard of the IETF or any other group.

---

[*] Sun has an annoying habit of getting this wrong in early releases of their software. The first release of the Mac JDK, and at least the first two releases of Jeeves, required some tags to be all lowercase.

HTML 2.0 adds images and interactive forms to the language. It was mostly driven by the desire of Marc Andreesen, Eric Bina, and others at NCSA to write a graphical web browser that could show pictures. HTML 2.0 is on the official IESG standards track. As of late 1996, it is a Proposed Elective Standard and seems likely to become an STD. RFC1866 documents this version of HTML. All current web browsers support HTML 2.0 very well.

HTML 3.0 was supposed to add tables, mathematical equations, figures, style sheets, and quite a bit more to the language. Some of these extensions have been implemented in different browsers, but no browsers support the full range of proposed extensions in HTML 3.0. However, there is no HTML 3.0 standard, and never will be; the standards effort fell apart, and was superseded by the rapid development of the web.

Several companies, notably Netscape, Microsoft, and Sun, have added nonstandard extensions to HTML. These include blinking text, inline movies, frames and, most importantly for this book, applets. Some of these extensions, like tables, are based on proposals for HTML 3.0. Others, like Netscape's notorious <BLINK>, come out of left field, and have no place in a semantically oriented language like HTML.

The standard currently under development is HTML 3.2, which codifies the existing practice of most browsers; it includes features like tables, refinements to the IMG tag, and quite a bit more. The most important addition is style sheets, which let documents request specific formatting for different tags. There was never an HTML 3.1. The World Wide Web Consortium (W3C), the organization currently developing HTML standards, decided to jump straight to version 3.2 from the unreleased 3.0.

HTML 4.0 will build on HTML 3.2 as well as add features that were originally planned for HTML 3.0, including mathematical equations. HTML 4.0 is barely being discussed as I write this. However, given the rate at which the web moves, it could well be passé by the second edition of this book.

HTTP

HTTP, the Hypertext Transport Protocol, is the standard protocol for communication between web browsers and web servers. HTTP is a stateless protocol that specifies how a client and server establish a connection, how the client requests data from the server, how the server responds to that request, and finally how the connection is closed. HTTP connections use the TCP/IP protocol for data transfer.

HTTP 1.0 is the currently accepted version of the protocol. It uses MIME to encode data. The basic protocol defines a sequence of four steps for each request from a client to the server.

1. *Making the connection*

   The client establishes a TCP connection to the server, on port 80 by default; other ports may be specified in the URL.

2. *Making a request*

   The client sends a message to the server requesting the page at a specified URL. The format of this request is typically something like:

   ```
   GET /index.html HTTP/1.0
   ```

   GET is a keyword. */index.html* is a relative URL to a file on the server. The file is assumed to be on the machine that receives the request, so there is no need to prefix it with *http://www.thismachine.com/*. HTTP/1.0 is the version of the protocol that the client understands. Two carriage return/linefeed pairs (\r\n\r\n in Java parlance) terminate the request, regardless of how lines are terminated on the client or server platform.

   Although the GET line is all that is required, a client request can include other information as well. These take the form:

   ```
   Keyword: Value
   ```

   The most common such keyword is Accept, which tells the server what kinds of data the client can handle. For example, the lines below say that the client can handle four MIME types, corresponding to HTML documents, plain text, GIF and JPEG images.

   ```
   Accept: text/html
   Accept: text/plain
   Accept: image/gif
   Accept: image/jpeg
   ```

   User-Agent is another common keyword that lets the server know what browser is being used. This allows the server to send files optimized for the particular browser type. The line below says that the request comes from version 2.4 of the Lynx browser:

   ```
   User-Agent: Lynx/2.4 libwww/2.1.4
   ```

   Finally, a blank line terminates the request; that is, two carriage return linefeed pairs, \r\n\r\n. A complete request might look like:

   ```
   GET /index.html HTTP/1.0
   Accept: text/html
   Accept: text/plain
   User-Agent: Lynx/2.4 libwww/2.1.4
   ```

The last line was intentionally left blank to end the request. In addition to GET, there are several other request types. HEAD retrieves only the header for the file, not the actual data. This is commonly used to check the modification date of a file, to see if a copy stored in the local cache is still valid. POST sends form data to the server, and PUT uploads a file to the server.

3. *The response*

The server sends a response to the client. The response begins with a response code, followed by MIME header information, then a blank line, then the requested document or an error message. Assuming the requested file is found, a typical response looks like this:

```
HTTP/1.0 OK 200
Server: NCSA/1.4.2
MIME-version: 1.0
Content-type: text/html
Content-length: 107

<html>
<Head>
<Title>
A Sample HTML file
</Title>
</Head>
<body>
The rest of the document goes here
</body>
</html>
```

The first line indicates the protocol the server is using (HTTP 1.0), followed by a response code. OK 200 is the most common response code, indicating that the request was successful. Table 3–1 is a complete list of the response codes used by HTTP 1.0; HTTP 1.1 will add still more to this list. The other header lines identify the server software (the NCSA server, version 1.4.2), the version of MIME in use, the MIME content type, and the length of the document delivered (not counting this header)—in this case, 107 bytes.

4. *Closing the connection*

Either the client or the server or both closes the connection. Thus, a separate network connection is used for each request. If the client connects again, the server retains no memory of the previous connection or its results. A protocol that retains no memory of past requests is called *stateless*; in contrast, a protocol like FTP can process many requests before the connection is closed. The lack of state is both a strength and a weakness of HTTP.

Table 3–1: HTTP 1.0 Response Codes

Response Code	Meaning
2xx Successful	Response codes between 200 and 299 indicate that the request was received, understood, and accepted.
200 OK	The most common response code. If the request used GET or POST, the requested data is contained in the response, along with the usual headers. If the request used HEAD, only the header information is included.
201 Created	The server has created a data file at a URL specified in the body of the response. The web browser should now attempt to load that URL. This is only sent in response to POST requests.
202 Accepted	This rather uncommon response indicates that a request (generally from POST) is being processed, but the processing is not yet complete so no response can be returned. The server should return an HTML page that explains the situation to the user, provides an estimate of when the request is likely to be completed, and, ideally, has a link to a status monitor of some kind.
204 No Content	The server has successfully processed the request but has no information to send back to the client. This is usually the result of a poorly written form-processing CGI program that accepts data but does not return a response to the user indicating that it has finished.
3xx Redirection	Response codes from 300 to 399 indicate that the web browser needs to go to a different page.
300 Multiple Choices	The page requested is available from one or more locations. The body of the response includes a list of locations from which the user or web browser can pick the most appropriate one. If the server prefers one of these choices, the URL of this choice is included in a Location header that web browsers can use to load the preferred page.
301 Moved Permanently	The page has moved to a new URL. The web browser should automatically load the page at this URL, and update any bookmarks that point to the old URL.
302 Moved Temporarily	This unusual response code indicates that a page is temporarily at a new URL, but that the document's location will change again in the foreseeable future, so bookmarks should not be updated.

Table 3–1: HTTP 1.0 Response Codes (continued)

Response Code	Meaning
304 Not Modified	The client has performed a GET request but used the If-Modified-Since header to indicate that it only wants the document if it has been recently updated. This status code is returned because the document has not been updated. The web browser will now load the page from a cache.
4xx Client Error	Response codes between 400 and 499 indicate that the client has erred in some fashion, though this may as easily be the result of an unreliable network connection as it is of a buggy or non-conforming web browser. The browser should stop sending data to the server as soon as it receives a 4xx response. Unless it is responding to a HEAD request, the server should explain the error status in the body of its response.
400 Bad Request	The client request to the server used improper syntax. This is rather unusual, though it is likely to happen if you're writing your own client.
401 Unauthorized	Authorization, generally username and password controlled, is required to access this page. Either the username and password have not yet been presented or the username and password are invalid.
403 Forbidden	The server understood the request, but is deliberately refusing to process it. Authorization will not help. This might be used when access to a certain page is restricted to a certain range of IP addresses.
404 Not Found	This most common error response indicates that the server cannot find the requested page. It may indicate a bad link, a page that has moved with no forwarding address, a mistyped URL, or something similar.
5xx Server Error	Response codes between 500 and 599 indicate that something has gone wrong with the server, and the server cannot fix the problem.
500 Internal Server Error	An unexpected condition occurred that the server does not know how to handle.
501 Not Implemented	The server does not have the feature that is needed to fulfill this request. A server that cannot handle POST requests might send this response to a client that tried to POST form data to it.

Table 3–1: HTTP 1.0 Response Codes (continued)

Response Code	Meaning
502 Bad Gateway	This response is only applicable to servers that act as proxies or gateways. It indicates that the proxy received an invalid response from a server it was connecting to in an effort to fulfill the request.
503 Service Unavailable	The server is temporarily unable to handle the request, perhaps due to overloading or maintenance.

HTTP 1.1 more than doubles the number of responses. However, a response code between 200 and 299 always indicates success; a response code between 300 and 399 always indicates redirection; 400 to 499 always indicates a client error; and 500 to 599 indicates a server error.

HTTP 1.0 is documented in the informational RFC1945; it is not an official Internet standard because it was developed primarily outside the IETF. HTTP 1.1 is a proposed standard (as of early 1997) being developed by the W3C and the HTTP working group of the IETF. It provides for much more flexible and powerful communication between the client and the server. However, it remains tied to the basic pattern of a client request, followed by a server response, consisting of a series of headers, followed by a blank line, followed by MIME encoded data.

Even further down the road is something currently called HTTP-NG (for Next Generation). HTTP-NG is designed to have much higher performance than HTTP 1.x, primarily through the use of state. Remember that HTTP 1.0 opens a new connection for every request. In practice, the time taken to open and close all the connections opened in a typical web session can outweigh the time taken to transmit the data, especially for sessions with many small documents. HTTP-NG allows a browser to send many different requests over a single connection; the connection remains open until it is explicitly closed. The requests and responses are all asynchronous. A browser doesn't need to wait for a response to its first request before sending a second or a third. Similarly, the server can reply to requests in any order. It can even send the responses to several requests in parallel using an application layer concept called "channels." A channel is essentially a way to divide a port into subparts. As of early 1997, HTTP-NG is nowhere near becoming an Internet standard, but given the rate at which Internet software is moving, it would not be surprising to see a commercial implementation in the near future.

MIME

MIME is an open standard for sending multipart, multimedia data through Internet email.[*] The data may be binary, or it may use multiple ASCII and non-ASCII character sets. Although MIME was originally intended for email, it has become a widely used technique to describe a file's contents so that client software can tell the difference between different kinds of data. For example, a web browser uses MIME to tell whether a file is a GIF image or a printable PostScript file.

MIME supports almost a hundred predefined types of content. Content types are classified at two levels: a type and a subtype. The type shows very generally what kind of data is contained: Is it a picture? Is it text? Is it a movie? The subtype identifies specifically the kind of data: GIF image, JPEG image, TIFF image. For example, HTML's content type is text/html; the type is text, and the subtype is html. The content type for a GIF image is image/gif; the type is image, and the subtype is gif. Table 3–2 lists the more common defined content types as of early 1997.[†] On most systems, a simple text file maintains a mapping between MIME types and the application used to process that type of data. On UNIX, this file is called *mime.types*.

The data returned by an HTTP 1.0 or 1.1 web server is sent in MIME format. Most web servers and clients understand at least two MIME text content types: text/html and text/plain, and two image formats, image/gif and image/jpeg. The Web also uses MIME for posting forms to web servers, a common way for an applet to communicate with a server. Finally, Java relies on MIME types to pick the appropriate content handler for a particular stream of data.

Table 3–2: Predefined MIME Content Types

Type	Subtype	Description
text		The document represents printable text.
	plain	This is supposed to imply raw ASCII text. However, some web servers use text/plain as the default MIME type for any file they can't recognize. Therefore, anything and everything, most notably, *.class* byte code files, can get identified as a text/plain file.

---

[*] Officially, MIME stands for "Multipurpose Internet Mail Extensions," which is the expansion of the acronym used in RFC1521. However, you will hear other versions—most frequently, "Multipart Internet Mail Extensions" and "Multimedia Internet Mail Extensions."

[†] For more details on MIME, see: Jerry Sweet, Ed Vielmetti, and Tim Goodwin, *The comp.mail.mime FAQ, http://www.netscape.com/assist/helper_apps/faq1.html*; N. Borenstein, Bellcore, "Multimedia Mail From the Bottom Up or Teaching Dumb Mailers to Sing," *ConneXions*, pp. 36–39, Sep. 92. The most current list of registered MIME types is available from *ftp://ftp.isi.edu/in-notes/iana/assignments/media-types/media-types*.

Table 3–2: Predefined MIME Content Types (continued)

Type	Subtype	Description
	richtext	This is an HTML-like markup for encoding formatting into pure ASCII text. It's never really caught on, in large part due to the popularity of HTML.
	tab-separated-values	The interchange format used by many spreadsheets and databases; records are separated by line breaks, and fields by tabs.
	html	Hypertext Markup Language as used by web browsers.
multipart		Multipart MIME messages encode several different files into one message.
	mixed	Several message parts intended for sequential viewing.
	alternative	The same message in multiple formats so a client may choose the most convenient one.
	digest	The popular format for merging many email messages into a single digest; used by many mailing lists and some FAQ lists.
	parallel	Several parts intended for simultaneous viewing.
	appledouble	A format used primarily on the AppleLink online service for encoding a two-fork Macintosh file into a single file.
message		An email message.
	rfc822	A standard email message including headers.
	partial	Part of a longer email message that has been split into multiple parts to allow transmission through email gateways.
	external-body	Just the headers of the email message; the message's body is not included, but exists at some other location, and is referenced, perhaps by a URL.
	news	A news article.
application		Data specific to some application.
	octet-stream	Unspecified binary data, which is usually saved into a file for the user. This MIME type is sometimes used to serve *.class* byte code files.
	java	A (not yet standard) subtype sometimes used to serve *.class* byte code files.
	postscript	Adobe Postscript.
	dca-rft	IBM's Document Content Architecture-Richly Formatted Text.

Table 3–2: Predefined MIME Content Types (continued)

Type	Subtype	Description
	rtf	An incompletely defined Microsoft format for word processing files.
	mac-binhex40	A means of encoding the two forks of a Macintosh ˙ document into a single ASCII file.
	pdf	An Adobe Acrobat file.
	zip	A zip compressed file.
	macwriteii	A MacWrite II word processing document.
	msword	A Microsoft Word document.
image		Pictures
	jpeg	The Joint Photographic Experts Group file format for bitmapped images with lossy compression.
	gif	A Graphics Interchange Format image. The format was originally developed by CompuServe. It uses certain compression algorithms on which Unisys holds a patent.
	tiff	The tagged image file format from Adobe.
audio		Sound
	basic	8-bit ISDN mu-law with a single channel and a sample rate of eight kilohertz. This is the format used by *.au* and *.snd* files.
video		Video
	mpeg	The Motion Picture Experts Group format for video data with lossy compression.
	quicktime	Apple's proprietary QuickTime movie format. Before being included in a MIME message QuickTime files must be "flattened."

A MIME-compliant program does not need to understand all these different types of data; it just needs to recognize what it can and cannot handle. Many programs, like Netscape, use various helper programs to display types of content they don't themselves understand.

MIME allows you to define additional non-standard subtypes by using the prefix x-. For example, the content type application/x-tex has the MIME type application and the non-standard subtype x-tex for a TEX document. These x-types are not guaranteed to be understood by any program other than the one that created them. Indeed, two programs may use the same x-type to mean two completely different things; or different programs may use different x-types to mean the same thing. However, many non-standard types have come into common use; some of the more common ones are listed in Table 3–3.

Table 3–3: x-types

Type	X-subtype	Description
application		Most x-types are subtypes of application; the name of the subtype is usually a file format name or an application name.
	x-aiff	SGI's AIFF audio data format
	x-bitmap	An X Window System bitmap image
	x-gzip	Data compressed in the GNU gzip format
	x-dvi	A TEX DVI document
	x-framemaker	A FrameMaker document
	x-latex	A LATEX document
	x-macbinhex40	Identical to `application/mac-binhex40`, but older software may use this x-type instead.
	x-mif	A FrameMaker MIF document
	x-sd	A session directory protocol announcement, used to announce MBONE events
	x-shar	A shell archive; this is the UNIX equivalent of a Windows or Macintosh self-extracting archive. Software shouldn't be configured to unpack shell archives automatically, because a shell archive can call any program that the user has the rights to call.
	x-tar	A tar archive
	x-gtar	A GNU tar archive
	x-tcl	A TCL (tool command language) program. You should never configure your web browser or email program to automatically run non-Java programs you download from the web or receive in email messages.
	x-tex	A TEX document
	x-texinfo	A GNU texinfo document
	x-troff	A troff document
	x-troff-man	A troff document written with the `man` macros
	x-troff-me	A troff document that should be processed using the `me` macros

Table 3–3: x-types (continued)

Type	X-subtype	Description
	x-troff-ms	A troff document that should be processed using the ms macros.
	x-wais-source	A WAIS source
	x-www-form-urlencoded	A CGI query string that has been encoded like a URL, with + replacing spaces and % escapes replacing non-alphanumeric characters that aren't separators
audio		Sound
	x-aiff	The same as application/x-aiff: an AIFF audio file
	x-wav	The Windows WAV sound format
image		Pictures
	x-fits	The FITS image format used primarily by astronomers
	x-macpict	A Macintosh PICT image
	x-pict	A Macintosh PICT image
	x-macpaint	A Macpaint image
	x-pbm	A portable bitmap image
	x-portable-bitmap	A portable bitmap image
	x-pgm	A PGM image
video		Video
	x-msvideo	Microsoft AVI Video for Windows
	x-sgi-movie	A Silicon Graphics movie
x-world		
	x-vrml	A Virtual Reality Modeling Language file, an evolving standard for 3-D data on the web

CGI

CGI, the common gateway interface, is used to generate Web pages dynamically; the browser invokes a program on the server that creates a new page. This web page may be based purely on server data, or it may process the results of a client form submission. You can write CGI programs in almost any language including Java, though currently most CGI programming is done in Perl, C, or AppleScript.

CGI programs run as independent processes, initiated by the HTTP server each time a request for services is received. This has three important consequences. First, CGI programs are relatively safe to run. A CGI program can crash without damaging the server, at least on preemptively multitasking, memory-protected operating systems like UNIX. Second, the CGI program has strictly limited access to the server. Third, CGI programs exact a performance penalty relative to serving a static file, due to the overhead of spawning a separate process for each request.

The simplest CGI programs run without any input from the user. From the view of the client, these are accessed like any other web page, and aren't of much concern to this book. The difference between a web page produced by a CGI program that takes no input and a web page written in static HTML is all on the server side. What happens on the server side has been adequately covered in several other books. For more information about writing server programs that process CGI input and create dynamic web pages, see William E. Weinman's *The CGI Book* from New Riders or Shishir Gundavaram's *CGI Programming on the World Wide Web* from O'Reilly & Associates.

This book takes an approach to CGI that isn't discussed frequently: how to write a client that sends data to a CGI program. The most common use of CGI is to process user input from HTML forms. In this capacity, CGI provides a standard, well understood and well supported means for Java applets and applications to talk to remote systems; therefore, I will cover how to use Java to talk to a CGI program on the server. There are other ways for Java programs to talk to servers, including remote method invocation (RMI) and servlets; I discuss these in Chapter 14, *Remote Method Invocation*, and Chapter 15, *The Java Server API and Servlets*. However, RMI and servlets are still alpha technologies at best. In contrast, CGI is mature, robust, better supported across multiple platforms and web servers, and better understood in the web development community.

Example 3–1 and Figure 3–1 show a simple form with two fields to collect a name and an email address. The values the user enters in the form are sent back to the server when the user presses the "Submit Query" button. The CGI program to run when the form data is received is */cgi-bin/register.pl*; the program is specified in the ACTION parameter of the FORM tag. The URL in this parameter is usually a relative URL, as it is in Example 3–1.

Example 3–1: A simple form with input fields for a name and an email address

```
<HTML>
<HEAD>
<TITLE>Sample Form</TITLE>
</HEAD>
<BODY>

<FORM METHOD=GET ACTION="/cgi-bin/register.pl">
```

Example 3–1: A simple form with input fields for a name and an email address (continued)

```
<PRE>
Please enter your name:          <INPUT NAME="username" SIZE=40>
Please enter your email address: <INPUT NAME="email" SIZE=40>
</PRE>
<INPUT TYPE="SUBMIT">
</FORM>
</BODY>
</HTML>
```

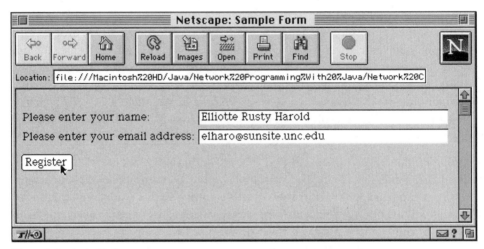

Figure 3–1: A simple form

The web browser reads the data the user enters and encodes it in a simple fashion. The name of each field is separated from its value by the equal sign. Different fields are separated from each other by an ampersand. Non-alphanumeric characters are encoded by a percent sign followed by two hexadecimal digits giving the ASCII value for that character. All characters in a URL are encoded *except* for the letters *a* through *z*, the capital letters *A* through *Z*, and the underscore (_). Spaces are a special case because they're so common. Instead of being encoded as %20, they become the + sign. The plus sign itself is encoded as %2b. For example, the data from the form in Figure 3–1 is encoded as:

```
username=Elliotte+Rusty+Harold&email=elharo%40sunsite%2eunc%2eedu
```

This is called the *query string*.

There are two ways the query string can be sent to the server: GET and POST. If the form specifies the GET method, the browser attaches the query string to the URL it sends to the server. CGI programs that use POST send the query string on an output stream. The form in Example 3–1 uses GET to communicate with the server, so it connects to the server and sends the following command (the actual command would be all one line, but this is too wide for the pages of this book):

```
GET /cgi-bin/register.pl?username=Elliotte+Rusty+Harold
&email=elharo%40sunsite%2eunc%2eedu HTTP/1.0
```

The server is responsible for recognizing that the URL contains the name of the CGI program plus input for the program; it passes the query string to the program, usually as an environment variable. Because of limitations in the lengths of environment variables on some platforms, the GET method is unreliable for sending more than about 200 characters of text. In these cases you're better off using POST.

With the POST method, the web browser sends the usual headers and follows them with a blank line (two successive carriage-return/linefeed pairs), and then sends the query string. The query string is passed to the CGI program on standard input. If the form in Figure 3–1 used POST, it would send this to the server:

```
POST /cgi-bin/register.pl HTTP/1.0
Content-type: application/x-www-form-urlencoded
Content-length: 65

username=Elliotte+Rusty+Harold&email=elharo%40sunsite%2eunc%2eedu
```

There are many different form tags in HTML that produce popup menus, radio buttons, and more. However, although these input widgets appear different to the user, the format of data they send to the server is the same. Each form element has a name and an encoded string value.

Applets and Security

Now that you understand how files are transferred across the web, you're ready to explore how applets are transferred. On one hand, applets are just more files that are transferred like any other. On the other hand, what an applet can do is closely related to where it came from. This isn't true of some other data types, including HTML and GIFs.

Where Do Applets and Classes Come From?

When a web browser sees an APPLET tag and decides to download and play the applet, it starts a long chain of events. Let's say your browser sees the applet tag below:

```
<APPLET CODEBASE=http://sunsite.unc.edu/javafaq/classes
code=animation.class width=200 height=100>
```

1. The browser sets aside a rectangular area on the page 200 pixels wide and 100 pixels high. In most web browsers this area is fixed and cannot be modified once created. (Sun's *appletviewer* is a notable exception.)

2. The web browser opens a connection to the server specified in the CODEBASE parameter, using port 80 unless another port is specified in the CODEBASE URL. If there's no CODEBASE parameter, the socket is opened to the same server that served the HTML page.

3. The browser requests the *.class* file from the web server just as it requests any other file. If a CODEBASE is present, it is prefixed to the requested filename. Otherwise the document base (the directory that contains the HTML page) is used. For example:

   ```
   GET /javafaq/classes/animation.class HTTP/1.0
   ```

4. The server responds by sending a MIME header followed by a blank line (\r\n) followed by the binary data in the *.class* file. A properly configured server sends *.class* files with MIME type application/octet-stream:

   ```
   HTTP/1.0 200 OK
   Date: Mon, 10 Jun 1996 17:11:43 GMT
   Server: Apache/1.0.5
   Content-type: application/octet-stream
   Content-length: 2782
   Last-modified: Fri, 08 Sep 1995 21:53:55 GMT
   ```

   Not all web servers are configured to send *.class* files correctly. Some send them as text/plain, which, though technically incorrect, works in most cases.

5. The web browser receives the data and stores it in a byte array.

6. The byte code verifier goes over the byte codes that have been received to make sure they don't do anything illegal.

7. If the byte code verifier is satisfied with the bytes that were downloaded, the raw data is converted into a Java class using the defineClass() and load-Class() methods of the current ClassLoader object. The class downloaded from the network is placed into a private name space associated with its origin. Thus, the above class may become edu.unc.sunsite.animation* instead of animation. This way, classes with the same name, but downloaded from different locations, will not conflict. This scheme is normally transparent to the programmer; you only have to write animation, not edu.unc.sunsite.animation in your source code.

---

* This isn't actually the name that's used, but it doesn't matter. All you need to know is that classes with the same name won't conflict with each other.

8. When an object of this class references another class, the Java interpreter first searches for the new class in the user's CLASSPATH. If the class is found in the user's CLASSPATH, it is created from the *.class* file on the user's hard drive. Otherwise, the web browser goes back to the site from which this class came, and downloads the *.class* file for the new class. The same procedure is followed for the new class, and any other class that is downloaded from the Net. If the new class cannot be found, a ClassNotFoundException is thrown.

Security: To Whom Can an Applet Talk and What Can It Say?

There is much FUD (fear, uncertainty, and doubt) in the universe about what Java applets can and cannot do. This is not a book about Java's SecurityManager, but I will mention a few things that applets loaded from the network are usually prohibited from doing.

1. Applets cannot access arbitrary addresses in memory. Unlike the other restrictions enforced by the browser's SecurityManager, this restriction is a property of the Java language itself and the byte code verifier.

2. Applets cannot access the local file system in any way. They cannot read from, or write to, the local file system; nor can they find out any information about files. Therefore, they cannot find out whether a file exists, or what its modification date may be.

3. Applets cannot launch other programs on the client. In other words, they cannot call System.exec() or Runtime.exec().

4. Applets cannot load libraries or define native method calls.

5. Applets are not allowed to use System.getProperty() in a way that reveals information about the user or the user's machine, such as a username or home directory. They may use System.getProperty() to find out what version of Java is in use.

6. Applets may not define any system properties.

7. In Java 1.1, applets may not create or manipulate any Thread or ThreadGroup that is not in the applet's own ThreadGroup. They may do this in Java 1.0.

8. Applets cannot define or use a new instance of ClassLoader, SecurityManager, ContentHandlerFactory, SocketImplFactory or URLStreamHandlerFactory. They must use the ones already in place.

9. An applet can only open network connections to the host from which the applet itself was downloaded.

10. Finally, and most important for this book, applets cannot accept connections from a client machine; an applet cannot create a server on the client.

Of these eight, only the second, ninth, and tenth are serious inconveniences for any significant number of applets. You can relax these restrictions in HotJava and the *appletviewer*, but not in Netscape. However, even if your audience uses HotJava, you should not expect to be allowed to open connections to arbitrary hosts or accept connections. If your program cannot work with these restrictions, it should be an application instead of an applet. Java applications are just like any other sort of application: they aren't restricted as to what they can do. If you are writing an application that will download and execute classes, you should consider carefully what restrictions to put in place, and write an appropriate subclass of `Security-Manager` to implement those restrictions.

Applet Network Security Levels

The Applet Viewer and HotJava have three security levels related to network access. The first security level for applets is "None." This is maximum security; the applet cannot use any of the classes in the `java.net` package. Therefore, the applet cannot make any network connections, or resolve any URLs or domain names. This security level makes this book completely useless. Applets that use networking may assume that this security level won't be in effect, if for no other reason than that they will be useless if it is. However, an applet may want to check first, and put up an error message if it is not allowed to make network connections.

The second network security level is "Unrestricted." This means that an applet can do anything it wants with the network. It can connect to any system the client running the applet can reach. It can open sockets to TFTP ports on machines around the Internet and try to retrieve */etc/passwd*, or launch other attacks across the network. It can gather information about the names and addresses of machines on the internal network behind a firewall that are not normally visible to the outside world, and send that information back to the applet host or some other machine. This level of trust is a little more than most people are willing to give. Therefore, you should not assume that the applets you write will have unrestricted access to the `java.net` classes.

The third and default network security level is "Applet Host." This allows the applets to make connections to the single site from which they were downloaded. This will almost always be the site from which the HTML page came, though there are some exceptions. In other words, applets can talk to the host specified by getCodeBase(), which is normally the same as the host retrieved by getDocument-Base(). You should write applets that use networking with the assumption that they need to work within these restrictions. If you need more access to the network than the Applet Host security level allows, you should consider writing an application instead.

4

Processing Internet Addresses

DNS, IP Addresses, and All That

Computers connected to the Internet are called *hosts*. Each host is identified by at least one unique 32-bit number called an Internet address, an IP address, or a host address, depending on who you talk to. You normally write an IP address as four unsigned bytes, each ranging from 0 to 255, with the most significant byte first. Bytes are separated by periods for human convenience. For example, the address for *rever.nmsu.edu* is 128.123.3.18. This takes up exactly four bytes in memory.

IP addresses are great for computers, but they are a problem for humans, who have a hard time remembering long numbers. In the 1950s, it was discovered that most people could remember about seven digits; some can remember as many as nine, while others remember as few as five. This is why phone numbers are broken into three- and four-digit pieces with three-digit area codes.[*] Obviously an IP address, which can have as many as twelve decimal digits, is beyond the capacity of most humans to remember. I can remember about two IP addresses, and then only if I use them both daily, and the second is a simple permutation of the first.

To avoid the need to carry around Rolodexes full of IP addresses, the designers of the Internet invented the Domain Name System (DNS). DNS associates hostnames that people can remember (like *rever.nmsu.edu*) with IP addresses computers can remember (like 128.123.3.18).[†] Most hosts have at least one hostname. An exception is made for computers that don't have a permanent IP address (like many

---

[*] G.A. Miller, "The Magic Number Seven, Plus or Minus Two: Some Limits on Our Capacity for Processing Information," *Psychological Review*, vol. 63, pp. 81–97.

[†] Colloquially, people often use "Internet address" to mean a hostname (or even an email address). In a book about network programming, it is crucial to be precise about addresses and hostnames. In this book, an address is always a numeric IP address, never a human-readable hostname.

PCs). Because they don't have a permanent address, they can't be used as servers, and since nobody will refer to them, they don't need a name.

Some machines have multiple names. For instance, both *www.macfaq.com* and *spacecadet.cnet.com* are the same SPARCstation in San Francisco. The name *www.macfaq.com* really refers to a web site rather than a particular machine; as this web site has moved from machine to machine, the name has been reassigned so that it always points to the web site's current server. This way, URLs around the web don't need to be updated just because the site has moved to a new host. Some common names like *www* and *news* are often aliases for the machines providing those services. For example, *www.ora.com* is an alias for ORA's public web server. Since the server may change over time, the alias can move with the service. On rare occasions, one name may map to multiple IP addresses. It is then the responsibility of the DNS server to randomly choose machines to respond to each request. This feature is most frequently used for very high-traffic web sites, where it splits the load across multiple systems.

Every computer connected to the Internet should have access to a machine called a domain name server, generally a UNIX box running special DNS software that knows the mappings between different hostnames and IP addresses. Most domain name servers only know the addresses of the hosts on their local network, plus the addresses of a few domain name servers at other sites. If a client asks for the address of a machine outside the local domain, the local domain name server asks a domain name server at the remote location, and relays the answer to the requestor.[*]

Most of the time, you can use hostnames and let DNS handle the translation to IP addresses. As long as you can connect to a domain name server, you don't need to worry about the details of how names and addresses are passed between your machine, the local domain name server, and the rest of the Internet. However, you will need to have access to at least one domain name server to use the examples in this chapter, and most of the rest of this book. These programs will not work on a standalone Mac or PC. Your machine must be connected to the Internet.

The InetAddress Class

The `java.net.InetAddress` class represents an Internet address. It contains two fields: `hostName` (a `String`), and `address` (an `int`). The `hostName` field contains the name of the host, for example, *www.ora.com*. The `address` field contains the 32-bit IP address. These fields are not public, so you can't access them directly. It will probably be necessary to change this representation to a byte array when 16-byte

---

[*] For more information about DNS see Paul Albitz and Cricket Liu, *DNS and BIND*, 2nd edition, O'Reilly & Associates, 1997.

IPv6 and 128-bit Addresses

The current IP address standard uses 32 bits, which is enough to address 4,294,967,296 computers, almost one for every person on Earth. You'd think it would be enough to handle even the explosive growth of the Internet for some time. However, we're currently in the middle of an address shortage. One relatively minor contribution to the shortage comes from machines that have many different IP addresses, either because they have multiple network interfaces (e.g., Ethernet cards), or because they use different IP addresses to provide different services. For instance, a Solaris 2.4 computer can pretend to be both *http://www.hotdogs.com/* and *http://www.badbreath.com/* by putting each of these services at a different IP address that attach to the same physical machine.

The real cause of the address shortage is that the addressees that are available aren't allocated very efficiently. Because of the way the addresses are parceled out, most organizations receive blocks of at least 256 numbers even if they only need a few of them. Other organizations receive blocks of 65,536 even if they only need a few thousand. Therefore, there's a lot of waste, and the addresses are beginning to run out.

Don't worry too much, though. A series of stopgap measures has been put in place to allocate addresses more efficiently; this should get the Internet through the next couple of years. After that, a new standard called IPv6 will begin using 16-byte, 128-bit addresses. This expands the available address space to 2^{128} or 1.6043703E32 different addresses. It's not enough to address every molecule in the universe, but it should be enough to get us well into the twenty-first century. IPv6 has been designed to be backwards compatible with 32-bit IP addresses to ease the transition.

As of 1996, Java doesn't yet support 128-bit IP addresses, nor are they in common use. However, Java's networking classes have been designed with 128-bit addresses in mind. When IPv6 does begin moving out of the labs and into the real world, it will be easy for Sun to modify the `java.net` classes to support the new address format; almost everything in this book will continue to work.

IPv6 addresses come into use. However, if you always use the `InetAddress` class to represent addresses, the changeover should not affect you; the class shields you from the details of how addresses are implemented.

Creating New InetAddress Objects

There are no public constructors in `java.net.InetAddress`. However, there are three static methods that return suitably initialized `InetAddress` objects, given a little information. They are:

```
public static InetAddress InetAddress.getByName(String hostname)
public static InetAddress[] InetAddress.getAllByName(String hostname)
public static InetAddress InetAddress.getLocalHost()
```

public static InetAddress InetAddress.getByName(String hostname)

The method you'll use most frequently is `InetAddress.getByName()`. This is a static method that takes the hostname you're looking for as its argument. It uses DNS to look up the host's IP address. Call `getByName()` like this:

```
java.net.InetAddress address = java.net.InetAddress.getByName("www.oreilly.com");
```

If you have already imported the `java.net.InetAddress` class, which will almost always be the case, you can call `getByName()` like this:

```
InetAddress address = InetAddress.getByName("www.oreilly.com");
```

In the rest of this book I will assume that there is an `import java.net.*;` statement at the top of every code fragment, as well as any other necessary import statements.

The `InetAddress.getByName()` method throws an `UnknownHostException` if the host can't be found, so you need to wrap it in a `try`-block like this.

```
try {
  InetAddress address = InetAddress.getByName("www.oreilly.com");
  System.out.println(address);
}
catch (UnknownHostException e) {
  System.out.println("Could not find www.oreilly.com");
}
```

Example 4–1 is a complete program that creates an `InetAddress` object for *www.oreilly.com* and prints it out.

Example 4–1: A program that prints the address of www.oreilly.com

```
import java.net.*;

class oreilly {

  public static void main (String args[]) {

    try {
      InetAddress address = InetAddress.getByName("www.oreilly.com");
      System.out.println(address);
```

Example 4–1: A program that prints the address of www.oreilly.com (continued)

```
    }
    catch (UnknownHostException e) {
      System.out.println("Could not find www.oreilly.com");
    }

  }

}
```

Here's the result:

```
% java oreilly
www.oreilly.com/204.29.207.217
```

On rare occasions, you will need to connect to a machine that does not have a hostname. In this case, you can pass a `String` containing the human-readable form of the IP address to `InetAddress.getByName()`:

```
    InetAddress address = InetAddress.getByName("204.29.207.217");
```

Example 4–2 uses the IP address for *www.oreilly.com* instead of the name.

Example 4–2: A program that prints the address of 204.29.207.217

```
import java.net.*;

class oreilly {

  public static void main (String args[]) {

    try {
      InetAddress address = InetAddress.getByName("204.29.207.217");
      System.out.println(address);
    }
    catch (UnknownHostException e) {
      System.out.println("Could not find 204.29.207.217");
    }

  }

}
```

Here's the result:

```
% java oreilly
204.29.207.217/204.29.207.217
```

When you call `getByName()` with an IP address as an argument, it doesn't do a reverse lookup to find out the corresponding hostname. That's because it thinks it already has one, in this case the string `"204.29.207.217"`. This is a bug in Java 1.0 which is fixed in Java 1.1.

Hostnames are much more stable than IP addresses. Some services like the MIT FAQ archives have lived at the same hostname (*rtfm.mit.edu*) for years but switched IP addresses several times. If you have a choice between using a hostname like *www.oreilly.com* or an IP address like 204.29.207.217, always choose the hostname. Only use an IP address when a hostname is not available.

public static InetAddress[ ]
InetAddress.getAllByName(String hostname)

Some computers have more than one Internet address. Given a hostname, `InetAddress.getAllByName()` returns an array that contains all the `InetAddresses` corresponding to a given hostname. Its use is straightforward:

```
InetAddress[] addresses = InetAddress.getAllByName("www.ora.com");
```

Like `InetAddress.getByName()`, `InetAddress.getAllByName()` can throw an `UnknownHostException`, so you need to enclose it in a `try-catch` block or declare that your method `throws UnknownHostException`.

Example 4–3 returns a complete list of the IP addresses for *www.apple.com.*

Example 4–3: A program that prints all the addresses of www.apple.com

```
import java.net.*;

class apple {

  public static void main (String args[]) {

    try {
      InetAddress[] addresses = InetAddress.getAllByName("www.apple.com");
      for (int i = 0; i < addresses.length; i++) {
        System.out.println(addresses[i]);
      }
    }
    catch (UnknownHostException e) {
      System.out.println("Could not find www.apple.com");
    }

  }

}
```

Here's the result:

```
% java apple
www.apple.com/17.254.3.61
```

It appears that *www.apple.com* has only one IP address. This is the case for almost every host on the Internet. Hosts with more than one address are the exception rather than the rule, and even in those cases, you rarely need to know more than one address.

public static InetAddress InetAddress.getLocalHost()

java.net.InetAddress contains one final means of getting an InetAddress object. The static method InetAddress.getLocalHost() returns the InetAddress of the machine on which it's running. Like InetAddress.getByName() and InetAddress.getAllByName() it throws an UnknownHostException when it can't find the address of the local machine. Its use is straightforward:

```
InetAddress thisComputer = InetAddress.getLocalHost();
```

Example 4–4 prints the address of the machine it's run on.

Example 4–4: Find the address of the local machine

```
import java.net.*;

class myAddress {

  public static void main (String args[]) {

    try {
      InetAddress address = InetAddress.getLocalHost();
      System.out.println(address);
    }
    catch (UnknownHostException e) {
      System.out.println("Could not find this computer's address.");
    }

  }

}
```

Here's the output; I ran the program on *helios.oit.unc.edu*.

```
% java myAddress
helios/152.2.22.3
```

The hostname is partially set here. Whether you see a fully qualified name like *helios.oit.unc.edu*, or a partial name like *helios*, is system-dependent.

Other sources of InetAddress objects

Four other methods in the java.net package also return InetAddress objects. These are DatagramPacket.getAddress(), ServerSocket.getInetAddress(), SocketImpl.getInetAddress(), and Socket.getInetAddress(). Each of these will be discussed along with their respective class in later chapters.

Getting the Values of the Fields

Only classes in the java.net package have access to the fields of the InetAddress class. Classes in other packages can read the fields of an InetAddress by calling getHostname() and getAddress(). There are no corresponding setHostName() and setAddress() methods; this means that packages outside of java.net can't change an InetAddress's fields behind its back. Therefore, Java can guarantee that the hostname and the IP address match each other, and that they in fact refer to a valid host.

public String getHostName()

The getHostName() method returns a String that contains the hostname of the InetAddress object. If the machine doesn't have a hostname, a String version of the numeric IP address is returned.

```
InetAddress thisMachine = InetAddress.getLocalHost();
System.out.println("This machine's name is " + thisMachine.getHostName());
```

Example 4–5 prints the hostname of the local machine.

Example 4–5: Find the hostname of the local machine

```
import java.net.*;

class myName {

  public static void main (String args[]) {

    try {
      InetAddress address = InetAddress.getLocalHost();
      System.out.println("Hello. My name is " +  address.getHostName());
    }
    catch (UnknownHostException e) {
      System.out.println("I'm sorry. I don't know my own name.");
    }

  }

}
```

Here's the result:

```
% java myName
Hello. My name is helios
```

Of course, the hostname you get depends on where you run the program. In this case, the program ran on a machine named *helios*. The hostname is partially set here. Whether you see a fully qualified name like *helios.oit.unc.edu*, or a partial name like *helios*, is system-dependent.

public byte[] getAddress()

If you want to know the IP address of a machine (and you almost never do),
getAddress() returns an IP address as an array of bytes in network byte order. The
most significant byte (i.e., the first byte in the address's dotted decimal form) is the
first byte in the array, or element zero—remember, Java array indices start with 0.
To be ready for 128-bit IP addresses, do not assume anything about the length of
this array. While currently this array has length 4, future implementations are
likely to return arrays with 16 bytes. If you need to know the length of the array,
use the array's length field.

```
InetAddress thisMachine = InetAddress.getLocalHost();
byte[] address = thisMachine.getAddress());
```

The bytes returned are unsigned, which leads to some difficulty. Unlike C, Java
doesn't have an unsigned byte primitive datatype. Bytes with values higher than
127 are treated as negative numbers. Therefore, if you want to do anything with
the bytes returned by getAddress(), you need to promote the bytes to ints, and
make appropriate adjustments. Here's one way to do it:

```
int unsignedByte = myByte < 0 ? myByte + 256 : myByte;
```

Here myByte may be either positive or negative. The conditional operator ? tests
whether myByte is negative. If it is, we add 256 to myByte to make it positive. Otherwise, we leave it alone. myByte is automatically promoted to an int before the addition is performed, so wrap-around is not a problem. Example 4–6 uses this
technique to print the IP address of the local machine in the customary format.

Example 4–6: Find the IP address of the local machine

```
import java.net.*;

class myAddress {

  public static void main (String args[]) {

    try {
      InetAddress thisComputer = InetAddress.getLocalHost();
      byte[] address = thisComputer.getAddress();
      System.out.print("My address is ");
      for (int i = 0; i < address.length; i++) {
        int unsignedByte = address[i] < 0 ? address[i] + 256 : address[i];
        System.out.print(unsignedByte + ".");
      }
      System.out.println();
    }
```

Example 4–6: Find the IP address of the local machine (continued)

```
    catch (UnknownHostException e) {
      System.out.println("I'm sorry. I don't know my own address.");
    }

  }

}
```

Here's the result.

```
% java myAddress
My address is 152.2.22.3.
```

As before, the exact address depends on where the program is run.

Object Methods

Like every other class, java.net.InetAddress inherits from java.lang.Object. Thus, it has access to all the methods of that class. It overrides three to provide more specialized behavior.

public boolean equals(Object anyObject)

An object will be equal to an InetAddress object if, and only if, it is an instance of the InetAddress class, and it has the same four-byte IP address. It does *not* need to have the same hostname. Thus, an InetAddress object for *www.macfaq.com* is equal to an InetAddress object for *spacecadet.cnet.com* since both names refer to the same IP address.[*] Example 4–7 creates InetAddress objects for *spacecadet.cnet.com* and *www.macfaq.com* and then tells you whether or not they're the same machine.

Example 4–7: Are spacecadet and macfaq the same?

```
import java.net.*;

class macfaq {

  public static void main (String args[]) {

    try {
      InetAddress macfaq = InetAddress.getByName("www.macfaq.com ");
      InetAddress spacecadet = InetAddress.getByName("spacecadet.cnet.com");
      if (macfaq.equals(spacecadet)) {
        System.out.println
          ("www.macfaq.com is the same as spacecadet.cnet.com");
      }
      else {
```

---

[*] In late 1996, *www.macfaq.com* moved from *spacecadet.cnet.com* to a new host. If you run this program now, you'll get the opposite results.

Example 4–7: Are spacecadet and macfaq the same? (continued)

```
    System.out.println
        ("www.macfaq.com is not the same as spacecadet.cnet.com");
    }
  }
  catch (UnknownHostException e) {
    System.out.println("Host lookup failed.");
  }
  }
}
```

When you run this program you discover:

```
% java macfaq
www.macfaq.com is the same as spacecadet.cnet.com
%
```

public int hashCode()

The hashCode() method returns an int needed when InetAddress objects are used as keys in hash tables. This is called by the various methods of java.util.Hashtable. You will almost certainly not need to call this directly.

Currently the int that hashCode() returns is the address field. This is different for every two unequal InetAddress objects (where unequal has the meaning provided by the equals() method). If two InetAddress objects have the same address, then they have the same hash code, even if their hostnames are different. Therefore, if you try to store two objects in a Hashtable using equivalent InetAddress objects as a key (for example, the InetAddress objects for *spacecadet.cnet.com* and *www.macfaq.com*), the second will overwrite the first. If this is a problem, use the String returned by getHostName() as the key instead of the InetAddress itself.

The hashCode() method is the single method in the InetAddress class that can't be easily modified to work with 16-byte addresses. The algorithm to calculate hash codes may become much more complex when 16-byte addresses are supported. Don't depend on the hashCode() method returning the IP address.

public String toString()

Like all good classes, java.net.InetAddress has a toString() method. Examples 4–1 through 4–6 all implicitly called this method when passing InetAddress objects to System.out.println(). As you saw there, the string produced by toString() has the form:

```
    hostname/IPaddress
```

Not all InetAddress objects have hostnames. If one doesn't, the hostname and the slash will be omitted from the result. This format isn't particularly useful, so you'll probably never call toString() explicitly. If you do, the syntax is simple:

```
InetAddress thisComputer = InetAddress.getLocalHost();
String address = thisComputer.toString();
```

Converting IP Addresses to Names

Reverse lookup—the conversion of an IP address like 152.2.22.3 into a hostname like *sunsite.unc.edu*—is not available in Java 1.0 due to a bug in Java's address caching scheme. This is regrettable because there are some applications, like processing web server log files, for which reverse lookup is invaluable. The bug is really quite simple. As we saw earlier, if we pass an IP address into getByName(), Java initializes the hostName field of the InetAddress to the original IP address string without doing a reverse lookup; it doesn't think the reverse lookup is necessary because it already has something it thinks is a name. That this "name" is really a numeric address in dotted quad format is irrelevant. Therefore, fixing the bug should be easy. The reverse lookup code is in the InetAddress class, and it does work; we only need a way to set the object's address field without setting hostName.

To make this fix, you need to use the InetAddress() constructor and the address field in java.net.InetAddress. These members are package protected; they are neither public, private, nor protected, and thus only available to classes in the java.net package. Therefore, we need to add a new class to java.net. As a rule, adding a class to a package you didn't write is a bad idea, because Sun can update java.net, and likely break any code that depends on the internal workings of the class. Furthermore different Java implementations may not share the same internals (though all the ones I've seen until now do). However, in this situation, there is no alternative, until Sun fixes the bug in InetAddress.[*]

To add this new class, you must put its compiled .class file in a *java/net* directory somewhere in your CLASSPATH. You can put it in the same place Sun's java.net files are stored. Otherwise you'll need to modify your CLASSPATH to point at the directory containing your *java/net* directory. Unfortunately, adding a class to java.net means that you can only use the class in applications that run on your own machine. It is not portable to other machines (unless you install the same file there), and it will certainly not work in an applet.

---

[*] This bug is fixed in Java 1.1. However, the InetAddressFactory that I develop below will still be useful as long as releases based on 1.0 are important (the near future). Several of the examples later in this book rely on the InetAddressFactory class. If you have Java 1.1, you can still install InetAddressFactory as suggested. If you don't want to do so, modifying the examples so they don't need the factory is relatively simple (and a good exercise).

Example 4–8 is an `InetAddressFactory` class that contains two public, static, overloaded `newInetAddress()` methods. The first returns an `InetAddress` given a byte array representation of the IP address. The second returns an `InetAddress` given a `String` representation of the numeric IP address.

Example 4–8: Get a hostname from an IP address

```
package java.net;

import java.util.StringTokenizer;

public class InetAddressFactory {

  // Use a byte array like {(byte) 199, (byte) 1, (byte) 32, (byte) 90} to build
  // to build an InetAddressObject
  public static InetAddress newInetAddress(byte addr[])
    throws UnknownHostException  {

    try {
      InetAddress ia = new InetAddress();
      ia.address  = addr[3] & 0xFF;
      ia.address |= ((addr[2] << 8) & 0xFF00);
      ia.address |= ((addr[1] << 16) & 0xFF0000);
      ia.address |= ((addr[0] << 24) & 0xFF000000);
      return ia;
    }
    catch (Exception e) { // primarily ArrayIndexOutOfBoundsExceptions
      throw new UnknownHostException(e.toString());
    }


  }// end newInetAddress


  // Use a String like 199.1.32.90 to build
  // an InetAddressObject
  public static InetAddress newInetAddress(String s)
   throws UnknownHostException {

    // be ready for IPv6
    int num_bytes_in_an_IP_address = 4;
    byte addr[] = new byte[num_bytes_in_an_IP_address];
    StringTokenizer st = new StringTokenizer(s, ".");

    // make sure the format is correct
    if (st.countTokens() != addr.length) {
      throw new UnknownHostException(s
        + " is not a valid numeric IP address");
    }

    for (int i = 0; i < addr.length; i++) {
      int thisByte = Integer.parseInt(st.nextToken());
      if (thisByte < 0 || thisByte > 255) {
```

Example 4–8: Get a hostname from an IP address (continued)

```
            throw new UnknownHostException(s
      + " is not a valid numeric IP address");
    }

    // check this
    if (thisByte > 127) thisByte -= 256;
    addr[i] = (byte) thisByte;

  } // end for

  return newInetAddress(addr);

 }// end newInetAddress

}// end InetAddressFactory
```

The InetAddressFactory class provides two versions of the method newInetAddress(). The first method takes a byte array as an argument, and returns an InetAddress object that's built from the bytes of this array; the second takes an Internet address in string (dotted decimal) form. Both versions throw an Unknown-HostException if they encounter any problems.

We'll look first at the method that takes a byte array for an argument. The address field of InetAddress is an int, so we need to turn the four bytes into an int. This requires bitwise manipulation with the bitshift left operator, <<, the bitwise and operator, &, and the bitwise or and assign operator, |=. Byte order is important. For example, suppose that the byte array passed into InetAddressFactory.newInetAddress() is {18, 81, 0, 21}. The lowest order byte is in addr[3], with the value 21. In binary, 21 is 00010101. A byte is automatically sign-extended to an int when it is used in a calculation, yielding the 32-bit quantity 00000000000000000000000000010101. This number is bitwise anded with 0xFF (00000000000000000000000011111111 in binary) so that the first three irrelevant bytes are thrown away. (In this case, the and operation has no effect; but, if we were working with a value greater than 127, it would be treated as a negative number, and we would need to mask off the leading ones resulting from sign extension.) This int is now assigned to ia.address. We treat the other elements of addr[] similarly, except that they need to be shifted before being merged into ia.address with an or operation. The most significant byte of the address is addr[0], which is 18 in this example (or 00010010 in binary). This byte will then be promoted to the int 00000000000000000000000000010010. Then this number is shifted 24 bits to the left yielding 00010010000000000000000000000000. This is bitwise anded with 0xFF000000 (11111111000000000000000000000000 in binary) to zero out all but the left eight bits. Finally this number is bitwise ored with ia.address to fill the leftmost eight bits of the address. In short, the bits of each byte are moved into the corresponding position of ia.address.

Working directly with bytes is rather painful in Java. First of all, numeric data types are signed, but the bytes in an IP address are unsigned. Second, bytes are automatically promoted to ints in calculations and there are no byte literals. To make it easier for programs to use this class, we add an overloaded newInetAddress() method to the InetAddressFactory that accepts numeric IP addresses as strings in dotted decimal form (e.g., 152.2.22.3). This method uses a StringTokenizer to split such a string into four pieces, each of which can be converted to a signed byte. The resulting byte array is passed to the previous newInetAddress() method for conversion into an InetAddress object. Various checks are performed to ensure that the string is indeed a valid numeric IP address. If it is not, an Unknown-HostException is thrown.

Example 4–9 demonstrates the use of the InetAddressFactory. It looks up the hostnames of the machines with addresses 18.81.0.21 and 152.2.22.3:

Example 4–9: Given the address, find the hostname

```
import java.net.*;

public class ReverseTest {

  public static void main (String args[]) {

    byte[] xcluster = {18, 81, 0, 21};
    try {
      InetAddress ia = InetAddressFactory.newInetAddress(xcluster);
      System.out.println(ia.getHostName());
    }
    catch (Exception e) {
      System.err.println(e);
    }

    String sunsite = "152.2.22.3";
    try {
      InetAddress ia = InetAddressFactory.newInetAddress(sunsite);
      System.out.println(ia.getHostName());
    }
    catch (Exception e) {
      System.err.println(e);
    }

  }

}
```

Here's the result:

```
% java ReverseTest
XCLUSTER.MIT.EDU
helios.oit.unc.edu
%
```

Some Useful Programs

You now know everything there is to know about the java.net.InetAddress class. The tools in this class alone let you write some genuinely useful programs. Here we'll look at two: one that queries your domain name server interactively, and another that can improve the performance of your web server by processing log files offline.

java lookup

nslookup is a UNIX utility that converts hostnames to IP addresses and IP addresses to hostnames. It has two modes: interactive and command-line. If you enter a hostname on the command line, *nslookup* prints the IP address of that host. If you enter an IP address on the command line, *nslookup* prints the hostname. If you do not enter a hostname or IP address on the command line, *nslookup* enters interactive mode, reads hostnames and IP addresses from standard input, and echoes back the corresponding IP addresses and hostnames until you type "exit."

Example 4–10 is a simple command-line application called javalookup that emulates *nslookup*. It doesn't implement any of *nslookup*'s more complex features, but it does enough to be useful. javalookup uses the InetAddressFactory class to do reverse lookups, so the InetAddressFactory class must be installed (as described in the last section).

Example 4–10: An nslookup clone

```
import java.net.*;
import java.io.*;

public class javalookup {

   public static void main (String args[]) {

   if (args.length > 0) {// use command line
     for (int i = 0; i < args.length; i++) {
        lookup(args[i]);
     }
   }
   else {
     DataInputStream myInputStream = new DataInputStream(System.in);
     System.out.println
       ("Enter names and IP addresses. Enter \"exit\" to quit.");
     while (true) {
       String s;
       try {
         s = myInputStream.readLine();
       }
       catch (IOException e) {
         break;
```

Example 4–10: An nslookup clone (continued)

```
    }
    if (s.equals("exit")) break;
    lookup(s);
  }


}

}/* end main */


private static void lookup(String s) {

  InetAddress thisComputer;
  byte[] address;

  // get the bytes of the IP address
  try {
    thisComputer = InetAddress.getByName(s);
    address = thisComputer.getAddress();
  }
  catch (UnknownHostException ue) {
    System.out.println("Cannot find host " + s);
    return;
  }

  if (isHostname(s)) {
    // Print the IP address
    for (int i = 0; i < address.length; i++) {
      int unsignedByte = address[i] < 0 ? address[i] + 256 : address[i];
      System.out.print(unsignedByte + ".");
    }
    System.out.println();
  }
  else { // this is an IP address
    try {
      System.out.println(InetAddressFactory.newInetAddress(s).getHostName());
    }
    catch (UnknownHostException e) {
      System.out.println("Could not lookup the address " + s);
    }
  }

} // end lookup

private static boolean isHostname(String s) {

  char[] ca = s.toCharArray();
  // if we see a character that is neither a digit nor a period
  // then s is probably a hostname
  for (int i = 0; i < ca.length; i++) {
    if (!Character.isDigit(ca[i])) {
      if (ca[i] != '.') {
```

Example 4–10: An nslookup clone (continued)

```
            return true;
          }
      }
  }

    // Everything was either a digit or a period
    // so s looks like an IP address
in dotted quad format
    return false;

  } // end isHostName

}// end javalookup
```

Here's some sample output; input typed by the user is in bold:

```
% java javalookup shock.njit.edu
128.235.252.184.
% java javalookup 128.235.252.184
shock.njit.edu
% java javalookup
Enter names and IP addresses. Enter "exit" to quit.
hertz.njit.edu
128.235.251.11.
199.1.32.90
star.blackstar.com
127.0.0.1
localhost
cs.nyu.edu
128.122.153.70.
cs.cmu.edu
128.2.222.173.
cs.med.edu
Cannot find host cs.med.edu
199.1.32.99
mars.blackstar.com
exit
%
```

The javalookup program is built out of three methods: main(), lookup(), and isHostname(). The main() method determines whether or not there were command-line arguments. If there were command-line arguments, main() calls lookup() to process each one. If there were no command-line arguments, it chains a DataInputStream to System.in and reads input from the user with the read-Line() method. If the line is "exit," the program exits. Otherwise the line is assumed to be a hostname or IP address, and is passed to the lookup() method.

The `lookup()` method uses `InetAddress.getByName()` to find the requested host, regardless of the input's format; remember that `getByName()` doesn't care if it gets a name or an address in string form. If `getByName()` fails, then `lookup()` prints a failure message, and returns. Otherwise it gets the address of the requested system. Then `lookup()` calls `isHostname()` to determine whether the input string s is a hostname (*shock.njit.edu*) or a numeric IP address (199.1.32.90). `isHostname()` looks at each character of the string; if all the characters are digits or periods, `isHostname()` guesses that the string is a numeric IP address and returns `false`. Otherwise, `isHostname()` guesses that the string is a hostname and returns `true`. What if the string is neither? That is very unlikely, since if the string is neither a hostname nor an address, `getByName()` won't be able to do a lookup, and will throw an exception. However, it would not be difficult to add a test ensuring the string looks valid; this is left as an exercise for the reader. If the user typed a hostname, `lookup()` prints the corresponding address; you have already saved the address in the byte array `address[]`, and the only complication is making sure that you don't treat byte values between 128 and 255 as negative numbers. If the user typed an IP address, you use `InetAddressFactory.newInetAddress()` to create an `InetAddress` object that doesn't have the `hostName` field initialized; call `getHostName()` to look up the host corresponding to the address, and print the result.

Processing Web Server Log Files

Web server logs track the hosts that access your web site. By default, the log reports the IP addresses of the sites that connect to you. However, you can often get more information from the names of those sites than from their IP addresses. Most web servers have an option to store hostnames instead of IP addresses, but this can hurt performance because the server needs to make a DNS request for each hit. It is much more efficient to log the IP addresses, and convert them to hostnames at a later time. You can do this when the server isn't busy, or even on another machine completely. Example 4–11 is a program called `weblog` that reads a web server log file and prints each line with IP addresses converted to hostnames. It uses the `InetAddressFactory` class to make the conversion.

Most web servers have standardized on the common log file format, although there are exceptions; if your web server is one of those exceptions, you'll have to adapt this program. A typical line in the common log file format looks like this:

```
205.160.186.76 unknown - [01/Jan/1996:22:53:58 -0500]
    "GET /bgs/greenbg.gif HTTP/1.0" 200 50
```

This means that a web browser at IP address 205.160.186.76 requested the file */bgs/greenbg.gif* from this web server at 10:53 P.M. (and 58 seconds) on January 1, 1996. The file was found, and 50 bytes of data were successfully transferred to the browser.

The first field is the IP address or, if DNS resolution is turned on, the hostname from which the connection was made. This is followed by a space. Therefore, parsing the log file is easy: everything before the first space is the IP address, and you do not need to change anything after it.

The Common Log File Format

If you want to expand weblog into a more general web server log processor, you need more information about the common log file format. A line in the file has the format:

```
remotehost rfc931 authuser [date] "request" status bytes
```

- *remotehost* is the hostname or IP address the browser connected from.

- *rfc931* is the username of the user on the remote system, as specified by Internet protocol RFC931. Very few browsers send this information, so it's almost always either unknown or a dash. This is followed by a space.

- *authuser* is the authenticated username as specified by RFC931. Once again, this is not supported by most popular browsers or client systems; this field usually is filled in with a dash, followed by a space.

- *[date]* is date and time of the request given in brackets. This is the local system time when the request was made. Days are a two-digit number ranging from 01 to 31. The Month is one of Jan, Feb, Mar, Apr, May, Jun, Jul, Aug, Sep, Oct, Nov or Dec. The year is given by four digits. This is followed by a colon, then the hour (from 00 to 23), another colon, then the minute (00 to 59), then a colon, then the seconds (00 to 59). Then comes the closing bracket and another space.

- *"request"* is the request line exactly as it came from the client. It is in quotes because it may contain embedded spaces. It is not guaranteed to be a valid HTTP request since client software may misbehave.

- *status* is a numeric HTTP status code returned to the client. A list of HTTP 1.0 status codes is given in Chapter 3, *Basic Web Concepts.* The most common response is 200, meaning the request was successfully processed.

- *bytes* is the length in bytes of the data that was sent to the client.

You convert the string version of the IP address into a byte array using the usual methods of java.net.InetAddress. This byte array is then passed to InetAddress-Factory.newInetAddress(s).getHostName() to find the hostname. Example 4–11 has the code.

Example 4–11: Process web server log files

```
import java.net.*;
import java.io.*;


class weblog {

  public static void main(String args[]) {

    String thisLine;
    String thisIP;
    String theRest;
    int index;
    InetAddress thisAddress;
    byte[] address;

    try {

      FileInputStream fin =  new FileInputStream(args[0]);
      DataInputStream myInput = new DataInputStream(fin);

        while ((thisLine = myInput.readLine()) != null) {
          index = thisLine.indexOf(" ", 0);
          thisIP = thisLine.substring(0, index);
          theRest = thisLine.substring(index, thisLine.length());
          try {
            thisAddress = java.net.InetAddress.getByName(thisIP);
            address = thisAddress.getAddress();
            System.out.println(InetAddressFactory.newInetAddress(address).getHostName()
                            + theRest);
          }
          catch (UnknownHostException e) {
            System.out.println(thisLine);
          }
        }// while loop ends here
    }
    catch (IOException e) {
      System.out.println("Exception: " + e);
    }

  } // end main


}
```

You pass the name of the file to be processed to weblog as the first argument on the command line. A FileInputStream fin is opened from this file and the DataInputStream myInput is chained to fin. The readLine() method of myInput processes the file line by line in a while loop. Each line is placed in the String variable thisLine. thisLine is then split into two substrings: thisIP, which contains everything before the first space, and theRest, which contains everything after the first space. The position of the first space is determined by `this-Line.indexOf(" ", 0)`. `thisAddress` is converted to a byte array using `java.net.InetAddress.getByName(thisIP)` and `getAddress()`. The byte array is passed to `InetAddressFactory.newInetAddress()`, which lets you look up the hostname by calling `getHostName()`. Finally the hostname, a space, and everything else on the line (`theRest`) is printed on `System.out`. You can send output to a new file through the standard means for redirecting output.

`weblog` is more efficient than you might expect. Most web browsers generate multiple log file entries per page served, since there's an entry in the log not just for the page itself but for each graphic on the page. And many web browsers request multiple pages while visiting a site. DNS lookups are expensive, and it simply doesn't make sense to look up each of those sites every time it appears in the log file. The `java.net.InetAddress` class has a `static Hashtable` it uses to cache requested addresses. If you request the same address again, it can be retrieved from the `InetAddress` cache much more quickly than from DNS.

5

Retrieving Data with URLs

The simplest way for a Java program to locate and retrieve data is to use a URL. You do not need to worry about the details of the protocol being used, the format of the data being retrieved, or how to communicate with the server; you simply tell Java the URL, and it gets the data for you. Although Java can only handle a few protocols and content types out of the box, in later chapters you'll learn how to write and install new content and protocol handlers that extend Java's capabilities to include new protocols and new kinds of data. In later chapters, you'll also learn how to open sockets and communicate directly with different kinds of servers. But that's later; for now, let's see how much you can do with a minimum of work.

The URL Class

The `java.net.URL` class is an abstraction of a uniform resource locator. Although storing a URL as a string would be trivial, it is helpful to think of URLs as objects with fields that include the protocol, hostname, port, path, filename, and document section, each of which may be set independently. Indeed, this is almost exactly how the `java.net.URL` class is arranged; the only difference is that the path and filename are contained in a single field.

The fields of `java.net.URL` are visible only to other members of the `java.net` package; classes that aren't in `java.net` can't access a URL's fields directly. However, you can set these fields using the URL constructors, and retrieve their values using various `get` methods (`getHost()`, `getPort()`, etc.). The URL class has a single method for setting the fields of a URL after it has been created, but this method is `protected`, and you won't need it unless you're implementing a new protocol handler. Once a URL has been constructed, you should not change its fields.

Finally, there are two methods that retrieve the contents of a file specified by a URL, and several methods like toString() and equals() that override methods of java.lang.Object. Let's investigate these methods in turn.

Creating New URLs

Unlike the InetAddress objects of the last chapter, you can construct instances of java.net.URL. There are four constructors, differing in the information they require. Which constructor you use depends on what information you have, and the form it's in. All these constructors throw a MalformedURLException if you try to create a URL for a protocol that is not supported. Sun's Java Developer's Kit 1.0.2 and later and Netscape 3.0 and later support HTTP, FTP, news, mailto, gopher, and file URLs, although this is somewhat platform-dependent. Surprisingly, Solaris Java 1.0.2 does not support as many protocols as Java on some other platforms. In particular, it is missing ftp. Solaris Java 1.1 does have all these protocols. More are likely to be supported in the future, and you can always install a protocol handler for a new kind of URL. Otherwise, it is up to you to make sure that any URL you create is valid. Java does not check the URL to make sure that it points at a valid host, or that it meets any other requirements for URLs.

public URL(String url) throws MalformedURLException

This is the simplest constructor; its argument is just a URL in string form. Like all constructors, you may only call URL() after the new operator; and, like all URL constructors, it can throw a MalformedURLException. The code below constructs a URL object from a String, catching the exception that might be thrown:

```
try {
  URL u = new URL("http://www.macfaq.com/vendor.html");
}
catch (MalformedURLException e)  {
  System.err.println(e);
}
```

Example 5-1 tries to create two URL objects, and print each one. However, the second URL, although it is valid, uses a protocol that is not supported by Java on this platform (FTP) and thus throws a MalformedURLException.

Example 5-1: Two URLs. One works. The other doesn't.

```
import java.net.*;

public class URLConstructorTest1 {

  public static void main (String args[]) {

    URL webURL, ftpURL;
```

Example 5–1: Two URLs. One works. The other doesn't. (continued)

```
try {
  webURL = new URL("http://www.macfaq.com/vendor.html");
  System.out.println(webURL);
  ftpURL = new URL("ftp://ftp.macfaq.com/pub/");
  System.out.println(ftpURL);
}
catch (MalformedURLException e)  {
  System.err.println(e);
}


}


}
```

Here's the result:

```
% java URLConstructorTest1
http://www.macfaq.com/vendor.html
java.net.MalformedURLException: ftp://ftp.macfaq.com/pub/: java.lang.Exception
```

public URL(String protocol, String host, String file) throws MalformedURLException

This constructor constructs a URL from separate strings specifying the protocol, hostname, and file. The port is set to −1 so the default port for the protocol will be used. You should begin the `file` string with a slash, and include a path, a filename, and, optionally, a reference to a named anchor. Forgetting the initial slash is a common mistake, and one that is not easy to spot. Like all constructors, `URL()` may only be called after the new operator, and like all URL constructors it can throw a `MalformedURLException`. For example:

```
try {
  URL u = new URL("http", "www.eff.org", "/blueribbon.html#intro");
}
catch (MalformedURLException e)  {
  System.err.println(e);
}
```

This creates a URL object that points to *http://www.eff.org/blueribbon.html#intro*, using the default port for the HTTP protocol (port 80). Note that the file specification includes a reference to a named anchor. The code catches the exception that would be thrown if the URL were invalid.

Example 5–2 tries to create two URL objects and print each one. However the second URL, although it is valid, uses a protocol that is not supported by Java (FTP) and thus throws a `MalformedURLException`.

Example 5–2: Two URLs. One works. The other doesn't.

```
import java.net.*;

public class URLConstructorTest2 {

  public static void main (String args[]) {

    URL webURL, ftpURL;

    try {
      webURL = new URL("http", "www.macfaq.com", "/vendor.html");
      System.out.println(webURL);
      ftpURL = new URL("ftp", "ftp.macfaq.com", "/pub");
      System.out.println(ftpURL);
    }
    catch (MalformedURLException e)  {
      System.err.println(e);
    }


  }


}
```

Here's the result:

```
% java URLConstructorTest2
http://www.macfaq.com/vendor.html
java.net.MalformedURLException: unknown protocol: ftp
```

public URL(String protocol, String host, int port, String file) throws MalformedURLException

For those rare occasions when the default port isn't correct, this constructor lets you specify the port explicitly, as an int. The other arguments are the same as for the URL(String protocol, String host, String file) constructor and carry the same caveats. For example:

```
try {
  URL u = new URL("http", "www.eff.org", 80, "/blueribbon.html#intro");
}
catch (MalformedURLException e)  {
  System.err.println(e);
}
```

The preceding code creates a URL object that points to *http://www.eff.org:80/ blueribbon.html#intro*, specifying port 80 explicitly.

Example 5–3 tries to create two URL objects and print each one. However the second URL, though valid, uses the FTP protocol, which is not supported by Sun's JDK 1.0 on Solaris; therefore, the constructor throws a MalformedURLException. This would work on the Mac or in Java 1.1.

Example 5–3: Two URLs. One works. The other doesn't.

```
import java.net.*;

public class URLConstructorTest3 {

  public static void main (String args[]) {

    URL webURL, ftpURL;

    try {
      webURL = new URL("http", "www.macfaq.com", 80, "/vendor.html");
      System.out.println(webURL);
      ftpURL = new URL("ftp", "ftp.macfaq.com", 21, "/pub");
      System.out.println(ftpURL);
    }
    catch (MalformedURLException e)  {
      System.err.println(e);
    }

  }

}
```

Here's the result:

```
% java URLConstructorTest3
http://www.macfaq.com:80/vendor.html
java.net.MalformedURLException: unknown protocol: ftp
```

public URL(URL u, String s)
throws MalformedURLException

This constructor builds an absolute URL from a relative URL; it is probably the constructor you'll use most frequently. For instance, you may be parsing an HTML document at *http://www.macfaq.com/index.html* and encounter a link to a file called *vendor.html* with no further qualifying information. In this case, you use the URL to the document that contains the link to provide the missing information. The constructor computes the new URL as *http://www.macfaq.com/vendor.html.* For example:

```
URL u1, u2;

try {
  URL u1 = new URL("http://www.macfaq.com/index.html");
  URL u2 = new URL (u1, "vendor.html");
}
catch (MalformedURLException e) {
   System.err.println(e);
}
```

The filename is removed from the path of u1, and the new filename *vendor.html* is appended to make u2. This constructor is particularly useful when you want to loop through a list of files that are all in the same directory. You can create a URL for the first file, and then use this initial URL to create URL objects for the other files by substituting their filenames. You also use this constructor when you want to create a URL relative to the applet's document or code base, which you retrieve using the getDocumentBase() or getCodeBase() methods of the Applet class. Example 5–4 is a very simple applet that uses getDocumentBase() to create a new URL object:

Example 5–4: A URL relative to the web page

```
import java.net.*;
import java.applet.Applet;

public class URLConstructorTest4 extends Applet {

public void init () {
    URL u1, u2;

    u1 = getDocumentBase();
    System.out.println(u1);
    try {
      u2 = new URL(u1, "vendor.html");
      System.out.println(u2);
    }
    catch (MalformedURLException e) {
      System.err.println(e);
    }

  }

}
```

Of course, the output from this applet depends on the document base. In the output shown below, the original URL (the document base) refers to the file *example1.html*; the constructor creates a new URL that points to the file *vendor.html* in the same directory:

```
file:/Mac HD/Java/Network Programming/Applets/Test4/example1.html
file:/Mac HD/Java/Network Programming/Applets/Test4/vendor.html
```

When using this constructor with getDocumentBase(), you frequently put the call to getDocumentBase() inside the constructor:

```
u2 = new URL(getDocumentBase(), "vendor.html");
```

Other sources of URL objects

As well as the constructors discussed here, a number of other methods in the Java class library return URL objects. You've already seen getDocumentBase() from java.applet.Applet. The other common source is getCodeBase(), also from java.applet.Applet. This works just like getDocumentBase(), except that it

returns the URL of the applet itself instead of the URL of the page that contains
the applet. Both getDocumentBase() and getCodeBase() come from the interface java.applet.AppletStub, which java.applet.Applet implements.
You're unlikely to implement this interface yourself unless you're building a web
browser or applet viewer. Finally, java.net.URLConnection (which you'll see
more of in Chapter 10, *The URLConnection Class*) has a URL field and a getURL()
method that returns this field.

Splitting a URL into Pieces

There are six fields in the URL class: the protocol, the host, the port, the file,
the URLStreamHandler, and the named anchor (commonly known as the section
or ref). All of these fields are private, except for URLStreamHandler, which is
accessible to other members of the java.net package, and static. Read-only
access to the other five fields is provided by five public methods: getFile(),
getHost(), getPort(), getProtocol(), and getRef().

public String getProtocol()

The getProtocol() method returns a String containing the protocol portion
of the URL: for example, "http" or "file."

```
URL thisPage = getCodeBase();
System.out.println("This applet was downloaded via " + thisPage.getProtocol())
```

public String getHost()

The getHost() method returns a String containing the hostname of the URL.

```
URL thisPage = getCodeBase();
System.out.println("This applet was downloaded from " + thisPage.getHost());
```

public int getPort()

The getPort() method returns the port number specified in the URL as an int.
If you do not specify a port, getPort() returns –1 to signify that the URL does not
specify the port explicitly, and will use the default port for the protocol. For example, if the URL is *http://www.ora.com/*, getPort() returns –1; if the URL is
http://www.ora.com:80/, getPort() returns 80. The code below prints –1 for the
port number, because it isn't specified in the URL:

```
try {
  URL u = new URL("http://www.ncsa.uiuc.edu/demoweb/html-primer.html#A1.3.3.3'
  System.out.println("The port part of " + u + " is\n" + u.getPort());
}
catch (MalformedURLException e) {
  System.err.println(e);
}
```

public String getFile()

The getFile() method returns a String that contains the path and file portion of a URL; remember that Java does not break a URL into separate path and file parts. Everything from the first slash after the hostname until the pound sign that begins a section is considered to be part of the file member. For example:

```
URL thisPage = getDocumentBase();
System.out.println("This page's path is " + thispage.getFile());
```

If the URL does not have a file part, Java appends a slash to the URL, and returns the slash as the filename. For example, if the URL is *http://www.ora.com* (rather than something like *http://www.ora.com/index.html*), getFile() returns a slash.

public String getRef()

The getRef() method returns the named anchor of the URL. If the URL doesn't have a named anchor, the method returns null. In the code below, getRef() returns the string xtocid1902914:

```
try {
  URL u = new URL("http://sunsite.unc.edu/javafaq/javafaq.html#xtocid1902914");
  System.out.println("This ref of " + u + " is " + u.getRef());
}
catch (MalformedURLException e) {
  System.err.println(e);
}
```

Example 5-5 uses all five methods to split URLs entered on the command line into their component parts.

Example 5-5: The parts of a URL

```
import java.net.*;

public class getURLParts {

  public static void main(String args[]) {

    for (int i = 0; i < args.length; i++) {
      try {
        URL u = new URL(args[0]);
        System.out.println("The URL is " + u);
        System.out.println("The protocol part is " + u.getProtocol());
        System.out.println("The host part is " + u.getHost());
        System.out.println("The port part is " + u.getPort());
        System.out.println("The file part is " + u.getFile());
        System.out.println("The ref part is " + u.getRef());
      } // end try
      catch (MalformedURLException e) {
        System.err.println(args[0] + "is not a URL I understand.");
      }
```

Example 5–5: The parts of a URL (continued)

```
    } // end for

  } // end main

} // end getURLParts
```

Here's the result:

```
% java getURLParts http://www.ncsa.uiuc.edu/demoweb/html-primer.html#A1.3.3.3
The URL is http://www.ncsa.uiuc.edu/demoweb/html-primer.html#A1.3.3.3
The protocol part is http
The host part is www.ncsa.uiuc.edu
The port part is -1
The file part is /demoweb/html-primer.html
The ref part is A1.3.3.3
```

In this case, the URL does not have an explicit port number, so getPort() returns −1 rather than the default port (80). If the URL had included the port (for example, in *http://www.ncsa.uiuc.edu:8080/demoweb/html-primer.html#A1.3.3.3*), that port would have been returned instead.

Getting Data From a URL

Naked URLs aren't very exciting. What's exciting is the data contained in the files they point to. The java.net.URL class has three methods to retrieve data from a URL. They are:

```
public final InputStream openStream() throws java.io.IOException
public URLConnection openConnection() throws java.io.IOException
public final Object getContent() throws java.io.IOException
```

public final InputStream openStream() throws java.io.IOException

The openStream() method connects to the resource referenced by the URL, performs any necessary handshaking between the client and the server, and then returns a InputStream that you can read data from. The data you get from this InputStream is the raw (i.e., uninterpreted) contents of the file the URL references: ASCII data if you're reading a text file, raw HTML if you're reading an HTML file, binary image data if you're reading an image file. It does not include any of the HTTP headers, or any other protocol-related information; if you want to see protocol headers, use the openConnection() method discussed later.

You can use the InputStream as you would any other InputStream. For example:

```
URL u;
InputStream is;
```

```
try {
  u  = new URL("http://www.ora.com");
  is = u.openStream();
}
catch (Exception e) {
  System.err.println(e);
}
```

This code catches a generic Exception; this is slightly easier (although less precise) than worrying about two different exceptions: the MalformedURLException that the URL constructor can throw, and the IOException that openStream() can throw.

Although openStream() is declared final in Java 1.0.2, a comment in the source code says this restriction is scheduled for removal; therefore, you may be able to override openStream() in the future. It is still final as of Java. 1.1beta2. However, most of the things you'd want to do by overriding openStream() are better implemented in a protocol handler.

Example 5–6 reads a URL from the command line, opens an InputStream from that URL, chains the resulting InputStream to a DataInputStream, and then uses DataInputStream's readLine() method to read successive lines of the file, each of which is printed on the standard output. That is, it prints the raw data located at the URL. If the URL references an HTML file, the program's output is raw HTML.

Example 5–6: Download a web page

```
import java.net.*;
import java.io.*;

public class viewsource {

  public static void main (String args[]) {

    String thisLine;
    URL u;

    if  (args.length > 0) {

      //Open the URL for reading
      try {
        u = new URL(args[0]);
        // now turn the URL into a DataInputStream
        try {
          DataInputStream theHTML = new DataInputStream(u.openStream());

          try {
            while ((thisLine = theHTML.readLine()) != null) {
              System.out.println(thisLine);
            }// while loop ends here
          } // end try
```

Example 5–6: Download a web page (continued)

```
        catch (Exception e) {
          System.err.println(e);
        }
      }// end try
      catch (Exception e) {
        System.err.println(e);
      }

    }// end try
    catch (MalformedURLException e) {
      System.err.println(args[0] + " is not a parseable URL");
      System.err.println(e);
    }
  }//  end if

 }// end main

} // end viewsource
```

Here are the first few lines of output when you use this program to retrieve *http://www.ora.com*:

```
% java viewsource http://www.ora.com
<!DOCTYPE HTML PUBLIC "-//Netscape Comm. Corp.//DTD HTML//EN>
<HTML>
<HEAD>
<LINK REV=MADE HREF="mailto:webmaster@ora.com>
<TITLE>O'Reilly Home Page</TITLE>
</HEAD>
<BODY  BGCOLOR="#ffffff>

<P>
<IMG ALT="O'Reilly & Associates" SRC="/www/graphics/oreilly.mast.gif>

<P>
<b>
```

There are quite a few more lines in that web page; but if you want to see them, you can fire up your web browser. viewsource assumes that the URL you give it points to an HTML file or a text file, so it uses the readLine() method of DataInput-Stream to read the input. If you were expecting a GIF image, an applet, or other binary data, you could read the InputStream a byte at a time with readByte() instead. We don't try to process the HTML in any way. If you wanted to process the HTML, the best approach would be to write a content handler for text/html files, and then call getContent().

public URLConnection openConnection()
throws java.io.IOException

The openConnection() method opens a socket to the specified URL and returns a URLConnection object. A URLConnection represents an open connection to a network resource. If the call fails, openConnection() throws an IOException:

```
try {
  URL u = new URL("http://sunsite.unc.edu/");
  try {
    URLConnection uc = u.openConnection();
  }// end try
  catch (IOException e) {
    System.err.println(e);
  }
}// end try
catch (MalformedURLException e) {
  System.err.println(e);
}
```

You use this method when you want to communicate directly with the server. The URLConnection gives you access to everything sent by the server; in addition to the document itself, in its raw form (i.e., HTML, plain text, binary image data), you see all the headers required by the protocol in use. For example, if you are retrieving an HTML document, the URLConnection will give you HTTP headers followed by raw HTML. URLConnections and what you can do with them will be the primary subject of Chapter 10.

public final Object getContent() throws java.io.IOException

The getContent() method is another way to download data referenced by a URL. The getContent() method retrieves the data referenced by the URL and tries to make it into some type of object. If the URL refers to some sort of text object like an ASCII or HTML file, the object returned is usually some sort of InputStream. If the URL refers to an image like a GIF or a JPEG file, getContent() usually returns an ImageProducer.

```
try {
  URL u = new URL("http://sunsite.unc.edu/");
  try {
    Object o = u.getContent();
  }// end try
  catch (Exception e) {
    System.err.println(e);
  }
}// end try
catch (MalformedURLException e) {
  System.err.println(args[0] + " is not a parseable URL");
  System.err.println(e);
}
```

Although this method is declared `final` in Java 1.0.2, this restriction is scheduled for removal. It is still final as of Java 1.1b2. Later releases of Java may allow you to override `getContent()`. However, it's probably better to write a content handler than to extend `java.net.URL`.

`getContent()` operates by looking at the `Content-type` field in the MIME header of data it gets from the server. If the server does not use MIME headers or sends an unfamiliar `Content-type`, `getContent()` throws a `ClassNotFoundException`. An `IOException` is thrown if the object can't be retrieved. Example 5–7 demonstrates.

Example 5–7: Download an object

```
import java.net.*;
import java.io.*;

public class getobject {

  public static void main (String args[]) {

    String thisLine;
    URL u;

    if  (args.length > 0) {

      //Open the URL for reading
      try {
        u = new URL(args[0]);
        try {
          Object o = u.getContent();
          System.out.println("I got a " + o.getClass().getName());
        }// end try
        catch (Exception e) {
          System.err.println(e);
        }
      }// end try
      catch (MalformedURLException e) {
        System.err.println(args[0] + " is not a parseable URL");
        System.err.println(e);
      }
    }//  end if

  }// end main

} // end getobject
```

Here's the result of trying to get the content of *http://www.ora.com/*:

```
% java getobject http://www.ora.com
java.lang.ClassNotFoundException: sun/net/www/content/text/html
        at java.net.URLConnection.getContentHandler(URLConnection.java)
        at java.net.URLConnection.getContent(URLConnection.java)
```

```
     at java.net.URL.getContent(URL.java)
     at getobject.main(getobject.java:18)
I got a sun.net.www.MeteredStream
```

This example demonstrates the two biggest problems when you use getContent().
First, many types of content aren't supported by the Java class libraries. The excep-
tions are thrown because Java 1.0.2 does not provide a content handler for the
MIME type text/html. The only content types that are likely to be supported in
Java 1.0 through 1.0.2 are text/plain, text/generic, image/gif and image/jpeg.
You can extend this list by writing content handlers for new MIME types; again,
this is covered in Chapter 12, *Content Handlers*.

Second, it's hard to predict what kind of object you'll get in return, but this may
not be as difficult as it seems. Right now, you either get some kind of InputStream
or an ImageProducer; it's easy to check what you get by using the instanceof operator. This should be enough knowledge to let you read a text file or display an
image. Of course, there may be more possibilities in the future.

Utility Methods of the URL Class

public boolean sameFile(URL other)

The sameFile() method tests whether two URL objects point to the same file. If
they do, sameFile() returns true; otherwise it returns false. The test that same-
File() performs is quite shallow; all it does is compare the corresponding fields
for equality. If the two URLs don't match, sameFile() returns false even if the two
files are the same. For example, sameFile() thinks that *http://helio.ora.com/
www/publishing/ttales/index.html* and *http://www.ora.com/www/publishing/ttales/
index.html* are different files because it cannot tell that *helio.ora.com* and
www.ora.com are different names for the same machine. sameFile() also gets confused if one URL has the port set explicitly and the other doesn't; thus
http://www.ora.com:80 appears to be different from *http://www.ora.com/*. sameFile()
is smart enough to ignore the ref part of a URL. It would be too much to expect
sameFile() to download the files and compare them, but one hopes that in a
future release, this method will understand default ports, and be able to find out
whether different hostnames are aliases for each other.

Here's a fragment of code that uses sameFile() to compare two URLs:

```
try {
  URL u1 = new URL("http://www.ncsa.uiuc.edu/HTMLPrimer.html#GS");
  URL u2 = new URL("http://www.ncsa.uiuc.edu/HTMLPrimer.html#HD");

  if u1.sameFile(u2) {
    System.out.println(u1 + " is the same file as \n" + u2);
  }
  else {
```

```
    System.out.println(u1 + " is not the same file as \n" + u2);
  }
}
catch (MalformedURLException e) {
  System.err.println(e);
}
```

The output is:

```
http://www.ncsa.uiuc.edu/HTMLPrimer.html#GS is the same file as
http://www.ncsa.uiuc.edu/HTMLPrimer.html#HD
```

The sameFile() method is similar to the equals() method of the URL class. The main difference between sameFile() and equals() is that any object may be passed to equals(); only URL objects can be passed to sameFile(). In fact, the equals() method just checks whether the object it gets is an instance of URL; if it is, it passes that object to sameFile().

public String toExternalForm()

The toExternalForm() method returns a human readable String representing the URL. It is identical to the toString() method. In fact, all toString() does is return toExternalForm(). Therefore, this method is currently redundant, and rarely used.

The Object Methods

java.net.URL inherits from java.lang.Object, so it has access to all the methods of the Object class. It overrides three methods to provide more specialized behavior: equals(), hashCode(), and toString().

public String toString()

Like all good classes java.net.URL has a toString() method. Examples 5–1 through 5–6 all implicitly called this method when URLs were passed to System.out.println(). As those examples demonstrated, the String produced by toString() is an absolute URL, like *http://sunsite.unc.edu/javafaq/javatutorial.html.*

It's uncommon to call toString() explicitly; in print statements, you can just print the URL, which calls toString() implicitly. Outside of print statements, it's usually more convenient to retrieve the individual pieces of the URL using the get methods. If you do call toString(), the syntax is simple:

```
URL thisApplet = getCodeBase();
String appletURL = thisApplet.toString();
```

public boolean equals(Object o)

An object is equal to a URL if it is also a URL, and both URLs point to the same file as determined by the sameFile() method. Thus equals() has the same limitations as sameFile(). For example, *http://helio.ora.com/* is not equal to *http://www.ora.com/*; and *http://www.ora.com:80/* is not equal to *http://www.ora.com/*. Whether this makes sense depends on whether you think of a URL as a string, or as a reference to a particular Internet resource.

What doesn't make sense under almost any scheme is that the comparison ignores references to named anchors. Thus *http://www.ncsa.uiuc.edu/HTMLPrimer.html#GS* equals *http://www.ncsa.uiuc.edu/HTMLPrimer.html#HD*. Ignoring the anchor makes sense for sameFile(), because two URLs with different anchors do indeed reference the same file; but when comparing URLs, ignoring named anchors is fishy, to say the least.

Example 5–8 creates URL objects for *http://helios.oit.unc.edu/javafaq/oldnews.html* and *http://sunsite.unc.edu/javafaq/oldnews.html* and then tells you whether they're the same.

Example 5–8: Are two URLs equivalent?

```
import java.net.*;

class URLEquality {

  public static void main (String args[]) {

    try {
      URL sunsite = new URL ("http://sunsite.unc.edu/javafaq/oldnews.html");
      URL helios = new URL("http://helios.oit.unc.edu/javafaq/oldnews.html");
      if (sunsite.equals(helios)) {
        System.out.println
          (sunsite + " is the same as " + helios);
      }
      else {
        System.out.println
          (sunsite + " is not the same as " + helios);
      }
    }
    catch (MalformedURLException e) {
      System.err.println(e);
    }

  }

}
```

When you run this program you discover:

```
% java URLEquality
http://sunsite.unc.edu/javafaq/oldnews.html is not the same as
http://helios.oit.unc.edu/javafaq/oldnews.html
```

public int hashCode()

The hashCode() method returns an int that is used when URL objects are used as keys in hash tables. Therefore, it is called by the various methods of java.util.Hashtable; you rarely need to call this method directly, if ever. Hash codes for two different URL objects are unlikely to be the same, but it is certainly possible; there are far more conceivable URLs than there are four-byte integers.

One Last Method

You use this last method in the context of protocol handlers, which are classes that implement particular protocols, like HTTP; it isn't used much in more prosaic network programming.

public static synchronized void setURLStreamHandlerFactory(URLStreamHandlerFactory fac)

This method sets the URLStreamHandlerFactory for the application, and throws an Error if the factory has already been set. A URLStreamHandler is responsible for parsing the URL, and then constructing the appropriate URLConnection object to handle the connection to the server. Most of this happens behind the scenes, and it's unwise to mess with it unless you're implementing a client of your own. You'll learn more about the URLStreamHandler and URLConnection classes in Chapter 11, *Protocol Handlers*.

The URLEncoder Class

One of the problems that the designers of the Web faced was differences between local operating systems. These differences can cause problems with URLs: for example, some operating systems allow spaces in filenames; URLs don't. Most operating systems won't complain about a # sign in a filename; in a URL, a # sign means that the filename has ended, and a named anchor follows. Similar problems are presented by other special characters, non-alphanumeric characters, etc., all of which may have a special meaning inside a URL or on another operating system. To solve these problems, you must encode all characters in a URL except for lower- and uppercase letters, digits, and underscores.

The encoding used is very simple. You represent any characters that are not numerals, underscores, or lower- or uppercase letters by a percent sign (%), followed by two hexadecimal digits giving the ASCII value for that character. Spaces are a special case because they're so common. According to the rule above, you can encode spaces as %20; you can also use a plus sign (+), which is usually more convenient. You encode the plus sign itself as %2b. You should encode the /, #, =, &, and ? characters when you use them as part of a name, and not as a separator between parts of the URL.

The java.net.URLEncoder class consists of a single static method called encode() that encodes a String according to these rules, changing any non-alphanumeric characters (except the space and underscore characters) into % sequences. There's no reason encode() couldn't have been included in the URL class, but it wasn't. The signature of encode() is:

```
public static String encode(String s)
```

It returns a new String suitably encoded. For example:

```
String s = URLEncoder.encode("This string has spaces");
```

Example 5–9 returns various encoded strings.

Example 5–9: x-www-form-urlencoded Strings

```
import java.net.URLEncoder;

public class encodeTest {

  public static void main(String args[]) {

    System.out.println(URLEncoder.encode("This string has spaces"));
    System.out.println(URLEncoder.encode("This*string*has*stars"));
    System.out.println(URLEncoder.encode("This%string%has%percent%signs"));
    System.out.println(URLEncoder.encode("This+string+has+pluses"));
    System.out.println(URLEncoder.encode("This/string/has/slashes"));
    System.out.println(URLEncoder.encode("This\"string\"has\"quote\"marks"));
    System.out.println(URLEncoder.encode("This:string:has:colons"));
    System.out.println(URLEncoder.encode("This.string.has.periods"));
    System.out.println(URLEncoder.encode("This=string=has=equals=signs"));
    System.out.println(URLEncoder.encode("This&string&has&ampersands"));
  }


}
```

Here is the output:

```
% java encodeTest
This+string+has+spaces
This%2astring%2ahas%2astars
This%25string%25has%25percent%25signs
This%2bstring%2bhas%2bpluses
```

```
This%2fstring%2fhas%2fslashes
This%22string%22has%22quote%22marks
This%3astring%3ahas%3acolons
This%2estring%2ehas%2eperiods
This%3dstring%3dhas%3dequals%3dsigns
This%26string%26has%26ampersands
```

There is no corresponding `decode()` method in Java. However, feel free to include Example 5–10 in your programs if you need it. This class contains a single public method, `decode()`, which takes a `String`, encoded in URL format, and returns it to normal ASCII. There is also a private constructor to ensure that no one instantiates this class.

Example 5–10: A class to decode x-www-form-urlencoded Strings

```java
import java.io.ByteArrayOutputStream;


/**
 * Turns Strings of x-www-form-urlEncoded format into regular text.
 *
 * @version 1.0, 4/3/1996
 * @author Elliotte Rusty Harold
 */

public class URLDecoder {

  private URLDecoder() {}

  /**
   * Translates String from x-www-form-urlEncoded format into text.
   * @param s String to be translated
   * @return the translated String.
   */
  public static String decode(String s) {

    ByteArrayOutputStream out = new ByteArrayOutputStream(s.length());

    for (int i = 0; i < s.length(); i++) {
      int c = (int) s.charAt(i);
      if (c == '+') {
        out.write(' ');
      }
      else if (c == '%') {
        int c1 = Character.digit(s.charAt(++i), 16);
        int c2 = Character.digit(s.charAt(++i), 16);
        out.write((char) (c1 * 16 + c2));
      }
      else {
        out.write(c);
      }
    }// end for
```

Example 5–10: A class to decode x-www-form-urlencoded Strings (continued)

```
    return out.toString();

  }

}
```

The decode() method begins by creating a new ByteArrayOutputStream out with the same length as the input string s. This length guarantees that the byte array will be long enough to contain the decoded result. It may be longer than necessary, since any % escapes in the string s (like %2b) are three characters long, but replaced by a single character. However, using an array that's too long won't cause any problems.

The for loop processes the string s, character by character. If the character is a plus sign, a space is written on the output stream out. If the character is a % sign, decode() reads the next two characters. Each is converted into a hexadecimal (base-16) digit using the java.lang.Character.digit() method. The first int is multiplied by 16 and added to the second. The result is the original character (i.e., the character represented by the escape sequence), so the int is cast to a char and written on the OutputStream. The loop counter is pre-incremented inside the loop (++i), so the next iteration through the loop will skip these two characters, and process a new character. Any character that is not a + or a % does not need to be decoded, and is passed onto the output stream without conversion. Finally, the OutputStream is converted to a String, which is returned to the caller.

Some Useful Programs

Query String

The following class uses the URLEncoder to encode successive name and value pairs in a Java object called QueryString, which will be used for posting data to CGI programs. Recall that a query string for a CGI program is composed of successive name-value pairs. You separate names from values by an equal sign (=), and successive pairs by an ampersand (&). Here's one QueryString that includes two name-value pairs:

```
    username=Elliotte+Rusty+Harold&email=elharo%40sunsite%2eunc%2eedu
```

The first pair in this string has the name username and the value Elliotte Rusty Harold. The second name-value pair has the name email and the value elharo@sunsite.unc.edu.

When you create a QueryString, you must supply the first name-value pair to the constructor; the arguments are a pair of Objects, which are converted to strings using their toString() methods, and then encoded. To add further pairs, call the add() method, which also takes two Objects as arguments, converts them to Strings, and encodes them. The QueryString class supplies its own toString() method, which simply returns the accumulated list of name-value pairs. toString() is called implicitly whenever you add a QueryString to another string, or print it on an output stream.

Example 5–11: The QueryString class

```
import java.net.URLEncoder;

public class queryString {

  String query;

  public queryString(Object name, Object value) {

    query = URLEncoder.encode(name.toString()) + "=" +
      URLEncoder.encode(value.toString());

  }

  public void add(Object name, Object value) {

      query += "&" + URLEncoder.encode(name.toString()) + "=" +
        URLEncoder.encode(value.toString());

  }

  public String toString() {
    return query;
  }

}
```

Page Saver

Most web browsers let you save a page on your hard drive as either HTML or text. However, both these formats lose track of images and relative links. The problem is that most pages are full of relative URLs; these all break when you move the page to another context by downloading it to your local machine. Example 5–12 is an application called PageSaver that downloads a web page to a local hard drive, while keeping all links intact by rewriting all relative URLs as absolute URLs.

The PageSaver class reads a series of URLs from the command line. It opens each one in turn and saves it on the local disk, using openStream() to get an input stream from which to read the document. As each file is downloaded, PageSaver searches it for link tags, like <IMG...>, <A HREF...>, and <APPLET...>. When it encounters one of these tags, PageSaver parses out the link that it refers to, and, if it is a relative URL, remaps it to an absolute URL. Absolute URLs are left alone. Note particularly the extensive use to which the URL class methods were put; Page-Saver could be rewritten with string replacements, but that would be considerably more complicated.

Example 5–12: PageSaver application

```
import java.net.*;
import java.io.*;

public class PageSaver {

  URL theURL;

  public static void main (String args[]) {

    // Loop through the command line arguments
    for  (int i = 0; i < args.length; i++) {

      //Open the URL for reading
      try {
        URL root = new URL(args[0]);
        PageSaver ps = new PageSaver(root);
        ps.saveThePage();
      }
      catch (MalformedURLException e) {
        System.err.println(args[0] + " is not a parseable URL");
        System.err.println(e);
      }
    }//  end for

  }// end main


  public PageSaver(URL u) {

    theURL = u;

  }

  // saveThePage opens a DataInputStream from the URL,
  // opens a PrintStream onto a file for the output,
  // and then copies one to the other while rewriting tags
  public void saveThePage() {

    char thisChar;
    String theTag;
    PrintStream  p = null;
```

Example 5–12: PageSaver application (continued)

```
try {
  DataInputStream theHTML = new DataInputStream(theURL.openStream());
  p = makeOutputFile();

  while (true) {
    thisChar = (char) theHTML.readByte();
    if (thisChar == '<') {
      theTag = readTag(theHTML);
      theTag = convertTag(theTag);
      p.print(theTag);
    }
    else {
      p.print(thisChar);
    }
  }// end while
} // end try
catch (EOFException e) { // This page is done
}
catch (Exception e) {
  System.err.println(e);
}
finally {
  p.close();
}

} // end SaveThePage


// We need open a file on the local file system
// with the same name as the remote file;
// then chain a PrintStream to the file
public PrintStream makeOutputFile() throws IOException {

  FileOutputStream fout;

  String theFile = theURL.getFile();

  // the getFile method returns the filename prefixed with a slash,
  // e.g. /index.html instead of index.html. That slash needs to be removed.
  theFile = theFile.substring(1);
  System.err.println("\n\n\n" + theFile + "\n\n\n");
  if (theFile.equals("")) theFile = "index.html";

  // At this point you should check to see whether
  // the file already exists and, if it does,
  // ask the user if they wish to overwrite it

  fout = new FileOutputStream(theFile);

  return new PrintStream(fout);

}
```

Example 5-12: PageSaver application (continued)

```
// The readTag method is called when a < is encountered
// in the input stream.  This method is responsible
// for reading the remainder of the tag.
// Note that when this method has been called the <
// has been read from the input stream but has not yet been sent
// to the output stream.
// This method has trouble (as do most web browsers)
// if it encounters a raw < sign in the Stream. Technically
// raw < signs should be encoded as &lt; in the original HTML.
public static String readTag(DataInputStream is) {

  StringBuffer theTag = new StringBuffer("<");
  char theChar = '<';

  try {
     while (theChar != '>') {
       theChar = (char) is.readByte();
       theTag.append(theChar);
     }// end while
  } // end try
  catch (EOFException e) {
    // Done with the Stream
  }
  catch (Exception e) {
     System.err.println(e);
  }

  return theTag.toString();

}


// The convertTag method takes a complete tag as
// a String and, if it's a relative link, converts it
// to an absolute link.  The converted tag is returned.
public String convertTag(String tag) {

  // temporary position variables
  int p1, p2, p3, p4;

  try {
    // HTML tags are cases insensitive so converting
    // it to upper case makes the problem slightly easier
    String s1 = tag.toUpperCase();
    // Find the beginning and the end of the URL
    //
    if (s1.startsWith("<A HREF")) {
      p1 = s1.indexOf("HREF");
    }
    else if (s1.startsWith("<IMG ")) {
      p1 = s1.indexOf("SRC");
    }
    else if (s1.startsWith("<APPLET ")) {
```

Example 5–12: PageSaver application (continued)

```
     p1 = s1.indexOf("CODEBASE");
   }
   else {// this is not a link based tag
     return tag;
   }
   // find the =
   p2 = s1.indexOf ("=", p1);
   if (p2 == -1) return tag;
   // Ideally the = sign is immediately followed by
   // a " mark followed by the URL which is closed by a ".
   // However since a lot of HTML is non-conforming we
   // need to be a little sneakier. In this case we read
   // characters in the URL until an character which is not
   // whitespace is encountered.
   p3 = p2+1;
   while (Character.isSpace(s1.charAt(p3))) {
     p3++;
   }
   if (s1.charAt(p3) == '"') p3++;

   // p3 now points to the beginning of the URL
   // The URL is read until a closing " or whitespace is seen
   p4 = p3+1;
   while (!Character.isSpace(s1.charAt(p4)) &&
    s1.charAt(p4) != '"') {
     p4++;
   }

   // The URL is the text between p3 and p4
   // URL's are in general NOT case insensitive so the URL
   // must be read from the original tag and not from s1
   // which was uppercased
   String link = tag.substring(p3, p4);

   // Is it a relative URL?  Relative URLs
   // don't contain colons.
   if (link.indexOf(":")  == -1) {
       // build an absolute URL from the relative URL
       URL newURL = new URL(theURL, link);
       // replace the old URL with the new URL
       tag = s1.substring(0,p3) + newURL + s1.substring(p4,s1.length());
   } // end if

 } // end try
 catch (StringIndexOutOfBoundsException e) {
   // Most of the time a StringIndexOutOfBoundsException here means
   // the tag was not standard conforming so
   // the algorithm for finding the URL crapped out.
   // If that's the case, the original tag is returned.
 }
 catch (Exception e) {
   System.err.println(e);
```

Example 5–12: PageSaver application (continued)

```
   }


   return tag;

  }

}
```

There's a lot you could add to this application. What's most needed is error check-ing; a lot of sites have imperfect URLs with missing quote marks and other errors, and that should be taken into account. PageSaver could also be more careful about overwriting existing files. Images and applets could actually be downloaded to the local hard drive rather than merely relinked. And this program will encounter problems if the name of the file on the remote system isn't a legal file-name on the local system. However, the basic networking code is here.

Communicating with CGI Programs Through GET

Since a query string can be embedded in a URL, it's simple to write a Java program that connects to a Web server and submits a query to a CGI script. Example 5–13 is a program called `lycos` that uses the Lycos search engine to look up topics speci-fied on the command line. The basic Lycos search engine is a simple form with one input field named `query`; input typed in this field is sent to a CGI program at *http://www.lycos.com/cgi-bin/pursuit*, which does the actual search. The HTML for the form looks something like this:

```
<form action="/cgi-bin/pursuit" method=GET>
<input name="query" >
<INPUT TYPE="submit" Value="Go Get It>
</form>
```

(The actual HTML Lycos uses is a bit more complicated because Lycos uses some non-standard tricks to lay out their page with tables.) Thus, to submit a search request to Lycos, you just need to collect the search string, encode that in a query string, and send it to *http://www.lycos.com/cgi-bin/pursuit*. For example, to do a search for "java" you would open a connection to the URL *http://www.lycos.com/cgi-bin/pursuit?query=java* and read the resulting input stream. Example 5–13 does exactly this.

Example 5–13: Do a Lycos search

```
import java.net.*;
import java.io.*;


public class lycos {
```

Example 5–13: Do a Lycos search (continued)

```java
public static void main (String[] args) {

  String querystring = "";

  for (int i = 0; i < args.length; i++) {
    querystring += args[i] + " ";
  }
  querystring.trim();
  querystring = "query=" + URLEncoder.encode(querystring);
  try {
    String thisLine;
    URL u = new URL("http://www.lycos.com/cgi-bin/pursuit?" + querystring);
    DataInputStream theHTML = new DataInputStream(u.openStream());
    while ((thisLine = theHTML.readLine()) != null) {
      System.out.println(thisLine);
    }// while loop ends here
  }
  catch (MalformedURLException e) {
    System.err.println(e);
  }
  catch (IOException e) {
    System.err.println(e);
  }

}

}
```

URLRequestor

The following program runs as an applet or as an application. URLRequestor has a single TextField where you can type a URL, a Button labeled "Get URL" that tells the application to retrieve the data at the URL, and a TextArea that displays the result (Figure 5–1). This isn't a full-fledged web browser by any means (for that you'd at least need to parse and display HTML), but it's very useful for testing. We will use URLRequestor in Chapter 11 and Chapter 12 to test content and protocol handlers.

URLRequestor uses getContent() to retrieve the objects that the URLs reference. As I said earlier, getContent() presents some problems. It returns an Object, but to do anything useful, you must cast that Object into a more specific class, and the actual classes of the Objects that getContent() returns are indeed far from obvious. For example, Sun's appletviewer returns a text/html page as a sun.net.www.MeteredStream, not a String. It returns an image/gif as a sun.awt.image.URLImageSource, not a java.awt.Image. The URLRequestor uses the instanceof operator to test the type of each object, and tries to match the object to something it knows how to handle. If it can't handle the type of object returned, it calls that object's toString() method and displays the result. If

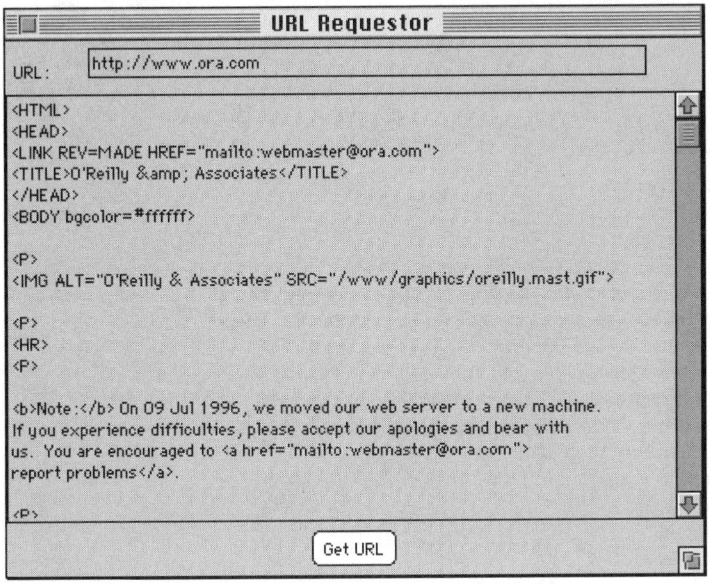

Figure 5–1: The URLRequestor applet

nothing else, this will tell you what class was returned so you can extend URLRequestor to handle the new kind of object. Example 5–14 just handles text. In the
next chapter and in Chapter 10, you'll learn how to download and display binary
files such as images, and applets.

Example 5–14: URLRequestor

```
import java.applet.*;
import java.awt.*;
import java.net.*;
import java.io.*;


public class URLRequestor extends Applet {

  TextField url;
  TextArea textDisplay;

  public static void main(String[] args) {

    URLRequestor a = new URLRequestor();
    Frame appletFrame = new Frame("URL Requestor");
    appletFrame.add("Center", a);
    appletFrame.resize(500,300);
    appletFrame.move(50,50);
    a.init();
    a.start();
    appletFrame.show();
```

Example 5–14: URLRequestor (continued)

```java
  }

  public void init() {


    setLayout(new BorderLayout());
    textDisplay = new TextArea();
    add("Center", textDisplay);

    // We don't want the buttons and fields in the north and south
    // to fill their respective sections so we'll add Panels there
    // and use FlowLayouts in the Panels
    Panel SouthPanel = new Panel();
    Panel NorthPanel = new Panel();
    NorthPanel.setLayout(new FlowLayout(FlowLayout.LEFT));
    SouthPanel.add(new Button("Get URL"));
    NorthPanel.add("North", new Label("URL: "));
    url = new TextField(40);
    NorthPanel.add("North", url);
    add("South", SouthPanel);
    add("North", NorthPanel);

  }

  public boolean action(Event e, Object o) {

    if (e.target instanceof Button) {
      fetchURL(url.getText());
      return true;
    }
    else if (e.target == url) {
      fetchURL(url.getText());
      return true;
    }
    else {
      return false;
    }

  }

public void fetchURL(String s) {

  try {
    URL u = new URL(s);
    try {
      Object o = u.getContent();
      if (o instanceof InputStream)  {
        showText((InputStream) o);
      }
      else {
        showText(o.toString());
      }
```

Example 5–14: URLRequestor (continued)

```
      }
      catch (IOException e) {
        showText("Could not connect to " + u.getHost());
      }
      catch (NullPointerException e) {
        showText("There was a problem with the content");
      }
    }
    catch (MalformedURLException e) {
      showText(url.getText() + " is not a valid URL");
    }

  }

  void showText(String s) {
    textDisplay.setText(s);
  }

  void showText(InputStream is) {

    String nextline;

    textDisplay.setText("");
    try {
      DataInputStream dis = new DataInputStream(is);
      while((nextline = dis.readLine()) != null) {
        textDisplay.appendText(nextline + "\n");
      }
    }
    catch (IOException e) {
      textDisplay.appendText(e.toString());
    }

  }

}
```

URLRequestor begins like many programs that double as applets and as applications: it starts with a main() method that creates a new instance of the applet, creates a Frame to hold that applet, adds the applet to the Frame, and then calls the applet's init() and start() methods.

The applet has three GUI components from the java.awt package: a TextField so the user can enter the URL to be retrieved, a TextArea to display the retrieved data, and a Button that tells the applet to get the URL. The Button is superfluous, because typing RETURN in the TextField also retrieves the data. These three components are placed in the Frame with a BorderLayout. Panels are used in the North and South sections of the BorderLayout; the Panels have a FlowLayout, which centers the components without resizing them.

The action() method is called when any of the GUI components generates an "action event." In this case, the events we're interested in are mouse clicks on the button or RETURNs in the text field. All we need to do is check whether the action was generated by a Button or a TextField. (It would be better style to check which Button or TextField the action occurred in, but since there's only one of each, we can be lazy. However, if we added another button to the user interface, it would break.) If it was, the applet should retrieve the URL that's in the TextField. action() returns true if the event was generated by our Button or TextField. If the event came from any other source, action() returns false to let the applet's container handle the event.

To retrieve data, action() calls the fetchURL() method, retrieving the contents of the TextField by calling getText(). fetchURL() uses this string to construct a new URL object u. Then u's getContent() method is called to return an object from the URL. This version of the URLRequestor class only understands one kind of object: an InputStream. If the object returned is an InputStream (as it will be for HTML and text files returned via HTTP), the InputStream is passed to the showText() method, which takes an InputStream as an argument; it reads the input line by line, and displays it in the TextArea. If the object has any other type, fetchURL() converts it to a String, and passes it to another (overloaded) version of show-Text() which takes a String as an argument. This version of showText() simply displays the String in the TextArea. If nothing else, this string tells the user the class of the object returned. Both versions of the showText() method put the resulting text in the TextArea for the user to see. The version that takes an Input-Stream as an argument displays the text line by line as it reads the incoming data.

If an error occurs at any point (for example, a bad URL is entered), the TextArea displays an error message.

6

The Network Methods of java.applet.Applet

Using the Applet Class to Download Data

By now, you should be familiar with applets, which are programs that can be embedded on a web page, and run in a secure environment within a browser. All applets extend the `java.applet.Applet` class, which includes methods that perform network-related operations. These methods allow an applet to find out where it came from, download images and sounds from a web server, and track the progress of the download. This chapter discusses interaction between applets and the network. It doesn't provide an introduction to the `Applet` class as a whole; for that, see an introductory book like Niemeyer and Peck's *Exploring Java* (O'Reilly & Associates, 1996) or my *Java Developer's Resource* (Prentice Hall, 1996).

NOTE   The methods of the `Applet` class are almost always called from within a subclass of `java.applet.Applet`. They are only rarely called using a reference variable. I assume all code fragments in this chapter exist inside a subclass of `java.applet.Applet`. Therefore, in this chapter, code fragments that demonstrate applet methods look like this:

```
URL u = getDocumentBase();
```

rather than this:

```
Applet a = new Applet();
URL u = a.getDocumentBase();
```

The methods of the Applet class that are discussed in this section are really just thin veneers over equivalent methods in the java.applet.AppletStub and java.applet.AppletContext classes. Applets that you instantiate yourself (for example, an applet that also runs as an application by supplying a main() method to call the applet's init() and start() methods) will generally have null Applet-Stub and AppletContext members. Therefore, if you try to use these methods in such an applet, a NullPointerException will be thrown.

Getting Related Information

Most often, applets want to retrieve image files or other data from one of two directories: the directory the applet came from, or the directory that contains the HTML page in which the applet is embedded. These directories are called the *codebase* and *document base*, respectively. To make it easy to find other files, the Applet class has methods that return URL objects for the current page and the current applet. These methods are called getDocumentBase() and getCodeBase() respectively.

public URL getDocumentBase()

The getDocumentBase() method returns the URL of the page containing the applet. The following code displays this URL on the screen:

```
public void paint(Graphics g) {

    g.drawString(getDocumentBase().toString(), 25, 50);

}
```

public URL getCodeBase()

The getCodeBase() method returns the URL of the applet's directory. Example 6-1 is an applet that displays its document base and codebase.

Example 6–1: An applet that displays its document base and its codebase

```
import java.applet.Applet;
import java.awt.*;

public class AppletBases extends Applet {

  public void paint(Graphics g) {

    g.drawString("Codebase:      " + getCodeBase().toString(), 10, 40);
    g.drawString("Document base: " + getDocumentBase().toString(), 10, 65);
  }

}
```

Figure 6–1 shows what happens when the applet runs; the result depends on the URLs of the applet, and the document. It's worth noting that getCodeBase() always returns the URL of a directory, not the URL of the applet itself, while get-DocumentBase() always returns the URL of a file. In practice, this rarely makes a difference; you almost always call getDocumentBase() and getCodeBase() within methods or constructors that build relative URLs.

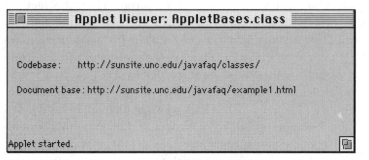

Figure 6–1: An applet that shows its codebase and its document base

Downloading Images

In the last chapter, you learned how to download data from an HTTP URL by using getContent() or getInputStream(). These methods are useful for data that can be read line-by-line like an HTML file, but they don't work well for binary data, since that usually requires some knowledge of the data's structure. The Applet class includes several methods that understand more about what they're downloading. The following group of methods is used to retrieve images.

TIP   Like the other methods in this chapter, the two getImage() methods in the Applet class rely on an AppletContext member that is not available to applets you instantiate yourself (in contrast to those instantiated by a web browser or applet viewer). However, the java.awt.Toolkit class includes identical getImage() methods that don't rely on an AppletContext. You can always get a Toolkit object by calling static java.awt.Toolkit.getDefaultToolkit(). Then you can use its getImage() methods in just the same way that you use the java.applet.Applet.getImage() methods described here. The one difference is that you'll need to prefix the calls to getImage() with a variable that refers to the Toolkit object. For example:

```
Toolkit t = java.awt.Toolkit.getDefaultToolkit();
URL u = new URL("http://www.macfaq.com/logo.gif")
Image theImage = t.getImage(u);
```

---

public Image getImage(URL u)

This method retrieves the image data at the specified URL and puts it in an `Image` object. For example:

```
Image myLogo = getImage(new URL("http://www.macfaq.com/logo.gif"));
```

The `getImage()` method relies on the `AppletContext` (provided by the web browser or applet viewer) to retrieve and interpret the image. Thus, this method can only get images in formats understood by the `AppletContext` that the applet is running in. Currently, all contexts that run in a graphical environment understand the GIF format. (IBM's Java environment for some of its mainframes and minicomputers is completely non-graphical because those platforms don't support graphics.) Most contexts also understand JPEG, though JPEG support was omitted from some vendors' early alpha and beta releases. Finally, Java implementations derived from Sun's source code often understand XBM. As of early 1997, no other formats are supported in any implementation. More are likely to be supported in the future, most notably PNG. Example 6–2 is a complete applet that loads and displays the image referenced by the `Image` parameter from a `<param>` tag in the HTML file.

Example 6–2: Display an image via a URL

```
import java.applet.Applet;
import java.awt.*;
import java.net.*;

public class ImageView extends Applet {

  Image theImage;

  public void init() {

    try {
      URL u = new URL(getCodeBase(), getParameter("Image"));
      theImage = getImage(u);
    }
    catch (MalformedURLException e) {
      System.err.println(e);
    }

  }

  public void paint (Graphics g) {
    g.drawImage(theImage, 0, 0, this);
  }

}
```

The `getImage()` method returns immediately, even before it knows whether or not the image actually exists. The image isn't loaded until some other part of the

program actually tries to draw it, or you explicitly force the image to start loading—we'll see how to do that shortly. At that point, the Java interpreter starts a
separate thread to download and process the image file.

public Image getImage(URL path, String filename)

This method is similar to the one above, except that it uses the path argument (a
URL) to find the image's directory, and the filename argument (a String) to get
the name of the image file:

```
Image myLogo = getImage(new URL("http://www.macfaq.com/"), "logo.gif");
```

This version of getImage() is frequently used with getCodeBase() or getDocument-
Base(). You would use getCodeBase() in an applet that might be used on many
different web servers, but whose images would always be in the same directory as
the applet. For example:

```
Image myImage = getImage(getCodeBase(), "logo.gif");
```

If the applet only exists on one web server, but is embedded on many pages that
load different images, you would use getDocumentBase() to locate the images:

```
Image myImage = getImage(getDocumentBase(), "logo.gif");
```

This technique would be useful in an animator applet; the applet would probably
read the names of some image files from parameters included in the HTML. You
can use the filename argument to add to the path you get from the URL component. For example, if the pictures are in a directory called *images*, which is in the
same directory as the HTML page, you would load the file *logo.gif* like this:

```
Image myImage = getImage(getDocumentBase(), "images/logo.gif");
```

Downloading Sounds

java.applet.Applet has four methods that download sounds from the web. The
two play() methods download a sound file and play it immediately. The two
getAudioClip() methods save a sound for later playing. The AppletContext provided by the web browser or applet viewer does the actual work of downloading
and playing the sound file. Netscape 2.0, Netscape 3.0, and the Java 1.0 and 1.1
appletviewers only support Sun's *.au* format. More formats are likely to be supported in the future through the Java Media API. In the meantime, there are a
number of freeware, shareware, and payware tools that convert sounds to the *.au*
format, including Lsox on Linux and UNIX systems, and SoundHack, Ulaw, and
SoundEdit 16 on the Mac.

public void play(URL u)

The play() method looks for a sound file at the URL u. If the sound file is found, then it is downloaded and played. Otherwise nothing happens. For example:

```
try {
  play(new URL("http://www.macfaq.com/sounds/gong.au"));
}
catch (MalformedURLException e) {
  System.err.println(e);
}
```

Example 6–3 is a simple applet that plays a sound file. The name of the file is taken from the parameter sound supplied by a <param> tag in the HTML file. The sound file should be in the same directory as the applet.

Example 6–3: Play a sound

```
import java.applet.Applet;
import java.awt.*;
import java.net.*;

public class PlaySound extends Applet {

  public void init() {

    try {
      URL u = new URL(getCodeBase(), getParameter("sound"));
      play(u);
    }
    catch (MalformedURLException e) {
      System.err.println(e);
    }
  }

}
```

public void play(URL u, String filename)

This method is similar to the one above, except that it uses the URL u to find the sound file's directory and the String filename to get the actual filename:

```
play(new URL("http://www.macfaq.com/", "gong.au"));
```

The URL argument is frequently a call to getCodeBase() or getDocumentBase(). You would use getCodeBase() if you know that the sound files will always be in the same directory as the applet, even if you don't know in advance where the applet will be located. For example:

```
play(getCodeBase(), "gong.au"));
```

If the sound files are always located in the same directory as the HTML file that loads the applet, you would use getDocumentBase(). In this scenario, one applet, residing on one server, might be used by several web pages located on different servers; each page might use a <param> tag to specify its own sound file. In this situation, you might call play() like this:

```
play(getDocumentBase(), getParameter("soundfile")));
```

You can use the filename argument to add to the path you get from the URL argument. For example, if the sounds are in a directory called *sounds*, a subdirectory of the directory containing the HTML page, you would call play() like this:

```
play (getDocumentBase(), "sounds/gong.au"));
```

public AudioClip getAudioClip(URL u)

The AudioClip interface represents a sound. You can download a sound from a web site with the getAudioClip() method. Once you have an AudioClip object, you play it at your leisure by calling the clip's play() and loop() methods; play() plays the file once, and loop() plays it repeatedly. Both of these methods let you keep the audio clip around for future use—unlike the play() method of the last section, which discards the audio data after it finishes.

Using the AudioClip interface is simple. Make sure that you have imported java.applet.AudioClip (many programmers only import java.applet.Applet out of habit), declare an AudioClip variable, and call getAudioClip() to retrieve the sound file. As usual, the creation of the URL needs to be wrapped in a try-catch block to catch MalformedURLExceptions. For example:

```
AudioClip theGong;
URL u;

try {
  u = new URL(http://sunsite.unc.edu/javafaq/gong.au);
  theGong = getAudioClip(u);
}
catch (MalformedURLException e) {
  System.err.println(e);
}
```

public AudioClip getAudioClip(URL u, String filename)

This method is similar to the one above, except that it uses the URL u to find the directory that the sound file is located in, and the String filename to supply the name of the audio file. For example:

```
AudioClip ac = getAudioClip(new URL("http://www.macfaq.com/", "gong.au"));
```

This version of getAudioClip() is frequently used with getCodeBase() or getDocumentBase(). For example, if you are writing an applet that will be stored on many different servers, but whose sound files will always be in the same directory as the applet, you would call getAudioClip() like this:

```
getAudioClip(getCodeBase(), "gong.au"));
```

Or, if you're writing an applet that will reside on one server, but be used by many web pages with different sound files, you might call getAudioClip() like this:

```
getAudioClip (getDocumentBase(), getParameter(soundfile));
```

Here, we're using getDocumentBase() to find the location of the HTML file, and getParameter() to retrieve the name of an audio file from a <param> tag in the HTML. You can use the filename argument to getAudioClip() to add to the path supplied by the URL. For example, in the following code, the sound file is located in the directory sounds, a subdirectory of the document's directory:

```
getAudioClip (getDocumentBase(), "sounds/gong.au"));
```

Example 6–4 is a complete applet that downloads a sound file called *gong.au*, located in the same directory as the applet, and then spawns a Thread to play the sound every five seconds.

Example 6–4: Download a sound via a relative URL and play it at five-second intervals

```
import java.applet.*;
import java.awt.*;

public class RelativeGong extends Applet implements Runnable {

  AudioClip theGong;
  Thread t;

  public void init() {

    theGong = getAudioClip(getDocumentBase(), "sounds/gong.au");
    if (theGong != null) {
      t = new Thread(this);
      t.start();
    }

  }

  public void start() {
    t.resume();
  }

  public void stop() {
    t.suspend();
  }
```

Example 6–4: Download a sound via a relative URL and play it at five-second intervals (continued)

```
public void run() {

  Thread.currentThread().setPriority(Thread.MIN_PRIORITY);
  while (true) {
    theGong.play();
    try {
      Thread.sleep(5000);
    }
    catch (InterruptedException e) {
    }
  }

}

}
```

The ImageObserver Interface

The World Wide Web is sometimes humorously referred to as the "World Wide Wait," primarily because of the amount of time it takes for graphics-heavy pages to load. Although reading large files off a hard drive can be time consuming, most users have trained themselves not to notice the time it takes; file loading appears to happen instantaneously. However, this is not the case when you load files from a network, particularly when that network is the Internet. It is not uncommon for small images to take several minutes to load. Since Java loads images in a different thread than the main execution of a program, the program can do something besides spin its wheels while the pictures are downloaded. However, programs don't get impatient; users do. It is a good idea to keeps users informed about how much of an image has been loaded and how much longer they can expect to wait. The java.awt.image.ImageObserver interface allows you to monitor the loading process so that you can keep the user informed, and use the image as quickly as possible once it is loaded.

When discussing getImage(), I said that the method returned immediately, before the image had been downloaded. Downloading begins when you try to display the image, or do something else that forces loading to start (for example, calling Component.prepareImage()). However, loading an image asynchronously creates a new problem: How do you know when the image is ready? An Image object exists as soon as getImage() returns, long before anything is known about the image. You can call an Image's methods before it has finished loading, but the results are rarely what you want or expect. For example, the getWidth() and getHeight() methods return −1 until enough data has been loaded for these values to be known.

The `ImageObserver` interface allows an object to monitor the progress of loading, and to take action (such as drawing the `Image`) when the `Image` is ready for use. You can also use `ImageObserver` objects to track the progress of an image that is being created from scratch, using `MemoryImageSource` or some other `ImagePro-ducer`. The `ImageObserver` interface consists of a group of constants, and a single method, `imageUpdate()`:

```
public boolean imageUpdate(Image img, int infoflags,
                    int x, int y, int width, int height)
```

`java.awt.Component` implements `ImageObserver`, so all its subclasses (including `java.applet.Applet`, `java.awt.Canvas`, `java.awt.Panel`, `java.awt.Button` and many more) do as well.

If you've done much Java programming at all, you've probably used the `ImageOb-server` class without thinking about it; the `this` that you stick at the end of a call to `drawImage()` says to use the current component as an `ImageObserver`:

```
g.drawImage(theImage, 0, 0, this);
```

If the image is complete, it's drawn and that's that. On the other hand, if the image is not ready, the component's `imageUpdate()` method will be called periodically, giving it the chance to check the status of the image and respond accordingly. Other methods that take `ImageObserver` objects as arguments include:

```
Image.getWidth(ImageObserver)
Image.getHeight(ImageObserver)
Image.getProperty(String, ImageObserver)
Component.checkImage(Image, ImageObserver)
Component.checkImage(Image, int, int, ImageObserver)
Component.prepareImage(Image, ImageObserver)
Component.prepareImage(Image, int, int, ImageObserver)
ComponentPeer.checkImage(Image, int, int, ImageObserver)
ComponentPeer.prepareImage(Image, int, int, ImageObserver)
```

Passing an `ImageObserver` object into any of these methods signals that the method is interested in the image, and should be notified when the image's status changes. Variables that are set using a method like `getWidth()` or `getHeight()`, and pictures that are drawn on the screen using `drawImage()`, are not updated automatically when `imageUpdate()` is called. It's your job to update them when the image changes.

If you want to create your own `ImageObserver`, you first create a subclass of any `Component`, or create your own class that implements the `ImageObserver` interface. Be sure to import `java.awt.image.ImageObserver` or `java.awt.image.*`. Importing `java.awt.*` does not automatically import `java.awt.image.ImageObserver`.

Your new class, or your Component subclass, must include an imageUpdate()
method. As you'll see in the next section, there are a series of tests that imageUp-
date() can perform to determine the current status of the image.

Example 6–5 is an applet that loads an image from the net. It supplies its own
imageUpdate() method (overriding the method in Applet) to see whether the
image has loaded. Until the image is finished loading, the the applet displays the
words "Loading Picture. Please hang on." Once the image has been fully loaded,
the applet displays it.

Example 6–5: Load an image

```
import java.awt.*;
import java.applet.*;
import java.awt.image.*;

public class showImage extends Applet {

  Image thePicture;

  public void init() {

    thePicture = getImage(getDocumentBase(), "logo.gif");

  }


  public void paint(Graphics g) {

    if(!g.drawImage(thePicture, 0, 0, this)) {
      g.drawString("Loading Picture. Please hang on", 25, 50);
    }

  }

public boolean imageUpdate(Image img, int infoflags,
                           int x, int y, int width, int height) {
    if ((infoflags & ImageObserver.ALLBITS) == ImageObserver.ALLBITS) {
      repaint();
      return false;
    }
    else {
      return true;
    }

  }

}
```

There are a couple of things to note about this example. First, the drawImage() methods of the Graphics class return a boolean. Many people don't realize this, since the return value of drawImage() is often ignored. However, that boolean tells you whether or not the image was drawn successfully. If it was, drawImage() returns true. Otherwise drawImage() returns false.

Second, the imageUpdate() method is called by the ImageObserver when necessary; you do not call it explicitly. It returns false if the image is complete, and no longer needs to be updated. It returns true if the image still needs to be updated.

TIP   Let's repeat that point, since it's easy to get backwards. Your image-
               Update() method should return false if the image is complete, and
               true if the image is not complete. The imageUpdate() method
               answers the question "Does this image need to be updated?" It does
               not answer the question "Is this image complete?"

Now, let's look at what imageUpdate() does. The Image being loaded is passed into imageUpdate() through the img argument. Various mnemonic constants are combined to form the infoflags argument, which indicates what information about the image is now available. For instance, ImageObserver.ALLBITS is 32, and means that the Image is complete. You test whether the ALLBITS flag is set in infoflags by bitwise *anding* it with the mnemonic constant ImageObserver.ALLBITS, and then seeing if the result is equal to ImageObserver.ALLBITS. This chunk of bitwise algebra looks complicated, but is more efficient than the alternatives.

The precise meaning of the x, y, width, and height arguments depends on the contents of the infoflags argument. The flags used in this argument are described in the next section.

The imageUpdate() method you write needs to do three things:

1. Check to see what has changed in this Image, using infoflags.

2. Perform any action needed to update the state of the running program.

3. Return true if further updates are needed, and false if all necessary information is available.

The ImageObserver Constants

The ImageObserver interface defines eight mnemonic constants, used as flags to report the image's status in calls to imageUpdate(). Table 6–1 lists the constants and their meanings.

Table 6–1: ImageObserver Constants

Flag	Meaning if the flag is set
ImageObserver.WIDTH	The width of the image is available in the width argument to imageUpdate(). Until this flag is set, calls to getWidth() return −1.
ImageObserver.HEIGHT	The height of the image is available in the height argument to imageUpdate(). Until this flag is set calls to getHeight() return −1.
ImageObserver.PROPERTIES	The properties of the image are now available, and can be accessed with the getProperty() method of the img object.
ImageObserver.SOMEBITS	Some portion of the data needed to draw the image has been delivered. The bounding box of the available pixels is given by the x, y, width, and height arguments to the imageUpdate() method.
ImageObserver.FRAMEBITS	Another complete frame of a multi-frame image is now available. The x, y, width, and height arguments to imageUpdate() have no meaning.
ImageObserver.ALLBITS	The image is now complete. The x, y, width, and height arguments to imageUpdate() have no meaning. At this point your imageUpdate() method should return false, to indicate that the image requires no further monitoring.
ImageObserver.ERROR	The image encountered an error while loading. No further information will be forthcoming, and attempts to draw the Image will fail. The ImageObserver.ABORT flag is set at the same time to indicate that image loading was aborted.
ImageObserver.ABORT	Loading aborted before the image was complete. No more information will become available without further action to reload the Image. If the ImageObserver.ERROR bit is not also set in infoflags, attempting to access any of the data in the image restarts the loading process.

For example, to test whether the width and the height of the image are known, you would put the following code into your imageUpdate() method:

```
if ((infoflags & ImageObserver.WIDTH) == ImageObserver.WIDTH &&
   (infoflags & ImageObserver.HEIGHT) == ImageObserver.HEIGHT) {

   ...
   }
```

The difference between the ERROR and ABORT flags can be confusing. You would get an ERROR if the image data was incorrect—for example, you tried to download a mangled file. If you try to load the image again, you'll get the same bad data. ABORT usually indicates some kind of network error, like a timeout; if you try to load the image again, you might succeed.

The MediaTracker Class

The `ImageObserver` interface is useful for monitoring a single image, but it starts to fall apart when faced with multiple images, and it does nothing for non-image media types like audio files. The `java.awt.MediaTracker` class can track the loading status of many different images, organize them into logical groups, and (in future versions of Java) monitor audio clips and other kinds of multimedia content. Unfortunately, the `MediaTracker` in Java 1.1 and earlier only works with images.

To use `java.awt.MediaTracker`, simply create an instance of `MediaTracker`, and then use the `MediaTracker`'s `addImage()` method to place each `Image` you care about under the `MediaTracker`'s control. When you add an `Image` to a `MediaTracker`, you give it a numeric ID. This ID does not have to be unique; it is really a group ID that is used to organize different images into groups. Before using the image, you call a method like `checkID()` to see if the image is ready. Other methods let you force loading to start, discover which images in a group have failed to load successfully, wait for images to finish loading, and so on.

NOTE   One difference between a `MediaTracker` and an `ImageObserver` is that the `MediaTracker` is called before the `Image` is used; an `Image-Observer` is called after the `Image` is used.

Example 6–6 is an applet that loads an image from the net. As usual, the image is loaded from the document base, and the name of the image file is read from a <param> tag; the name of the parameter is `imagefile`. The applet uses a `Media-Tracker` to see whether the image has loaded. The applet displays the words "Loading Picture. Please hang on" until the image has finished loading.

Example 6–6: Load an image

```
import java.awt.*;
import java.applet.*;

public class trackImage extends Applet implements Runnable {

  Thread play;
  Image thePicture;
```

Example 6–6: Load an image (continued)

```
MediaTracker theTracker;

public void init() {

    thePicture = getImage(getDocumentBase(), getParameter("imagefile"));
    theTracker = new MediaTracker(this);
    theTracker.addImage(thePicture, 1);

    play = new Thread(this);
    play.start();

}

public void run() {

    try {
      theTracker.waitForID(1);
      repaint();
    }
    catch (InterruptedException ie) {
    }

}

public void paint(Graphics g) {

    if (theTracker.checkID(1, true)) {
      g.drawImage(thePicture, 0, 0, this);
      play.stop();
    }
    else {
      g.drawString("Loading Picture. Please hang on", 25, 50);
    }

}

}
```

The init() method reads the name of the image to be loaded, prepares an Image
object, thePicture, to hold it by calling getImage(), constructs a new Media-
Tracker called theTracker, and then adds thePicture to theTracker with an ID of
1. Next it constructs a new Thread, and starts it.

The Thread that's spawned just makes sure that the applet is repainted as soon as
the image has finished loading. It calls theTracker.waitForID(1), which blocks
until all media with this ID number have finished loading. When that's true, the
method returns and repaint() is called. I used a separate thread so the call to
waitForID() won't block the rest of the applet.

The paint() method calls theTracker.checkID(1, true) to see if the media with ID 1 is available. If this method returns true, the image is available, and the applet calls drawImage() to render the image on the screen. Then it stops the thread. Otherwise, the picture is not available, so the applet displays the string "Loading Picture. Please hang on." A more sophisticated applet could put up a progress bar, showing the percentage of the Image that had been loaded, and the approximate time remaining.

The Constructor

public MediaTracker(Component comp)

The MediaTracker class has one constructor. This constructor creates a Media-Tracker object that tracks images for a given Component. It's usually called like this:

```
MediaTracker theTracker = new MediaTracker(this);
```

The constructor's argument is the component that will display the images you want to track. You almost always call the constructor within the definition of the component that will be rendering your images; therefore, the argument to Media-Tracker() is usually this.

Adding Images to MediaTrackers

public void addImage(Image img, int id)

addImage() adds the Image img to the list of images being tracked by this Media-Tracker object, and assigns it the ID number id. The image will eventually be displayed at its normal (unscaled) size. For example, the following code fragment sets up a tracker for an image, called *logo.gif*, that's in the same directory as the web page. It's given the ID number 1.

```
Image thePicture = getImage(getDocumentBase(), "logo.gif");
MediaTracker theTracker = new MediaTracker(this);
theTracker.addImage(thePicture, 1);
```

Images are loaded in order of their IDs; that is, image 1 is loaded before image 2, and so on.[*] If multiple images have the same ID, there's no guarantee which will be loaded first. Adding an Image to a MediaTracker does not start loading the image data. You have to call checkID(ID, true), checkAll(true), or one of the three wait() methods first. If you are going to scale the image, you must use the next version of addImage().

---

[*] It's probably not wise to rely on the implicit prioritization of image loading by ID number. This is how the JDK currently behaves, but the behavior isn't guaranteed for future versions or other development environments.

public synchronized void addImage(Image img, int id, int w, int h)

This version of `addImage()` adds the `Image` `img` with the ID number `id` to the list of `Image` objects being tracked by this `MediaTracker`. The image will eventually be displayed scaled to the width `w` and the height `h`. The following code fragment sets up a tracker for an image called *logo.gif* that's in the same directory as the web page. This image will be scaled into a 30- by 30-pixel square when it's displayed. It's given the id number 1.

```
Image thePicture = getImage(getDocumentBase(), "logo.gif");
MediaTracker theTracker = new MediaTracker(this);
theTracker.addImage(thePicture, 1, 30, 30);
```

It is inconvenient, to say the least, that you have to remember what scaling will be applied when you draw the image. It is unclear what happens if the dimensions you give the `MediaTracker` are incorrect; presumably, it may not give you accurate information about when the image is ready.

Checking the Status of Media

public boolean checkID(int id)

This method checks whether all the images with the indicated ID that are tracked by this `MediaTracker` have finished loading. If they have, it returns `true`; otherwise it returns `false`. Multiple `Image` objects may have the same ID. The images do not start loading if they are not already loading. For example, the `paint()` method below only draws `thePicture` if all the `Image` objects with ID 1 have completely finished loading:

```
public void paint(Graphics g) {

    if (theTracker.checkID(1)) {
      g.drawImage(thePicture, 0, 0, this);
    }
    else {
      g.drawString("Loading Picture. Please hang on", 25, 50);
    }

  }
```

WARNING   There's something a little funny about how this operates. The `Image` with ID 1 is not necessarily the same `Image` as `thePicture`. There may be zero or more `Image` objects with ID 1, and none of them is necessarily `thePicture`. It's up to the programmer to make sure the ID you check is the ID for the `Image` you want to load. Although there are times when you want to check one picture, and display another, this is rare. There should be a `MediaTracker` method with the signature `check(Image I)` but there isn't, in 1.1 and earlier.

---

public synchronized boolean checkID(int id, boolean load)

This method checks whether all the Image objects with the indicated ID that are tracked by this MediaTracker have finished loading. If they have, it returns true; otherwise it returns false. Multiple Image objects may have the same ID. If the boolean argument load is true, all images with that ID that are not yet being loaded will begin loading.

The following paint() method checks whether the Image objects with ID 1 have finished loading. If they have, thePicture is drawn. Otherwise the Image objects with ID 1 start loading (if they aren't already), and the String "Loading Picture. Please hang on" is displayed.

```
public void paint(Graphics g) {

    if (theTracker.checkID(1, true)) {
      g.drawImage(thePicture, 0, 0, this);
    }
    else {
      g.drawString("Loading Picture. Please hang on", 25, 50);
    }

}
```

public boolean checkAll()

This method checks whether all the Image objects that are tracked by this object have finished loading. ID numbers are not considered. If they have, it returns true; otherwise it returns false. It does not start loading Images that are not already loading.

public synchronized boolean checkAll(boolean load)

This version of checkAll() checks whether all the Image objects that are tracked by this MediaTracker have finished loading. If they have, it returns true; otherwise it returns false. If the boolean argument load is true, it starts loading any Image objects that are not already being loaded.

Waiting for Media to Load

The next three methods start loading images tracked by the MediaTracker, and then wait for the images to finish loading (they *block*). Your code will not continue until the images have finished loading. If you don't want your program to hang while you wait for images to download, call these methods inside a separate thread.

public void waitForID(int id) throws InterruptedException

This method forces the images with the ID number id that are tracked by this MediaTracker to start loading, and then waits until each one has either finished loading, aborted, or received an error. An InterruptedException is thrown if another thread interrupts this thread. For example, to begin loading Image objects with ID 1, and then wait for them to finish loading, you would write:

```
try {
    theTracker.waitForID(1);
}
catch (InterruptedException e) {
}
```

public synchronized boolean waitForID(int id, long ms)
throws InterruptedException

This version of waitForID() begins loading all the images that are tracked by this MediaTracker with the ID number id, and then waits until each one has either finished loading, aborted, or received an error, or until ms milliseconds have passed. An InterruptedException is thrown if another thread interrupts. For example, to begin loading all Image objects with ID 1, and wait no longer than two minutes (120,000 milliseconds) for them to finish loading, you would write:

```
try {
    theTracker.waitForID(1, 120000);
}
catch (InterruptedException e) {
}
```

public synchronized boolean waitForAll()
throws InterruptedException

This method starts loading all the images that are tracked by this MediaTracker, and waits until each one has either finished loading, aborted, or received an error. An InterruptedException is thrown if another thread interrupts. This method might be used by an animation applet that wants to load all frames before it begins playing. The applet would add each frame to the MediaTracker, and then call waitForAll() before starting the animation. The following code fragment begins loading all Image objects tracked by the MediaTracker theTracker.

```
try {
    theTracker.waitForAll();
}
catch (InterruptedException e) {
}
```

As with any time-consuming operation, you should display some sort of progress bar so the user has an idea how long the operation is likely to take, and give the user an option to cancel the download.

public synchronized boolean waitForAll(long ms)
throws InterruptedException

This method is similar to the previous waitForAll() method. It too starts loading all the images that are tracked by this MediaTracker, and waits until each one has either finished loading, aborted, or received an error. However, this method times out if ms milliseconds have passed before all images are complete. An InterruptedException is thrown if another thread interrupts. The following code fragment begins loading all Image objects tracked by the MediaTracker theTracker, and waits not more than two minutes (120,000 milliseconds) for them to finish loading.

```
try {
  theTracker.waitForAll(120000);
}
catch (InterruptedException e) {
}
```

As with any time consuming operation, you should display some sort of progress bar so the user has an idea how long the operation is likely to take, and give the user an option to cancel the download.

Error Checking

If there is an error as an Image is loaded or scaled, that Image is considered "complete"; no further loading of that image's data takes place. The following methods let you check whether an error has occurred, and find out which image is at fault. However, there are not any methods that tell you what sort of error has occurred.

public synchronized boolean isErrorAny()

This method checks whether an error occurred while loading any image tracked by this object.

```
if (theTracker.isErrorAny()) {
  System.err.println("There was an error while loading media");
}
```

This method does not tell you which image failed or why. If there was an error, you can use getErrorsAny() to find out which objects returned errors. Do not assume that a single Image caused the error; it is common for an entire group of Images to fail to load due to errors.

public synchronized Object[] getErrorsAny()

This method returns an array containing all the objects tracked by this Media-Tracker that encountered an error while loading. If there were no errors, it returns null.

```
if (theTracker.isErrorAny()) {
  System.err.println("The following media encountered errors while loading:");
  Object[] failedMedia = theTracker.getErrorsAny();
  for (int i = 0; i < ; i++) {
    System.err.println(failedMedia[i]);
  }
}
```

public synchronized boolean isErrorID(int id)

This method returns true if any of the media with the specified ID encountered an error while loading; otherwise it returns false. If there was an error, use getErrorsID() to find out which objects returned errors. Remember, a single ID may refer to several Image objects, any of which may have encountered errors.

```
if (theTracker.isErrorID(2)) {
  System.err.println("There was an error while loading media with ID" + 2);
}
```

public synchronized Object[] getErrorsID(int id)

This method returns an array containing all the objects with this ID that encountered an error while loading. If there were no errors, it returns null.

```
if (theTracker.isErrorID(2)) {
  System.err.println("The following media encountered errors while loading:");
  Object[] failedMedia = theTracker.getErrorsID(2);
  for (int i = 0; i < ; i++) {
    System.err.println(failedMedia[i]);
  }
}
```

Checking the Status of Media

In this section, we'll discuss a number of methods that report the status of image groups. Unfortunately, the class only lets you check the status of image groups, not individual images—a good argument for keeping image groups small. To report the status, the MediaTracker class defines a group of flag constants that are combined to tell you whether the images in question are loading, aborted, errored out, or completed. These constants are shown in Table 6–2.

Table 6–2: Media Status Constants

Constant	Value	Meaning
MediaTracker.LOADING	1	At least one image in the group is still being downloaded.
MediaTracker.ABORTED	2	The loading process aborted for at least one image in the group.
MediaTracker.ERRORED	4	An error occurred during loading for at least one image in the group.
MediaTracker.COMPLETE	8	At least one image in the group was downloaded successfully.

You use these constants are used to test the values returned by the following status methods and determine whether particular conditions or combinations of conditions are true. Since each constant is an integral power of two, each one has exactly one set bit, and thus the different constants can be easily combined with the bitwise operators to test combinations of conditions.

public int statusAll(boolean load)

This method returns the status of all of the media tracked by this MediaTracker object. Thus to test whether any of the media tracked by MediaTracker m have finished loading you would write:

```
if ((m.statusAll(false) & ImageObserver.COMPLETED) == ImageObserver.COMPLETED) {
```

If the argument load is true, any media that have not yet begun loading will start loading. If it is false, they will not.

public int statusID(int id, boolean load)

This method returns the status of the media sharing the ID id that are tracked by this MediaTracker. If the load argument is true, the media with the given id will begin loading if they haven't already started. If load is false, they won't. Thus, to test whether any of the media tracked by MediaTracker m with ID 2 have finished loading, you would write:

```
if ((m.statusAll(2, false) & ImageObserver.COMPLETED)
            == ImageObserver.COMPLETED) {...}
```

Because of the nature of the flags, if any of the images with ID 2 have finished loading, this will be true. Similarly, if any of the images with ID 2 have errored out, then the following expression will also be true:

```
(m.statusAll(2, false) & ImageObserver.ABORTED)
        == ImageObserver.ABORTED)
```

The same is true for the `ImageObserver.LOADING` and `ImageObserver.ERRORED` flags. Because there isn't any way to check a single image (other than putting the image into a group by itself), `statusID()` and `statusAll()` can return apparently contradictory results. For example, if there are four images in the group, it's entirely possible that `statusID()` will return the value:

```
MediaTracker.LOADING | MediaTracker.ABORTED |
    MediaTracker.ERRORED | MediaTracker.COMPLETE
```

This means that, of the four images, one is still loading, one aborted, an error occurred in another, and one loaded successfully. A single group of images can appear to simultaneously have completed loading, still be loading, have aborted, and encountered an error. There is no way to test the status of a single `Image` if it shares an ID with another `Image`. For this reason, it's probably not a good idea to let too many images share the same ID.

The Network Methods of the AppletContext Interface

`AppletContext` is an interface that lets an applet manipulate the environment that it is running in. Every applet has an `AppletContext` field that refers to an object implementing `AppletContext`; this object is provided by the web browser or applet viewer running the applet. (In rare cases, mostly applets started from the command line and instantiated in the `main()` method, the `AppletContext` may be null.) To access the applet's context, call the applet's `getAppletContext()` method.

The `AppletContext` must provide several methods for the use of the applet, including `getAudioClip()` and `getImage()` methods; the `getAudioClip()` and `getImage()` methods of the last section merely call the corresponding method in the applet's `AppletContext`. There are two methods in `java.applet.AppletContext` relevant to network programming and not mirrored in `java.applet.Applet`: `showDocument(URL)` and `showDocument(URL, String)`.

public void showDocument(URL u)

This method shows the document at URL u in the `AppletContext`'s window. It is not supported by all web browsers and applet viewers, but it is supported by Netscape and HotJava. This method is useful in fancy imagemap applets, where it is used to send the user to a new page after clicking on a hot button. For example, to send the user to the O'Reilly home page you would write:

```
AppletContext ac = getAppletContext();
try {
  URL oraHomePage = new URL("http://www.ora.com/");
  ac.showDocument(oraHomePage);
}
catch (Exception e) {
}
```

public void showDocument(URL u, String name)

This method displays the document u in a new window with the title name. show-Document() is not supported by all web browsers and applet viewers. However, it is supported by Netscape and HotJava. Here's a typical use:

```
try {
  AppletContext ac = getAppletContext();
  ac.showDocument(new URL("http://www.ora.com/"), "The O'Reilly Home Page");
}
catch (Exception e) {
  System.err.println(e);
}
```

There are four special strings you can use for the name argument. These define where the document is shown rather than the title of the window. Here the word Frame refers to a Java Frame object: i.e., a window, not an HTML frame. Table 6–3 lists the different possible target strings.

Table 6–3: Targets for showDocument()

String	Target
__self	Show the document in the current Frame.
_parent	Show the document in the parent Frame.
_top	Show the document in the top-most Frame.
_blank	Show the document in a new, unnamed, top-level Frame.

For example, to send the browser to the O'Reilly home page in a new untitled window, you might write:

```
AppletContext ac = getAppletContext();
try {
  URL oraHomePage = new URL("http://www.ora.com/");
  ac.showDocument(oraHomePage, "_blank");
}
catch (Exception e) {
}
```

Most web servers allow you to redirect requests from one URL to another; this feature can save you a lot of work when a site moves. For example, "The Well Connected Mac" began its life at *http://rever.nmsu.edu/~elharo/faq/*, but eventually went commercial at *http://www.macfaq.com/*. When this happened, a redirector was set up to redirect any request for files in *http://rever.nmsu.edu/~elharo/faq/* to *http://www.macfaq.com/*. That way I didn't have to update thousands of links and references to the old site overnight.

Fortunately, the old site had an exceedingly friendly system administrator, who was willing to modify his server configuration files to perform the necessary redirection. However, some administrators aren't so friendly or willing to help you leave their site. In these cases, if you don't have the privileges to modify the server configuration, you can write a simple redirector in Java that will send people along their merry way.

Example 6–7 is an applet that reads the new URL from the newhost parameter in the HTML, and sends the browser from the old site to the new site. For maximum effect, place any text that should appear on the page between the opening and closing <APPLET> tags. This way, people with Java-capable browsers will be redirected without realizing they took a roundabout route.

Example 6–7: Redirector

```
import java.applet.*;
import java.net.*;

public class Redirector extends Applet {

  public void init() {

    AppletContext ac = getAppletContext();
    URL oldURL = getDocumentBase();
    try {
      URL newURL = new URL(getParameter("newhost") + oldURL.getFile());
      ac.showDocument(newURL);
    }
    catch (MalformedURLException e) {
    }

  }
}
```

The Redirector class is extremely simple. It reads the newhost parameter from a <PARAM> tag in the HTML file, adds the name of the file being requested, and constructs a new URL. It then calls showDocument() to jump to the new URL.

Some Useful Programs

Image Sizer

Some of the most useful extensions to HTML are the height and width parameters to the <IMG> tag. To the user, it seems much faster to load a page that includes height and width parameters for all its images than one that doesn't. Actually, the time it takes to load the page is the same either way; but browsers like Netscape can start displaying text and partial images as soon as they know how much space to reserve for each image. Consequently, if the width and height of each image is specified in the HTML, the browser can lay out the page and display the text immediately, without forcing the user to wait for everything to load. However, it takes a lot of time to measure every image on a page manually, and rewrite the HTML, especially for pages that include many different sized images.

Example 6–8 is a program that gets a URL from the user, reads the requested page, and outputs the HTML with height and width parameters added to all the <IMG> tags that didn't have them. It uses the default Toolkit object's getImage() method to retrieve the Image objects, the Image's getWidth() and getHeight() methods to measure them, and an ImageObserver to make sure the height and width are available.

Example 6–8: A program that adds height and width tags to the IMGs on a web page

```
import java.net.*;
import java.io.*;
import java.awt.*;
import java.awt.image.*;

public class ImageSizer extends Frame {

  TextField theURL;
  TextArea theOutput;
  Button getURL;

  public static void main(String[] args) {

    ImageSizer is = new ImageSizer();
    is.resize(300, 200);
    is.show();

  }

  public ImageSizer() {

    setLayout(new BorderLayout());
    theURL = new TextField(40);
    add("North", theURL);
    theOutput = new TextArea(80, 40);
```

Example 6–8: A program that adds height and width tags to the IMGs on a web page (continued)

```
    add("Center", theOutput);
    add("South", new Button("Get URL"));

}

public boolean action(Event e, Object o) {
  if (e.target instanceof Button) {
    fixThePage(theURL.getText());
    return true;
  }
  return false;

}

public void fixThePage(String thePage) {

  String thisLine;
  URL root;

  if  (thePage != null) {

    //Open the URL for reading
    try {
      if (thePage.indexOf(":") != -1) {
        root = new URL(thePage);
      }
      else {
        root = new URL("http://" + thePage);
      }
      sizeAPage(root);
    }
    catch (MalformedURLException e) {
      System.err.println(thePage + " is not a parseable URL");
      System.err.println(e);
    }
  }//  end if

}// end main


public void sizeAPage(URL u) {

 char thisChar;
 String theTag;

 try {
   DataInputStream theHTML = new DataInputStream(u.openStream());
   try {
     while (true) {
       thisChar = (char) theHTML.readByte();
       if (thisChar == '<') {
         theTag = readTag(theHTML);
```

Example 6–8: A program that adds height and width tags to the IMGs on a web page (continued)

```
            if (theTag.startsWith("<IMG")) {
              theTag = sizeImage(u, theTag);
            }
            theOutput.appendText(theTag);
          }
          else {
            theOutput.appendText(String.valueOf(thisChar));
          }
        }// end while
      } // end try
      catch (EOFException e) {
        // Done with the Stream
      }
    } // end try
    catch (IOException e) {
      System.err.println(e);
    }

  } // end SaveAPage


  public String readTag(DataInputStream is) {

    StringBuffer theTag = new StringBuffer("<");
    char theChar = '<';

    try {
      while (theChar != '>') {
        theChar = (char) is.readByte();
        theTag.append(theChar);
      }// end while
    } // end try
    catch (EOFException e) {
      // Done with the Stream
    }
    catch (Exception e) {
        System.err.println(e);
    }

    return theTag.toString();

  }


  public String sizeImage(URL u, String tag) {

    String s1 = tag.toUpperCase();

    boolean hasHeightTag = s1.indexOf("HEIGHT") != -1;
    boolean hasWidthTag = s1.indexOf("WIDTH") != -1;

    if (hasHeightTag && hasWidthTag) {
```

Example 6–8: A program that adds height and width tags to the IMGs on a web page (continued)

```
      return tag;
    }
    else {
      String newTag;
      Image thePicture;
      int p1, p2, p3, p4;
      p1 = s1.indexOf("SRC");
      p2 = s1.indexOf ("=", p1);
      p3 = s1.indexOf("\"", p2);
      p4 = s1.indexOf("\"", p3+1);
      String theURL = tag.substring(p3+1, p4);
      URL thePictureURL;
      try {
        if (theURL.indexOf(":")  == -1) {
          // it's not an absolute URL
          thePictureURL = new URL(u, theURL);
        } // end if
        else {
          thePictureURL = new URL(theURL);
        }
        Toolkit t = Toolkit.getDefaultToolkit();
        thePicture = t.getImage(thePictureURL);
        thePicture.getHeight(this);
        int last = tag.indexOf(">");
        newTag = tag.substring(0,last);
        if (!hasWidthTag) {
          while (thePicture.getWidth(this) == -1) {
            try {
              Thread.currentThread().sleep(100);
            }
            catch (InterruptedException e) {
            }
          }
          newTag = newTag + " width=" + thePicture.getWidth(this);
        }
        if (!hasHeightTag) {
          while (thePicture.getHeight(this) == -1) {
            try {
              Thread.currentThread().sleep(100);
            }
            catch (InterruptedException e) {
            }
          }
          newTag = newTag + " height=" + thePicture.getHeight(this);
        }
        newTag = newTag +  >";
      }
      catch (MalformedURLException e) {
        newTag = tag;
      }
      return newTag;
    }
```

Example 6–8: A program that adds height and width tags to the IMGs on a web page (continued)

```
    }

    // For this applet you don't need to
    // download an entire Image, just enough to get the height and width
    public boolean imageUpdate(Image img, int infoflags,
                               int x, int y, int width, int height) {
        if ((infoflags & ImageObserver.HEIGHT) == ImageObserver.HEIGHT &&
            (infoflags & ImageObserver.WIDTH) == ImageObserver.WIDTH)  {
            return false;
        }
        else {
            return true;
        }

    }

}
```

This is a standalone application that extends `java.awt.Frame`. It will normally be started from the command line so it has a `main()` method that merely constructs a new `ImageSizer` object. The constructor inserts three `Components` into the frame: a `TextField` for the user to type the URL, a `TextArea` to display the modified URL, and a `Button` to get the URL.

When the user clicks on the `Button`, the `Button` generates an action event. The `action()` method is called to handle the event; it reads the contents of the `TextField`, `theURL`, and calls the `fixThePage()` method. `fixThePage()` converts the text in `theURL` to a URL object, and passes the URL to the `sizeAPage()` method.

The `sizeAPage()` method is reminiscent of `PageSaver` in Chapter 5, *Retrieving Data with URLs*. It gets an `InputStream` for the URL, and reads the text. As the text is read, `sizeAPage()` searches for HTML tags. Any text that is not a tag is copied to the output. When a tag is found, it is passed to the `readTag()` method; if the tag is not an `IMG` tag, it is also copied to the output. However, if the tag is an `IMG` tag, the URL in the tag's `SRC` parameter is passed to the `sizeImage()` method, and this finds out the image's width and height. To find the width and height, `sizeImage()` requests the image by calling `getImage()`, and forces it to start downloading by calling `getWidth()`. It then calls `getWidth()` and `getHeight()` in loops, waiting until these methods return some value other than –1. When `getWidth()` and `get-Height()` return a positive value, `sizeImage()` knows that it has read the actual size of the image. It uses these to write a new tag, including height and width parameters, which it passes to the output.

As usual, there's a lot that remains to be added to this program. It tends to monopolize control of the computer until it's done. You could move a lot of the work into lower priority threads. Furthermore, this program relies on you copying the modified data, and pasting it into another program. It would be better if you saved a file on the hard drive or, better yet, on the network server itself. However, this example is already overly long, so I leave those additions as exercises.

Animation Player

One of the first uses of Java was to create animations by displaying a sequence of images. To create an animation, you need to download a series of images, each of which will be one cell of the animation. Downloading the images is easy, using the URL class: just create URL objects that point to each image, and call getImage() with each URL. Use a MediaTracker to force the images to load, wait until loading is complete, and then call drawImage() to display the images in sequence.

Example 6–9 is a simple animation applet called Animator. It reads a list of filenames from <PARAM> tags in the applet; the parameter names are Cell1, Cell2, Cell3, and so on. The value of the parameter Cell*n* should be the name of the *n*th file in the animation sequence. This makes it easy to retrieve an indefinite number of images; the init() method continues reading parameters until it finds a parameter name that doesn't exist. init() then builds URLs from the filenames and the document base, and uses getImage() to retrieve each image. The Image objects are stored in a Vector since it's not known in advance how many there will be. The applet assumes that the files reside in the same directory as the HTML page; therefore, one applet on a site can play many different animations, just by changing the <PARAM> tags and the image files. When an image is retrieved, it's added to the MediaTracker theTracker. theTracker's checkAll() method starts loading the images. Then a new thread is spawned to display the images in sequence. However, before displaying an image, the run() method calls theTracker.waitForID() to make sure that the image is ready.

Example 6–9: A very simple animator applet

```
import java.net.*;
import java.awt.*;
import java.awt.image.*;
import java.applet.*;
import java.util.*;

public class Animator extends Applet implements Runnable {

    boolean running = false;
    int thisCell = 0;
    Vector cells;
    Thread play;
    MediaTracker theTracker;
```

Example 6–9: A very simple animator applet (continued)

```java
public void init() {

    String nextCell;
    cells = new Vector();
    theTracker = new MediaTracker(this);
    for (int i = 0; (nextCell = getParameter("Cell" + i)) != null ; i++) {
        Image img = getImage(getDocumentBase(), nextCell);
        cells.addElement(img);
        theTracker.addImage(img, i);
    }

    // start loading the images
    theTracker.checkAll(true);
    play = new Thread(this);
    play.start();
    running = true;

}

public void run() {

    for (thisCell=0; thisCell < cells.size(); thisCell++) {

        try {
            // make sure this cell is loaded
            theTracker.waitForID(thisCell);
            // paint the cell
            repaint();
            // sleep for a tenth of a second
            // i.e. play ten frames a second
            play.sleep(100);
        }
        catch (InterruptedException ie) {
        }
    }

}

public void stop() {

    play.suspend();

}

public void start() {

    play.resume();

}
```

Example 6–9: A very simple animator applet (continued)

```
public void paint(Graphics g) {

  g.drawImage((Image) cells.elementAt(thisCell), 0, 0, this);

}

// The convention is that a mouseClick starts
// a stopped applet and stops a running applet.
public boolean mouseUp(Event e, int x, int y) {

  if (running) {
    play.suspend();
    running = false;
  }
  else {
    play.resume();
    running = true;
  }

  return true;

}

}
```

This example demonstrates the power of Java's networking classes. There is only one line of network code:

```
Image img = getImage(getDocumentBase(), nextCell);
```

The rest of the applet is dedicated to building up and tearing down threads, painting the images, and other things. A language like C would require dozens of lines to open a connection, interact with the server, and transfer the data.

It's easy to imagine ways to enhance this applet. The most important addition would be a timing engine; otherwise, this applet is little more than a slide show, not true animation. Another possibility would be sprites that follow a path across a constant background. Adding these extensions is up to you; they won't require any changes to the applet's networking code.

Implementing an Image Map in Java

This program loads an image and a series of map locations, and sends browsers to other web pages when the user clicks in a sensitive spot on the image. Unlike a traditional image map, an image map implemented in Java only needs to access the server once. This image map applet doesn't need any special support from the server because it can do everything locally: figure out where the user clicked, use those coordinates to look up the new Web page, and send the user to the new page. In a traditional image map, the server does all the work: the client sends the coordinates of the click to the server, which then redirects the client to the appropriate page.

The first thing you need for an image map is an image. Figure 6–2 shows a simple button bar with three buttons: one pointing to O'Reilly & Associates, one to Sunsite, and one to the Well Connected Mac.

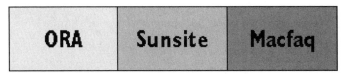

Figure 6–2: A sample image to be mapped

When users click on the first rectangle, they go to *http://www.ora.com/*; the second rectangle sends them to *http://sunsite.unc.edu/*; and the third sends them to *http://www.macfaq.com/*. The following three lines show how to split the image into rectangles for an image map, using the NCSA image map format:

```
rect http://www.macfaq.com 227,0 340,65
rect http://sunsite.unc.edu 114,0 227,65
rect http://www.ora.com/ 1,0 114,65
```

This applet uses the NCSA image map format because it's simple, easy to parse, and many freely available tools can be used to write the mappings. To communicate the map to the applet, we'll use a series of HTML <param> tags, one for each region in the map. That way, we can embed the map information into the HTML, rather than wiring it into the applet itself. (You could also read the map from a file on the server, but that is more likely to run into restrictions.) Here are the <param> tags for our simple map; the names of the tags are in a sequence (area1, area2, area3, etc.), and the values are the tag lines themselves.

```
<PARAM NAME="area1" VALUE="rect http://www.macfaq.com 227,0 340,65">
<PARAM NAME="area2" VALUE="rect http://sunsite.unc.edu 114,0 227,65">
<PARAM NAME="area3" VALUE="rect http://www.ora.com/ 1,0 114,65">
```

Now for the applet itself. This is an applet where thinking about design pays off. It splits naturally into several classes: an ImageMap class extends java.awt.Canvas, and also responds to mouse clicks; the ImageMapApplet class extends java.applet.Applet, and is responsible for loading the Image, and parsing the <param> tags; an abstract MapArea class represents a mapped area, and is subclassed to define the behavior of different types of areas, like rectangles and circles. Example 6–10 shows this abstract MapArea class; Example 6–11 shows the RectArea class, a concrete class that extends MapArea.

Example 6–10: An abstract MapArea class

```
import java.net.URL;

public abstract class MapArea {

  URL u;

  public abstract boolean contains(int x, int y);

  public URL getURL() {
    return u;
  }

  public abstract String toString();

}
```

The `MapArea` class has an abstract method called `contains()` that determines whether or not the user has clicked within the area; subclasses need to implement this method in a way that's appropriate for their geometry. The `MapArea` also has a URL field u that holds the URL to which users will be sent when they click in the area. There's also a `getURL()` method that returns this URL, and an abstract `toString()` method, which forces anyone extending the class to follow good coding practice and supply an implementation of `toString()`.

Since this class is abstract, you must subclass it to implement different types of map areas. The only subclass you need for this example is a `RectArea`. Circle, polygon, and oval `MapAreas` could be implemented similarly, with appropriate modifications to the constructor and the `contains()` method. Example 6–11 shows the `RectArea` class.

Example 6–11: A RectArea class

```
import java.awt.Rectangle;
import java.util.StringTokenizer;
import java.net.*;

public class RectArea extends MapArea {

  Rectangle r;

  // An NCSA format String looks like
  // rect http://www.macfaq.com 227,0 340,65
  public RectArea (String s) throws MalformedURLException {

    int x1, y1, x2, y2;

    StringTokenizer st = new StringTokenizer(s, " \n\t\r,");
    // throw away the first token
    // This should be "rect";
    st.nextToken();
```

Example 6–11: A RectArea class (continued)

```
    u = new URL(st.nextToken());
    x1 = Integer.parseInt(st.nextToken());
    y1 = Integer.parseInt(st.nextToken());
    x2 = Integer.parseInt(st.nextToken());
    y2 = Integer.parseInt(st.nextToken());
    r = new Rectangle(x1, y1, x2 - x1, y2 - y1);
  }

  public boolean contains(int x, int y) {
    return r.inside(x, y);
  }

  public String toString() {

    return "rect " + u + " " + r.x + "," + r.y + " "
      + (r.x + r.width) + "," + (r.y + r.height);
  }
}
```

The RectArea constructor takes a line in NCSA image map format as its argument.
It uses a StringTokenizer to split the line into tokens; it discards the first (which
must be the string "rect"), uses the second token to create a URL object, and uses
the remaining tokens to create a Rectangle (a class in the java.awt package). The
URL and the Rectangle are the class's instance variables. Implementing contains()
is easy; to tell whether a point is contained in the RectArea, you simply call the
Rectangle class's inside() method. Finally, toString() returns a string that provides useful debugging information.

Different mapped areas plus an Image are combined to form an ImageMap. Example 6–12 shows the ImageMap class:

Example 6–12: An ImageMap component

```
import java.awt.*;
import java.net.*;
import java.util.*;
import java.applet.*;

public class ImageMap extends Canvas {

  Image theMap;
  Vector areas;
  AppletContext ac;

  public ImageMap(Image img, AppletContext browser) {

    theMap = img;
    // make sure the Image is loading
    theMap.getWidth(this);
    ac = browser;
```

Example 6–12: An ImageMap component (continued)

```
   areas = new Vector();
}

public void addMapArea(String s) {

  if (s.startsWith("rect")) {
    try {
      RectArea r = new RectArea(s);
      areas.addElement(r);
    }
    catch (MalformedURLException e) {
      System.err.println(e);
    }
  }
  else if (s.startsWith("circle")) {
    ;
  }
  else if (s.startsWith("poly")) {
    ;
  }
  else if (s.startsWith("oval")) {
    ;
  }
  else { // unrecognized tag
    ;
  }

}

public boolean mouseDown(Event evt, int x, int y) {
  for (Enumeration e = areas.elements() ; e.hasMoreElements() ;) {
    MapArea a = (MapArea) e.nextElement();
    if (a.contains(x, y)) {
      ac.showDocument(a.getURL());
      break;
    }
  }
  return true;

}

public void paint(Graphics g) {

  if(!g.drawImage(theMap, 0, 0, this)) {
    g.drawString("Loading Picture. Please hang on", 25, 50);
  }

}

public Dimension minimumSize() {

  return new Dimension(theMap.getWidth(this), theMap.getHeight(this));
```

Example 6–12: An ImageMap component (continued)

```
    }

    public Dimension preferredSize() {

        return minimumSize();

    }

}
```

The ImageMap constructor takes an AppletContext and an Image as arguments. The image, of course, is the image you display for the map, and is saved in the field theMap; the constructor calls theMap.getWidth(this) to force the image to start loading. The AppletContext is used to redirect the browser. Finally, the constructor creates the Vector areas, used to hold the different mapped areas in the image.

The addMapArea() method installs a new hot spot in the image map; it looks at the beginning of an NCSA-format image map line to determine the area's shape. The version given here only supports rectangular areas, but positions are provided where you can plug in new shapes after implementing other MapArea subclasses.

The mouseDown() method loops through all the map areas in the ImageMap to see if the mouse click hit any of them. You test each MapArea by calling its contains(int x, int y) method. The ImageMap does not need to know the geometry of the map area; that information is encapsulated in the map area itself. If the mouse click did occur inside a map area, the browser is redirected to the URL of the area that was hit. If the mouse click hits more than one map area (that is, if map areas overlap), the browser is redirected to the first one found. There are no guarantees about which one this will be.

The minimumSize() method returns the dimensions of the image. The preferred-Size() method returns minimumSize(). It's important to include these methods in custom components like this, so LayoutManagers know how much space to allot for the Component.

Finally, there is the applet itself. This applet is very simple. It creates an ImageMap object, puts it in the center of the applet's display, reads the parameters, and passes them to the addMapArea() method of the newly created ImageMap object.

Example 6–13: An ImageMap applet

```
import java.applet.*;
import java.awt.*;

public class ImageMapApplet extends Applet {

  public void init() {

    String nextarea;
    int i = 1;

    setLayout(new BorderLayout());
    String filename = getParameter("filename");
    Image theMap = getImage(getDocumentBase(), filename);
    ImageMap im = new ImageMap(theMap, getAppletContext());
    add("Center", im);
    while ((nextarea = getParameter("area" + i++)) != null) {
      im.addMapArea(nextarea);
    }

  }

}
```

Multihoming

Some operating systems (like Solaris) allow *multihoming*: one machine can respond to different IP addresses. It is then possible to attach a different web server to each IP address, and run several different sites that look independent but share the same hardware. This is quite common at web server farms.

Some operating systems, like the MacOS, do not support multiple IP addresses. Therefore, if you want to serve multiple web sites with a single Mac, the sites' URLs must all look like *http://www.mysite.com/siteA/* and *http://www.mysite.com/siteB/*. You can use DNS to attach multiple hostnames to a single server (for example, *http://www.siteA.com/siteA/* and *http://www.siteB.com/siteB/*), but that doesn't help. The HTTP protocol does not tell the server the hostname requested; remember, the request to the web server looks like:

```
GET / HTTP/1.0
```

It does not look like:

```
GET http://www.macfaq.com/ HTTP/1.0
```

Nowhere does the client tell the server the hostname it is trying to connect to. Therefore, there is no way to distinguish between *http://www.siteA.com/* and *http://www.siteB.com/* if both hostnames refer to the same machine, and that machine does not support multiple addresses.

However, Java applets provide a clever solution to this problem. Because an applet runs on the client, not on the server, it can ask the client for the URL it requested with getDocumentBase(). Then the applet can use the hostname portion of the URL to distinguish between *http://www.siteA.com/* and *http://www.siteB.com/*, rewrite the URL to reflect the hostname, and redirect the browser to a new page. Example 6–14 is a simple applet that redirects requests for *http://www.siteA.com/* and *http://www.siteB.com/*:

Example 6–14: Multihome server

```
import java.applet.*;
import java.net.*;


public class Multihome extends Applet {

  public void init() {

    AppletContext ac = getAppletContext();
    URL oldURL = getDocumentBase();
    try {
      URL newURL = new URL(oldURL.getProtocol() + "://" + oldURL.getHost() + "/"
        + oldURL.getHost() + oldURL.getFile());
      ac.showDocument(newURL);
    }
    catch (Exception e) {
    }

  }

}
```

The Multihome applet will redirect requests for *http://www.siteA.com/somedirectory/ somefile.html* to *http://www.siteA.com/www.siteA.com/somedirectory/somefile.html*, requests for *http://www.siteA.com/somedirectory/somefile.html* to *http://www.siteA.com/ www.siteA.com/somedirectory/somefile.html*, and so on.

The lines

```
    URL newURL = new URL(oldURL.getProtocol() + "://" + oldURL.getHost() + "/"
      + oldURL.getHost() + oldURL.getFile());
```

build the new URL from the pieces of the old, while ac.showDocument(newURL) actually moves the browser from the old URL to the new URL. There are a number of things you could do to make this applet more flexible, including runtime configuration of the different hostname directory mappings through <PARAM> tags, but Example 6–14 demonstrates how to approach the problem.

7

Sockets for Clients

What Is a Socket?

Data is transmitted across the Internet in packets of finite size called *datagrams.* Each datagram contains a *header* and a *payload.* The header contains the address and port the packet is going to, the address and port the packet came from, and various other housekeeping information used to ensure reliable transmission. The payload contains the data itself. However, since datagrams have finite length, it's often necessary to split the data across multiple packets and reassemble it at the destination. It's also possible that one or more packets may be lost or corrupted in transit, and need to be retransmitted, or that packets will arrive out of order. Keeping track of this—splitting the data into packets, generating headers, parsing the headers of incoming packets, keeping track of what packets you have and haven't received, etc.—is a lot of work, and requires a lot of intricate software.

Fortunately, you don't have to do the work yourself. Sockets are an innovation of Berkeley UNIX. They allow the programmer to treat a network connection as another stream that bytes can be written onto or read from. Historically, sockets are an extension of one of UNIX's most important ideas: that all I/O should look like file I/O to the programmer, whether you're working with a keyboard, a graphics display, a regular file, or a network connection. Sockets shield the programmer from low-level details of the network, like media types, packet sizes, packet retransmission, network addresses, and more. This abstraction has proved to be immensely useful, and has long since traveled from its origins in Berkeley UNIX to all breeds of UNIX, plus Windows, the Macintosh, and of course Java.

A socket can perform seven basic operations:

- Connect to a remote machine (i.e., prepare to send or receive data)

- Send data

- Receive data

- Close a connection

- Bind to a port

- Listen for incoming data

- Accept connections from remote machines on the bound port

Java's `Socket` class, which is used by both clients and servers, has methods that correspond to the first four of these operations. The last three operations are only needed by servers that need to wait for clients to connect to them. They are implemented by the `ServerSocket` class, discussed in the next chapter. Client sockets are normally used in the following fashion:

1. The new socket is created using a `Socket()` constructor.

2. The socket attempts to connect to a remote host.

3. Once the connection is established, the local and remote hosts get input and output streams from the socket, and use those streams to send data to each other. This connection is *full-duplex*; both hosts can send and receive data simultaneously. What the data means depends on the protocol; you send different commands to an FTP server than to an HTTP server. There will normally be some agreed upon handshaking followed by the transmission of data from one to the other.

4. When the transmission of data is complete, one or both sides closes the connection. Some protocols, such as HTTP, require the connection to be closed after each request is serviced. Others, like FTP, allow multiple requests to be processed in a single connection.

Investigating Protocols with Telnet

In this chapter, you'll see clients that communicate with a number of well-known Internet services including HTTP, echo, and more. The sockets themselves are simple enough; however, the protocols that you use to communicate with different servers make life complex.

To get a feel for how a protocol operates, you can use *telnet* to connect to a server, type different commands at it, and watch its responses. By default, *telnet* attempts to connect to port 23. To connect to servers on different ports, specify the port as in this example:[*]

```
% telnet localhost 25
```

This example requests a connection to port 25, the SMTP port, on the local machine; SMTP is the protocol used to transfer email between servers, or between a mail client and a server. Now, if you know the commands to interact with an SMTP server, you can send email without going through a mail program. This trick can be used to forge email. For example, a few years ago the summer students at the National Solar Observatory in Sunspot, New Mexico made it appear that the party one of the scientists was throwing after the annual volleyball match was in fact a victory party for the students. (Of course the author of this book had absolutely nothing to do with such despicable behavior. '-)) The interaction with the SMTP server went something like Example 7–1; what you type is shown in bold. Lines beginning with a three-digit number are responses from the server. (The names have been changed to protect the gullible.)

Example 7–1: Direct connection to an SMTP server

```
flare% telnet localhost 25
Trying 127.0.0.1 ...
Connected to localhost.sunspot.noao.edu.
Escape character is '^]'.
220 flare.sunspot.noao.edu Sendmail 4.1/SMI-4.1 ready at Fri, 5 Jul 93 13:13:01 MDT
HELO sunspot.noao.edu
250 flare.sunspot.noao.edu Hello localhost [127.0.0.1], pleased to meet you
MAIL FROM: bart
250 bart... Sender ok
RCPT TO: local@sunspot.noao.edu
250 local@sunspot.noao.edu... Recipient ok
DATA
354 Enter mail, end with "." on a line by itself

In a pitiful attempt to reingratiate myself with the students
after their inevitable defeat of the staff on the volleyball
court at 4:00 P.M., July 24, I will be throwing a
victory party for the students at my house that evening at 7:00.
Everyone is invited.

Beer and Ben-Gay will be provided so the staff may drown
their sorrows and assuage their aching muscles after their
public humiliation.

sincerely,
```

---

[*] This example, and the other examples using *telnet*, assume that you're using a UNIX system. However, *telnet* clients exist on all common operating systems, and they are all pretty similar; for example, on Windows, you might have to type the hostname and the port into a dialog rather than on the command line, but otherwise, the clients work the same.

Example 7–1: Direct connection to an SMTP server (continued)

Bart
.
```
250 Mail accepted
```
QUIT
```
221 flare.sunspot.noao.edu delivering mail
Connection closed by foreign host.
```

Several members of the staff asked Bart why he, a staff member, was throwing a victory party for the students. The moral of this story is that you should never trust email, especially patently ridiculous email like this, without independent verification. The other moral of this story is that you can use *telnet* to simulate a client, see how the client and the server interact, and thus learn what your Java program needs to do. Although this session doesn't demonstrate all the features of the SMTP protocol, you should be able to deduce what a simple email client has to do to talk to a server.

The Socket Class

The Constructors

The four public Socket constructors in Java 1.1 are simple. Each lets you specify the host and the port you want to connect to. Hosts may be specified as an InetAddress or a String. Ports are always specified as int values between 0 and 65,535. Two of the constructors also specify the local address and local port from which data will be sent. You might need to specify a local address when you want to select one particular network interface on a multihomed host.

In Java 1.1, the Socket class also has two protected constructors. Network clients and servers will probably never need to use these; they become important if you're creating a subclass of Socket (perhaps to implement a new type of Socket that automatically does encryption, authentication, or data compression).

public Socket(String host, int port) throws UnknownHostException, IOException

This constructor creates a TCP socket to the specified port on the specified host, and attempts to connect to the remote host. For example:

```
try {
  Socket toOra = new Socket("www.ora.com", 80);
}
catch (UnknownHostException e) {
  System.err.println(e);
}
```

```
  catch (IOException e) {
    System.err.println(e);
  }
```

In this constructor, the host argument is just a hostname, expressed as a String—not a URL like *http://www.ora.com*, or an InetAddress object. If the host is unknown or the domain name server is not functioning, the constructor throws an Unknown-HostException. If the socket cannot be opened for some other reason, the constructor throws an IOException. There are many reasons why a connection attempt might fail: the host you're trying to reach may not be accepting connections, your Internet connection may be down, or some routing problem may be preventing your packets from reaching their destination.

Since this constructor doesn't just create a Socket object, but also tries to connect the socket to the remote host, you can use it to determine whether connections to a particular port are allowed, as in Example 7–2.

Example 7–2: Find out which of the first 1024 ports seem to be hosting TCP servers

```
import java.net.*;
import java.io.*;


public class lookForPorts {

  public static void main(String[] args) {

    Socket theSocket;
    String host = "localhost";

    if (args.length > 0) {
      host = args[0];
    }
    for (int i = 0; i < 1024; i++) {
      try {
        theSocket = new Socket(host, i);
        System.out.println("There is a server on port " + i + " of " + host);
      }
      catch (UnknownHostException e) {
        System.err.println(e);
        break;
      }
      catch (IOException e) {
        // must not be a server on this port
      }
    }// end for

  } // end main

} // end look for ports
```

Here's the output this program produces on my local host. Your results will vary, depending on ports occupied. As a rule, more ports will be occupied on a UNIX workstation than on a PC or a Mac.

```
% java lookForPorts
There is a server on port 7 of localhost
There is a server on port 9 of localhost
There is a server on port 13 of localhost
There is a server on port 19 of localhost
There is a server on port 21 of localhost
There is a server on port 23 of localhost
There is a server on port 25 of localhost
There is a server on port 37 of localhost
There is a server on port 79 of localhost
There is a server on port 111 of localhost
There is a server on port 512 of localhost
There is a server on port 513 of localhost
There is a server on port 514 of localhost
There is a server on port 515 of localhost
%
```

If you're curious about what servers are running on these ports, try experimenting with *telnet*. On a UNIX system, you may be able to find out which services reside on which ports by looking in the file */etc/services*. If lookForPorts finds any ports that are running servers but are not listed in */etc/services*, then that's interesting.

This program, though it looks simple, is not without its uses. The first step to securing a system is understanding it. This program helps you understand what your system is doing so you can find (and close) possible entrance points for attackers. You may also find rogue servers. For example, lookForPorts might tell you that there's a server on port 1020; this, on further investigation, turns out to be an HTTP server that somebody is running to serve erotic GIFs, and that is overloading your Internet connection. However, like most security tools, this program should not be misused. Don't run lookForPorts to probe a machine you do not own; most system administrators would consider that a hostile act.

public Socket(InetAddress host, int port) throws IOException

Like the previous constructor, this constructor creates a TCP socket to the specified port on the specified host, and tries to connect. It differs by using an InetAddress object (discussed in Chapter 4, *Processing Internet Addresses*) to specify the host, rather than a hostname. It throws an IOException if it can't connect, but does not throw an UnknownHostException; if the host is unknown, you will find out when you create the InetAddress object. For example:

```
InetAddress ORA = null;
Socket ORASocket;
try {
  ORA = new InetAddress("www.ora.com");
```

```
  }

  catch (UnknownHostException e) {
    System.err.println(e);
  }
  try {
    ORASocket = new Socket(ORA, 80);
  }
  catch (IOException e) {
    System.err.println(e);
  }
```

In the rare case where you open many sockets to the same host, it is marginally more efficient to convert the hostname to an InetAddress, and then repeatedly use that InetAddress to create sockets. Example 7–3 uses this technique to improve on the efficiency of **UNKNOWN XREF**.

Example 7–3: Find out which of the ports at or above 1024 seem to be hosting TCP servers

```java
import java.net.*;
import java.io.*;


public class lookForPorts2 {

  public static void main(String[] args) {

    Socket theSocket;
    String host = "localhost";

    if (args.length > 0) { 155

      host = args[0];
    }

    try {
      InetAddress theAddress = InetAddress.getByName(host);
      for (int i = 1024; i < 65536; i++) {
        try {
          theSocket = new Socket(theAddress, i);
          System.out.println("There is a server on port " + i + " of " + host);
        }
        catch (IOException e) {
          // must not be a server on this port
        }
      }// end for
    }// end try
    catch (UnknownHostException e) {
      System.err.println(e);
    }

  } // end main

} // end lookForPorts2
```

The results are much the same as before, except that lookForPorts2 now checks ports above 1023, and reports any servers it finds.

public Socket(String host, int port, InetAddress interface, int localPort) throws IOException (Java 1.1 only)

This constructor creates a TCP socket to the specified port on the specified host, and tries to connect. It connects *to* the host and port specified in the first two arguments. It connects *from* the network interface and local port specified in the last two arguments. The network interface may either be physical (e.g. a different Ethernet card) or virtual (a multihomed host). If 0 is passed for the localPort argument, a random available port (also known as an "anonymous port") will be chosen between 1024 and 65,535. For example, if I am running a program on *calzone.oit.unc.edu*, and want to make sure that my connection goes over the 100 megabit-per-second FDDI interface (*sunsite.unc.edu*) instead of the 10-Mbps Ethernet interface, I open a socket like this:

```
InetAddress sunsite;
Socket ORASocket;
try {
  sunsite = new InetAddress("sunsite.unc.edu");
}
catch (UnknownHostException e) {
  System.err.println(e);
}
try {
  ORASocket = new Socket("www.ora.com", 80, sunsite, 0);
}
catch (IOException e) {
  System.err.println(e);
}
```

By passing 0 for the local port number, I say that I don't care what port is used but I do want to use the FDDI network interface.

This constructor can throw an IOException for all the usual reasons given in the previous constructors. Furthermore, an IOException (specifically it would be an UnknownHostException, though that's not declared in the throws clause of this constructor) will also be thrown if the String host cannot be located.

Finally, an IOException (probably a BindException, though again, that's not declared in the throws clause of this method) will be thrown if the socket is unable to bind to the requested network interface. This tends to limit the portability of applications that use this constructor. You could take deliberate advantage of this and restrict a compiled program to run only on a predetermined host. This would require customizing distributions for each computer, and is certainly overkill for cheap products. Furthermore, Java programs are so easy to disassemble, decompile, and reverse engineer that this scheme is far from foolproof. Nonetheless, it might be part of a scheme to enforce a software license, or to prevent disgruntled employees from emailing your proprietary software to your competitors.

public Socket(InetAddress host, int port, InetAddress interface, int localPort) throws IOException (Java 1.1 only)

This constructor is identical to the previous one except that the host to connect to is passed as an `InetAddress`, not a `String`. It creates a TCP socket to the specified port on the specified host from the specified interface and local port, and tries to connect. If it fails, it throws an `IOException`. For example:

```
InetAddress sunsite, ora;
Socket ORASocket;
try {
  sunsite = new InetAddress("sunsite.unc.edu");
  ora = new InetAddress("www.ora.com");
}
catch (UnknownHostException e) {
  System.err.println(e);
}
try {
  ORASocket = new Socket(ora, 80, sunsite, 0);
}
catch (IOException e) {
  System.err.println(e);
}
```

protected Socket() (Java 1.1 only)

The `Socket` class also has two protected constructors that initialize the superclass without connecting the socket. You use these if you're subclassing `Socket`, perhaps to implement a special kind of `Socket` that encrypts transactions or understands your local proxy server. Most of your implementation of a new socket class will be written in a `SocketImpl` object.

The noargs `Socket()` constructor, available only in Java 1.1, installs the default `SocketImpl` (either from the factory or a `java.net.PlainSocketImpl`). It creates a new `Socket` without connecting it, and is usually called by subclasses of `java.net.Socket`. In Java 1.0, `java.net.Socket` is declared `final` so it cannot be subclassed, and this constructor does not exist.

protected Socket(SocketImpl impl) (Java 1.1 only)

This constructor, available only in Java 1.1, installs the SocketImpl object impl when it creates the new Socket object. The Socket object is created but is not connected. This constructor is usually called by subclasses of java.net.Socket. In Java 1.0, java.net.Socket is final so it cannot be subclassed, and this constructor does not exist. You can pass null to this constructor if you don't need a SocketImpl. However, in this case you must override all the base class methods that depend on the underlying SocketImpl.

NOTE   Java 1.0 has two more Socket constructors that are deprecated in Java 1.1:

```
public Socket(String host, int port, boolean useStreams)
        throws IOException
public Socket(InetAddress host, int port, boolean useStreams)
        throws IOException
```

These constructors allow the programmer to specify whether the socket is used for reliable, connection-oriented TCP stream traffic, or unreliable, UDP datagram traffic. If the useStreams argument is true, the TCP datagrams are combined into a reliable stream of data, just as all the other Socket constructors do. However, if useStreams is false, the socket transmits data as UDP datagrams instead.

These constructors are deprecated in Java 1.1, and their inclusion in Java 1.0 was probably a mistake. Sockets are normally thought of as applying to TCP traffic only, and there are two other Java classes to handle UDP traffic. Therefore, this constructor was always on the flaky side. The documentation for these constructors was never very clear. Different versions of the Java 1.0 documentation said different things about how this constructor was used, and you had to dig into the source code to figure out what was really happening.

Getting Information about a Socket

To the programmer, Socket objects appear to have several private fields that are accessible through various *get* methods. Actually, sockets have only one field, a SocketImpl; the fields that appear to belong to the Socket actually belong to the SocketImpl. This way, you can change socket implementations without disturbing the program; the actual SocketImpl in use is almost completely transparent.

public InetAddress getInetAddress()

Given a Socket object, the getInetAddress() method tells you what host the Socket is connected to, or, if the connection is now closed, what host the Socket will be connected to when it is connected. For example:

```
try {
  Socket theSocket = new Socket("www.javasoft.com", 80);
  InetAddress host = theSocket.getInetAddress();
  System.out.println(host);
} // end try
catch (UnknownHostException e) {
  System.err.println(e);
}
catch (IOException e) {
  System.err.println(e);
}
```

public int getPort()

The getPort() method tells you to which port the Socket is (or will be) connected on the remote host. For example:

```
try {
  Socket theSocket = new Socket("www.javasoft.com", 80);
  int port = theSocket.getPort();
  System.out.println(port);
} // end try
catch (UnknownHostException e) {
  System.err.println(e);
}
catch (IOException e) {
  System.err.println(e);
}
```

public int getLocalPort()

There are two ends to a connection: a remote and a local end. To find the port number for the local end of a connection, call getLocalPort(). For example:

```
try {
  Socket theSocket = new Socket(hostname, 80);
  int localPort = theSocket.getLocalPort();
  System.out.println(localPort);
} // end try
catch (UnknownHostException e) {
  System.err.println(e);
}
catch (IOException e) {
  System.err.println(e);
}
```

Unlike the remote port (usually a well-known port, and preassigned by a standards committee), the local port is usually chosen by the system at runtime from the available unused ports. This way, many different clients on a system can access the same service at the same time. The local port is embedded in the IP packet along with the local host's IP address, so the server can send data back to the client.

public InetAddress getLocalAddress() (Java 1.1 only)

The getLocalAddress() method tells you which network interface a socket is bound to. You normally use this on a multihomed host, or one with multiple network interfaces. For example:

```
try {
  Socket theSocket = new Socket(hostname, 80);
  InetAddress localAddress = theSocket.getLocalAddress();
  System.out.println(localAddress);
} // end try
catch (UnknownHostException e) {
  System.err.println(e);
}
catch (IOException e) {
  System.err.println(e);
}
```

Example 7–4 reads a list of hostnames from the command line, attempts to open a socket to each one, and then uses these three methods to print the remote host, the remote port, the local address, and the local port.

Example 7–4: Get a socket's information

```
import java.net.*;
import java.io.*;

public class getSocketInfo {

  public static void main(String[] args) {

    for (int i = 0; i < args.length; i++) {
      try {
        Socket theSocket = new Socket(args[i], 80);
        System.out.println("Connected to " + theSocket.getInetAddress()
          + " on port "  + theSocket.getPort() + " from port "
          + theSocket.getLocalPort() + " of " + theSocket.getLocalAddress());
      } // end try
      catch (UnknownHostException e) {
        System.err.println("I can't find " + args[i]);
      }
      catch (SocketException e) {
        System.err.println("Could not connect to " + args[i]);
      }
      catch (IOException e) {
        System.err.println(e);
      }
    }// end for

  } // end main

} // end getSocketInfo
```

Here's the result. I included *www.ora.com* on the command line twice to demonstrate that each connection was assigned a different local port, regardless of the remote host; the local port assigned to any connection is unpredictable, and depends mostly on what other ports are in use. The connection to *shock.njit.edu* failed because that machine does not allow connections on port 80.

```
% java getSocketInfo www.ora.com www.ora.com www.macfaq.com shock.njit.edu
Connected to www.ora.com/198.112.208.23 on port 80 from port 46770 of
calzone.oit.unc.edu/152.2.22.81
Connected to www.ora.com/198.112.208.23 on port 80 from port 46772 of
calzone.oit.unc.edu/152.2.22.81
Connected to www.macfaq.com/204.162.81.201 on port 80 from port 46773 of
calzone.oit.unc.edu/152.2.22.81
Could not connect to shock.njit.edu
%
```

public InputStream getInputStream() throws IOException

The getInputStream() method returns a raw input stream you can use to read data from the socket into your program. You usually chain this InputStream to a stream that offers more functionality—DataInputStream, for example—before reading input.

Now that we can get an input stream, we can read data from a socket, and start experimenting with some actual Internet protocols. One of the simplest protocols is called "daytime," and is defined in RFC867. There's almost nothing to it. The client opens a socket to port 13 on the daytime server; in response, the server sends the time in a human-readable format, and closes the connection. You can test the daytime server with *telnet* like this:

```
% telnet localhost 13
Trying 127.0.0.1...
Connected to localhost.
Escape character is '^]'.
Fri Apr 19 09:27:07 1996
Connection closed by foreign host.
%
```

The daytime server sends the line "Fri Apr 19 09:27:07 1996"; when you read your Socket's InputStream, this is what you will get. The UNIX shell or *telnet* program produces the other lines. Example 7–5 uses the InputStream returned by getInputStream() to read the time sent by the daytime server.

TIP   The daytime protocol doesn't specify a format for the time it returns. Thus is difficult to convert the character data the server returns to a Java Date in a reliable fashion. If you want to create a Date object based on the time at the server, it's easier to use the Time protocol from RFC868, which specifies a format for the time.

Example 7–5: A daytime protocol client

```
import java.net.*;
import java.io.*;

public class daytimeClient {

  public static void main(String[] args) {

    Socket theSocket;
    String hostname;
    DataInputStream theTimeStream;

    if (args.length > 0) {
      hostname = args[0];
    }
    else {
      hostname = "localhost";
    }

    try {
      theSocket = new Socket(hostname, 13);
      theTimeStream = new DataInputStream(theSocket.getInputStream());
      String theTime = theTimeStream.readLine();
      System.out.println("It is " + theTime + " at " + hostname);
    } // end try
    catch (UnknownHostException e) {
      System.err.println(e);
    }
    catch (IOException e) {
      System.err.println(e);
    }

  } // end main

}// end daytimeClient
```

daytimeClient reads the hostname of a daytime server from the command line, and uses it to construct a new Socket that connects to port 13 on the server. The client then calls theSocket.getInputStream() to get theSocket's input stream, and this is immediately fed into the constructor for a DataInputStream to produce theTimeStream. You could read the response using the methods of the Input-Stream class, but it's much easier to read ASCII text with a DataInputStream. Finally, daytimeClient prints the result. Here's what happens:

```
% java daytimeClient
It is Fri Apr 19 09:22:17 1996 at localhost
% java daytimeClient www.ora.com
It is Fri Apr 19 09:25:01 1996 at www.ora.com
```

You can see the clocks on the *localhost* and *www.ora.com* aren't synchronized. Differences of a few seconds can also be caused by the time it takes packets to travel across the Internet. More details about network time keeping can be obtained from *http://tycho.usno.navy.mil/*.

public OutputStream getOutputStream() throws IOException

The getOutputStream() method returns a raw OutputStream that you can use to write data from your application to the other end of the socket. You usually chain this stream to a more powerful stream class like DataOutputStream before using it.

The echo protocol, defined in RFC862, is one of the simplest interactive TCP services. The client opens a socket to port 7 on the echo server, sends data, and the server sends the data back. This continues until the client closes the connection. The echo protocol is useful for testing the network to make sure that data is not mangled by a misbehaving router or firewall. You can test echo with *telnet* like this:

```
% telnet localhost 7
Trying 127.0.0.1...
Connected to localhost.
Escape character is '^]'.
This is a test
This is a test
This is another test
This is another test
9876543210
9876543210
^]
telnet> close
Connection closed.
%
```

Example 7–6 uses getOutputStream() and getInputStream() to implement a simple echo client. The program exits when the user types a period on a line by itself.

Example 7–6: An echo client

```
import java.net.*;
import java.io.*;

public class echoClient {

  public static void main(String[] args) {

    Socket theSocket;
    String hostname;
    DataInputStream theInputStream;
    DataInputStream userInput;
    PrintStream theOutputStream;
    String theLine;

    if (args.length > 0) {
      hostname = args[0];
    }
```

Example 7–6: An echo client (continued)

```
else {
  hostname = "localhost";
}

try {
  theSocket = new Socket(hostname, 7);
  theInputStream = new DataInputStream(theSocket.getInputStream());
  theOutputStream = new PrintStream(theSocket.getOutputStream());
  userInput = new DataInputStream(System.in);
  while (true) {
    theLine = userInput.readLine();
    if (theLine.equals(".")) break;
    theOutputStream.println(theLine);
    System.out.println(theInputStream.readLine());
  }
} // end try
catch (UnknownHostException e) {
  System.err.println(e);
}
catch (IOException e) {
  System.err.println(e);
}

} // end main

} // end echoClient
```

As usual, echoClient reads the host to connect to from the command line. You use the hostname is to create a new Socket object on port 7, called theSocket. The socket's InputStream is returned by getInputStream(), and chained to a DataInputStream called theInputStream, which is used to read server responses. Next, echoClient calls theSocket.getOutputStream() to get theSocket's output stream, which is used to construct a new PrintStream, called theOutputStream. This client also needs to read input from the user, so it creates a second DataInputStream, this one called userInput, which reads data from System.in.

Now that the three streams have been created, it's simply a matter of reading from userInput, and writing whatever you type to theOutputStream. Once data has been sent to the echo server, theInputStream waits for a response. When theInputStream receives a response, it's printed on System.out. In theory, this client could get hung waiting for a response that never comes. However, this is unlikely if the connection can be made in the first place, since the TCP protocol checks for bad packets, and automatically asks the server for replacements. When we implement a UDP echo client in Chapter 9, *UDP Datagrams and Sockets*, we will need a different approach because UDP does not check for errors. Here's a sample run:

```
% java echoClient
This is a test
This is a test
This is another test
This is another test
9876543210
9876543210
.
%
```

Closing the Socket

That's almost everything you need to know about client-side sockets. When you're writing a client application, almost all the work goes into handling the streams and interpreting the data. The sockets themselves are very easy to work with; all the hard parts are hidden. That is one reason sockets are such a popular paradigm for network programming. After we cover a couple of remaining methods, you'll know everything you need to know to write TCP-based clients.

public synchronized void close() throws IOException

Until now, our examples have assumed that sockets close on their own; they haven't done anything to clean up after themselves. It is true that sockets are closed automatically when the program ends or when they're garbage collected. However, it is a bad practice to assume that the system will close sockets for you, especially for programs that may run for an indefinite period of time. The look-ForPorts programs we wrote earlier are particularly bad offenders in this respect, since it may take a long time for the program to run through all the ports. Shortly, we'll write a new version that doesn't have this problem.

When you're through with a socket, you should call its close() method to disconnect. The syntax is trivial:

```
try {
  Socket theSocket = new Socket("www.ora.com", 13);
  theSocket.close();
} // end try
catch (UnknownHostException e) {
  System.err.println(e);
}
catch (IOException e) {
  System.err.println(e);
}
```

Once you have closed a Socket, its InetAddress, port number, local address, and local port number are still accessible through the getInetAddress(), getPort(), getLocalAddress(), and getLocalPort() methods. However, although you can still call getInputStream() or getOutputStream(), attempting to read data from the InputStream or write data to the OutputStream throws an IOException.

Example 7–7 is a revision of the lookForPorts program that closes each socket once it's through with it:

Example 7–7: Look for ports with socket closing

```
import java.net.*;
import java.io.*;

public class lookForPorts3 {

  public static void main(String[] args) {

    Socket theSocket;
    String host = "localhost";

    if (args.length > 0) {
      host = args[0];
    }

    try {
      InetAddress theAddress = InetAddress.getByName(host);
      for (int i = 1; i <= 65536; i++) {
        try {
          // the next line will fail and drop into the catch block if
          // the connection to the specified port is refused by the remote
          // host
          theSocket = new Socket(host, i);
          System.out.println("There is a server on port " + i + " of " + host);
          theSocket.close();
        }
        catch (IOException e) {
          // must not be a server on this port
        }
      }// end for
    }// end try
    catch (UnknownHostException e) {
      System.err.println(e);
    }

  }

}
```

The Object Methods

public String toString()

The Socket class overrides only one method from java.lang.Object, toString(). As shown earlier, the toString() method produces a string that looks like this:

```
Socket[addr=www.ora.com/198.112.208.11,port=80,localport=50055]
```

This is ugly and useful primarily for debugging. You shouldn't rely on this format; it will probably change in the future. All parts of this string are accessible directly through other methods (`getInetAddress()`, `getPort()`, and `getLocalPort()`).

Socket Implementations

`SocketImpl` is an abstract class consisting of about two dozen protected members and methods that construct new sockets, connect the sockets, close the sockets, and so on. A `Socket` itself is little more than a `SocketImpl` field that the `Socket` calls when you call its `getInetAddress()`, `getInputStream()`, and other methods. This hides changes in socket implementations from the programmer. For example, a program that installs a different `SocketImpl` to accommodate some firewall or proxy server doesn't need different socket code; the behavior of the `Socket` class is unchanged.

You can extend a `Socket` by subclassing `java.net.SocketImpl`, and providing a `SocketImplFactory` that returns the new classes as needed. A *factory* is an object whose job is to create new objects of a class that's determined at runtime. In this case, the `SocketImplFactory`'s job is to choose and create a `SocketImpl` that is appropriate for the runtime environment; thus, the `SocketImplFactory` mechanism allows Java applications to be portable across environments that use different transport mechanisms. A client application that uses the `Socket` class can use a `java.net.PlainSocketImpl` in normal situations; in environments where sockets must do something strange, like connect from behind a firewall where connections to the Internet must be passed through a SOCKS proxy server, the client's `SocketImplFactory` can install a specialized `SocketImpl` that understands how to communicate through the firewall. An application can also affect the choices that are being made by installing a new `SocketImplFactory` with the method `Socket.setSocketImplFactory(SocketImplFactory fac)`.

In Java 1.0 and 1.1, there is only one `SocketImpl` available, and that is `java.net.PlainSocketImpl`. This is a non-public class that does not understand anything about firewalls; it makes direct connections over the Internet. The class and its various fields and methods are only accessible within the `java.net` package. You should only need to access this package if you're writing a specialized socket implementation; for example, one that understands your local firewall. Another possible subclass of `SocketImpl` could encrypt the connection.

public static synchronized void
setSocketImplFactory(SocketImplFactory fac)
throws SocketException

This static method sets the *system's* client `SocketImplFactory`. The `SocketImplFactory` is an interface that the `Socket` class uses to create socket implementations. The `SocketImplFactory` may only be set once. This method throws a `SocketException` if it is called a second time.

Setting Socket Options

In Java 1.1 and later, you can set several advanced options for your sockets. These change how the low-level sockets send and receive data. There are five socket options you can set in Java: TCP_NODELAY, SO_BINDADDR, IP_MULTICAST_IF, SO_TIMEOUT, and SO_LINGER. Not all options are appropriate for all sockets. Regular client `Socket` objects support the TCP_NODELAY, SO_LINGER, and SO_TIMEOUT options.

TCP_NODELAY

```
public void setTcpNoDelay(boolean on) throws SocketException
public boolean getTcpNoDelay() throws SocketException
```

Setting `TCP_NODELAY` to true ensures that packets are sent as quickly as possible regardless of their size. Normally small (one-byte) packets are combined into larger packets before being sent.[*] Before sending another packet, the local host waits to receive a packet from the remote system. This is known as *Nagle's algorithm*. The problem with Nagle's algorithm is that if the remote system doesn't send *something* back to the local system the connection can get stuck. Setting TCP_NODELAY to `true` defeats this buffering scheme, so that all packets are sent as soon as they're ready.

`setTcpNoDelay(true)` turns off this buffering for the socket. `setTcpNoDelay(false)` turns it back on. `getTcpNoDelay()` returns `true` if buffering is off and `false` if buffering is on. For example, the following fragment turns off buffering (that is, it turns on TCP_NODELAY) for the socket s if it isn't already off.

```
if (!s.getTcpNoDelay()) s.setTcpNoDelay();
```

SO_LINGER

```
public void setSoLinger(boolean on, int seconds) throws SocketException
public int getSoLinger() throws SocketException
```

The `SO_LINGER` option specifies what to do with datagrams that have yet to be sent when a socket is closed. By default the `close()` method returns immediately, and the system tries to deliver any remaining data. If a linger time is set to zero, then any unsent packets are thrown away when the socket is closed. If the linger time is any positive value, the `close()` method blocks while waiting the specified number of seconds for the data to be sent, and the acknowledgments to be received. When that number of seconds has passed, the socket is closed and any remaining data is

---

[*] In practice, it's a little more complicated that that, but that's the main thing you need to know.

not sent, with or without acknowledgment. If the linger time is –1, this option is disabled, and as much time as is needed is taken to deliver the remaining data.

For example, to set the linger timeout for the Socket s to four minutes, if it's not already set to some other value:

```
if (s.getTcpNoLinger() != -1) s.setSoLinger(240);
```

SO_TIMEOUT

```
public synchronized void setSoTimeout(int ms) throws SocketException
public synchronized int getSoTimeout() throws SocketException
```

Normally, when you try to read data from a socket, the read() call blocks as long as necessary to get enough bytes. By setting SO_TIMEOUT, you ensure that the call will not block for more than a fixed number of milliseconds. When the TIMEOUT expires, an InterruptedException is thrown, and you should be prepared to catch it. However, the socket is still connected even though the read call failed.

Timeouts are given in milliseconds. 0 is interpreted as an infinite timeout, and is the default value. For example, to set the timeout value of s to three minutes, if it isn't already set:

```
if (s.getSoTimeout() == 0) s.setSoTimeout(180000);
```

It is a good idea to set the timeout to some reasonable (nonzero) period, so your program won't hang if the remote system crashes.

Socket Exceptions

In Java 1.0, a problem with a socket method is likely to throw a SocketException, a subclass of java.io.IOException. However, knowing that a problem occurred is often not sufficient to deal with the problem. Did the remote host refuse the connection because it was busy? Did the remote host refuse the connection because no service was listening on the port? Did the connection attempt timeout because of network congestion or because the host was down? Java 1.1 adds three new subclasses of SocketException that provide more information about what went wrong: BindException, ConnectException and NoRouteToHostException.

A BindException is thrown if you try to construct a Socket or ServerSocket object on a local port that is in use, or that you do not have sufficient privileges to use. A ConnectException is thrown when a connection is refused at the remote host, usually because the host is busy or no process is listening on that port. Finally, a NoRouteToHostException indicates that the connection has timed out.

Code that you write in Java 1.0 should catch SocketException and IOException. Since all three of these new exceptions are subclasses of SocketException, such code should continue to work in Java 1.1. New code that you write in Java 1.1 can take advantage of these three subclasses to provide more informative error messages, or to decide if you are likely to be successful if you retry the operation.

Some Useful Programs

One of the first large-scale Java programs was HotJava, a web browser that was easily the equal of the early versions of Mosaic. It is completely possible to write commercial-quality applications in Java, and it is especially possible to write network-aware applications, both clients and servers. This section shows two network clients, finger and whois, to prove this point. I do stop short of what could be done, but only in the user interface. All the necessary networking code is present. Again we find out that network code is easy; it's user interfaces that are hard.

Finger

Finger is a straightforward protocol. The client makes a TCP connection to the server on port 79, and sends a one-line query; the server responds to the query, and closes the connection. The format of the query is precisely defined, the format of the response somewhat less so. All data transferred must be pure ISO-Latin-1 text, and all lines must end with a carriage-return/linefeed pair (\r\n).

The simplest allowable request from the client is a bare carriage-return/linefeed pair. This is usually interpreted as a request to show a list of the currently logged-in users.[*] For example:

```
% telnet president.oit.unc.edu 79
Trying 152.2.22.97...
Connected to president.oit.unc.edu.
Escape character is '^]'.
Login      Name                TTY        Idle    When     Where
josmith  John Smith            console     17: Mon 04:02
uncpress UNCPress              pts/4               Tue 08:45 garamond.uncpress.un
Connection closed by foreign host.
%
```

It is also possible to request information about a specific user or username by including that user or username on the query line:

```
% telnet sunsite.unc.edu 79
Trying 152.2.254.81...
Connected to sunsite.unc.edu.
```

---

[*] Vending machines connected to the Internet return a list of items available for purchase instead. A few servers put finger to other uses; for example, one site gives you a list of recent earthquake activity.

```
Escape character is '^]'.
elharo
Login       Name              TTY        Idle   When    Where
elharo    Elliotte Harold - ja  pts/45            Tue 08:47   port112.dialup.inch.
Connection closed by foreign host.
%
```

The information that finger servers return typically includes the user's full name, where they're connected from, how long they've been connected, and any other information they've chosen to make available in their *.plan* file.[*] It is possible to request information about users via their first name, last name, or login name. You can also request information about more than one user at a time like this:

```
% telnet sunsite.unc.edu 79
Trying 152.2.254.81...
Connected to sunsite.unc.edu.
Escape character is '^]'.
elharo josmith Jane
Login       Name              TTY        Idle   When    Where
elharo    Elliotte Harold - ja  pts/45            Tue 08:47   port112.dialup.inch.
josmith   John Smith          pts/30     17: Mon 13:26   president.oit.unc.ed
josmith   John Smith          pts to/11   5d Mon 17:25
josmith   John Smith          pts/29      1d Fri 09:31
josmith   John Smith          pts/33      1d Fri 09:31
janed     Jane Doe            pts/41     6:26 Mon 14:13   moe.oit.unc.edu
janed     Jane Doe            pts/12     6:26 Mon 15:21   moe.oit.unc.edu
Connection closed by foreign host.
%
```

In this section, we'll develop a Java finger client that allows users to specify a hostname on the command line, followed by zero or more user names. For example, a typical command line will look like this:

```
% java finger hostname user1 user2 ...
```

finger connects to port 79 on the specified host. The Socket's OutputStream is chained to a PrintStream that sends a line consisting of all the names on the command line, followed by a carriage return and a line feed. Next, the output from the server (input to the program) is taken from theSocket.getInputStream() and chained to a DataInputStream so the server response can be read line by line. Each line of the server's output is presented to the user on System.out. Example 7–8 shows the code.

Example 7–8: A Java command-line finger client

```
import java.net.*;
import java.io.*;
```

---

[*] The *.plan* file is a peculiarity of UNIX; you won't find this file on other operating systems.

Example 7–8: A Java command-line finger client (continued)

```
public class finger {

  public final static int port = 79;

  public static void main(String[] args) {

    String hostname;
    Socket theSocket;
    DataInputStream theFingerStream;
    PrintStream ps;

    try {
      hostname = args[0];
    }
    catch (Exception e) {
      hostname = "localhost";
    }

    try {
      theSocket = new Socket(hostname, port, true);
      ps = new PrintStream(theSocket.getOutputStream());
      for (int i = 1; i < args.length; i++) ps.print(args[i] + " ");
      ps.print("\r\n");
      theFingerStream = new DataInputStream(theSocket.getInputStream());
      String s;
      while ((s = theFingerStream.readLine()) != null) {
        System.out.println(s);
      }
    }
    catch (IOException e) {
      System.err.println(e);
    }
  }
}
```

Here are some samples of this program running:

```
% java finger sunsite.unc.edu elharo
Login      Name                TTY        Idle   When      Where
elharo     Elliotte Harold - ja pts/45      52 Tue 08:47  port112.dialup.inch.
% java finger sunsite.unc.edu elharo Jane
Login      Name                TTY        Idle   When      Where
elharo     Elliotte Harold - ja pts/45      52 Tue 08:47  port112.dialup.inch.
janed      Jane Doe            pts/41    7:22 Mon 14:13  moe.oit.unc.edu
janed      Jane Doe            pts/12    7:22 Mon 15:21  moe.oit.unc.edu
% java finger president.oit.unc.edu
Login      Name                TTY        Idle   When      Where
josmith    John Smith          console     18: Mon 04:02
elharo     Elliotte Harold - ja pts/3           Tue 10:04  port252.dialup.inch.
uncpress   UNCPress            pts/4        44 Tue 08:45  garamond.uncpress.un
%
```

Whois

Whois is a simple directory service protocol defined in RFC954; it was originally designed to keep track of administrators responsible for Internet hosts and domains. A whois client connects to one of several central servers, and requests directory information for a person or persons; it can usually give you a phone number, an email address, and a US mail address.

With the explosive growth of the Internet, flaws have become apparent in the whois protocol, most notably its centralized nature. A more complex replacement called whois++ is under development. This new protocol is documented in RFC1834 and RFC1835; from the client's perspective, whois++ is similar to the original whois protocol. As of publication, it is unclear whether whois++ will succeed, or whether whois will be replaced by a standards effort outside of the IETF, such as X.400, or by a commercial directory service like *www.switchboard.com* or *www.411.com.*

Let's begin with a simple client to connect to a whois server. The basic structure of the whois protocol is:

1. The client opens a TCP socket to port 43 on the server *whois.internic.net.* When you're using whois, you almost always connect to this server; there are a few other private servers, but these are relatively rare. (There's also a separate whois server for the U.S. Department of Defense.) This is actually the protocol's biggest problem: all the information is concentrated in one place.

2. The client sends a search string terminated by a carriage-return/linefeed pair, (\r\n). The search string can be a name, a list of names, or a special command discussed below. You can also search for domain names, like *ora.com* or *netscape.com*, which gives you information about a network.

3. The server sends an unspecified amount of human-readable information in response to the command and closes the connection.

4. The client displays this information to the user.

The search string the client sends has a fairly simple format. At its most basic, it's just the name of the person you're searching for. Example 7–9 shows a simple whois search for "Harold." The phone numbers have been changed, and about two-thirds of the hits have been deleted. If this is what you get with a search for "Harold," imagine a search for "John" or "Smith."

Example 7–9: A manual connection to a whois server

```
% telnet whois.internic.net 43
Trying 198.41.0.7...
Connected to rs.internic.net.
Escape character is '^]'.
Harold
Bates, Harold (HB358)              harold@FAITH-REALTY.COM            (719)555-9497
Bloomenthal, Harold S. (HSB)      harold@AUTH.COM                    (303) 555-0353
Carey, Harold (HC186)             harold@IBIC.COM                     801-555-9202
Carey, Jr (JC2039)                harold@IBIC.COM                     801-555-9202
Christensen, Harold (HC40)        harold@THECOO.EDU                   605-555-6755
Dull, Harold (HD123)              harold@WABA.EDU                     707-555-3801
Fink, Harold (HF31)               harold@HBF.LIII.COM                (516) 555-3430
Fritz, Harold (HF51)              harold@USWEST.COM                   303-555-4864
Gregg, Harold (HG20)              harold@ZILKER.NET                  (512) 555-2323
HAROLD ZIELGER FORD (NET-ADP-AUTONET-C114352) ADP-AUTONET-C114352  206.89.58.0
Harold Blair (BLAIR6-DOM)                                             BLAIR.ORG
Harold Bloomenthal, Author (AUTH-DOM)                                 AUTH.COM
Harold Brehe (INFO-ADS-DOM)                                        INFO-ADS.COM
Harold C. Brown & Co., Inc. (HCB-DOM)                                 HCB.COM
Harold Cabano (SALES-PEOPLE-NET-DOM)                        SALES-PEOPLE-NET.COM
Harold Chev Inc (NET-C101957)   C101957                         192.110.86.0
Harold Gershuny (RAINWALKER-DOM)                               RAINWALKER.COM
Harold Gwatney Chevy (NET-C106080) C106080                       198.249.45.0
harold lawrence productions (BAYAREAVIDEO-DOM)                 BAYAREAVIDEO.COM

The InterNIC Registration Services Host contains ONLY Internet Information
(Networks, ASNs, Domains, and POCs).
Please use the whois server at nic.ddn.mil for MILNET Information.
Connection closed by foreign host.
%
```

Each response contains a *handle*, which, in the preceding output, is in parentheses. Handles are guaranteed to be unique, and are used to get more specific information about a person or a network. If you search for a handle, you will get at most one match. If your search only has one match, either because you get lucky when searching for a name, or because you're searching for a handle, the server returns a more detailed record. Example 7–10 shows a search for *ora.com*. Because there is only one *ora.com* in the database, the server returns all the information it has on this domain.

Example 7–10: A whois search for ora.com

```
% telnet whois.internic.net 43
Trying 198.41.0.5...
Connected to rs.internic.net.
Escape character is '^]'.
ora.com
O'Reilly & Associates (ORA-DOM1)
   103A Morris Street
   Sebastopol, CA  95472
```

Example 7–10: A whois search for ora.com (continued)

```
Domain Name: ORA.COM

Administrative Contact, Technical Contact, Zone Contact:
   Pearce, Eric  (EP86)  eap@ORA.COM
   707-829-0515 x221

Record last updated on 17-Aug-95.
Record created on 14-Jun-89.

Domain servers in listed order:

RUBY.ORA.COM                198.112.208.25
NIC.NEAR.NET                192.52.71.4
NOC.CERF.NET                192.153.156.22
NS.WEST.ORA.COM             198.112.209.1


The InterNIC Registration Services Host contains ONLY Internet Information
(Networks, ASNs, Domains, and POCs).
Please use the whois server at nic.ddn.mil for MILNET Information.
Connection closed by foreign host.
%
```

It's easy to implement a simple whois client that connects to *whois.internic.net* and searches for names entered on the command line. Example 7–11 is such a client.

Example 7–11: A command-line whois client

```java
import java.net.*;
import java.io.*;

public class whois {

  public final static int port = 43;
  public final static String hostname = "whois.internic.net";

  public static void main(String[] args) {

    Socket theSocket;
    DataInputStream theWhoisStream;
    PrintStream ps;

    try {
      theSocket = new Socket(hostname, port, true);
      ps = new PrintStream(theSocket.getOutputStream());
      for (int i = 0; i < args.length; i++) ps.print(args[i] + " ");
      ps.print("\r\n");
      theWhoisStream = new DataInputStream(theSocket.getInputStream());
      String s;
      while ((s = theWhoisStream.readLine()) != null) {
        System.out.println(s);
      }
```

Example 7–11: A command-line whois client (continued)

```
    }
    catch (IOException e) {
      System.err.println(e);
    }


  }

}
```

The class has two final static fields: the port, 43, and the hostname, *whois.internic.net*. This client always connects to this host and port; it doesn't give the user a choice because there are very few situations in which you need to use another server. The main() method begins by opening a stream socket to *whois.internic.net* on port 43. The Socket's OutputStream is chained to a PrintStream. Then each argument on the command line is printed on this stream, and thus sent out over the socket to the whois server. Next, the Socket's Input-Stream is chained to the DataInputStream theWhoisStream. Lines are read from this stream with readLine() until null is returned, signaling the end of the server's response. Each line is simply copied onto System.out.

There is a series of rules you can use to restrict or expand your search. For example, if you know you want to search for a person named "Elliott" but you aren't sure whether he spells his name "Elliot," "Elliott," or perhaps even something as unlikely as "Elliotte," you would type:

```
    java whois Person Partial Elliot
```

This tells the whois server that you only want matches for people (not domains, gateways, groups or the like) whose name begins with the letters "Elliot." Unfortunately, you need to do a separate search if you want to find someone who spells his name "Eliot." The rules for modifying a search are summarized in Table 7–1. Each prefix should be placed before the search string on the command line.

Table 7–1: Whois Prefixes

Prefix	Meaning
Domain	Find only domain records.
Gateway	Find only gateway records.
Group	Find only group records.
Host	Find only host records.
Network	Find only network records.
Organization	Find only organization records.
Person	Find only person records.
ASN	Find only autonomous system number records.

Table 7–1: Whois Prefixes (continued)

Prefix	Meaning
Handle or leading !	Only search for matching handles.
Mailbox or @	Only search for matching email addresses.
Name or leading :	Only search for matching names.
Expand or '*'	Only search for group records and show all individuals in that group.
Full or =	Show complete record for each match.
Partial or suffix .	Match records that start with the given string.
Summary or $	Just show the summary, even if there's only one match.
SUBdisplay or %	Show the users of the specified host, the hosts on the specified network, etc.

These keywords are all useful, and you could use them with the command-line client of Example 7–11, but they're way too much trouble to remember. In fact, most people don't even know that they exist. They just type "whois Harold" at the command line, and sort through the mess that comes back. A good whois client doesn't rely on you remembering arcane keywords. Rather, it shows you the options you have to choose from. This requires a graphical user interface.

Figure 7–1 shows one possible interface for a graphical whois client. This interface has a TextField to enter the name to be searched for, and a Checkbox to determine whether the match should be exact or partial. A group of radio buttons lets you specify the group of records you want to search. Another group of radio buttons chooses the fields that should be searched. By default, this client searches all fields of all records for an exact match.

When you enter a string in the Whois: TextField, the applet makes a connection to *whois.internic.net*, and retrieves records that match that string. These are placed in a List component on the left-hand side of the applet. When you double-click a record in that List, the client uses the record's handle to retrieve an individual record, and displays the result in the TextArea on the bottom right. Example 7–12 is the program that produces this interface.

Example 7–12: A graphical whois client

```
import java.applet.Applet;
import java.awt.*;
import java.net.*;
import java.io.*;

public class whoisApplet extends Applet {

  public final static int port = 43;
```

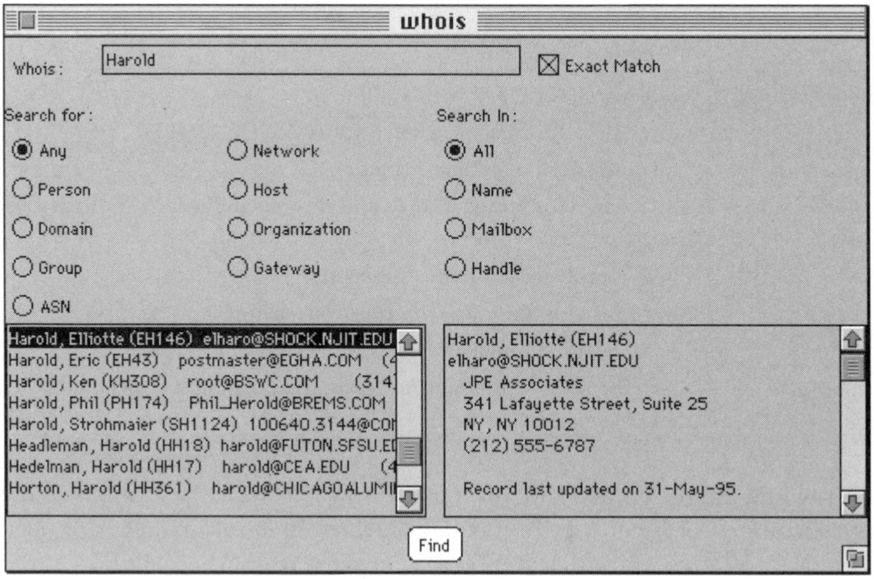

Figure 7–1: The graphical whois client

Example 7–12: A graphical whois client (continued)

```
public final static String hostname = "whois.internic.net";

TextField searchString;
TextArea detailView;
List names;
Button findButton;
CheckboxGroup searchIn;
CheckboxGroup searchFor;
Checkbox exactMatch;

public static void main(String[] args) {

  whoisApplet a = new whoisApplet();
  a.init();
  a.start();

  Frame appletFrame = new Frame("whois");
  appletFrame.add("Center", a);
  appletFrame.resize(500,300);
  appletFrame.move(50,50);
  appletFrame.show();

}

public void init() {

  setLayout(new BorderLayout());
```

Example 7–12: A graphical whois client (continued)

```
      // The TextArea in the center will expand to fill the
      // center of the BorderLayout
      detailView = new TextArea(12, 40);
      detailView.setEditable(false);
      names = new List(12, false);
      Panel CenterPanel = new Panel();
      CenterPanel.setLayout(new GridLayout(1, 2, 10, 10));
      CenterPanel.add("Center", names);
      CenterPanel.add(detailView);
      add("Center", CenterPanel);

      // You don't want the buttons in the south and north
      // to fill the entire sections so add Panels there
      // and use FlowLayouts in the Panel
      Panel NorthPanel = new Panel();
      Panel NorthPanelTop = new Panel();
      NorthPanelTop.setLayout(new FlowLayout(FlowLayout.LEFT));
      NorthPanelTop.add(new Label("Whois: "));
      searchString = new TextField(30);
      NorthPanelTop.add("North", searchString);
      exactMatch = new Checkbox("Exact Match", null, true);
      NorthPanelTop.add(exactMatch);
      NorthPanel.setLayout(new BorderLayout(2,1));
      NorthPanel.add("North", NorthPanelTop);
      Panel NorthPanelBottom = new Panel();
      NorthPanelBottom.setLayout(new GridLayout(1,2,5,5));
      NorthPanelBottom.add(initRecordType());
      NorthPanelBottom.add(initSearchFields());
      NorthPanel.add("Center", NorthPanelBottom);
      Panel SouthPanel = new Panel();
      findButton = new Button("Find");
      SouthPanel.add("South", findButton);
      add("South", SouthPanel);
      add("North", NorthPanel);

  }

public Panel initRecordType() {

  Panel p = new Panel();
  p.setLayout(new GridLayout(6, 2, 5, 2));
  searchFor = new CheckboxGroup();
  p.add(new Label("Search for:"));
  p.add(new Label(""));
  p.add(new Checkbox("Any", searchFor, true));
  p.add(new Checkbox("Network", searchFor, false));
  p.add(new Checkbox("Person", searchFor, false));
  p.add(new Checkbox("Host", searchFor, false));
  p.add(new Checkbox("Domain", searchFor, false));
  p.add(new Checkbox("Organization", searchFor, false));
  p.add(new Checkbox("Group", searchFor, false));
  p.add(new Checkbox("Gateway", searchFor, false));
```

Example 7–12: A graphical whois client (continued)

```java
    p.add(new Checkbox("ASN", searchFor, false));
    return p;

  }

  public Panel initSearchFields() {

    Panel p = new Panel();
    p.setLayout(new GridLayout(6, 1, 5, 2));
    searchIn = new CheckboxGroup();
    p.add(new Label("Search In:"));
    p.add(new Checkbox("All", searchIn, true));
    p.add(new Checkbox("Name", searchIn, false));
    p.add(new Checkbox("Mailbox", searchIn, false));
    p.add(new Checkbox("Handle", searchIn, false));
    return p;

  }

  public boolean action(Event e, Object o) {

    if (e.target == searchString || e.target == findButton) {
      lookUpNames(searchString.getText());
      return true;
    }
    else if (e.target == names) {
      getFullRecord(names.getSelectedItem());
      return true;
    }
    else {
      return false;
    }

  }

  public String makeSuffix() {

    String suffix = "";
    if (!exactMatch.getState()) suffix = ".";
    return suffix;

  }

  public String makePrefix() {

    String searchForLabel = searchFor.getCurrent().getLabel() + " ";
    String searchInLabel = searchIn.getCurrent().getLabel() + " ";
    if (searchInLabel.startsWith("A")) searchInLabel = "";
    if (searchForLabel.startsWith("A")) searchForLabel = "";
    return searchForLabel + searchInLabel + "$";

  }
```

Example 7–12: A graphical whois client (continued)

```java
public void lookUpNames(String name) {

  Socket theSocket;
  DataInputStream theWhoisStream;
  PrintStream ps;
  String s;

  try {
    theSocket = new Socket(hostname, port, true);
    ps = new PrintStream(theSocket.getOutputStream());
    theWhoisStream = new DataInputStream(theSocket.getInputStream());
    ps.print(makePrefix() + searchString.getText() + makeSuffix() + "\r\n");
    names.clear();
    while ((s = theWhoisStream.readLine()) != null) {
      names.addItem(s);
    }
  }
  catch (IOException e) {
    System.err.println(e);
  }

}

public void getFullRecord (String summary) {

  Socket theSocket;
  DataInputStream theWhoisStream;
  PrintStream ps;
  String s;
  String handle = getHandle(summary);

  try {
    theSocket = new Socket(hostname, port, true);
    ps = new PrintStream(theSocket.getOutputStream());
    theWhoisStream = new DataInputStream(theSocket.getInputStream());
    ps.print("!" + handle + "\r\n");
    detailView.setText("");
    while ((s = theWhoisStream.readLine()) != null) {
      detailView.appendText(s + "\n");
    }
  }
  catch (IOException e) {
    System.err.println(e);
  }

}

String getHandle(String s) {

  int begin = s.indexOf("(") + 1;
  int end = s.indexOf(")", begin);
```

Example 7–12: A graphical whois client (continued)

```
    return s.substring(begin,end);

  }

}
```

The main() method is the usual block of code to allow an applet to run as a standalone application. The init(), initRecordType(), and initSearchFields() methods draw the user interface. As usual with LayoutManager-based interfaces, the setup is fairly involved. Since you'd probably use a visual designer to build such an application, I won't describe it in detail here.

The action() method needs to respond to three logical types of events: first, the user may be requesting a list of names that match a search string; to do so, he presses the Button, or types RETURN in the TextField. In this case, action() gets the string in the TextField, and passes it to the lookUpRecords() method. The second kind of event is a request for more detailed information about a record. This is indicated by a double-click in the List box. In this case, action() passes the selected name to getFullRecord(). Finally, all other events are grouped into the broad category of "Events we don't care about"; action() handles these by returning false, and this passes the event up the component hierarchy to the container.

The lookUpNames() method checks the state of the different radio buttons and checkboxes. It uses this information to set up a search string to send to the whois server. After making the connection, it sends the data in much the same way as our previous whois client. Any data that returns is placed in the List names as a selectable item, rather than printed on System.out.

The getFullRecord() method is called when the user double-clicks on a name in the List box names. This method looks up the complete information about the selected individual. To do this, you need a unique way of identifying that individual. We saw earlier that the whois database assigns unique strings called "handles" to look up complete information. In the summary records, the handle is enclosed in parentheses. Therefore, the first thing getFullRecord() does is call getHandle() to parse the String between the parentheses. Once you know the handle, it is a simple matter to tell the whois server to return its record. Just precede the handle with an exclamation point:

```
    !EH146
```

getFullRecord() communicates with the server in the same way as lookUpNames(). The only differences are the modified search string (to look up a handle), and the output; the data that's returned is placed in the detailView TextArea, rather than the List selector names.

This is not a perfect client, by any means. The most glaring omission is that it doesn't provide a way to save the data and quit the program. It might also be useful to provide a list of whois servers to choose from; though there are really very few choices, unless you're in the military. It would be a good idea to add labels to the List (names) and the TextArea (detailView), and there should also be a Button to get the detailed data, in case it isn't obvious to the user that double-clicking on a name will work. However, these are all user-interface issues that would take us too far afield from the topic of network programming.

8

Sockets for Servers

What Is a Server Socket?

The last chapter discussed sockets from the standpoint of clients: programs that open a socket to a server that's listening for connections. However, client sockets themselves aren't enough; clients aren't much use unless they can talk to a server, and if you think about it, the sockets we discussed in the last chapter aren't sufficient for writing servers. To create a Socket, you need to know the Internet host that you want to connect to. When you're writing a server, you don't know in advance who will contact you; even if you did, you wouldn't know when that host wants to contact you. In other words, a server is like a person who sits by the phone, and waits for incoming calls. This person doesn't know who will call or when, only that when the phone rings, he has to pick it up and talk to whoever is there. We can't program that behavior with the Socket class alone. Granted, there's no reason that clients written in Java have to talk to Java servers—in fact, a client doesn't care what language the server was written in, or what platform it runs on. However, if Java didn't let us write servers, there would be a glaring hole in its capabilities.

Java provides a ServerSocket class to allow you to write servers. Basically, a server socket's job is to sit by the phone and wait for incoming calls. More technically, a ServerSocket runs on the server, and listens for incoming connections. Each ServerSocket listens on a particular port on the local host. When a client socket on a remote host attempts to connect to that port, the server wakes up, negotiates the connection between the client and the server, and opens a regular Socket between the two hosts. In other words, server sockets wait for connections while client sockets initiate connections. Once the server socket has set up the connection, the server uses a regular Socket to send data to the client. Data always travels over the regular socket.

The ServerSocket Class

The ServerSocket class contains everything you need to write servers in Java. It has constructors that create new ServerSocket objects, methods that listen for connections on a specified port, and methods that return a Socket when a connection is made, so you can send and receive data. In addition, it has the usual miscellaneous methods, like toString().

The basic life cycle of a server is:

1. A new ServerSocket is created on a particular port using a ServerSocket() constructor.

2. The ServerSocket listens for incoming connection attempts on that port using its accept() method. accept() blocks until a client attempts to make a connection, at which point accept() returns a Socket object that connects the client to the server.

3. Depending on the type of server, either the Socket's getInputStream() method, getOutputStream() method, or both, are called to get input and output streams that communicate with the client.

4. The server and the client interact according to an agreed upon protocol until it is time to close the connection.

5. The server, the client, or both, close the connection.

6. The server returns to step 2, and waits for the next connection.

If step 4 is likely to take a long or indefinite amount of time, traditional UNIX servers like *wu-ftpd* create a new process to handle each connection. In Java, you should spawn a thread to interact with the client so that the server can be ready to process the next connection sooner. Threads place far smaller loads on the server than a complete child process. In fact, the overhead of forking too many processes is why the typical UNIX FTP server can't handle more than roughly 400 connections without becoming unusable. On the other hand, if the protocol is simple, quick, and allows the server to close the connection when it's through, it will be more efficient for the server to process the client request immediately without spawning a thread.

The operating system stores incoming connections addressed to a particular port in a first-in, first-out queue. The default length of the queue is normally 50, though this can vary from operating system to operating system. Some operating systems (though not Solaris) have a maximum queue length, typically five. On these systems, the queue length will be the largest possible value less than or equal to 50. After the queue fills to capacity with unprocessed connections, the host refuses additional connections on that port until slots in the queue open up. Many (though not all) clients will try to make a connection multiple times if their initial attempt is refused. Managing incoming connections and the queue is a service provided by the operating system; your program does not need to worry about it. Several ServerSocket constructors allow you to change the length of the queue if its default length isn't large enough; however, you won't be able to increase the queue beyond the maximum size that your operating system supports.

The Constructors

public ServerSocket(int port)
throws IOException, BindException

This constructor creates a server socket on the specified port. If you pass 0 for the port number, the system selects an available port for you. A port chosen for you by the system is sometimes called an *anonymous port* since you don't know its number. For servers, anonymous ports aren't very useful because clients need to know in advance which port to connect to; however, there are a few situations (which we will discuss later) in which an anonymous port might be useful.

For example, to create a server socket that would be used by an HTTP server on port 80 you would write:

```
try {
  ServerSocket httpd = new ServerSocket(80);
}
catch (IOException e) {
  System.err.println(e);
}
```

The constructor throws an IOException if you cannot create and bind the socket to the requested port. (In Java 1.1, a BindException, which inherits from IOException, is thrown instead.) An IOException when you create a ServerSocket almost always means one of two things. Either the specified port is already in use, or you do not have root privileges on UNIX, and you're trying to connect to a port between 1 and 1023.

You can use this constructor to write a variation on the lookForPorts program of the last chapter. Example 8–1 checks for ports on the local machine by attempting to create ServerSocket objects on them, and seeing on which ports that fails. If you're using UNIX and are not root (superuser), this program only works for ports 1024 and above.

Example 8–1: Look for local ports

```
import java.net.*;
import java.io.*;

public class lookForLocalPorts {

  public static void main(String[] args) {

    ServerSocket theServer;

    for (int i = 1024; i <= 65535; i++) {
      try {
        // the next line will fail and drop into the catch block if
        // there is already a server running on port i
        theServer = new ServerSocket(i);
        theServer.close();
      }
      catch (IOException e) {
        System.out.println("There is a server on port " + i + ".");
      }// end try
    }// end for

  }

}
```

public ServerSocket(int port, int queuelength)
throws IOException, BindException

This constructor creates a `ServerSocket` on the specified port with a queue length of your choosing. The `queuelength` argument sets the length of the queue for incoming connections—that is, how many incoming connections can be stored at one time before the host starts refusing connections. If you try to expand the queue past the maximum queue length, the maximum queue length is used instead. If you pass 0 for the port number, the system selects an available port.

For example, to create a server socket on port 5776 that would hold up to 100 incoming connections in the queue, you would write:

```
try {
  ServerSocket httpd = new ServerSocket(5776, 100);
}
catch (IOException e) {
  System.err.println(e);
}
```

The constructor throws an `IOException` if the socket cannot be created and bound to the requested port. (In Java 1.1, a `BindException`, which inherits from

IOException, is thrown instead.) This almost always means one of two things. Either the specified port is already in use, or you do not have root privileges on UNIX and you're trying to connect to a port between 1 and 1023.

public ServerSocket(int port, int queuelength, InetAddress bindAddress) throws IOException (Java 1.1 only)

This constructor, which is only available in Java 1.1 and later releases, creates a ServerSocket on the specified port with the specified queue length. The Server-Socket only binds to the specified local IP address. This constructor is useful for servers that run on systems with several IP addresses (a common practice at web server farms) because it allows you to choose the address that you'll listen to. That is, this ServerSocket only listens for incoming connections on the specified address; it won't listen for connections that come in through the host's other addresses. The other constructors bind to all local IP addresses by default.

For example, *sunsite.unc.edu* is a particular SPARCstation in North Carolina. It's connected to the Internet via an extremely fast 100 megabit/second (MBPS) FDDI interface with the IP address 152.2.254.81. The same SPARCstation is also called *calzone.oit.unc.edu*, but *calzone* is connected to the Internet via a 10 MBPS Ethernet card, using a different IP address (152.2.22.81). To create a server socket that listens on port 5776 of *sunsite.unc.edu* but not on port 5776 of *calzone.oit.unc.edu*, you would write:

```
try {
  ServerSocket httpd = new ServerSocket(5776, 100,
    InetAddress.getHostByName("sunsite.unc.edu"));
}
catch (IOException e) {
  System.err.println(e);
}
```

The constructor throws an IOException if the socket cannot be created and bound to the requested port. (In Java 1.1, a BindException, which inherits from IOException, is thrown instead.) This almost always means one of two things. Either the specified port is already in use, or you do not have root privileges on UNIX, and you're trying to connect to a port between 1 and 1023.

protected ServerSocket() (Java 1.1 only)

This protected constructor is for the use of subclasses of ServerSocket that want to provide their own SocketImpl, perhaps to pass through a proxy server or implement security protocols. It is available only in Java 1.1 and later. This constructor creates a default SocketImpl, impl, in the superclass but does not initialize impl. That is, it does not invoke impl.create(), impl.bind(), or impl.listen(). You can therefore use a different SocketImpl object of your own to do all the work.

To subclass ServerSocket you must also override accept(). The SocketImpl impl in the superclass isn't accessible from your subclass. The protected final void implAccept(Socket s) method is provided instead. When implAccept() returns, the socket is connected. This method can throw an IOException.

Accepting and Closing Connections

public Socket accept() throws IOException

When your setup is done, and you're ready to accept a connection, call the ServerSocket's accept() method. This method blocks: it stops the flow of execution, and waits until a client connects. When a client does connect, the accept() method returns a Socket object. You use the streams returned by this Socket's getInputStream() and getOutputStream() methods to communicate with the client. For example:

```
try {
  ServerSocket theServer = new ServerSocket(5776);
  while (true) {
    Socket theConnection = theServer.accept();
    PrintStream p = new PrintStream(theConnection.getOutputStream());
    p.println("You've connected to this server. Bye-bye now.");
    theConnection.close();
  }
}
catch (IOException e) {
  System.err.println(e);
}
```

If you don't want your program to halt while it waits for a connection, put the call to accept() in a separate thread.

Example 8–2 implements a simple daytime server, as per RFC867. Since this server sends a single line of text in response to each connection, it processes each connection immediately. More complex servers should spawn a thread to handle each request. In this case, the overhead of spawning a thread would be greater than the time needed to process the request.

NOTE   If you run this program on a UNIX box, you need to run it as root in order to connect to port 13. If you don't want to, or can't, run it as root, change the port number to something above 1024, say 1313.

Example 8–2: A daytime server

```
import java.net.*;
import java.io.*;
import java.util.Date;

public class daytimeServer {

  public final static int daytimePort = 13;

  public static void main(String[] args) {

    ServerSocket theServer;
    Socket theConnection;
    PrintStream p;

    try {
      theServer = new ServerSocket(daytimePort);
      try {
        while (true) {
          theConnection = theServer.accept();
          p = new PrintStream(theConnection.getOutputStream());
          p.println(new Date());
          theConnection.close();
        }
      }
      catch (IOException e) {
        theServer.close();
        System.err.println(e);
      }

    } // end try
    catch (IOException e) {
      System.err.println(e);
    }

  }

}
```

Example 8–2 is straightforward. The first three lines import the usual packages, java.io and java.net, as well as java.util.Date. There is a single public final static int field (i.e., a constant) in the class, daytimePort, which is set to the well-known port for a daytime server (port 13). The class has a single method, main(), which does all the work.

The main() method has three local variables: the ServerSocket theServer, the Socket theConnection, and a PrintStream p. After the variables are declared, a try-catch block traps any IOExceptions that may arise while the ServerSocket theServer is constructed on the daytime port. Then another try block watches for exceptions thrown while the connections are accepted and processed. accept() is called within an infinite loop to watch for new connections; like many servers, this program never terminates, but continues listening until an exception is thrown or you stop it manually.*

When a client makes a connection, accept() returns a Socket, which is placed in theConnection, and the program continues. We call getOutputStream() to get the output stream associated with that Socket, and then chain that output stream to a new PrintStream, p. To get the current date, we construct a new Date object, and send it to the client by printing it on the PrintStream with println().

After sending the data, we call theConnection's close() method. Always close a socket when you're finished with it. In the last chapter, we said that a client shouldn't rely on the other side of a connection to close the socket. That goes triple for servers. Clients can time out or crash; users cancel transactions; networks may go down in high-traffic periods. For any of these or a dozen more reasons, you cannot rely on clients to close sockets.

public void close() throws IOException

If you're finished with a server socket, you should close it, especially if your program is going to continue to run for some time. This frees up the port for other programs that may wish to use it. Closing a ServerSocket should not be confused with closing a Socket. Closing a ServerSocket frees a port on the local host, allowing another server to bind to the port; closing a Socket breaks the connection between the local and the remote hosts.

Server sockets are closed automatically when a program dies, so it's not absolutely necessary to close them in programs that terminate shortly after the ServerSocket is no longer needed. Nonetheless, it doesn't hurt to do it.

The get Methods

public InetAddress getInetAddress()

This method returns the address being used by the server (the local host). If the local host has a single IP address (as most do), this is the address returned by InetAddress.getLocalHost(). If the local host has more than one IP address, the

---

* The command for stopping a program manually depends on your system; under UNIX and many other systems, Control-C will do the job. If you are running the server in the background on a UNIX system, stop it by finding the server's process ID, and killing it with the kill command (**kill** *pid*).

specific address returned is one of the host's IP addresses; in Java 1.0, you can't predict which address you will get. For example:

```
try {
  ServerSocket httpd = new ServerSocket(80);
  InetAddress ia = httpd.getInetAddress();
}
catch (IOException e) {
}
```

public int getLocalPort()

The ServerSocket constructors allow you to listen on an unspecified port by passing 0 for the port number. This method lets you find out what port you're listening on. You might use this in a peer-to-peer multisocket program when you already have a means to inform other peers of your location. Or a server might spawn several smaller servers to perform certain operations. The well-known server could inform clients on what ports they can find smaller servers. Of course, you can also use getLocalPort() to find a non-anonymous port, but why would you need to?

Example 8–3: A random port

```
import java.net.*;
import java.io.*;

public class anon {

  public static void main(String[] args) {

    try {
      ServerSocket httpd = new ServerSocket(0);
      System.out.println("This server runs on port " + httpd.getLocalPort());
    }
    catch (IOException e) {
      System.err.println(e);
    }
  }
}
```

Here's the output of one run:

```
% java anon
This server runs on port 61209
```

Socket Options

The only socket option supported for server sockets in Java 1.1 is SO_TIMEOUT. SO_TIMEOUT is the amount of time, in milliseconds, accept() waits for an incoming connection before throwing a java.io.InterruptedIOException. This time must be non-negative. If SO_TIMEOUT is 0, accept() will never time out.

Using SO_TIMEOUT on the ServerSocket is rather rare. You might need it if you were implementing a complicated and secure protocol that required multiple connections between the client and the server, and where some responses needed to occur within a fixed amount of time. Most servers are designed to run for indefinite periods of time, and thus use the default timeout value, 0 (never time out).

public synchronized void setSoTimeout(int timeout) throws SocketException

The setSoTimeout() method sets the SO_TIMEOUT field for this server socket object. When the timeout expires, an InterruptedException is thrown. You should set this option before calling accept(); you cannot change the timeout value while accept() is waiting for a connection. The timeout argument must be greater than or equal to zero; if it isn't, the method throws a SocketException:

```
try {
  ServerSocket ss = new ServerSocket(2048);
  ss.setSoTimeout(30000); // block for no more than 30 seconds
  try {
    Socket s = ss.accept();
    // handle the connection
    ...
  }
  catch (InterruptedException e) {
    ss.close();
    System.err.println("No connection within 30 seconds");
  }
}
catch (SocketException e) {
  System.err.println(e);
}
catch (IOException e) {
  System.err.println("Unexpected IOException: " + e);
}
```

public synchronized int getSoTimeout() throws IOException

The getSoTimeout() method returns the current value of this ServerSocket object's SO_TIMEOUT field. For example:

```
public void printSoTimeout(ServerSocket ss) {

  int timeout = ss.getSoTimeOut();
  if (timeout > 0) {
    System.out.println(ss + " will time out after " + timeout + "milliseconds.");
  }
  else if (timeout == 0) {
    System.out.println(ss + " will never time out.");
  }
```

```
    else {
      System.out.println("Something is seriously wrong with " + ss);
    }

  }
```

The Object Methods

public String toString()

The `ServerSocket` class overrides one method from `java.lang.Object`, `toString()`. In Java 1.0, a `String` returned by `toString()` looks like:

```
    ServerSocket[addr=0.0.0.0,port=0,localport=5776]
```

In Java 1.1, the `String` returned by `toString()` looks like:

```
    ServerSocket[addr=0.0.0.0/0.0.0.0,port=0,localport=4000]
```

`addr` is always 0.0.0.0, and `port` is always 0. Presumably, these may become something more interesting in the future. The `localport` is the local port on which the server is listening for connections, and is the only element in the string that changes to reflect the state of the `ServerSocket`.

Implementation

public static synchronized void setSocketFactory(SocketImplFactory fac) throws IOException

This method sets the *system's* server `SocketImplFactory`, the factory used to create `ServerSocket` objects. This is not the same factory that is used to create client `Socket` objects, though the syntax is similar; you can have one factory for `Socket` objects, and a different factory for `ServerSocket` objects. You can only set this factory once in a program, however. A second attempt to set the `SocketImplFactory` throws a `SocketException`. It is unlikely that you will need to call this.

protected final void implAccept(Socket s) throws IOException (Java 1.1)

Subclasses of `ServerSocket` use this method to implement `accept()`. You would pass an unconnected `Socket` object to `implAccept()`. When the method returns, the `Socket s` will be connected to a client. Presumably, s is an instance of some subclass of `Socket`.

Some Useful Servers

This section shows several servers you can build with server sockets. It starts with a server you can use to test client responses and requests, much as you use *telnet* to test server behavior. Then we present three different HTTP servers, each with a different special purpose, and each slightly more complex than the previous one.

Client Tester

In the last chapter you learned how to use *telnet* to experiment with servers. There's no equivalent program to test clients, so let's create one. Example 8–4 is a program called `clientTester` that runs on a port specified on the command line, shows all data sent by the client, and allows you to send a response to the client by typing it on the command line. For example, you can use this program to see the commands Netscape Navigator sends to a server.

NOTE   Clients are rarely as forgiving about unexpected server responses as
                servers are about unexpected client responses. If at all possible, try to
                run the clients that connect to this program on a UNIX system, or
                some other platform that is moderately crash-proof. Don't run them
                on a Mac or Windows 95; they are less stable.

This program uses two threads: one to handle input from the client, and the other to send output from the server. Using two threads allows the program to handle input and output simultaneously; it can be sending a response to the client while receiving a request—or, more to the point, it can send data to the client while waiting for the client to respond. This is convenient because different clients and servers talk in unpredictable ways. With some protocols, the server talks first; with others, the client talks first. Sometimes the server sends a one-line response; often, the response is much larger. Our program must be flexible enough to handle all these cases.

Once a connection is established, the resulting socket is split into input and output streams, each in its own thread. The client's request is transferred to the screen a byte at a time. Because command-line input in Java is line by line, I use a `PrintStream` to send responses back to the client. Example 8–4 shows the code.

Example 8–4: A client tester

```
import java.net.*;
import java.io.*;

public class clientTester {
```

Example 8–4: A client tester (continued)

```
  public static void main(String[] args) {

    int thePort;
    ServerSocket ss;
    Socket theConnection;

    try {
      thePort = Integer.parseInt(args[0]);
    }
    catch (Exception e) {
      thePort = 0;
    }

    try {
      ss = new ServerSocket(thePort);
      System.out.println("Listening for connections on port " + ss.getLocalPort());

      while (true) {
        theConnection = ss.accept();
        System.out.println("Connection established with " + theConnection);
        InputThread it = new InputThread(theConnection.getInputStream());
        it.start();
        OutputThread ot = new OutputThread(theConnection.getOutputStream(), it);
        ot.start();
        // need to wait for ot and it to finish
        try {
          ot.join();
          it.join();
        }
        catch (InterruptedException e) {
        }
      }
    }
    catch (IOException e) {

    }

  }

}

class InputThread extends Thread {

  InputStream is;

  public InputThread(InputStream is) {
    this.is = is;
  }

  public void run()   {

    try {
```

Example 8–4: A client tester (continued)

```
      while (true) {
        int i = is.read();
        if (i == -1) break;
        char c = (char) i;
        System.out.print(c);
      }
    }
    catch (IOException e) {
      System.err.println(e);
    }

  }

}


class OutputThread extends Thread {

  PrintStream ps;
  DataInputStream is;
  InputThread it;

  public OutputThread(OutputStream os, InputThread it) {
    ps = new PrintStream(os);
    this.it = it;
    is = new DataInputStream(System.in);
  }

  public void run() {

    String line;
    try {
      while (true) {
        line = is.readLine();
        if (line.equals(".")) break;
        ps.println(line);
      }
    }
    catch (IOException e) {

    }
    it.stop();
  }

}
```

The `clientTester` application is split into three classes: `clientTester`, `Input-Thread`, and `OutputThread`. The `clientTester` class reads the port from the command line, opens a `ServerSocket`, `ss`, on that port, and listens for incoming connections. You can only make one connection at a time, because this program is designed for experimentation, and a slow human being has to provide all responses. Further connections will be refused until you close the first one.

An infinite while loop waits for connections with the accept() method. When a connection is detected, its InputStream is used to construct a new InputThread, and its OutputStream is used to construct a new OutputThread. After starting these threads, we wait for them to finish by calling their join() methods.

The InputThread is contained almost entirely in the run() method. It has a single field, is, the InputStream that data will be read from one byte at a time. Each byte is cast to a char, c, printed on System.out. The run() method ends when an IOException is thrown, presumably because the end of stream was encountered.

The OutputThread sends output to the client. Its constructor has two arguments: an output stream for sending data to the client, and the InputThread. Output-Thread reads input from the user on System.in, which is chained to a DataInput-Stream is. The OutputStream that was passed to the constructor is chained to a PrintStream for convenience. The run() method for OutputThread reads lines from the DataInputStream is, and copies them onto the PrintStream ps, which sends them to the client. A period typed on a line by itself signals the end of user input. When this occurs, run() exits the loop, and stops the InputThread by calling it.stop().

HTTP Servers

HTTP is a large protocol. As you saw in Chapter 3, *Basic Web Concepts*, a full-blown HTTP server must respond to requests for files, convert URLs into filenames on the local system, respond to POST and GET requests, handle requests for files that don't exist, interpret MIME types, and much, much more. However, many HTTP servers don't need all these features. For example, in 1996, the web server at *www.oreilly.com* simply chunked out a page saying the machine belonged to Jim O'Reilly and not O'Reilly & Associates, who were at *www.ora.com*. The Netscape commerce server is clearly overkill for this site. Such a site is a candidate for a custom server that only does one thing. Writing this kind of server in Java is simple.

Custom servers aren't only useful for small sites. High-traffic sites like Yahoo are also candidates for custom servers because a server that only does one thing can often be much faster than a general purpose server like Apache or Netscape. It is easy to optimize a special purpose server for a particular task; the result is often much more efficient than a general purpose server that needs to respond to many different kinds of requests.

A single file server

Our investigation of HTTP servers begins with a server that always sends out the same file, no matter who or what the request. The filename and the local port are read from the command line. If the port is omitted, port 80 is assumed.

Example 8–5: An HTTP server that chunks out the same file

```
import java.net.*;
import java.io.*;
import java.util.*;

public class onefile extends Thread {

  static String theData = "";
  static String ContentType;
  static int ContentLength;
  Socket theConnection;

  public static void main(String[] args) {

    int thePort;
    ServerSocket ss;
    Socket theConnection;
    FileInputStream theFile;

    // cache the file
    try {
      theFile = new FileInputStream(args[0]);
      DataInputStream dis = new DataInputStream(theFile);
      if (args[0].endsWith(".html") || args[0].endsWith(".htm")) {
        ContentType = "text/html";
      }
      else {
        ContentType = "text/plain";
      }

      try {
        String thisLine;
        while ((thisLine = dis.readLine()) != null) {
          theData += thisLine + "\n";
        }
      }
      catch (Exception e) {
        System.err.println("Error: " + e);
      }
    }
    catch (Exception e) {
      System.err.println(e);
      System.err.println("Usage: java onefile filename port");
      System.exit(1);
    }

    // set the port to listen on
    try {
      thePort = Integer.parseInt(args[1]);
      if (thePort < 0 || thePort > 65535) thePort = 80;
    }
    catch (Exception e) {
      thePort = 80;
```

Example 8–5: An HTTP server that chunks out the same file (continued)

```java
    }

    try {
      ss = new ServerSocket(thePort);
      System.out.println("Accepting connections on port "
        + ss.getLocalPort());
      System.out.println("Data to be sent:");
      System.out.println(theData);
      while (true) {
        onefile fs = new onefile(ss.accept());
        fs.start();
      }
    }
    catch (IOException e) {
    }
  }

  public onefile(Socket s) {
    theConnection = s;
  }

  public void run() {

    try {
      PrintStream os = new PrintStream(theConnection.getOutputStream());
      DataInputStream is = new DataInputStream(theConnection.getInputStream());
      String request = is.readLine();
      // If this is HTTP/1.0 or later send a MIME header
      if (request.indexOf("HTTP/") != -1) {
        while (true) { // read the rest of the MIME header
          String thisLine = is.readLine();
          if (thisLine.trim().equals("")) break;
        }

        os.print("HTTP/1.0 200 OK\r\n");
        Date now = new Date();
        os.print("Date: " + now + "\r\n");
        os.print("Server: OneFile 1.0\r\n");
        os.print("Content-length: " + ContentLength + "\r\n");
        os.print("Content-type: " + ContentType + "\r\n\r\n");
      }// end if
      os.println(theData);
      theConnection.close();
    } // end try
    catch (IOException e) {
    }

  }

}
```

This server starts a new thread for every incoming request. Because the server is so simple, it is arguable whether using separate threads helps or hurts performance. A lot depends on the size of the file being served, the number of connections expected per hour, and the thread model of Java on the host machine. When in doubt, threading is generally a good idea, so it's been used here. Using multiple threads would be a clear win for a server that was even slightly more sophisticated than this one.

The main() method of the onefile class handles all initialization tasks; it then enters a while loop that accepts connections, and spawns threads to process each connection. The name of the file to be served is read from the first command-line argument. If no file is specified or the file cannot be opened, an error message is printed, and the program exits. Assuming the file can be read, its contents are stored in the static variable theData. A reasonable guess is made about the content type of the file, and that guess is stored in the static variable ContentType.

For efficiency's sake, the file is cached in memory (the variable theData) when the server starts; this is faster than reading the file from disk for each connection.[*] If the file is so large that it requires a significant fraction of the available memory, you shouldn't be sending it over the web. However, caching the file means that you can't change the file without restarting the server. If this is a problem, it would be simple to extend this server to listen for connections on an additional administrative port, and reread the file when a connection is detected. A more advanced server could use this technique to change many more aspects of its configuration.[†]

onefile reads the port to listen on from the second command-line argument. If no port is specified, or if the second argument is not an integer between 0 and 65,535, port 80 is used. After initialization is complete, onefile opens a ServerSocket on the specified port, and prints a message saying what port is being used, and what data will be sent to the clients.

Next, the program enters an infinite loop that continually accepts connections, and spawns threads to process them. A thread is spawned by constructing a new instance of the onefile class with ss.accept() as an argument. Then the thread is started, transferring control to the thread's run() method.

The run() method of the thread creates a PrintStream for output to the socket, and a DataInputStream for input from the socket. Then it reads the request from the client. It looks at the first line to see whether it contains the String HTTP/. If it

---

[*] This should be true even if you have a file system that does a good job of caching; making system calls to read the file is expensive, even if the file is already in cache.

[†] This technique is similar to a trick used by most UNIX servers; when the administrator sends the server a signal, the server rereads its configuration files. Java doesn't support anything like signals, but there's no reason you can't use a connection attempt to serve the same purpose.

sees this, the server assumes that the client understands HTTP 1.0 or later, and therefore sends a MIME header for the file; then it sends the data. If the client request doesn't contain the string HTTP/, our server omits the header, sending the data by itself. Finally, the server closes the connection, and the thread dies.

Here's what you see when you connect to this server via *telnet*; the specifics depend on the exact server and file:

```
% telnet sunsite.unc.edu 2000
Trying 152.2.254.81...
Connected to sunsite.unc.edu.
Escape character is '^]'.
GET / HTTP/1.0

HTTP/1.0 200 OK
Date: Sat May 04 08:54:31 EDT 1996
Server: OneFile 1.0
Content-length: 6877
Content-type: text/html

<html>
<head>
<title>Cafe Au Lait</title>
<body>

<h1>Cafe Au Lait</h1>
```

A redirector

Another simple but useful application for a special purpose HTTP server is redirection. In this section, we develop a server that redirects users from one web site to another, for example, from *ora.com* to *www.ora.com*. Example 8–6 reads a URL and port number from the command line, and redirects all requests that it receives to the site indicated by the new URL, using a 302 FOUND code.

Example 8–6: An HTTP redirector

```
import java.net.*;
import java.io.*;
import java.util.*;

public class Redirector extends Thread {

  Socket theConnection;
  static String theSite;

  public Redirector(Socket s) {
    theConnection = s;
  }

  public static void main(String[] args) {
```

Example 8–6: An HTTP redirector (continued)

```
    int thePort;
    ServerSocket ss;

    try {
      theSite = args[0];
    }
    catch (Exception e) {
      theSite = "http://www.ora.com";
    }

    // trim trailing slash
    if (theSite.endsWith("/")) {
      theSite = theSite.substring(0, theSite.length()-1);
    }

    try {
      thePort = Integer.parseInt(args[1]);
    }
    catch (Exception e) {
      thePort = 80;
    }

    try {
      ss = new ServerSocket(thePort);
      System.out.println("Redirecting connections on port " + ss.getLocalPort()
        + " to " + theSite);

      while (true) {
        Redirector rd = new Redirector(ss.accept());
        rd.start();
      }
    }
    catch (IOException e) {

    }

  } // end main

  public void run() {
    try {
      PrintStream os = new PrintStream(theConnection.getOutputStream());
      DataInputStream is = new DataInputStream(theConnection.getInputStream());
      String get = is.readLine();
      // The StringTokenizer parses out the requested document
      // so a proper URL can be built for the document at
      // the new site
      StringTokenizer st = new StringTokenizer(get);
      st.nextToken();  // the method, e.g. "GET" or "POST"
      String theFile = st.nextToken();

      // Does the client understand HTTP/1.0 or later?
      try {
```

Example 8–6: An HTTP redirector (continued)

```
        if (st.nextToken().startsWith("HTTP/")) {
          // wait for a blank line
          while (true) {
            String thisLine = is.readLine();
            if (thisLine.trim().equals("")) break;
          }

          // Send the HTTP 1.0 Header
          os.print("HTTP/1.0 302 FOUND\r\n");
          Date now = new Date();
          os.print("Date: " + now + "\r\n");
          os.print("Server: MiniRedirector 1.0\r\n");
          os.print("Location: " + theSite + theFile + "\r\n");
          os.print("Content-type: text/html\r\n\r\n");
        }// end if
      }// end try
      catch (NoSuchElementException e) {
        // No big deal. This client
        // doesn't understand HTTP/1.0
        // so don't send a MIME header
      }
      // Not all browsers support redirection so we need to
      // produce HTML that says where the document has moved to.
      os.println("<HTML><HEAD><TITLE>Document moved</TITLE></HEAD>");
      os.println("<BODY><H1>Document moved</H1>");
      os.println("The document " + theFile +
        " has moved to <A HREF=\"" + theSite + "\>" + theSite +
        "</A>. Please update your bookmarks<P>");
      os.println("</BODY></HTML>");
      theConnection.close();
    }
    catch (IOException e) {

    }

  } // end run

}
```

To start the redirector on port 2000, and redirect incoming requests to *http://www.ora.com*, you would type:

```
% java redirector http://www.ora.com 2000
Redirecting connections on port 2000 to http://www.ora.com
```

If you connect to this server via telnet, this is what you'll see:

```
% telnet sunsite.unc.edu 2000
Trying 152.2.254.81...
Connected to sunsite.unc.edu.
Escape character is '^]'.
GET / HTTP/1.0
```

```
HTTP/1.0 302 FOUND
Date: Sat May 04 09:16:08 EDT 1996
Server: MiniRedirector 1.0
Location: http://www.ora.com/
Content-type: text/html

<HTML><HEAD><TITLE>Document moved</TITLE></HEAD>
<BODY><H1>Document moved</H1>
The document / has moved to <A HREF="http://www.ora.com>http://www.ora.com</A>.
 Please update your bookmarks<P>
</BODY></HTML>
Connection closed by foreign host.
%
```

If you connect with a web browser, you should be seamlessly sent to
http://www.ora.com with only a slight delay. You should never see the HTML added
after the response code; this is provided to support older browsers that don't redirect automatically.

This server is large enough to take advantage of multithreading, so it is implemented as a subclass of Thread. The main() method accepts connections and
spawns new threads while the run() method processes each connection. Initialization is straightforward; main() reads the URL that connections are redirected to
and the port on which to listen from the command line. If there are any errors,
because a command-line argument is missing or some other reason, Redirector
listens on port 80, and redirects requests to *http://www.ora.com*.

Next, Redirector opens a ServerSocket on the specified port. Assuming this is
successful, main() enters an infinite while loop to accept() incoming connections, and spawn new threads to deal with each one. Inside of this loop, main()
calls the constructor for Redirector. This takes a Socket object (returned by
accept()) as its argument, and then calls the Redirector's run() method to start
the thread.

The run() method does most of the work. It begins by creating a PrintStream os
from the Socket's output stream, and a DataInputStream is from the Socket's
input stream. Then the run() method waits for the client to start talking. This is
done in the line:

```
String get = is.readLine();
```

The first line the client sends should be of the format:

```
GET /directory/filename.html HTTP/1.0
```

It is possible that the first word will be POST or PUT instead, or that there will be
no HTTP version. The second word is the file the client wants to retrieve. This

must begin with a slash (/). Browsers are responsible for converting relative URLs to absolute URLs that begin with a slash; the server does not do this. The third word is the version of the HTTP protocol the browser understands. Possible values are nothing at all (pre-HTTP 1.0 browsers), HTTP 1.0 (almost all browsers as of December 1996), or HTTP 1.1.

To handle a request like this, `Redirector` ignores the first word. The second word is attached to the URL of the target server (stored in the variable `theSite`) to give a full redirected URL. The third word is used to determine whether or not to send a MIME header; MIME headers are not used for old browsers that do not understand HTTP 1.0. The easiest way to split these three words apart is to use a `String-Tokenizer`. The first token in the `String` is `GET`, which we discard with the line:

```
st.nextToken();
```

This line retrieves the token but doesn't do anything with it. The next time `st.nextToken()` is called, it returns the file. The third time `st.nextToken()` is called, it returns the HTTP version. You have to watch out for a `NoSuchElementException` which is thrown if there isn't an HTTP version. If there is a version, a MIME header is sent, otherwise, it is omitted.

Sending the data is almost trivial. The `PrintStream os` is used. The only trick here is that the end of line character for HTTP requests is \r\n—a carriage return followed by a line feed. Since `println()` only adds a linefeed to the end of each line, you need to use `print()`, and insert manual carriage return-linefeed pairs.

The next lines each send one line of text to the client. The first line printed is:

```
HTTP/1.0 302 FOUND
```

This is an HTTP 1.0 response code that tells the client to expect to be redirected. The second line is a `Date:` header that gives the current time at the server. This line is optional. The third line is the name and version of the server; this is also optional, but is used by spiders that try to keep statistics about the most popular web servers. (It would be very surprising to ever see `MiniRedirector` break into single digits in lists of the most popular servers.) The next line is the `Location:` header, which is required for this server. It tells the client where it has been redirected to. Last the standard `Content-type:` header. We send the content type `text/html` to indicate that the client should expect to see HTML. Finally, a blank line is sent to signify the end of the header data.

Everything after this will be HTML, which is processed by the browser and displayed. At this point it is permissible to go back to regular `println()` statements, and stop using the funny line endings. The next several lines print a message for browsers that do not support redirection, so those users can manually jump to the new site. That message looks like:

```
<HTML><HEAD><TITLE>Document moved</TITLE></HEAD>
<BODY><H1>Document moved</H1>
The document has moved to <A HREF="http://www.ora.com">http://www.ora.com"</A>.
Please update your bookmarks<P></BODY></HTML>
```

Finally, the connection is closed and the thread dies.

A full-fledged HTTP server

Enough with special purpose HTTP servers. This section develops a full-blown HTTP server, called jhttp, that can serve an entire document tree including images, applets, HTML files, text files, and more. It will be very similar to the one-file server, except that it pays attention to the GET requests. This server is still fairly lightweight; after looking at the code, we'll discuss other features you might want to add.

Jeeves, a Java Web Server

While this book was being written, Sun released its own HTTP server built in Java, called "Jeeves." Jeeves isn't real competition for the Netscape Commerce Server. Instead, it's a reference implementation of a server class library. The primary addition to the server class library is *servlets*, Java programs that run on the server similar to the way applets run on the client. Servlets produce similar results to CGI programs, NSAPI programs, and server-side includes. However, they have the advantages provided by Java's SecurityManager and Java's cross-platform nature. Furthermore, the servlet library is specifically designed for writing web applications in a way that neither C nor Perl are. Servlets are explored in detail in Chapter 15, *The Java Server API and Servlets*.

As of December 1996, Jeeves is only in alpha, so it's still very much subject to change. However, it looks like it will be composed of an HTTP server, a proxy server, and a chat server. These three main servers will be built on top of five packages: a database access package for connecting to legacy databases, and executing SQL queries; a security package for authentication and authorization of users; an HTML package for dynamic generation of HTML; a utility package for logging, configuration, and account management; and a tools package. These packages can also be used by other web servers. For more information see *http://www.javasoft.com/jeeves/*.

As in the previous two examples, the main() method of jhttp handles initialization, and an infinite while loop accepts connections. A subclass of Thread called Request handles processes of each request. Example 8–7 shows the complete code.

Example 8–7: The jhttp web server

```java
import java.net.*;
import java.io.*;
import java.util.*;

public class jhttp extends Thread {

  Socket theConnection;
  static File docroot;
  static String indexfile = "index.html";

  public jhttp(Socket s) {
    theConnection = s;
  }

  public static void main(String[] args) {

    int thePort;
    ServerSocket ss;

    // get the Document root
    try {
      docroot = new File(args[0]);
    }
    catch (Exception e) {
      docroot = new File(".");
    }

    // set the port to listen on
    try {
      thePort = Integer.parseInt(args[1]);
      if (thePort < 0 || thePort > 65535) thePort = 80;
    }
    catch (Exception e) {
      thePort = 80;
    }

    try {
      ss = new ServerSocket(thePort);
      System.out.println("Accepting connections on port "
        + ss.getLocalPort());
      System.out.println("Document Root:" + docroot);
      while (true) {
        jhttp j = new jhttp(ss.accept());
        j.start();
      }
    }
    catch (IOException e) {
      System.err.println("Server aborted prematurely");
    }

  }
```

Example 8–7: The jhttp web server (continued)

```
public void run() {

   String method;
   String ct;
   String version = "";
   File theFile;

   try {
     PrintStream os = new PrintStream(theConnection.getOutputStream());
     DataInputStream is = new DataInputStream(theConnection.getInputStream());
     String get = is.readLine();
     StringTokenizer st = new StringTokenizer(get);
     method = st.nextToken();
     if (st.hasMoreTokens()) {
       file = st.nextToken();
       if (file.endsWith("/")) file += indexfile;
       }
       if (st.hasMoreTokens()) version = st.nextToken();
       if (method.equals("GET")) {
         ct = guessContentTypeFromName(file);
         // loop through the rest of the input lines

         while ((get = is.readLine()) != null) {
           if (get.trim().equals("")) break;
       }

       try {
         theFile = new File(docroot, file.substring(1,file.length()));
         FileInputStream fis = new FileInputStream(theFile);
         byte[] theData = new byte[(int) theFile.length()];
         // need to check the number of bytes read here
         fis.read(theData);
         fis.close();

         if (version.startsWith("HTTP/")) { // send a MIME header
           os.print("HTTP/1.0 200 OK\r\n");
           Date now = new Date();
           os.print("Date: " + now + "\r\n");
           os.print("Server: jhttp 1.0\r\n");
           os.print("Content-length: " + theData.length + "\r\n");
           os.print("Content-type: " + ct + "\r\n\r\n");
         } // end try

         // send the file
         os.write(theData);
         os.close();
       } // end try
       catch (IOException e) { // can't find the file
         if (version.startsWith("HTTP/")) { // send a MIME header
           os.print("HTTP/1.0 404 File Not Found\r\n");
           Date now = new Date();
           os.print("Date: " + now + "\r\n");
```

Example 8–7: The jhttp web server (continued)

```
            os.print("Server: jhttp 1.0\r\n");
            os.print("Content-type: text/html" + "\r\n\r\n");
          }
          os.println("<HTML><HEAD><TITLE>File Not Found</TITLE></HEAD>");
          os.println("<BODY><H1>HTTP Error 404: File Not Found</H1></BODY></HTML>");
          os.close();
        }
      }
      else { // method does not equal "GET"
        if (version.startsWith("HTTP/")) { // send a MIME header
          os.print("HTTP/1.0 501 Not Implemented\r\n");
          Date now = new Date();
          os.print("Date: " + now + "\r\n");
          os.print("Server: jhttp 1.0\r\n");
          os.print("Content-type: text/html" + "\r\n\r\n");
        }
        os.println("<HTML><HEAD><TITLE>Not Implemented</TITLE></HEAD>");
        os.println("<BODY><H1>HTTP Error 501: Not Implemented</H1></BODY></HTML>");
        os.close();
      }
    }
    catch (IOException e) {

    }
    try {
      theConnection.close();
    }
    catch (IOException e) {
    }

  }

  public String guessContentTypeFromName(String name) {
    if (name.endsWith(".html") || name.endsWith(".htm")) return "text/html";
    else if (name.endsWith(".txt") || name.endsWith(".java")) return "text/plain";
    else if (name.endsWith(".gif") ) return "image/gif";
    else if (name.endsWith(".class") ) return "application/octet-stream";
    else if (name.endsWith(".jpg") || name.endsWith(".jpeg")) return "image/jpeg";
    else return "text/plain";
  }

}
```

The main() method of the jhttp class is almost identical to the main() methods of the previous two HTTP servers, with the single difference that you use args[0] to set the document root directory. As usual, most of the processing occurs inside the run() method. Let's look at what it does.

The run() method begins by getting input and output streams from the socket. run() then reads the first line of input from the input stream, and parses the line with a StringTokenizer to get the request method, the file requested, and the HTTP version. Assuming the method is GET, the file that is requested is converted to a filename on the local file system; if the file requested was a directory (i.e., its name ended with a slash), you add the name of an index file. You then discard the rest of the client input, until you reach a blank line, signaling that the client is ready to receive output. (A more advanced web server would read some of this data, particularly the User-Agent, for the logfile.)

Then you open the requested file, and read its contents into a byte array. If the HTTP version is 1.0 or later, you write the appropriate MIME headers on the output stream. To figure out the content type, you call the guessContentTypeFrom-Name() method to map file extensions like *.html* onto MIME types like text/html. You write the byte array containing the file's contents onto the output stream, and close the connection. Exceptions may be thrown at various places if, for example, the file cannot be found or opened. If an exception occurs, you send an appropriate HTTP error message to the client instead of the file's contents.

This server is functional but still rather austere. Here are a few features you might want to think about adding:

1. A Server Administration Interface
2. Support for CGI programs
3. Support for other commands such as POST, HEAD, and PUT
4. A logfile in the common web logfile format
5. Server-side includes
6. Support for multiple document roots, so individual users can have their own sites

Finally, you should spend a little time thinking about ways to optimize this server. If you really want to use jhttpd to run a high-traffic site, there are a couple of things you can do to speed this server up.

The first and most important is to use a Just-in-Time compiler like Symantec's or Borland's. JITs often improve program performance by as much as two orders of magnitude.

The second thing you should do is implement smart caching. Keep track of the requests you've received, and store the most frequently requested files in a Hashtable so they're kept in memory. Use a low priority thread to update this cache.

9

UDP Datagrams and Sockets

What Is a UDP Datagram?

In the previous chapters, we discussed how to write several kinds of applications using the TCP protocol. TCP is designed for reliable transmission of data. If data is lost or damaged in transmission, TCP ensures that the data is sent again; if packets of data arrive out of order, TCP puts them back in the correct order for you. A program never needs to worry about receiving data that is out of order or incorrect. However, this reliability comes at a price: speed. Establishing and tearing down TCP connections can take a fair amount of time, particularly for protocols like HTTP that tend to require many short transmissions.

TCP's "poor cousin" is UDP, User Datagram Protocol. It is an alternative protocol for sending data over IP that is very quick, but not reliable. That is, when you send UDP data, you have no way of knowing whether it arrived, much less whether different pieces of data arrived in the order in which you sent them. The obvious question to ask is why anyone would ever use such a protocol. Surely if we have data worth sending, we care about whether the data arrives correctly?

Clearly, UDP isn't a good match for applications like FTP that require reliable transmission of data over potentially unreliable networks. However, there are many kinds of applications in which raw speed is more important than getting every bit right. For example, if you're sending real-time audio or video data, lost or misplaced packets of data will simply appear as static. Static is tolerable, but awkward pauses in the audio stream, when TCP requests a retransmission or waits for a wayward packet to arrive, are unacceptable. In other applications, reliability tests can be implemented in the application layer. For example, if a client sends a short UDP request to a server, it may assume that the packet is lost if no response is returned within an established period of time; this is how the Domain Name System (DNS) works. In fact, you could implement a file transfer protocol using UDP, and many people have: the NFS (Network File System), TFTP (Trivial FTP), and FSP (a more distant relative of FTP) all use UDP.[*] In these cases, the application is responsible for reliability; UDP doesn't do it for you. That is, the application must take care of missing or out-of-order packets. This is a lot of work, but there's no reason it can't be done—though if you find yourself writing this code, you should think carefully about whether you wouldn't be better off with TCP.

To understand the difference between TCP and UDP, it's helpful to think about the difference between the phone system and the post office. TCP is like the phone system. When you dial a number, the phone is answered, and a connection is established between the two parties. As you talk, you know the other party hears your words in the order in which you say them. If the phone is busy or no one answers, you find out right away. UDP, by contrast, is like the postal system. You send packets of mail to an address. Most of the letters arrive, but some may be lost on the way. The letters probably arrive in the order in which you sent them, but there's no guarantee. The further away you are from your recipient, the more likely it becomes that mail will be lost on the way or arrive out of order. If this is a problem, you can write sequential numbers on the envelopes, ask the recipients to arrange them in the correct order, and send you mail requesting a resend of any letters that did not arrive. However, you and your correspondent need to agree on this protocol in advance. The post office will not do it for you.

Both the phone system and the postal system have their uses. Although either can be used for almost any communication, in some cases one is definitely superior to the other. The same is true of UDP and TCP. The last four chapters have all focused on TCP applications, which are far more common than UDP applications. However, UDP also has its place; in this chapter, we'll look at what you can do with UDP in Java. If you want to go further, look at Chapter 13, *Multicast Sockets*. Multicasting is an important area of experimentation, and relies on UDP; a multicast socket is a fairly simple variation on a UDP socket.

Java's implementation of UDP is split into two classes: `DatagramPacket` and `DatagramSocket`. The `DatagramPacket` class stuffs bytes of data into UDP packets called datagrams, and lets you unstuff datagrams that you receive. A `DatagramSocket` both sends and receives UDP datagrams. Therefore, to send data, you put the data in a `DatagramPacket`, and send the packet using a `DatagramSocket`; to receive data, you receive a `DatagramPacket` object from a `DatagramSocket`, and then read the contents of the packet. The sockets themselves are very simple animals. In UDP,

---

[*] The latest version of NFS can use either UDP or TCP.

everything about a datagram, including the address to which it is directed, is included in the packet itself; the socket only needs to know the local port on which to listen or send.

This division of labor contrasts with the Socket and ServerSocket classes used by TCP. First, UDP doesn't have any notion of a server socket. You use the same kind of socket to send data and to listen for incoming connections. Second, although TCP ultimately packetizes the data you send, TCP sockets allow you to treat a network connection as a stream; you send and receive with input and output streams that you get from the socket. UDP doesn't allow this; you always work with individual datagram packets. All the data you stuff into a single datagram is sent as a single packet, and is either received or lost as a group. One packet is not related to the next, and there is no way to determine which packet is first and which is second. Instead of the orderly queue of data that's necessary for a stream, datagrams try to crowd into the recipient as quickly as possible, like a crowd of people pushing their way onto a bus. A third difference, a consequence of the first two, is that a single DatagramSocket can receive data from many independent hosts. The socket isn't dedicated to a single connection, as it is in TCP. In fact, UDP doesn't have any concept of a connection between two hosts; it only knows about individual datagrams. Figuring out who sent what data is the application's responsibility.

The DatagramPacket Class

The Constructors

There are two constructors for DatagramPacket objects. You use the first constructor when you want to receive data from the net; the second is for data that you will send to the net. This is a little unusual. Normally constructors are polymorphic, to let you provide different kinds of information when you create an object, not to give you objects of the same class that will be used in different ways. In this case, both constructors accept a byte array that is used as a buffer for data, and the length of that buffer. When you want to receive a datagram, these are the only arguments you provide; in addition, the data buffer should be empty. When you use this DatagramPacket to receive data, Java fills in its data buffer and several of its fields: the remote Internet address, and the port from which the packet came.

You use the second DatagramPacket constructor to create a datagram you will send to the net. Like the first, this constructor requires a buffer and length, but it also requires the InetAddress and port the packet is to be sent to. In this case, you will pass a buffer containing the data you want to send (not an empty buffer) to the constructor. The DatagramSocket reads the destination address and port from the packet; the address and port aren't stored within the socket, as they are in TCP.

public DatagramPacket(byte buffer[], int length)

This constructor creates a new DatagramPacket that receives data. buffer is a byte array in which the data will be placed. When a datagram is received, the data is stored in buffer, beginning at buffer[0] and continuing until the packet is completely stored, or until length bytes have been written into the buffer. length must be less than or equal to buffer.length. If you try to construct a Datagram-Packet with a length that is greater than buffer.length, the constructor will throw an IllegalArgumentException. This is a RuntimeException, so your code is not required to catch it; however, you should do so if you want your application to be robust. It is all right to construct a DatagramPacket with a length that is less than buffer.length. In this case, at most, the first length bytes of buffer[] will be filled when the datagram is received.

Although the constructor does not really care how large the buffer is, a datagram can be, at most, 64 kilobytes in length (65,535 bytes). Some of this space is taken up by the headers: 8 bytes for the UDP header, and at least 20 bytes (though possibly as many as 60) for the IP header. Therefore, the largest datagram that you could receive would actually have only 65,507 bytes of data.

Choosing a Packet Size

The amount of data that you can stuff into one packet depends on the situation. Some protocols dictate the size of the packet. For example, *rlogin* transmits each character to the remote system almost as soon as the user types it. Therefore, the packets it sends tend to be short: a single byte of data, plus a few bytes of headers. Other applications aren't so picky. For example, file transfer is more efficient with large buffers; the only requirement is that you split files into packets that are smaller than the maximum allowable packet size (64 kilobytes).

Several factors are involved in choosing the optimal packet size. If the network is highly unreliable, such as a packet radio network, smaller packets are preferable, since they are less likely to be corrupted in transit. On the other hand, very fast and reliable LANs should use the largest packet size possible. Newer technologies, like gigabit Ethernet, will most likely require a revision of the IP protocol to allow for packets larger than 64K, in order to achieve maximum efficiency. Eight kilobytes, that is, 8192 bytes, is a good compromise for many types of networks.

Example 9–1 creates a new DatagramPacket for receiving a datagram of up to 8096 bytes.

Example 9–1: Construct a DatagramPacket to receive data

```
import java.net.*;

public class UDPReceiver {

  public static void main(String args[]) {

    byte[] buffer = new byte[8096];
    DatagramPacket dp = new DatagramPacket(buffer, buffer.length);

  }

}
```

public DatagramPacket(byte buffer[], int length, InetAddress ia, int port)

This constructor creates a new DatagramPacket to be sent to another host. You fill the packet with the data already stored in the buffer array. length is the number of bytes to be sent. If you try to construct a DatagramPacket with a length that is greater than buffer.length, the constructor throws an IllegalArgumentException. It's OK to construct a DatagramPacket with a length less than buffer.length. In this case, only the first length bytes of buffer[] will be sent over the network. The InetAddress object ia points to the packet's destination host; the int argument port is the destination port.

Although the constructor doesn't care how large the buffer is, a datagram can be at most 64 kilobytes in length (65,535 bytes). Some of this is taken up by headers: 8 bytes for the UDP header, and at least 20 bytes (possibly as many as 60) for the IP header. Therefore, the largest datagram you can send has 65,467 bytes of data; you can send more if you know which IP options are in effect, but Java doesn't give you access to most of them. Assuming the largest possible IP header makes your code simpler and only wastes 40 bytes per datagram.

It's customary to convert the data to a byte array and place it in buffer before creating the DatagramPacket, but it's not absolutely necessary. Changing the data in buffer after the datagram has been constructed and before it has been sent changes the data in the datagram; the data isn't copied into a private buffer. In some applications, you can take advantage of this. For example, you could store data that changes over time in buffer[] and send out the current datagram (with the most recent data) every minute. However, it's more important to make sure that your data doesn't change when you don't want it to. This is especially true if your program is multithreaded, and different threads may write into the data buffer. If this is the case, synchronize the buffer variable or copy the data into a temporary buffer before you construct the DatagramPacket.

Example 9–2 creates a new DatagramPacket filled with the data "This is a test." As you see, most of the effort in creating a new DatagramPacket involves translating the data into a byte array. Since you are sending an ASCII String, you use the getBytes() method of java.lang.String to convert the String into a byte array.

TIP   Since getBytes() only returns the low order eight bits of each character in the string, this code won't work for full Unicode strings, only for ISO-Latin-1 strings. If you want to convert Unicode strings into bytes, you'll have to use getChars(), and then convert each Unicode character into two bytes. At present, most Internet services only understand ASCII, so Unicode only makes sense when you're working with a custom protocol.

Example 9–2: Construct a DatagramPacket to send data

```
import java.net.*;

public class UDPSender {

  public static void main(String args[]) {

    String s = "This is a test.";

    byte[] data = new byte[s.length()];
    s.getBytes(0, s.length(), data, 0);
    try {
      InetAddress ia = InetAddress.getByName("sunsite.unc.edu");
      int port = 7;
      DatagramPacket dp = new DatagramPacket(data, data.length, ia, port);
    }
    catch (UnknownHostException e) {
    }

  }

}
```

The get Methods

These four methods let you retrieve different parts of a datagram: its contents, plus several fields from its header. The datagram starts with an IP header, which contains the address of the host the packet came from, and the address of the host to which it is going. The IP header is followed by a UDP header that is 8 bytes long and is defined by RFC768. The first two bytes are an unsigned integer containing the port from which the datagram was sent. The second pair of bytes (the third and fourth bytes) is the port to which the datagram is sent. The third pair of bytes is the length of the datagram, including this header, and the final pair of bytes is a checksum that can be used to ensure reliable transmission, but is often set to zero instead. Everything after the two headers is the datagram's contents.

public InetAddress getAddress()

getAddress() returns an InetAddress object that is the address of the remote host. If the datagram was received from the Internet, the address returned is the address of the machine from which it was sent. On the other hand, if the datagram was created locally in order to be sent to a remote machine, this method returns the address of the host to which the datagram is addressed. This is most commonly used to determine the address of the host that sent a UDP datagram, so that you can reply.

public int getPort()

getPort() returns an integer that is the datagram's port on the remote machine. If this datagram was received from the Internet, this is the port on the host that sent the packet. If the datagram was created locally to be sent to a remote host, this is the port to which this packet is addressed on the remote machine.

public byte[] getData()

The getData() method returns a byte array that contains the bytes of data from the datagram. It is usually necessary to convert the bytes into some other form of data before they'll be useful to your program. The most common way to do this is to change the byte array into a String using the following String constructor:

```
public String(byte[] buffer, int high_byte, int start, int num_bytes)
```

In this constructor, the first argument, buffer, is the array of bytes that contains the data from the datagram. This constructor presumes that each byte represents an ASCII character. However, Java strings are made up of two-byte Unicode characters, so an extra byte must be added to each character. This is the high_byte argument, and it is almost always 0. The start argument is the first element of the array to convert; elements prior to array[start] are ignored. getData() places the data in the byte array, starting with the first element (0), so that start will always be 0. Finally, num_bytes is the number of bytes in the array to use. This is

not necessarily the same as the length of the array, because the buffer may not
have been completely filled. To get the number of elements that were actually
used, call getLength() (discussed later) to tell you how much of the buffer was
actually filled. Thus, given a DatagramPacket dp received from the network, you
can convert it to a String s like this:

```
String s = new String(dp.getData(), 0, 0, dp.getLength());
```

If the String has special formatting or significance, it can be parsed with
java.util.StringTokenizer.

If the data in the datagram is not ASCII text, converting it to Java data is more difficult. One approach is to convert the byte array returned by getData() into a
ByteArrayInputStream using this constructor:

```
public ByteArrayInputStream(byte[] buffer, int offset, int num_bytes)
```

buffer is the byte array to be used as an InputStream. It's important to specify the
portion of the buffer that you want to use as an InputStream using the offset and
num_bytes arguments. When converting datagram data into InputStream objects,
offset is always 0, and num_bytes is given by the DatagramPacket object's
getLength() method:

```
ByteArrayInputStream bis =
    new ByteArrayInputStream(dp.getData(), 0, dp.getLength());
```

The ByteArrayInputStream can then be chained to a DataInputStream:

```
DataInputStream dis = new DataInputStream(bis);
```

You can read the data using the DataInputStream's readInt(), readLong(), read-
Char(), and other methods. Of course, you are assuming that the datagram's
sender uses the same data formats as Java; this will always be the case when the
sender is written in Java, and will usually (but not necessarily) be the case otherwise. (Most modern computers use the same floating-point format as Java, and any
well-behaved network software should send multibyte data in Network Byte Order,
which also matches Java's requirements.) DataInputStreams are also useful for
reading large ASCII datagrams a line at a time with readLine(). Another approach
would be to use a StreamTokenizer to read successive words in the byte array. Both
of these approaches are rather unusual, though, since most UDP datagrams contain a line's worth of data at most.

public int getLength()

The getLength() method returns the number of bytes of the data in the datagram.
If the datagram was received from the network, the int returned by getLength()

should be equal to the length of the array returned by getData() (i.e., get-Data().length). If the datagram was created on the local host, it is possible that the int returned by getLength() is less than the length of the array returned by getData().

Example 9–3 expands on Example 9–2 by using all the methods covered in this section to print the information in the DatagramPacket. This example is a little artificial; because you create the DatagramPacket, you already know what's in it. More often, you'll use these methods on a DatagramPacket received from the net, but that will have to wait for the introduction of the DatagramSocket class in the next section.

Example 9–3: Construct a DatagramPacket to receive data

```
import java.net.*;

public class getDatagramExample {

  public static void main(String args[]) {

    String s = "This is a test.";

    byte[] data = new byte[s.length()];
    s.getBytes(0, s.length(), data, 0);
    try {
      InetAddress ia = InetAddress.getByName("sunsite.unc.edu");
      int port = 7;
      DatagramPacket dp = new DatagramPacket(data, data.length, ia, port);
      System.out.println("This packet is addressed to " + dp.getAddress() +
                      " on port " + dp.getPort());
      System.out.println("There are " + dp.getLength() +
                      " bytes of data in the packet");
      System.out.println(new String(dp.getData(), 0, 0, dp.getLength()));
    }
    catch (UnknownHostException e) {
      System.err.println(e);
    }

  }

}
```

Here's the output:

```
% java getDatagramExample
This packet is addressed to sunsite.unc.edu/152.2.254.81 on port 7
There are 15 bytes of data in the packet
This is a test.
%
```

The DatagramSocket Class

To send or receive a DatagramPacket, open a DatagramSocket. As with Datagram-Packets, the DatagramSocket class has two constructors, to be used in different situations. All DatagramSockets are bound to a local port on which they listen for incoming data. The local port is placed in the header of outgoing datagrams. If you're writing a client, you don't care what the local port is, so you call a constructor that lets the system assign an unused port (an anonymous port). The server sends its reply to the local port from which the datagram originated. If you're writing a server, clients need to know the port the server will be listening on for incoming datagrams; therefore, when a server constructs a DatagramSocket, it must specify the local port. However, the sockets used by clients and servers are otherwise identical: they differ only in whether they use an anonymous (system-assigned) or a well-known port. There's no distinction between plain sockets and server sockets, as there is with TCP; there is no such thing as a DatagramServer-Socket.

The Constructors

public DatagramSocket() throws SocketException

This constructor creates a socket that is bound to an anonymous port. (The destination port is part of the DatagramPacket, not the DatagramSocket.) You use this constructor in a client that initiates a conversation with a server. In this situation, you don't care what port you're using; the server will send its response to the port the datagram originated from. Letting the system assign a port means you don't have to worry about finding an unused port. If for some reason you need to know the local port, you can find it with the getLocalPort() method described later.

The same socket may be used to receive the datagrams a server sends back to it. A SocketException is thrown if the socket can't be created. It's unusual for this constructor to throw an exception; it's hard to imagine situations in which the socket could not be opened, especially since the system gets to choose the local port.

Example 9–4: Create a DatagramSocket on an unspecified port

```
import java.net.*;

public class DatagramSocketExample {

  public static void main(String[] args) {

    try {
      DatagramSocket theClient = new DatagramSocket();
    }
    catch (SocketException e) {
    }
```

Example 9–4: Create a DatagramSocket on an unspecified port (continued)

```
  }

}
```

public DatagramSocket(int port) throws SocketException

This constructor creates a socket that listens for incoming datagrams on a specific port, specified by the port argument. You can use this constructor to write a server that listens on a preassigned port; if servers listened on anonymous ports, clients wouldn't be able to contact them. A SocketException is thrown if the socket can't be created. There are two common reasons this constructor fails: the specified port is already in use, or you're trying to connect to a port below 1024 and you don't have sufficient privileges (i.e., you're not root on a UNIX system; for better or worse, other platforms let anyone connect to low-numbered ports).

TCP ports and UDP ports aren't related. Two unrelated servers or clients can use the same port if one uses UDP and the other uses TCP. Example 9–5 is a port scanner that looks for UDP ports in use on the local host. It decides the port is in use if the DatagramSocket constructor throws an exception. As written, it looks at ports from 1024 up. You can easily extend it to check ports below 1024.

Example 9–5: Look for local UDP ports

```
import java.net.*;

public class lookForLocalUDPPorts {

  public static void main(String[] args) {

    DatagramSocket theServer;

    for (int i = 1024; i <= 65535; i++) {
      try {
        // the next line will fail and drop into the catch block if
        // there is already a server running on port i
        theServer = new DatagramSocket(i);
        theServer.close();
      }
      catch (SocketException e) {
        System.out.println("There is a server on port " + i + ".");
      }// end try
    }// end for

  }

}
```

The speed at which lookForLocalUDPPorts runs depends strongly on the speed of your machine and its UDP implementation. I've clocked Example 9–5 at as little as

two minutes on a moderately powered SPARCstation and as long as an hour on a
PowerBook 5300. Here are the results from one SPARCstation:

```
% java lookForLocalUDPPorts
There is a server on port 2049.
There is a server on port 4045.
There is a server on port 32771.
There is a server on port 32773.
There is a server on port 32778.
There is a server on port 32779.
There is a server on port 32787.
There is a server on port 32788.
There is a server on port 32790.
There is a server on port 32793.
There is a server on port 32797.
There is a server on port 32804.
There is a server on port 32812.
There is a server on port 32822.
There is a server on port 32834.
There is a server on port 32852.
There is a server on port 32857.
There is a server on port 32858.
There is a server on port 32860.
There is a server on port 32871.
There is a server on port 32877.
There is a server on port 33943.
There is a server on port 34955.
There is a server on port 35977.
There is a server on port 35982.
There is a server on port 36000.
There is a server on port 36159.
There is a server on port 36259.
%
```

The high-numbered UDP ports in the 30,000 range are Remote Procedure Call
(RPC) services. Aside from RPC, some common protocols that use UDP are NFS,
TFTP, and FSP.

public DatagramSocket(int port, InetAddress intf)
throws SocketException (Java 1.1 only)

This constructor is primarily used on multihomed hosts; it creates a socket that listens for incoming datagrams on a specific port and network interface. The port
argument is the port this socket listens for datagrams on. As with TCP sockets, you
need to be root on a UNIX system to create a DatagramSocket on a port below
1024. The intf argument is an InetAddress object for one of the host's network
addresses. A SocketException is thrown if the socket can't be created. There are
three common reasons for this constructor to fail: the specified port is already

occupied, you are trying to connect to a port below 1024, and you don't have sufficient privileges (i.e., you are not root on a UNIX system), or intf is not the
address of one of the system's network interfaces.

Sending and Receiving Datagrams

public void send(DatagramPacket dp) throws IOException

Once a DatagramPacket is created and a DatagramSocket is constructed, you send
the packet by passing it to the socket's send() method. For example, if theSocket
is a DatagramSocket object, and theOutput is a DatagramPacket object, you send
theOutput using theSocket like this:

```
theSocket.send(theOutput);
```

If there's a problem sending the data, an IOException may be thrown. Most of the
time this means that the SecurityManager won't let you communicate with the
host the packet is addressed to. This is primarily a problem for applets. You don't
get an exception if the packet doesn't arrive at its destination.

Example 9–6 is a UDP-based discard client. It reads lines of user input from Sys-
tem.in, and sends them to a discard server that simply discards all the data. Each
line is stuffed in a DatagramPacket. Many of the simpler Internet protocols like discard have both TCP and UDP implementations.

Example 9–6: A UDP discard client

```
import java.net.*;
import java.io.*;

public class UDPDiscardClient {

  public final static int port = 9;

  public static void main(String[] args) {

    String hostname;

    if (args.length > 0) {
      hostname = args[0];
    }
    else {
      hostname = "localhost";
    }

    try {

      String theLine;
      DatagramPacket theOutput;

      InetAddress server = InetAddress.getByName(hostname);
```

Example 9–6: A UDP discard client (continued)

```
      DataInputStream userInput = new DataInputStream(System.in);
      DatagramSocket theSocket = new DatagramSocket();
      while (true) {
        theLine = userInput.readLine();
        if (theLine.equals(".")) break;
        byte[] data = new byte[theLine.length()];
        theLine.getBytes(0, theLine.length(), data, 0);
        theOutput = new DatagramPacket(data, data.length, server, port);
        theSocket.send(theOutput);
      } // end while
    } // end try
    catch (UnknownHostException e) {
      System.err.println(e);
    }
    catch (SocketException se) {
      System.err.println(se);
    }
    catch (IOException e) {
      System.err.println(e);
    }

  } // end main

}
```

The `UDPDiscardClient` class should look familiar. It has a single field, `port`, set to the default port for the discard protocol (port 9), and a single method, `main()`. The `main()` method reads a hostname from the command line, and converts that hostname to the `InetAddress` object called `server`. A `DataInputStream` is chained to `System.in` to read user input from the keyboard. You then create a `Datagram-Socket` object called `theSocket`. After creating the socket, you enter an infinite while loop that reads user input, line by line. In the `while` loop, each line is converted to a byte array using the `getBytes()` method, and the bytes are stuffed in a new `DatagramPacket`, `theOutput`. Finally, the `theOutput` is sent over `theSocket`, and the loop restarts. If at any point the user types a period on a line by itself, the program exits. The `DatagramSocket` constructor may throw a `SocketException`, so that needs to be caught. Because this is a discard client, you don't need to worry about data coming back from the server.

public void receive(DatagramPacket dp) throws IOException

This method receives a single UDP datagram from the network and converts it to a `DatagramPacket` object. Like the `accept()` method in the `ServerSocket` class, this method stops program execution, and waits until a datagram arrives. If your program does anything besides wait for datagrams, you should call `receive()` in a separate thread.

The datagram's buffer should be large enough to hold the data received. If not, receive() places as much data in the buffer as it can hold; the rest is lost. It may be useful to remember that the maximum size of the data portion of a UDP datagram is 65,507 bytes. Some application protocols that use UDP further restrict the maximum number of bytes in a packet; for instance, NFS uses a maximum packet size of 8192 bytes.

NOTE   Why 65,507 bytes? Remember that the UDP protocol includes an
              eight-byte header. Two of those bytes are an unsigned two-byte inte-
              ger whose value ranges from 0 to 65,535. This integer is the length of
              the datagram including the header. Once eight bytes for the UDP
              header and a minimum of twenty bytes for the IP header are sub-
              tracted, the maximum space available for data is 65,507 bytes.

If there's a problem receiving the data, an IOException may be thrown. Example 9–7 is a UDP discard server that receives incoming datagrams. Just for fun, it logs the data in each datagram to System.out so you can see who's sending what to your discard server.

Example 9–7: The UDPDiscardServer

```
import java.net.*;
import java.io.*;

public class UDPDiscardServer {

  public final static int discardPort = 9;
  static byte[] buffer = new byte[65507];

  public static void main(String[] args) {

    int port;

    try {
      port = Integer.parseInt(args[0]);
    }
    catch (Exception e) {
      port = discardPort;
    }

    try {
      DatagramSocket ds = new DatagramSocket(port);
      while (true) {
        DatagramPacket dp = new DatagramPacket(buffer, buffer.length);
        try {
          ds.receive(dp);
          String s = new String(dp.getData(), 0, 0, dp.getLength());
          System.out.println(dp.getAddress() + " at port " + dp.getPort() +
            " says " + s);
```

Example 9–7: The UDPDiscardServer (continued)

```
      }
      catch (IOException e) {
        System.err.println(e);
      }
     }// end while
  } // end try
  catch (SocketException se) {
    System.err.println(se);
  } // end catch

 } // end main

}
```

This is a simple class with a single method, `main()`. It reads the port for the server to listen to from the command line. If the port is not specified on the command line, it is set to 9. We open a `DatagramSocket` on that port, and create a `Datagram-Packet` with a 65,507 byte buffer—large enough to receive any possible packet. The server enters an infinite loop that receives packets and prints the contents and the originating host on the console. A high-performance discard server would skip this step. Try running the discard client on one machine and connecting to the discard server on a second machine to verify that both these programs work.

public int getLocalPort()

A `DatagramSocket`'s `getLocalPort()` method returns an `int` that represents the local port on which this socket is listening. You use this method if you create a `DatagramSocket` with an anonymous port and want to find out what port you've been assigned. Example 9–8 creates a `DatagramSocket` and prints its local port.

Example 9–8: Create a DatagramSocket on an unspecified port

```
import java.net.*;

public class getLocalPortExample {

  public static void main(String[] args) {

    try {
      DatagramSocket ds = new DatagramSocket();
      System.out.println("The DatagramSocket is on port " + ds.getLocalPort());
    }
    catch (SocketException e) {
    }

  }

}
```

public synchronized void close()

Calling a `DatagramSocket` object's `close()` method frees the port occupied by that socket. For example:

```
try {
  DatagramSocket theServer = new DatagramSocket();
  theServer.close();
}
```

It's never a bad idea to close a `DatagramSocket` when you're through with it; it's particularly important to close an unneeded socket if your program will continue to run for a significant amount of time. For example, the `close()` method was essential in Example 9–5, `lookForLocalUDPPorts`; if this program did not close the sockets it opened, it would tie up every UDP port on the system for a significant amount of time. On the other hand, if the program ends as soon as you're through with the `DatagramSocket`, you don't need to close the socket explicitly; the socket is automatically closed on garbage collection. However, closing unneeded sockets never hurts, and is good programming practice.

Socket Options (Java 1.1)

The only socket option that is supported for datagram sockets in Java 1.1 is SO_TIMEOUT. SO_TIMEOUT is the amount of time, in milliseconds, that `receive()` waits for an incoming connection before throwing an `Interrupte-dIOException`. Its value must be non-negative. If SO_TIMEOUT is 0, `receive()` never times out.

There are few situations in which you would need to set SO_TIMEOUT. You might need it if you were implementing a secure protocol that required responses to occur within a fixed amount of time. You might also decide that the host you're communicating with is dead (unreachable or not responding) if you don't receive a response in a certain amount of time.

public synchronized void setSoTimeout(int timeout)
throws SocketException

The `setSoTimeout()` method sets the SO_TIMEOUT field for a datagram socket. When the timeout expires, an `InterruptedException` is thrown. You should set this option *before* you call `receive()`. You cannot change it while `receive()` is waiting for a connection. The `timeout` argument must be greater than or equal to zero; if it is not, `setSoTimeout()` throws a `SocketException`. For example:

```
try {
  buffer = new byte[2056];
  DatagramPacket dp = new DatagramPacket(buffer, buffer.length);
  DatagramSocket ds = new ServerSocket(2048);
```

```
ds.setSoTimeout(30000); // block for no more than 30 seconds
try {
 ds.receive(dp);
   // process the packet
   ...
 }
 catch (InterruptedException e) {
   ss.close();
   System.err.println("No connection within 30 seconds");
 }
catch (SocketException e) {
  System.err.println(e);
}
catch (IOException e) {
  System.err.println("Unexpected IOException: " + e);
}
```

public synchronized int getSoTimeout() throws IOException

The getSoTimeout() method returns the current value of this DatagramSocket object's SO_TIMEOUT field. For example:

```
public void printSoTimeout(DatagramSocket ds) {

  int timeout = ds.getSoTimeOut();
  if (timeout > 0) {
    System.out.println(ds + " will time out after " + timeout + "milliseconds.");
  }
  else if (timeout == 0) {
    System.out.println(ds + " will never time out.");
  }
  else {
    System.out.println("Something is seriously wrong with " + ds);
  }

}
```

The Object Methods

The only method from java.lang.Object overridden by either DatagramSocket or DatagramPacket is the finalize() method of DatagramSocket. Neither class has a toString() method, much less a clone() or hashCode() method.

protected synchronized void finalize()

This method is called before a DatagramSocket object is garbage collected. Its primary purpose is to close the socket. It is protected, and you should not need to call it directly.

A Higher Level of Abstraction

DatagramPackets and DatagramSockets are a little too close to the metal for easy programming. Especially when writing client software, there's no good reason why you should need to worry about DatagramPackets. As an application programmer, you care about sending and receiving data, perhaps in the form of byte arrays, perhaps in the form of strings, perhaps in some other form; but you almost certainly don't care about DatagramPackets. The following UDPClient class takes you away from all that.

The UDPClient class sends and receives UDP data in its native format (as byte arrays or strings). You do not need to convert data to DatagramPacket objects before sending it, and you don't need to construct an empty DatagramPacket before data is received. You construct a UDPClient object by passing it an Internet address and a port. The address may be an InetAddress, a string containing a hostname, or a string containing the host's numeric IP address in "dotted quad" format. To send data, pass it to the send() method. Example 9–9 has overloaded send() methods for byte arrays and Strings; you can subclass or modify this class to add additional send() methods for other datatypes if you need them. To receive data, call receive() to get a byte array or receiveString() to get a String.

This class is more robust than raw UDP sockets. Among other things, it checks to see that the data sent will fit in a single datagram, and that incoming data is coming from the correct remote server.

Example 9–9: The UDPClient class

```java
import java.net.*;
import java.io.*;

/**
 * This class allows you to send and receive Strings and byte arrays via UDP
 * without concerning yourself with DatagramPackets and DatagramSockets.
 * @version 1.0 of June 1, 1996
 * @author Elliotte Rusty Harold
 */
public class UDPClient {

  InetAddress ia;
  int port;
  DatagramSocket ds;

  /**
   * Creates a new UDPClient.
   * @param ia The InetAddress of the remote host to which data will be sent
   * @param port The port on the remote host to which data will be sent
   * @throws SocketException
```

Example 9–9: The UDPClient class (continued)

```
  */
  public UDPClient(InetAddress ia, int port) throws SocketException {

    this.ia = ia;
    this.port = port;
    ds = new DatagramSocket();

  }

  public UDPClient(String hostname, int port)
      throws UnknownHostException, SocketException {

    this(InetAddress.getByName(hostname), port);

  }

  /**
   * This method sends data to the remote host via UDP. If the byte is longer than
   * the maximum reliable length of a UDP Datagram (64900) bytes then an
   * IOException is thrown
   * @param buffer A byte array containing the data to be sent
   * @throws IOException
   */
  public void send(byte[] buffer) throws IOException {

    if (buffer.length > 64900) throw new IOException();
    DatagramPacket dp = new DatagramPacket(buffer, buffer.length, ia, port);
    ds.send(dp);

  }

  /**
   * This method sends an ISO-Latin-1 string to the remote host via UDP.
   * The string will be truncated to ISO-Latin-1 even if it's Unicode.
   * @param s The string to be sent
   * @throws IOException
   */
  public void send(String s) throws IOException {

    byte[] data = new byte[s.length()];
    s.getBytes(0, s.length(), data, 0);
    send(data);

  }

  /**
   * This method sends an empty datagram to the remote host via UDP.
   * @throws IOException
   */
  public void send() throws IOException {

    byte[] b = new byte[1];
```

Example 9–9: The UDPClient class (continued)

```java
    send(b);

  }

  /**
   * This method blocks until a UDP Datagram is received from the host with
   * which this UDPClient communicates. This can be an indefinite amount of time
   * if the host is unreachable so calls to this method should be placed in a
   * separate thread from the main program.
   * @return the data received as a byte array
   * @throws IOException
   */
  public synchronized byte[] receive() throws IOException {

    byte[] buffer = new byte[65507];
    DatagramPacket incoming = new DatagramPacket(buffer, buffer.length);
    ds.receive(incoming);
    // a client should only receive data from the host to
    while ( !incoming.getAddress().equals(ia)) {
      ds.receive(incoming);
    }
    return incoming.getData();

  }

  /**
   * This method blocks until a UDP Datagram is received from the host with
   * which this UDPClient communicates. This can be an indefinite amount of time
   * if the host is unreachable so calls to this method should be placed in a
   * separate thread from the main program. When data is received it is
   * converted into an ISO-Latin-1 String and returned.
   * @return the data received as a byte array
   * @throws IOException
   */
  public synchronized String receiveString() throws IOException {

    byte[] data = receive();
    return new String(data, 0, 0, data.length);

  }

  /**
   * @return the port which this object sends data to
   */
  public int getPort() {

    return port;

  }

  /**
   * @return the port which this client is bound to
```

Example 9–9: The UDPClient class (continued)

```
  */
  public int getLocalPort() {

    return ds.getLocalPort();

  }

  /**
   * @return the InetAddress which this client sends data to
   */
  public InetAddress getAddress() {

    return ia;

  }

  /**
   * @return a String showing the remote host and port which this client
   * sends data to
   */
  public String toString() {

    return ia + ":" + port;

  }

}
```

Some Useful Applications

In this section, you'll see several Internet servers and clients that use Datagram-
Packets and DatagramSockets. Some of these will be familiar from the last two
chapters.

Many simple Internet protocols have both TCP and UDP implementations. When
an IP packet is received by a host, the host determines whether the packet is a TCP
packet or a UDP datagram by inspecting the IP header. As I said earlier, there's no
connection between UDP and TCP ports; TCP and UDP servers can share the
same port number without problems. By convention, if a service has both TCP and
UDP implementations, it uses the same port for both, though there's no absolute
reason this has to be the case.

Simple UDP Clients

Several Internet services only need to know the client's address and port; they discard any data the client sends in its datagrams. Daytime, quote of the day, and

chargen are three such protocols. Each of these responds the same way, regardless of the data contained in the datagram, or even regardless of whether there is data in the datagram. Clients for these protocols simply send a UDP datagram to the server and read the response that comes back. Therefore, let's begin with a simple client that sends an empty UDP packet to a specified host and port; we will design this class so it can be subclassed to provide specific clients for different protocols.

The UDPPoke class has two fields, both protected so they may be overridden by subclasses. The defaultPort field holds the port the client sends data to, if no other port is specified. In this class it's set to 0. Subclasses override this field with the default port appropriate for their protocol. bufferLength is the length of the buffer needed for incoming data. An 8192-byte buffer is large enough for most of the protocols that UDPPoke is useful for, but it can be increased in a subclass or set from the command line if necessary.

The main() method is invoked from the command line with the hostname, the port, and the buffer length passed as command-line arguments. If you do not include the hostname, the localhost is used. If the port is not included, the defaultPort is used. If the buffer length is not specified, 8192 bytes is used. For example, to send a packet to the daytime server on port 13 of *sunsite.unc.edu* you would type:

```
% java UDPPoke sunsite.unc.edu 13
Sat May 18 15:56:36 1996
```

Once the port and host are known, a new DatagramSocket object ds is created on an anonymous local port. We use the hostname to construct an InetAddress that we then use to create a new DatagramPacket called outgoing, aimed at the host and port specified on the command line. Although in theory, you should be able to send a datagram with no data at all, bugs in some Java implementations require that you add at least one byte of data to the datagram. The simple servers we're currently considering ignore this data.

Next we create a new DatagramPacket with a 8192-byte buffer for the returning datagram. An 8192-byte buffer is large enough for most protocols. However, you can override it in a subclass if necessary. The DatagramSocket ds sends the outgoing packet and then waits to receive the response. When the response is received, UDPPoke converts it into a String and prints it on System.out.

Example 9–10: The UDPPoke class

```
import java.net.*;
import java.io.*;

public class UDPPoke {

  protected static int defaultPort = 0;
```

Example 9–10: The UDPPoke class (continued)

```
protected static int bufferLength = 8192;

public static void main(String[] args) {

  String hostname;
  int port;
  int len;

  if (args.length > 0) {
    hostname = args[0];
  }
  else {
    hostname = "localhost";
    port = defaultPort;
    len = bufferLength;
  }
  try {
    port = Integer.parseInt(args[1]);
  }
  catch (Exception e) {
    port = defaultPort;
  }
  try {
    len = Integer.parseInt(args[2]);
  }
  catch (Exception e) {
    len = bufferLength;
  }

  try {
    DatagramSocket ds = new DatagramSocket(0);
    InetAddress ia = InetAddress.getByName(hostname);
    DatagramPacket outgoing = new DatagramPacket(new byte[512], 1, ia, port);
    DatagramPacket incoming = new DatagramPacket(new byte[len], len);
    ds.send(outgoing);
    ds.receive(incoming);
    System.out.println(new String(incoming.getData(), 0, 0, incoming.getLength()));
  } // end try
  catch (UnknownHostException e) {
    System.err.println(e);
  } // end catch
  catch (SocketException e) {
    System.err.println(e);
  } // end catch
  catch (IOException e) {
    System.err.println(e);
  } // end catch

} // end main


}
```

A daytime client is a trivial extension of UDPPoke; all you need to do is override the default port, as in Example 9–11. The chargen and "quote of the day" protocols are equally trivial, and are left as exercises for you.

Example 9–11: The UDP daytime client

```
public class UDPdaytime extends UDPPoke {

  protected static int defaultPort = 13;

}
```

UDPServer

Clients aren't the only programs that benefit from an object-oriented implementation. The servers for these protocols are also very similar. They all wait for UDP datagrams on a specified port, and reply to each datagram with another datagram. The servers differ only in the content of the datagram that they return. Example 9–12 is a UDPServer class. It will be subclassed to provide specific servers for different protocols. The only reason it isn't implemented as an abstract class is the difficulty of combining both static and abstract methods in one class. (In brief, a static method needs to instantiate a class before it can call a non-static method in that class, but an abstract class can't be instantiated.)

The UDPServer class has two fields, defaultPort and defaultBufferLength, which are protected so they can be overridden by subclasses. The main() method is invoked from the command line, with the port and the buffer length passed as command-line arguments. If the port is not included, the defaultPort is used (though this will be of more use for subclasses). If the buffer length is not specified, 65,507 bytes is used. Once the port and buffer length are known, UDPServer creates a new DatagramSocket ds on the specified port. A new DatagramPacket called ingoing is constructed, with the buffer length specified on the command line. Then UDPServer enters an infinite loop in which the DatagramSocket receives packets. When UDPServer receives a packet, both the packet and the Datagram-Socket ds are passed to the respond() method.

The respond() method sends the response to the originating host, using the Data-gramSocket ds. In this class, the respond() method does nothing. It should be overridden in subclasses that implement particular protocols. It would not be a bad idea to make respond() an abstract method, except that methods may not be both abstract and static.

UDPServer is a very flexible class. Subclasses can send zero, one, or many datagrams in response to each incoming datagram. If a lot of processing is required to respond to a packet, the respond() method can spawn a thread to do it. However, UDP servers tend not to have extended interactions with a client. Each incoming packet is treated independently of other packets, so the response can usually be handled directly in the respond() method without spawning a thread.

Example 9–12: The UDPServer class

```
import java.net.*;
import java.io.*;

public class UDPServer {

  protected static int defaultPort = 0;
  protected static int defaultBufferLength = 65507;

  public static void main(String[] args) {

    DatagramPacket incoming;

    int port;
    int len;

    try {
      port = Integer.parseInt(args[0]);
    }
    catch (Exception e) {
      port = defaultPort;
    }
    try {
      len = Integer.parseInt(args[1]);
    }
    catch (Exception e) {
      len = defaultBufferLength;
    }

    try {
      DatagramSocket ds = new DatagramSocket(port);
      byte[] buffer = new byte[len];
      while (true) {
        incoming = new DatagramPacket(buffer, buffer.length);
        try {
          ds.receive(incoming);
          respond(ds, incoming);
        }
        catch (IOException e) {
          System.err.println(e);
        }
      }// end while
    } // end try
    catch (SocketException se) {
      System.err.println(se);
    } // end catch
```

Example 9–12: The UDPServer class (continued)

```
  } // end main

  public static void respond(DatagramSocket ds, DatagramPacket dp) {
    ;
  }

}
```

As written, `UDPServer` is almost a functional discard server. All you need to change is the port. Example 9–13 adds the proper `defaultPort` for a high-performance UDP discard server that does nothing with incoming packets.

Example 9–13: A high-performance UDP discard server

```
public class FastUDPDiscardServer extends UDPServer {

  static int defaultPort = 9;

}
```

Example 9–14 is a discard server that prints the incoming packets on `System.out`.

Example 9–14: A UDP discard server

```
import java.net.*;

public class UDPDiscardServer extends UDPServer {

  static int defaultPort = 9;

  public static void respond(DatagramSocket ds, DatagramPacket dp) {

    String s = new String(dp.getData(), 0, 0, dp.getLength());
    System.out.println(dp.getAddress() + " at port " + dp.getPort() + " says " +s);

  }

}
```

It isn't much harder to implement an echo server, as Example 9–15 shows.

Example 9–15: A UDP echo server

```
import java.net.*;
import java.io.*;

public class UDPEchoServer extends UDPServer {

  static int defaultPort = 7;

  public static void respond(DatagramSocket ds, DatagramPacket dp) {

    DatagramPacket outgoing;
```

Example 9–15: A UDP echo server (continued)

```
    try {
      outgoing = new DatagramPacket(dp.getData(), dp.getLength(),
                                    dp.getAddress(), dp.getPort());
      ds.send(outgoing);
    }
    catch (IOException e) {
      System.err.println(e);
    }

  }

}
```

A daytime server is only mildly more complex. The server listens for incoming
UDP datagrams on port 13. When a datagram is detected, a response is returned
with the date and time at the server in a one-line ASCII string. Example 9–16
demonstrates this.

Example 9–16: The UDP daytime server

```
import java.net.*;
import java.io.*;
import java.util.Date;

public class UDPDaytimeServer extends UDPServer {

  static int defaultPort = 13;

  public static void respond(DatagramSocket ds, DatagramPacket dp) {

    DatagramPacket outgoing;

    Date now = new Date();
    String s = now.toString();
    byte[] data = new byte[s.length()];
    s.getBytes(0, s.length(), data, 0);
    try {
      outgoing = new DatagramPacket(data, data.length, dp.getAddress(), dp.getPort());
      ds.send(outgoing);
    }
    catch (IOException e) {
      System.err.println(e);
    }

  }

}
```

A UDP Echo Client

The UDPPoke class implemented earlier isn't flexible enough for many protocols. In particular, protocols that require multiple datagrams require a separate implementation. The echo protocol has both TCP and UDP implementations. Implementing the echo protocol with TCP was simple; it's more complex with UDP because you don't have I/O streams or the concept of a connection to work with. A TCP-based echo client can send a message, and wait for a response on the same connection. However, a UDP-based echo client has no guarantee that the message it sent was received. Therefore, it cannot simply wait for the response; it needs to be prepared to send and receive data asynchronously.

This behavior is fairly simple to implement using threads. One thread can process user input, and send it to the echo server, while a second thread accepts input from the server, and displays it to the user. The client is divided into three classes: the main UDPEchoClient class, the echoInputThread class, and the echoOutputThread class.

The UDPEchoClient class should look familiar. It reads a hostname from the command line, and converts that to an InetAddress object. It then creates a DatagramSocket pointing to that server on the echoPort (7), and passes the InetAddress and the DatagramSocket into the constructor for the echoInputThread. This constructor can throw a SocketException, so you must catch the exception. Then we start the echoInputThread. Finally, we use the same DatagramSocket to construct an echoOutputThread, that we then start. It's important to use the same DatagramSocket for both sending and receiving data, because the echo server will send the response back to the port the data was sent from. Example 9–17 lists the code for our UDPEchoClient.

Example 9–17: The UDPEchoClient class

```
import java.net.*;
import java.io.*;

public class UDPEchoClient {

  public static void main(String[] args) {

    String hostname;
    int echoPort = 7;

    if (args.length > 0) {
    hostname = args[0];
    }
    else {
      hostname = "localhost";
    }
```

Example 9–17: The UDPEchoClient class (continued)

```
    try {
       InetAddress ia = InetAddress.getByName(hostname);
       DatagramSocket theSocket = new DatagramSocket();
       echoInputThread eit = new echoInputThread(ia, theSocket);
       eit.start();
       echoOutputThread eot = new echoOutputThread(theSocket);
       eot.start();
    }
    catch (UnknownHostException e) {
      System.err.println(e);
    }
    catch (SocketException se) {
      System.err.println(se);
    }

  } // end main

}
```

The echoInputThread class reads input from the user, a line at a time, and sends it to the echo server. The input is provided by System.in, but a more advanced echoClient could include an option to read input from a different stream—perhaps opening a FileInputStream to read from a file. The three fields of this class define the server to which it sends data, the port on that server, and the DatagramSocket that does the sending. echoInputThread has a single constructor that takes an InetAddress and a DatagramSocket as arguments and sets the equivalent fields in the object.

The run() method processes user input, a line at a time. To do this, the DataInputStream userInput is chained to System.in. Then you enter an infinite loop that reads lines of user input. Each line is stored in the String theLine. A period on a line by itself signals the end of user input and breaks out of the loop. Otherwise, the bytes of data are stored in the data array, using the getBytes() method from java.lang.String. Next the data array is placed in the payload part of the DatagramPacket theOutput, along with information about the server, the port and the data length. This packet is then sent to its destination by theSocket. This thread then yields to give other threads an opportunity to run.

Example 9–18: The echoInputThread class

```
import java.net.*;
import java.io.*;

public class echoInputThread extends Thread {

  InetAddress server;
  int echoPort = 7;
  DatagramSocket theSocket;
```

Example 9–18: The echoInputThread class (continued)

```
public echoInputThread(InetAddress ia, DatagramSocket ds) {

  server = ia;
  theSocket = ds;

}

public void run() {

  DataInputStream userInput;
  String theLine;
  DatagramPacket theOutput;

  try {
    userInput = new DataInputStream(System.in);
    while (true) {
      theLine = userInput.readLine();
      if (theLine.equals(".")) break;
      byte[] data = new byte[theLine.length()];
      theLine.getBytes(0, theLine.length(), data, 0);
      theOutput = new DatagramPacket(data, data.length, server, echoPort);
      theSocket.send(theOutput);
      Thread.yield();
    }

  } // end try
  catch (IOException e) {
    System.err.println(e);
  }

 } // end run

}
```

The echoOutputThread class waits for datagrams to arrive from the network. When a datagram is received, it is converted to a String, and printed on System.out for display to the user. A more advanced echoClient could include an option to send the output elsewhere; it might also check to make sure that the datagrams were in fact returned by the server you're talking to. It's rather unlikely that some other server on the Internet is going to bombard this particular port with extraneous data, so this is not a big flaw. However, it's a good habit to make sure the packets you receive come from the right place, particularly if security is a concern.

This class has two fields. The first field is the DatagramSocket, theSocket, which must be the same DatagramSocket used by the echoInputThread. Data arrives on the port used by that DatagramSocket, and any other DatagramSocket would not be allowed to connect to the same port. The second field is the DatagramPacket dp, simply a buffer in which to place incoming datagrams. The constructor for echoOutputThread initializes both of these fields. It constructs the DatagramPacket dp with a buffer of 65,507 bytes, the maximum size of an incoming packet.

The run() method is an infinite loop that uses theSocket's receive method to wait for incoming datagrams. When an incoming datagram appears, it is converted into a String with the same length as the incoming data and printed on System.out. As in the input thread, this thread then yields to give other threads an opportunity to execute.

Example 9–19: The echoOutputThread class

```
import java.net.*;
import java.io.*;

class echoOutputThread extends Thread {

  DatagramSocket theSocket;
  protected DatagramPacket dp;

  public echoOutputThread(DatagramSocket s) {
    theSocket = s;
    byte [] buffer = new byte[65507];
    dp = new DatagramPacket(buffer, buffer.length);
  }

  public void run() {

    while (true) {
      try {
        theSocket.receive(dp);
        String s = new String(dp.getData(), 0, 0, dp.getLength());
        System.out.println(s);
        Thread.yield();
      }
      catch (IOException e) {
        System.err.println(e);
      }

    }

  }

}
```

Try running the echo client on one machine and connecting to the echo server on a second machine to verify that both these programs work.

10

The URLConnection Class

The URLConnection Class

URLConnection is an abstract class that represents an active connection to a resource specified by a URL. The URLConnection class has two different but related purposes. First, it provides more control over the interaction with a server than the URL class. With a URLConnection, you can inspect the MIME headers sent by an HTTP server and respond accordingly. You can also use a URLConnection to download binary files. In addition, a URLConnection lets you send data back to a web server with POST. We will explore all of these techniques in this chapter.

Second, the URLConnection class is a part of the *protocol handler mechanism,* which also includes the URLStreamHandler class. The idea behind protocol handlers is simple: they let you separate the details of processing a protocol from processing particular datatypes, provide user interfaces, and do the other work that a monolithic web browser performs. The base java.net.URLConnection class is abstract; to implement a specific protocol, you write a subclass. These subclasses can be loaded at runtime by your own applications or by the HotJava browser; in the future, it may be possible for Java applications to download protocol handlers over the net as needed, making them automatically extensible. For example, if your browser runs across a URL with a strange prefix, like compress:, rather than throwing up its hands and issuing an error message, it will be able to download a protocol handler for this unknown protocol, and use it to work with the server. Writing protocol handlers is the subject of Chapter 11, *Protocol Handlers.*

In the Java 1.0 reference release, there are no URLConnection subclasses in the java.net package. However, Sun provides two subclasses of URLConnection that handle file and HTTP URLs. They are in the sun.net package hierarchy; the fully qualified package names are sun.net.www.protocol.file.FileURLConnection and sun.net.www.protocol.HttpURLConnection. In Java 1.1, HttpURLConnection has moved into the java.net package.

Opening URLConnections

When you first create a URLConnection, it is closed; that is, there is no actual connection between the local and remote host that data can be sent and received over. The URLConnection's connect() method establishes an actual connection— normally using TCP sockets but possibly through some other mechanism— between the local and remote host so you can send and receive data.

The constructor for the URLConnection class is protected, so unless you're subclassing it to handle a new kind of URL (that is, writing a protocol handler), you can only get a reference to one of these objects through the openConnection() methods of the URL or URLStreamHandler classes. Example 10–1 demonstrates.

Example 10–1: Open a URLConnection to http://www.ora.com

```
import java.net.*;
import java.io.IOException;

public class getURLConnection {

  public static void main(String args[]) {

    URL u;
    URLConnection uc;

    try {
      u = new URL("http://www.ora.com");
      try {
        uc = u.openConnection();
      }
      catch (IOException e) {
        System.err.println(e);
      }
    }
    catch (MalformedURLException e) {
      System.err.println(e);
    }

  }

}
```

Although the URLConnection class is abstract, all but one of its methods are implemented. The single method that subclasses are forced to implement is connect(); this makes a connection to a server, and thus depends on the type of service you're implementing (HTTP, FTP, etc.). Of course, you may find it convenient or necessary to override other methods in the class.

NOTE   In practice, the openConnection() method of java.net.URL is the same as the openConnection() method of java.net.URL StreamHandler. All a URL object's openConnection() method does is call its URLStreamHandler's openConnection() method.

Many of the methods and fields in the URLConnection class are *protected*. In other words, you can only access them by instances of the URLConnection class or its subclasses. It is rare to instantiate or access URLConnection objects directly in your source code; instead, the runtime environment creates these objects as needed, depending on the protocol in use. The class (unknown at compile time) is then instantiated using the forName() and newInstance() methods of the class java.lang.Class.

Methods to Get Data From a Server

public abstract void connect() throws IOException

The connect() method is an abstract method that opens the connection to a server. The name of the server is taken from a URL that is stored as a field within the URLConnection, and is set by the class's constructor. Subclasses of URLConnection override this method to handle a specific kind of connection. For example, a FileURLConnection's connect() method converts the URL to a filename in the appropriate directory, creates MIME information for the file, and opens a buffered FileInputStream to the file. The connect() method of HttpURLConnection creates an HttpClient object (from sun.net.www.http.HttpClient) that is responsible for connecting to the server. A URL object's openConnection() method calls the appropriate connect() method, and returns an opened connection. Therefore, you rarely need to call connect() directly.

public Object getContent() throws IOException

This method is virtually identical to the getContent() method of the URL class. In fact, URL.getContent() just calls this method. getContent() downloads the object selected by the URL of this URLConnection. For getContent() to work, the environment needs to recognize and understand the content type. Currently, the only content types that are understood are text/plain, image/gif, and image/jpeg. You can install additional content handlers that understand other content types.

getContent() only works for protocols like HTTP that have a clear understanding of MIME content types. If the content type is unknown, or the protocol doesn't understand content types, an UnknownServiceException is thrown.

public InputStream getInputStream()

The getContent() method only works when Java has a content handler for the content type. If this is not the case, you'll probably want to get a generic Input-Stream, which lets you read and parse the data yourself. To do so, call getInput-Stream(). This method is also useful when the built-in content handler does not do exactly what you want. Example 10–2 uses the getInputStream() method to download a web page.

Example 10–2: Download a web page with a URLConnection

```
import java.net.*;
import java.io.*;

public class viewsource2 {

  public static void main (String args[]) {

    String thisLine;
    URL u;
    URLConnection uc;

    if  (args.length > 0) {

      //Open the URL for reading
      try {
        u = new URL(args[0]);
        try {
          uc = u.openConnection();

            // now turn the URLConnection into a DataInputStream
            DataInputStream theHTML = new DataInputStream(uc.getInputStream());

            try {
              while ((thisLine = theHTML.readLine()) != null) {
                System.out.println(thisLine);
              }// while loop ends here
            } // end try
            catch (Exception e) {
              System.err.println(e);
            }
        }// end try
        catch (Exception e) {
          System.err.println(e);
        }

      }// end try
      catch (MalformedURLException e) {
```

Example 10–2: Download a web page with a URLConnection (continued)

```
        System.err.println(args[0] + " is not a parseable URL");
        System.err.println(e);
    }
  }//  end if

 }// end main

} // end viewsource2
```

It is no accident that this program is almost the same as Example 5–5. The open-
Stream() method of the URL class just returns an InputStream from its own URL-
Connection object.

public OutputStream getOutputStream()

Sometimes you need to write data to a URLConnection—for example, when you
want to send data to a web server using POST. The getOutputStream() method
gives you an OutputStream on which you can write data for transmission to a
server. Since a URLConnection doesn't allow output by default, you have to call
setDoOutput() before asking for an output stream. Once you've got the Output-
Stream, you generally chain it to a DataOutputStream or another subclass of OutputStream that provides more features. For example:

```
    try {

      URL u = new URL("http://www.somehost.com/cgi-bin/acgi");
      // open the connection and prepare it to POST
      URLConnection uc = u.openConnection();
      uc.setDoOutput(true);

      DataOutputStream dos = new DataOutputStream(uc.getOutputStream());
      dos.writeBytes("Here is some data");
      dos.close();

    }
    catch (Exception e) {
      System.err.println(e);
    }
```

Parsing the Header

HTTP servers provide a substantial amount of information in the MIME headers
that precede each response. The information in the MIME headers may include
the content encoding scheme used, the date and time, the length of the content
returned in bytes, the expiration date for the content, and the date the content
was last modified. However, the information sent depends on the server; some

send all this information for each request, others send some information, and a few servers don't send anything. The methods of this section allow you to query a URLConnection to find out what MIME information the server has provided.

Aside from HTTP, very few protocols use MIME headers. When writing your own subclass of URLConnection, it is often necessary to override these methods so they return sensible values. The most important piece of information you may be lacking is the MIME content type. URLConnection provides some utility methods that help you guess the data's content type, based on its file name or (in the worst case) the first few bytes of the data itself. (These methods are also used by the HTTP protocol handler to deal with servers that don't use MIME headers.)

public String getContentType()

This method returns the MIME content type of the data. It relies on the web server to send a proper MIME header, including a valid content type. (In a later section, we'll see how recalcitrant servers are handled.) It throws no exceptions, and returns null if the content type isn't available. text/html will be by far the most common content type you'll encounter when connecting to web servers. Other commonly used types include text/plain, image/gif, and image/jpeg.

public int getContentLength()

This method tells you how many bytes there are in the content. Many servers only send Content-length headers when they're transferring a binary file, not when transferring a text file. If there is no Content-length header, getContentLength() returns –1. The method throws no exceptions. It is used when you need to know exactly how many bytes to read, or when you need to create a buffer large enough to hold the data in advance.

TIP   Every version of Java I've tested has an annoying bug: getContentLength() returns –1 if it's the first header method you call. To avoid this bug, make sure you call at least one other header method first.

---

public String getContentEncoding()

This method returns a String that tells you how the content is encoded. If the content is sent unencoded (as is commonly the case with HTTP servers), this method returns null. It throws no exceptions. Commonly used content encodings are Base-64 and quoted-printable, though you're not very likely to see these on the web.

When writing your own URLConnection subclass, you need to override this method if you expect to be dealing with encoded data. This might be the case for a news or SMTP protocol handler; in these applications, many different encoding schemes like BinHex and uuencode are used to pass 8-bit binary data through a 7-bit ASCII connection.

public long getDate()

The getDate() method returns a long integer that tells you when the document was sent, in seconds since midnight, GMT, January 1, 1970. You can convert it to a java.util.Date. For example:

```
Date docSent = new Date(uc.getDate());
```

This is the time the document was sent on the server; it may not agree with the time on your local machine. If the MIME header does not include a Date header, getDate() returns 0, meaning 12:00 A.M., GMT, January 1, 1970.

public long getExpiration()

Some documents have server-based expiration dates that indicate when the document should be expired from the cache and reloaded from the server. getExpiration() is very similar to getDate(), differing only in how the return value is interpreted. It returns a long indicating the number of seconds after 12:00 A.M., GMT, January 1, 1970 at which time the document expires. In practice, few servers send expiration dates. If the MIME header does not include an expiration header, getExpiration() returns 0, meaning 12:00 A.M., GMT, January 1, 1970. The only reasonable interpretation of this date is that the document does not need to be expired, and can remain in the cache indefinitely.

public long getLastModified()

The final date method, getLastModified(), returns the date the document was last modified. Again, the date is given as the number of seconds since midnight, GMT, 1970. If the MIME header does not include a Last-modified header (and many don't), this method returns 0, meaning 12:00 A.M., GMT, January 1, 1970.

Example 10–3 reads URLs from the command line, and uses these six methods to print their content type, content length, content encoding, date of last modification, expiration date, and current date.

Example 10–3: Return the MIME header

```
import java.net.*;
import java.io.IOException;

public class getMIMEHeader {
```

Example 10–3: Return the MIME header (continued)

```
public static void main(String args[]) {

  for (int i=0; i < args.length; i++) {
    try {
      URL u = new URL(args[0]);
      URLConnection uc = u.openConnection();
      System.out.println("Content-type: " + uc.getContentType());
      System.out.println("Content-encoding: " + uc.getContentEncoding());
      System.out.println("Date: " + new java.util.Date(uc.getDate()));
      System.out.println("Last modified: "
                          + new java.util.Date(uc.getLastModified()));
      System.out.println("Expiration date: "
                          + new java.util.Date(uc.getExpiration()));
      System.out.println("Content-length: "   + uc.getContentLength());
    } // end try
    catch (MalformedURLException e) {
      System.err.println(args[i] + " is not a URL I understand");
    }
    catch (IOException e) {
      System.err.println(e);
    }
    System.out.println();

  } // end for

} // end main

} // end getMIMEHeader
```

Here's the result:

```
% java getMIMEHeader http://www.ora.com/
Content-type: text/html
Content-encoding: null
Date: Mon Jul 29 09:25:50 EDT 1996
Last modified: Fri Jul 26 13:55:21 EDT 1996
Expiration date: Wed Dec 31 19:00:00 EST 1969
Content-length: -1

%
```

The MIME type of the file at *http://www.ora.com* is text/html. No content encoding was used. The file was sent on Monday, July 29, 1996 at 9:25 A.M., Eastern Daylight Time. It was last modified on Friday, July 26, at 1:55 P.M., EDT; and it expires on Wednesday, December 31, 1969 at 7:00 P.M, Eastern Standard Time. Did this document really expire over twenty years ago? No. Remember that what's being checked here is whether the copy in your cache is more recent than 7:00 P.M. EST, December 31, 1969. If it is, you don't need to reload it. More to the point, this date looks suspiciously like 12:00 A.M., GMT, January 1, 1970, the default if the server doesn't send an expiration date. (Most don't.)

Finally, the content length of –1 means that there was no Content-length header.
Many servers don't bother to provide a Content-length header for text files. However, a Content-length header should always be sent for a binary file. Here is the
MIME header that you will receive when you request the GIF image
http://www.ora.com/graphics/space.gif. Now the server sends a Content-length header
with a value of 57.

```
% java getMIMEHeader http://www.ora.com/graphics/space.gif
Content-type: image/gif
Content-encoding: null
Date: Mon Jul 29 12:12:13 EDT 1996
Last modified: Fri Mar 01 14:55:02 EST 1996
Expiration date: Wed Dec 31 19:00:00 EST 1969
Content-length: 57

%
```

Retrieving Arbitrary MIME Header Fields

The last six methods requested specific fields from a MIME header, but there's no
theoretical limit to the number of header fields a MIME message can contain. The
next five methods inspect arbitrary fields in a MIME header. Indeed, the methods
of the last section are just thin wrappers over the methods discussed here; you can
use these methods to get MIME headers that Java's designers did not plan for.

FileURLConnections don't have real MIME headers, so these methods all return
null when you are dealing with a file: URL, their default behavior. HttpURLCon-
nections do attempt to find a header field to match your request. If it's found, it is
returned; otherwise the method returns null.

public String getHeaderField(String name)

The getHeaderField() method returns the value of a named MIME header field.
The name of the header is not case-sensitive and does not include a closing colon.
For example, to get the value of the Content-type and Content-encoding header
fields of a URLConnection object uc you would write:

```
uc.getHeaderField("content-type");
uc.getHeaderField("content-encoding");
```

To get the Date, Content-length or Expiration date headers you'd do the same:

```
uc.getHeaderField("date");
uc.getHeaderField("expires");
uc.getHeaderField("last-modification");
uc.getHeaderField("Content-length");
```

These methods all return Strings, not ints or longs like the getContentLength(),
getExpirationDate(), getLastModified(), and getDate() methods of the last

section did. If you are interested in a numeric value, you must convert the String to a long or an int.

Do not assume the value returned by getHeaderField() is valid. You must check to make sure it is non-null.

public String getHeaderFieldKey(int n)

This method returns the key (that is, the field name: for example, Content-length or Server) of the nth MIME header field. The first header is 0. For example, to get the sixth key of the MIME header of the URLConnection uc, you would write:

```
String header5 = uc.getHeaderFieldKey(5);
```

TIP   In Java 1.0.2, this method is not implemented by either HttpURLConnection or FileURLConnection. It always returns null.

---

public String getHeaderField(int n)

This method returns the value of the nth MIME header field. The first MIME header is one. Example 10–4 uses this method in conjunction with getHeaderFieldKey() to print the entire MIME header.

Example 10–4: Print the entire MIME header

```
import java.net.*;
import java.io.IOException;

public class printMIMEHeader {

  public static void main(String args[]) {

    URL u;
    URLConnection uc;
    String header;

    for (int i=0; i < args.length; i++) {
      try {
        u = new URL(args[i]);
        uc = u.openConnection();
        for (int j = 1; ; j++) {
          header = uc.getHeaderField(j);
          if (header == null) break;
          System.out.println(uc.getHeaderFieldKey(j) + " " + header);
        } // end for
      } // end try
      catch (MalformedURLException e) {
        System.err.println(args[i] + " is not a URL I understand.");
      }
```

Example 10–4: Print the entire MIME header (continued)

```
      catch (IOException e) {
        System.err.println(e);
      }
    } // end for

  } // end main

} // end printMIMEHeader
```

public long getHeaderFieldDate(String name, long default)

This method first retrieves the header field specified by the name argument and
tries to convert the string to a long that specifies the seconds since midnight, January 1, 1970, GMT. You can use getHeaderFieldDate() to retrieve a MIME header
that represents a date: for example, the expires, date or last-modified headers.
To convert the String to an integer, getHeaderFieldDate() uses the parseDate()
method of java.util.Date. The parseDate() method does a decent job of understanding and converting most common date formats, but it can be stumped; one
assumes that parseDate() will be stumped if you ask for a header field that contains something other than a date. If parseDate() doesn't understand the date, or
if getHeaderFieldDate() is unable to find the requested header field, getHeader-
FieldDate() returns the default argument. For example:

```
    uc.getHeaderFieldDate("expires", -1);
    uc.getHeaderFieldDate("last-modification", -1);
    uc.getHeaderFieldDate("date", -1);
```

You can use the methods of the Date class to convert the long to a String. However, if that's if you want, you should probably use getHeaderField() instead.

public int getHeaderFieldInt(String name, int default)

This method retrieves the value of the MIME header field name, and tries to convert it into an int. If it fails, either because it can't find the requested header field
or because that field does not contain a recognizable integer, getHeaderField-
Int() returns the default argument. This method is often used to retrieve the
Content-length field. For example, to get the content length from a URLConnection uc you would write:

```
    int cl = uc.getHeaderFieldInt("content-length", -1);
```

In this code fragment, getHeaderFieldInt() returns –1 if the Content-length
header doesn't exist or is garbled.

The RequestProperty Methods

These four methods don't do anything in the base URLConnection class, nor are they implemented in the FileURLConnection or HttpURLConnection classes. You may wish to override them in a subclass to implement hashtable lookup—for example, to build a hashtable containing all the request's MIME headers.

public String getRequestProperty(String property_name)

This method throws an IllegalAccessError if the connection is open. Otherwise it returns null. If you override it, your method should return the value associated with the given property as a string.

public static void setDefaultRequestProperty(String property_name, String property_value)

This method does nothing. If you override it, you would use it to store a default value for the given property.

public void setRequestProperty(String property_name, String property_value)

This method throws an IllegalAccessError if the connection is open. Otherwise it does nothing. If you override it, you would use it to store the value of a given property.

public String getDefaultRequestProperty(String property_name)

This method always returns null. If you override it, you should return the default value assigned to the given property as a String.

The Constructor

protected URLConnection(URL u)

The single constructor in URLConnection takes one argument, the URL, to connect to. All the other properties of a URLConnection are initially set to their default values, and you may change them with the various *set* methods of the next section. Since the constructor is protected, only objects in the java.net package can create a URLConnection. Since URLConnection is an abstract class, you can only call its constructor from the constructor of one of its subclasses.

If you are subclassing URLConnection, you must call this constructor in the first line of your subclass's constructor like this:

```
myURLConnectionSubclass(URL u) {
  super(u);
}
```

If you don't put an explicit call to the constructor in your subclass, Java attempts to call the no-argument constructor of the superclass: i.e., URLConnection(). Since the URLConnection class doesn't have a no-argument constructor, omitting the explicit call to the constructor causes a compile-time error.

The Fields and Associated Methods

There are thirteen fields in java.net.URLConnection. Seven are static variables that define defaults for all URLConnection instances. The other six define the state of a particular URLConnection. Several of these have public *get* and *set* methods to change their values.

Most of the methods that set fields throw IllegalAccessExceptions if you call them while the connection is open. In general, you can only set the properties of a URLConnection object while the connection is closed.

protected URL url
public URL getURL()

The url field specifies the URL this URLConnection connects to. It is set by the constructor when you create the URLConnection, and should not change. You can retrieve the value by calling the getURL() method. Example 10–5 opens a URLConnection to *http://www.ora.com/*, gets the URL of that connection, and prints it.

Example 10–5: Print the URL of a URLConnection to http://www.ora.com/

```
import java.net.*;
import java.io.IOException;

public class printURLConnection {

  public static void main(String args[]) {

    URL u;
    URLConnection uc;

    try {
      u = new URL("http://www.ora.com/");
      try {
        uc = u.openConnection();
        System.out.println(uc.getURL());
      }
      catch (IOException e) {
        System.err.println(e);
      }
    }
```

Example 10–5: Print the URL of a URLConnection to http://www.ora.com/ (continued)

```
  catch (MalformedURLException e) {
    System.err.println(e);
  }
 }
}
```

Here's the result, which should be no great surprise. The URL that is printed is the one used to create the URLConnection.

```
% java printURLConnection
http://www.ora.com/
%
```

protected boolean connected

The boolean field connected is true if the connection is open, false if it's closed. Since you have not opened the connection when a new URLConnection object is created, its initial value is false. You can only access this variable by instances of java.net.URLConnection and its subclasses. There are no methods that read or change its value.

When writing a protocol handler, you're responsible for setting this variable to true when connected, and resetting it to false when the connection closes. Many methods in java.net.URLConnection read this variable to determine what they can do. If it's set incorrectly, your program will have severe bugs that are not easy to diagnose.

protected boolean allowUserInteraction
public void setAllowUserInteraction(boolean allowuserinteraction)
public boolean getAllowUserInteraction()

Some URLConnections need to interact with users. For example, a web browser may ask for a username and password. However, many applications cannot assume that a user is present to interact with it. As its name suggests, the allowUserInteraction field specifies whether user interaction is allowed. It is false by default.

Since this variable is protected, use the public getAllowUserInteraction() method to read its value, and the public setAllowUserInteraction() method to set it. The value true indicates that user interaction is allowed; false indicates that there is no user interaction. The value may be read at any time, but it may only be set when the connection is closed. Calling setAllowUserInteraction() when the connection is open throws an IllegalAccessError (not an IllegalAccessException!). Programs usually don't catch errors (unlike exceptions); an uncaught error usually forces the program to terminate.

Example 10–6 creates a new HttpURLConnection, uses getAllowUserInteraction() to see whether user interaction is allowed, and, if it isn't, uses setAllowUserInteraction() to allow user interaction.

Example 10–6: Allow user interaction

```
import java.net.*;
import java.io.*;

public class allowUserInteraction {

  public static void main(String[] args) {

    URL u;
    URLConnection uc;
    myHttpHandler handler;

    try {
      u = new URL("http://www.ora.com");
      handler = new myHttpHandler();
      uc = handler.openConnection(u);
      if (!uc.getAllowUserInteraction()) {
        uc.setAllowUserInteraction(true);
      }
    }
    catch (MalformedURLException e) {
      System.err.println(e);
    }
    catch (IOException e) {
      System.err.println(e);
    }
  }
}


class myHttpHandler extends sun.net.www.protocol.http.Handler {

  public URLConnection openConnection(URL u) throws IOException {
    return super.openConnection(u);
  }
}
```

private static boolean defaultAllowUserInteraction
public static void setDefaultAllowUserInteraction(boolean
defaultAllowUserInteraction)
public static boolean getDefaultAllowUserInteraction()

The defaultAllowUserInteraction field defines the default behavior for the URLConnection. It may be read by calling the public method getDefaultAllowUserInteraction(), and set by setDefaultAllowUserInteraction(). Since this variable is static (i.e., a class variable instead of a member variable), setting it changes the default behavior for all instances of the URLConnection class created after setDefaultAllowUserInteraction() is called.

Example 10–7 uses getDefaultAllowUserInteraction() to see if user interaction is allowed by default; if user interaction isn't allowed, the example uses setDefaultAllowUserInteraction() to allow user interaction by default.

Example 10–7: Make allowing user interaction the default

```
import java.net.*;

public class allowDefaultUserInteraction {

  public static void main(String[] args) {

    if (!URLConnection.getDefaultAllowUserInteraction()) {
      URLConnection.setDefaultAllowUserInteraction(true);
    }
  }
}
```

protected boolean doInput
public void setDoInput(boolean doinput)
public boolean getDoInput()

Many URLConnections provide input to a client program. For example, a connection to a web server with the GET method would produce input for the client. However, a connection to a web server with the POST method wouldn't. You can use a URLConnection for input to the program, output from the program, or both. The protected boolean field doInput is true if the URLConnection can be used for input, false if it cannot be. The default is true unless you explicitly set doOutput to true, in which case doInput defaults to false. To access this protected variable, use the public getDoInput() and setDoInput() methods. You may call both on an open URLConnection. For example:

Example 10–8: Make sure a URLConnection can be used for input

```
import java.net.*;
import java.io.IOException;

public class allowUserInput {

  public static void main(String[] args) {

    URL u;
    URLConnection uc;

    try {
      u = new URL("http://www.ora.com");
```

Example 10–8: Make sure a URLConnection can be used for input (continued)

```
      try {
        uc = u.openConnection();
        if (!uc.getDoInput()) {
          uc.setDoInput(true);
        }
      }
      catch (IOException e) {
        System.err.println(e);
      }
    }
    catch (MalformedURLException e) {
      System.err.println(e);
    }
  }
}
```

protected boolean doOutput
public void setDoOutput(boolean dooutput)
public boolean getDoOutput()

Programs can use a URLConnection to send output back to the server. For example, a program that needs to send data to the server using the POST method could do so by getting an output stream from a URLConnection. The protected boolean variable doOutput is true if the URLConnection can be used for output, false if it cannot be; it is false by default in Sun's Virtual Machine. To access this protected variable, use the getDoOutput() and setDoOutput() methods. You can call these methods when the URLConnection is open. See Example 10–9.

Example 10–9: Make sure a URLConnection can be used for output

```
import java.net.*;
import java.io.IOException;

public class allowUserOutput {

  public static void main(String[] args) {

    URL u;
    URLConnection uc;

    try {
      u = new URL("http://www.ora.com");
      try {
        uc = u.openConnection();
        if (!uc.getDoOutput()) {
          uc.setDoOutput(true);
        }
      }
      catch (IOException e) {
        System.err.println(e);
```

Example 10–9: Make sure a URLConnection can be used for output (continued)

```
      }
    }
    catch (MalformedURLException e) {
      System.err.println(e);
    }
  }
}
```

protected long ifModifiedSince
public void setIfModifiedSince(long ifmodifiedsince)
public long getIfModifiedSince()

Some servers, particularly web servers, tell clients when an object was last modified. The client can use this information to avoid fetching an object unless it has been modified since some point in time—typically the last time the client fetched the object.

The ifModifiedSince field counts time as seconds since midnight, January 1, 1970, GMT. Because ifModifiedSince is protected, programs should call the getIfModifiedSince() and setIfModifiedSince() methods to read or modify it. Example 10–10 prints the default value of ifModifiedSince, sets its value to 24 hours ago, and prints the new value.

Example 10–10: Set ifModifiedSince to 24 hours prior to now

```
import java.net.*;
import java.io.*;
import java.util.Date;

public class last24 {

  public static void main (String[] args) {

    URL u;
    URLConnection uc;
    String thisLine;
    // Initialize a Date object with the current date and time
    Date today = new Date();

    try {
      u = new URL("http://www.ora.com");
      uc = u.openConnection();
      System.out.println("Will retrieve file if it's been modified since "
        + new Date(uc.getIfModifiedSince()).toLocaleString());
      uc.setIfModifiedSince(Date.UTC(today.getYear(), today.getMonth(),
        today.getDate() - 1, today.getHours(), today.getMinutes(),
        today.getSeconds())));
      System.out.println("Will retrieve file if it's been modified since "
        + new Date(uc.getIfModifiedSince()).toLocaleString());
    }
```

Example 10–10: Set ifModifiedSince to 24 hours prior to now (continued)

```
    catch (Exception e) {
      System.err.println(e);
    }
  }
}
```

Here's the result. First, you see the default value: midnight, January 1, 1970, GMT, converted to Eastern Daylight Time. Next, you see the new time you set to 24 hours before the current time. Again, the time appears to be off by four hours because of the conversion from GMT to EDT.

```
% java last24
Will retrieve file if it's been modified since Wed Dec 31 19:00:00 1969
Will retrieve file if it's been modified since Mon Apr 15 13:30:36 1996
% date
Tue Apr 16 17:30:44 EDT 1996

%
```

protected boolean useCaches
public void setUseCaches(boolean usecaches)
public boolean getUseCaches()

Some clients, notably web browsers, can retrieve a document from a local cache instead of from a server. The useCaches variable determines whether a cache will be used if it's available. The default value is true, meaning that the cache will be used; false means it won't be used. Because useCaches is protected, programs access it via getUseCaches() and setUseCaches() methods. Example 10–11 disables caching to ensure the most recent version of the document is retrieved.

Example 10–11: Disable caching

```
import java.net.*;
import java.io.IOException;

public class disableCache {

  public static void main(String[] args) {

    URL u;
    URLConnection uc;

    try {
      u = new URL("http://www.ora.com");
      try {
        uc = u.openConnection();
        if (uc.getUseCaches()) {
          uc.setUseCaches(false);
        }
```

Example 10–11: Disable caching (continued)

```
      }
    catch (IOException e) {
       System.err.println(e);
    }
  }
  catch (MalformedURLException e) {
    System.err.println(e);
  }
 }
}
```

protected static boolean defaultUseCaches
public static void setDefaultUseCaches(boolean defaultusecaches)
public static boolean getDefaultUseCaches()

defaultUseCaches is the default state for the useCaches field. The value of this field can be read and modified by the public getDefaultUseCaches() and setDefaultUseCaches() methods. Since this variable is static (i.e., a class variable instead of a member variable), setting it changes the default behavior for all instances of the URLConnection class created after the change. Example 10–12 disables caching by default; after this code runs, URLConnections that want caching must enable it explicitly using setUseCaches(true).

Example 10–12: Disable caching by default

```
public class disableDefaultCache {

  public static void main(String[] args) {


    try {
      URL u = new URL("http://www.ora.com/");
      URLConnection uc = u.openConnection();

      if (uc.getDefaultUseCaches()) {
        uc.setDefaultUseCaches(false);
      }
    }
    catch (IOException e) }
      System.err.println(e);
    }
  }
}
```

static ContentHandlerFactory factory
public static synchronized void
setContentHandlerFactory(ContentHandlerFactory fac)

This method sets the `ContentHandlerFactory`. The `ContentHandlerFactory`, which you'll learn more about in Chapter 12, *Content Handlers*, instantiates the appropriate content handler for a particular MIME type. That is, a content handler factory tells the program where it can find a content handler for a `text/html` file, an `image/gif` file, or some other kind of file. You may only set the `ContentHandlerFactory` once per application; this method throws an `Error` if called a second time.

Figuring Out MIME Types

In the best of all possible worlds, every protocol and server would use the MIME typing method to specify what kind of file it was transferring. Unfortunately, that's not the case. Not only do you have to deal with older protocols, like FTP; many HTTP servers that should use MIME either don't provide MIME headers at all, or they lie and provide headers that are incorrect (usually because the server has been misconfigured). Java provides two methods to help programs figure out the MIME type of some data; you can use these if the content type just isn't available, or if you have reason to believe that the content type you're given isn't correct.

protected static String guessContentTypeFromName(String name)

This method tries to guess the content type of an object based on the extension in the filename portion of the object's URL. It returns its best guess about the content type as a `String`. This guess is likely to be correct; people follow some fairly regular conventions when thinking up filenames. It's unfortunate that `guessContentTypeFromName()` is `protected`. It's useful for any program that needs to deal with MIME types (for example, mail clients and HTTP servers), not just for URL-Connections. Table 10–1 shows the guesses Java makes.

Table 10–1: Java Extension-Content-type Mappings (Case-Insensitive)

Extension	MIME Content Type
No extension	content/unknown
.uu, .saveme, .dump, .hqx, .arc, .o, .a, .bin, .exe, .z, .gz	application/octet-stream
.oda	application/oda
.pdf	application/pdf
.eps, .ai, .ps	application/postscript
.rtf, .rtx	application/rtf
.dvi	application/x-dvi
.hdf	application/x-hdf
.latex	application/x-latex
.cdf	application/x-netcdf

Table 10–1: Java Extension-Content-type Mappings (Case-Insensitive) (continued)

Extension	MIME Content Type
.nc	application/x-netcdf
.tex	application/x-tex
.texinfo, .texi	application/x-texinfo
.t, .tr, .roff	application/x-troff
.man	application/x-troff-man
.me	application/x-troff-me
.ms	application/x-troff-ms
.src, .wsrc	application/x-wais-source
.zip	application/zip
.bcpio	application/x-bcpio
.cpio	application/x-cpio
.gtar	application/x-gtar
.shar, .sh	application/x-shar
.sv4cpio	application/x-sv4cpio
.sv4crc	application/x-sv4crc
.tar	application/x-tar
.ustar	application/x-ustar
.snd, .au	audio/basic
.aifc, .aif, .aiff	audio/x-aiff
.wav	audio/x-wav
.gif	image/gif
.ief	image/ief
.jfif, .jfif-tbnl, .jpe, .jpg, .jpeg	image/jpeg
.tif, .hiff	image/tiff
.ras	image/x-cmu-rast
.pnm	image/x-portable-anymap
.pbm	image/x-portable-bitmap
.pgm	image/x-portable-graymap
.ppm	image/x-portable-pixmap
.rgb	image/x-rgb
.xbm	image/x-xbitmap
.xpm	image/x-xpixmap
.xwd	image/x-xwindowdump
.htm, .html	text/html

Table 10–1: Java Extension-Content-type Mappings (Case-Insensitive) (continued)

Extension	MIME Content Type
.text, .c, .cc, .c++, .h, .pl, .txt, .java	text/plain
.tsv	text/tab-separated-values
.etx	text/x-setext
.mpg, .mpe, .mpeg	video/mpeg
.mov, .qt	video/quicktime
.avi	application/x-troff-msvideo
.movie, .mv	video/x-sgi-movie
.mime	message/rfc822

In Java 1.1, URLConnection has a field `fileNameMap` that implements the `FileNameMap` interface. This interface allows you to look up MIME types given a filename; it has a single method called `getContentTypeFor()`.

static protected String
guessContentTypeFromStream(InputStream is)

`guessContentTypeFromStream()` tries to guess the content type by looking at the first few bytes of data in the stream. For this to work, the `InputStream` must support marking, so you can return to the beginning of the stream after the first bytes have been read. Java inspects the first six bytes of the `InputStream`, though sometimes fewer than six bytes are needed to make an identification. Table 10–2 shows how Java 1.0 guesses. Java 1.1 can also identify files of types `audio/x-wav`, `audio/basic`, and `application/java-vm`. These guesses are not as reliable as the guesses made by the previous method; there's no reason a text file can't start with the bytes GIF8, causing `guessContentTypeFromStream()` to misidentify the text file as an image. Therefore, you should only use this method as a last resort.

Table 10–2: Java First Bytes-Content-type Mappings (Case-Sensitive)

First bytes	MIME Content Type
GIF8	image/gif
#def	image/x-bitmap
! XPM2	image/x-pixmap
<!	text/html
<html>	text/html
<body>	text/html
<head>	text/html

These mappings are case-sensitive. For example, guessContentTypeFromStream() does not recognize <HTML> as the beginning of a text/html file. It shouldn't be difficult for Sun to fix this bug in future versions.

The Object Methods

The URLConnection class overrides one of the methods from java.lang.Object, toString().

```
public String toString()
```

Even so, there is little reason to print a URLConnection object or to convert one to a String, except perhaps for debugging. toString() is called the same way as every other toString() method.

Some Useful Programs

URLConnections let you do things that aren't possible with plain URL objects. First, they let you download binary data like images and applets. Second, they let you talk back to a server—necessary if you want to communicate with CGI programs through POST or PUT.

Saving Binary Data from HTTP Connections

In Chapter 5, *Retrieving Data with URLs*, you saw how to use the openStream() method of the URL class to download text files from an HTTP server. Although you should be able to use the same method to download a binary file, like a GIF image or a *.class* byte code file, this procedure presents a problem in practice. HTTP servers don't always close the connection and give you an EOF character where you need it; therefore, you don't know when to stop reading. To download a binary file, it is more reliable to use a URLConnection's getContentLength() method to find the file's length, and read exactly the number of bytes indicated. Example 10–13 is a program called saveBinaryFile that uses this technique to save a binary file on a disk.

Example 10–13: Download a binary file and save it to disk

```
import java.net.*;
import java.io.*;

public class saveBinaryFile {

  public static void main (String args[]) {

    for (int i = 0; i < args.length; i++) {

      try {
```

Example 10–13: Download a binary file and save it to disk (continued)

```
        URL root = new URL(args[i]);
        saveBinaryFile(root);
    }
    catch (MalformedURLException e) {
      System.err.println(args[i] + " is not URL I understand.");
    }
  }// end for

}// end main

public static void saveBinaryFile(URL u) {

  int bfr = 128;

  try {
    URLConnection uc = u.openConnection();
    String ct = uc.getContentType();
    int cl = uc.getContentLength();
    if (ct.startsWith("text/") || cl == -1 ) {
      System.err.println("This is not a binary file.");
      return;
    }

    InputStream theImage = uc.getInputStream();
    byte[] b = new byte[cl];
    int bytesread = 0;
    int offset = 0;
    while (bytesread >= 0) {
       bytesread = theImage.read(b, offset, bfr);
       if (bytesread == -1) break;
       offset += bytesread;
    }
    if (offset != cl) {
      System.err.println("Error: Only read " + offset + " bytes");
      System.err.println("Expected " + cl + " bytes");
    }

    String theFile = u.getFile();
    theFile = theFile.substring(theFile.lastIndexOf('/') + 1);
    FileOutputStream fout = new FileOutputStream(theFile);
    fout.write(b);
  } // end try
  catch (Exception e) {
   System.err.println(e);
  }

  return;

}// end saveBinaryFile

}
```

As usual, the main() method loops over the URLs entered on the command line, passing each URL to the saveBinaryFile() method. saveBinaryFile() opens a URLConnection uc to the URL u. It puts the type into the variable ct, and the content length into the variable cl. Note that ct is set before cl to avoid the bug in getContentLength(). Next, an if statement checks whether the MIME type is text, or the Content-length header is missing or invalid (cl == -1). If either of these is true, an error message is printed and the method returns. If these assertions are both false, you are dealing with a binary file of known length. (That's what you want.)

Assuming you have a genuine binary file on your hands, prepare to read it into an array of bytes called b. b is initialized with the number of bytes required to hold the binary object: cl, the content length. Ideally, you would like to fill b with a single call to InputStream.read(), but that doesn't work. You have to work around a bug in the read(byte b[]) method by reading the bytes in small chunks. Here you read them in chunks of bfr=128 bytes at a time. The read() method returns the number of bytes read, or −1 when there are no bytes left to read. The number of bytes read up to this point is accumulated into the offset variable that also keeps track of the location in the array b at which to start placing the data retrieved by the next call to read(). You break out of the while loop if read() returns −1, indicating that there is no more data. The offset variable now contains the total number of bytes read that should be equal to the content length, cl. If they are not equal, an error has occurred, so saveBinaryFile() prints an error message and returns.

Now you are ready to save the data in a file. saveBinaryFile() retrieves the filename from the URL using the getFile() method, and strips any path information by calling theFile.substring(theFile.lastIndexOf('/') + 1). A new FileOutputStream fout is opened into this file, and the data is written in one large burst with fout.write(b). (Fortunately, there's no bug in OutputStream.write() that requires the write to be buffered.)

Loading Classes From the Network

Images and sounds aren't the only binary files you're likely to load over the network. The other type of file commonly loaded from the network is a *.class* byte code file. To load a class from the network, you define a subclass of the abstract class, java.lang.ClassLoader. This class must implement the loadClass() method. This takes a name as an argument, and returns an instance of java.lang.Class. Given a class name, the ClassLoader is responsible for knowing where to find the class's byte code, and for converting those raw bytes into a Class object.

Example 10–14 is a URLClassLoader that attempts to load classes from the URL that
was passed to its constructor. The URL is used to specify the directory in which
class files are located on some server. The file portion of the URL, if any, is
ignored; the class loader assumes that the filename can be derived by adding the
extension *.class* to the class name given in the call to loadClass(). The class has a
Hashtable field to cache classes already loaded, so that it doesn't define the same
class twice. If a class fails to load for any reason, a ClassNotFoundException is
thrown.

Example 10–14: The URLClassLoader

```
import java.util.Hashtable;
import java.net.*;
import java.io.*;

public class URLClassLoader extends ClassLoader {

    Hashtable cache;
    URL u;

    public URLClassLoader(URL u) {

      this.u = u;
      cache = new Hashtable();

    }


    public synchronized Class loadClass(String  name, boolean resolve)
     throws ClassNotFoundException {

      // first look for the class in the cache
      Class c = (Class) cache.get(name);

      // If it's not in the cache, then look
      // in the system classes
      if (c == null) {
        try {
          c = findSystemClass(name);
        }
        catch (ClassNotFoundException e) {

        }
      }

      // if the class still hasn't been found,
      // load it from the network
      if (c ==  null) {
        byte b[] = loadClassData(name);
        c = defineClass(b, 0, b.length);
        cache.put(name, c);
      }
```

Example 10–14: The URLClassLoader (continued)

```
    if (resolve) {
      resolveClass(c);
    }

    return  c;

  } // end loadClass

  private byte[] loadClassData(String name)
    throws ClassNotFoundException {

    byte[] b;
    InputStream theClass = null;
    int bfr = 128;

    try {

      URL classURL = new URL(u, name + ".class");

      URLConnection uc = classURL.openConnection();
      uc.setAllowUserInteraction(false);

      // I don't know why, but uc.getInputStream absolutely
      // has to come before uc.getContentLength or you'll
      // get a nasty NullPointerException
      try {
        theClass = uc.getInputStream();
      }
      catch (NullPointerException e) {
        System.err.println(e);
        throw new ClassNotFoundException(name + " input stream problem");
      }
      int cl = uc.getContentLength();

      // A lot of web servers don't send content-lengths
      // for .class files
      if (cl == -1 ) {
        b = new byte[bfr * 16];
      }
      else {
        b = new byte[cl];
      }

      int bytesread = 0;
      int offset = 0;

      while (bytesread >= 0) {
        bytesread = theClass.read(b, offset, bfr);
        if (bytesread == -1) break;
        offset += bytesread;
        if (cl == -1 && offset == b.length) {// grow the array
          byte temp[] = new byte[offset * 2];
```

Example 10–14: The URLClassLoader (continued)

```
            System.arraycopy(b, 0, temp, 0, offset);
            b = temp;
          }
        else if (offset > b.length) {
          throw new ClassNotFoundException(name
            + " error reading data into the array");
          }
        }

      if (offset < b.length) {// shrink the array
        byte temp[] = new byte[offset];
        System.arraycopy(b, 0, temp, 0, offset);
        b = temp;
        }


      // Make sure all the bytes were received
      if (cl != -1 && offset != cl) {
        throw new ClassNotFoundException("Only " + offset +
          " bytes received for " + name +
          "\n Expected " + cl + " bytes");
        }
      }// end try
    catch (Exception e) {
     throw new ClassNotFoundException(name + " " + e);
      }
    finally {
      try {
        if (theClass != null) theClass.close();
        }
      catch (IOException e) {
        }


      }

    return b;

  } // end loadClassData

} // end URLClassLoader
```

There are two fields in this class: the Hashtable cache and the URL u. The cache
stores classes that you have already loaded. This hashtable is always consulted
before loading a class from the network. The URL field u is the URL of the directory
that ClassLoader searches for classes. It is initialized in the loader's constructor,
URLClassLoader().

The single public method loadClass() tries to find and return the requested class.
First it looks in the cache. If the class isn't in the cache, it looks for the class in the

CLASSPATH by calling findSystemClass(name). If the class isn't found there, it looks on the network by calling loadClassData(), a private utility method that returns a byte array containing the class's data. loadClass() converts the byte array into a Class object using the defineClass() method of java.lang.ClassLoader, and stores the newly created class in the cache for future use. If the resolve argument to loadClass() is true, the class is resolved with java.lang.ClassLoader's resolveClass() method; resolving a class makes it possible to create a new instance of the class and call the class's methods. Finally, load-Class() returns the class as a Class object.

The loadClassData() method does the dirty work of retrieving the data from a server somewhere. It makes the connection to the URL and downloads the bytes in the file name, returning the class data as an array of bytes, b. The code for reading the class file is similar to the code in saveBinaryFile() (in the previous section). However, many web servers return *.class* files with the MIME type text/plain, and omit a Content-length header. Therefore, the bytes need to be read in chunks, and the array b grown or shrunk as necessary to accommodate them. If anything goes wrong, loadClassData() throws a ClassNotFoundException. This exception isn't caught by loadClass(), so it is propagated up the chain.

If you're writing your own class loader, here are the key points to remember:

1. The class must extend the abstract class java.lang.ClassLoader.

2. It must have a public synchronized method called loadClass() that returns a Class object (an instance of java.lang.Class), and throws ClassNot-FoundException. Its signature is:

    ```
    public synchronized Class loadClass(String  name, boolean resolve)
        throws ClassNotFoundException
    ```

    The String name is the name of the class. The boolean argument resolve specifies whether this class should be resolved before it is returned.

3. Each class should be converted into one, and only one, Class object. That is, if you are asked to load a class twice, the second request shouldn't produce a new Class object; instead, you should return the Class you produced the first time. Therefore, you must store any classes you load in a cache (commonly a Hashtable), and try to retrieve the classes from the cache before loading them from somewhere else.

4. For security reasons, you should always load classes in the user's CLASSPATH preferentially to classes elsewhere. Giving preference to classes installed on your local hard drive means that they can't be replaced by potentially dangerous classes from the network. To see if a class is in the CLASSPATH, call findSystemClass(name).

5. If you are downloading classes from the network, you should think carefully
    about what these classes should and should not be allowed to do. Your applica-
    tion should install a security manager that prevents these classes from doing
    anything you consider undesirable.

As long as your class loader follows these rules, the rest of the implementation is
up to you. Different class loaders can look for byte codes in different places, and
implement different strategies for reading the bytes.

Example 10–15 shows how to load an applet from a URL using the URLClass-
Loader. This program is essentially a very simple applet viewer. It reads the URL of
an applet from the command line, and uses this URL to create a new URLClass-
Loader. It then extracts the name of the requested class from the URL, and asks
the ClassLoader to load and resolve that class. Finally, loadApplet creates a new
instance of the class by calling newInstance(). The resulting Object is cast to an
Applet, which is added to a Frame, and then started by calling its init() and
start() methods.

Example 10–15: Load an applet from a URL

```
import java.applet.*;
import java.awt.*;
import java.net.*;

public class loadApplet {

  public static void main(String args[]) {

    int x = 50;
    int y = 50;

    for (int i = 0; i < args.length; i++) {
      try {
        if (!args[i].endsWith(".class")) {
          System.err.println("That doesn't look like a byte code file!");
          break;
        }

        URL u = new URL(args[i]);
        URLClassLoader ucl = new URLClassLoader(u);

        // parse out the name of the class from the URL
        String s = u.getFile();
        String classname = s.substring(s.lastIndexOf('/'),
         s.lastIndexOf(".class"));
        System.err.println(classname);
        Class AppletClass = ucl.loadClass(classname, true);
        Applet apl = (Applet) AppletClass.newInstance();

        Frame f = new Frame();
        f.resize(200, 200);
```

Example 10–15: Load an applet from a URL (continued)

```
        f.move(x, y);
        x += 50;
        y += 50;
        f.add("Center", apl);
        apl.init();
        apl.start();
        f.show();

      } // end try
      catch (MalformedURLException e) {
        System.err.println(args[i] + " is not a URL I understand.");
      }
      catch (Exception e) {
        System.err.println(e);
      }

    } // end for

  } // end main

} // end loadApplet
```

It's worth taking an extra look at how you instantiate a class that was loaded by a class loader. You are used to creating new objects with the new operator. You can't use this strategy with classes that are loaded dynamically because you don't know the new class at compile time—in this case, you read the class name from the command line, and therefore do not know it until you run the program. Java does not let you write:

```
Object o = new args[i]();
```

To create a class dynamically, you must first create a class loader (in this case, our URLClassLoader) using its constructor. The class loader's loadClass() method is called to load the byte codes, and convert them into a Class object. Then the Class object's newInstance() method is used to instantiate the object. In short, the three steps are:

1. Construct a ClassLoader.

2. Call the ClassLoader's loadClass() method to return a Class object.

3. Call the Class's newInstance() method to instantiate the class.

loadApplet demonstrates the basics of loading a class over a network. However, it isn't a full-fledged applet viewer. It doesn't provide the applet with either an AppletStub or an AppletContext, so the applet can't call getImage() or similar methods. Worse, it doesn't have any provision for loading classes other than the applet itself (i.e., helper classes that the applet may require). However, it's enough to get you started. Loading classes at runtime is central to writing dynamically extensible programs; the ability to write programs that can be extended on the fly is one of Java's most interesting features, and one that few people have taken advantage of.

Posting Forms

In Chapter 5, you saw how to send data to CGI programs with GET. Sending data with POST is almost as easy. Instead of attaching the query string to the URL, you use a URLConnection's getOutputStream() method to send the query string on an output stream. The URLConnection creates and sends a MIME header for you. The request looks something like this:

```
POST /cgi-bin/register.pl HTTP/1.0
Content-type: application/x-www-form-urlencoded

username=Elliotte+Rusty+Harold&email=elharo%40sunsite%2eunc%2eedu
```

The request above contains two name-value pairs, separated by an ampersand. When using POST, you can also put each name-value pair on a line by itself; this avoids problems if the server doesn't like lines greater than some maximum length. For example:

```
% telnet hoohoo.ncsa.uiuc.edu 80
Trying 141.142.103.54...
Connected to hoohoo.ncsa.uiuc.edu.
Escape character is '^]'.
POST /cgi-bin/post-query HTTP/1.0
ACCEPT: text/plain
Content-type: application/x-www-form-urlencoded
Content-length: 66

username=Elliotte+Rusty+Harold
email=elharo%40sunsite%2eunc%2eedu
HTTP/1.0 200 Document follows
Date: Tue, 30 Jul 1996 15:10:41 GMT
Server: NCSA/1.5.2
Content-type: text/html

<H1>Query Results</H1>You submitted the following name/value pairs:<p>
<ul>
<li> <code>name = Elliotte Rusty Harold</code>
<li> <code>email = elharo@sunsite.unc.edu</code>
</ul>
Connection closed by foreign host.
%
```

For that matter, as long as you control both the client and the server, you can use any other sort of data encoding you like. However, if you deviate from the standard, you'll find that your non-conforming client can't talk to most CGI programs, or that your non-conforming CGI program can't process requests from most clients. The query string format used here, in which either an & or a \r\n separates name-value pairs, is used by all web browsers, and is expected by most CGI programs.

Example 10–16 is a program called postform that sends the name "Elliotte Rusty Harold" and the email address *elharo@sunsite.unc.edu* to the CGI program *http://hoohoo.ncsa.uiuc.edu/cgi-bin/post-query*. This CGI program is a simple form tester that accepts any input using the POST method, and returns an HTML page showing the names and values that were submitted. Once you understand this example, it should be easy to write Java programs that communicate with other CGI scripts. postform encodes the data according to the URL standard, posts it to *http://hoohoo.ncsa.uiuc.edu/cgi-bin/post-query*, and displays the results. The data returned is HTML; this example simply displays the HTML, rather than attempting to parse it. You could easily extend this program by adding a user interface that lets you enter the name and email address to be posted, but since that triples the size of the program while showing nothing more of network programming, it is left as an exercise.

Example 10–16: Posting a form

```
import java.net.*;
import java.io.*;

public class postform {

  URL u;

  public static void main(String args[]) {

    String s;

    try {
      s = args[0];
    }
    catch (ArrayIndexOutOfBoundsException e) {
      s = "http://hoohoo.ncsa.uiuc.edu/cgi-bin/post-query";
    }

    try {
      postform pf = new postform();
      pf.u = new URL(s);
      pf.submitData();
    }
    catch (MalformedURLException e) {
      System.err.println(args[0] + "is not a URL I understand");
    }
```

Example 10–16: Posting a form (continued)

```
  }

  void submitData() {

    String query = "name=" + URLEncoder.encode("Elliotte Rusty Harold");
    query += "&";
    query += "email=" + URLEncoder.encode("elharo@sunsite.unc.edu");


    try {

      // open the connection and prepare it to POST

      URLConnection uc = u.openConnection();
      uc.setDoOutput(true);
      uc.setDoInput(true);
      uc.setAllowUserInteraction(false);
      DataOutputStream dos = new DataOutputStream(uc.getOutputStream());

      // The POST line, the Accept line, and
      // the content-type headers are sent by the URLConnection.
      // We just need to send the data
      dos.writeBytes(query);
      dos.close();

      // Read the response
      DataInputStream dis = new DataInputStream(uc.getInputStream());
      String nextline;
      while((nextline = dis.readLine()) != null) {
        System.out.println(nextline);
      }
      dis.close();

    }
    catch (Exception e) {
      System.err.println(e);
    }

  }

}
```

Here's the response from the CGI program:

```
% java postform
<H1>Query Results</H1>You submitted the following name/value pairs:<p>
<ul>
<li> <code>name = Elliotte Rusty Harold</code>
<li> <code>email = elharo@sunsite.unc.edu</code>
</ul>
%
```

The main() method tries to read the first command-line argument from args[0]. The argument is optional; if there is an argument, it is saved in the variable s, and assumed to be the URL of a CGI script. If there are no arguments, attempting to read args[0] throws an exception; main() catches the exception and initializes the string s with a default URL, *http://hoohoo.ncsa.uiuc.edu/cgi-bin/post-query.* main() then calls the implied constructor for postform, and converts the command line argument into a URL object, u.

WARNING   This program does not work on the Mac using Sun's JDK 1.0.2, because of bugs in Sun's networking code.

After initialization, main() calls the submitData() method, which sends the request to the server. This method is the heart of this program. First, it initializes the data it will send: two input fields called name and email. (Again, it would be easy to collect this data from a pair of text fields.) The fields and their content are encoded and formatted into a query string. Next, the method opens a connection to the URL stored in u. It sets the doInput and doOutput fields of this connection to true since this URLConnection needs to send output and read input. Then it chains the OutputStream for this URL to a DataOutputStream that sends the data. After the data is sent, submitData() closes the OutputStream. Next, the URLConnection's InputStream is chained to a DataInputStream so the response can be read. Any data sent by the server is read line by line and printed on System.out.

To summarize, posting data to a form requires these steps:

1. Decide what name-value pairs you'll use to send data to the CGI program.

2. Write the CGI! If it doesn't use any custom data encoding, you can test the CGI program using a regular HTML form, and your web browser.

3. Create a query string in your Java program. The string should look like this:

    ```
    name1=value1&name2=value2&name3=value3
    ```

    Pass each value in the query string to URLEncoder.encode() before adding it to the query string.

4. Open a URLConnection to the CGI program.

5. Set doOutput to true. If you want to read the response, also set doInput to true.

6. Chain the URLConnection's OutputStream to a DataOutputStream.

7. Use the DataOutputStream's writeBytes() method to send the query string to the server. Then close the DataOutputStream.

8. Chain the URLConnection's InputStream to a DataInputStream.

9. Use the DataInputStream's readLine() method to read the response in a while loop. Then close the DataInputStream.

Posting forms is considerably more complex than using the GET method described in Chapter 5. However, with POST you get more control over the connection. More important, GET has an annoying habit of failing once the query string grows past 200 characters. (The exact point where GET fails varies from operating system to operating system, and from web server to web server.) POST lets you send long strings of data reliably.

In this chapter:
- *What Is a Protocol Handler?*
- *Writing a URLStreamHandler*
- *Writing a Protocol Handler*
- *Factories for URLStreamHandlers*
- *More Protocol Handler Examples and Techniques*

11

Protocol Handlers

What Is a Protocol Handler?

When trying to design a mechanism that would allow them to build a self-extensible browser, the engineers at Sun divided the problem into two parts: handling protocols and handling content. Handling a protocol means taking care of the interaction between a client and a server: generating requests in the correct format, interpreting the headers that come back with the data, acknowledging that the data has been received, etc. Handling the content means doing something appropriate to the data that you received; for example, displaying a GIF image file. These two problems, handling protocols and handling content, are distinct. The software that displays a GIF image doesn't care whether the image was retrieved via FTP, HTTP, gopher, or some new protocol. Likewise, the protocol handler, which manages the connection and interacts with the server, doesn't care if it's receiving an HTML file or an MPEG movie file; at most, it will extract a content type from the headers to pass along to the content handler.

The task of working with protocols was further divided into a number of pieces. As a result, there is no single class called ProtocolHandler. Instead, pieces of the protocol handler mechanism are implemented by four different classes in the java.net package: URL, URLStreamHandler, URLConnection, and URLStreamHandlerFactory. URL is the only concrete class in this group; URLStreamHandler and URLConnection are both abstract classes, and URLStreamHandlerFactory is an interface. Therefore, if you are going to implement a new protocol handler, you have to write concrete subclasses for the URLStreamHandler and the URLConnection. To use these classes, you may also have to write a class that implements the URLStreamHandlerFactory interface.

The way these classes work together can be confusing. Everything starts with a URL that represents a pointer to a particular Internet resource. Each URL specifies the protocol used to access the resource; common values for the protocol are mailto, http, and ftp. When you construct a URL object from the URL's string representation, the constructor strips the protocol field and uses it to call the URLStreamHandlerFactory. The factory's job is to take the protocol, locate an appropriate subclass of URLStreamHandler for the protocol, and create a new instance of that stream handler, which is stored as a field within the URL object. Each application has at most one URLStreamHandlerFactory; once the factory has been installed, attempting to install another is a security violation.

Now that the URL object has a stream handler, it can use the stream handler to finish parsing the URL string and to create a subclass of URLConnection that knows how to deal with servers for this protocol. URLStreamHandlers and URLConnections are always paired; the stream handler for a protocol always knows how to find an appropriate URLConnection for its protocol. It is worth noting that the stream handler does most of the work of parsing the URL. The format of the URL, although it is standard, depends on the protocol; therefore, it must be parsed by a URLStreamHandler that knows about a particular protocol, and not by the URL object (which is generic, and thus should have no knowledge of specific protocols). This also means that, if you are writing a new stream handler, you can define a new URL format that's appropriate to your task.

The URLConnection, which we saw in Chapter 10, *The URLConnection Class*, represents an active connection to the Internet resource. It is responsible for interacting with the server. URLConnections know how to generate requests, and interpret the headers that the server returns. The output from a URLConnection is raw data, with all traces of the protocol (headers, etc.) stripped, ready for processing by a content handler.

In most applications, you don't need to worry about URLConnections and stream handlers; they are hidden by the URL class, which provides a simple interface to the methods you need. When you call the getInputStream(), getOutputStream(), and getContent() methods of the URL class, you are really calling similarly named methods in the URLConnection and URLStreamHandler classes. We have seen that interacting directly with a URLConnection can be convenient when you need a little more control over communication with a server, most commonly when downloading binary files.

However, if that was the only reason these classes were of interest, they wouldn't be worth the effort. The URLConnection and URLStreamHandler classes become very important when you want to add new protocols. By writing subclasses of these classes, you can add support for old protocols, like gopher, whois, or the time protocol. You're not limited to established protocols with well-known services, either. You can create new protocols that perform database queries, search across multiple Internet search engines, view pictures from binary newsgroups, and more. You can add new kinds of URLs as needed to represent the new types of resources. Furthermore, you can build Java applications so that they can load new protocol handlers at runtime. Unlike current browsers such as Netscape Navigator and Internet Explorer, which contain explicit knowledge of all the protocols and content types they can handle, a Java browser can be a relatively lightweight skeleton that loads new handlers as needed. Supporting a new protocol just means adding some new classes in predefined locations, not writing an entirely new release of the browser.

What's involved in adding support for a new protocol? As I said earlier, you need to write two new classes: a URLConnection subclass, and a URLStreamHandler subclass. You may also need to write a class that implements the URLStreamHandlerFactory interface. Your URLConnection subclass handles the interaction with the server, converts anything the server sends into an InputStream, and converts anything the client sends into an OutputStream. This subclass must implement the abstract method connect(); it may also override the concrete methods getInputStream(), getOutputStream(), and getContentType().

The URLStreamHandler subclass parses the string representation of the URL into its separate parts, and creates a new URLConnection object that understands that URL's protocol. This subclass must implement the abstract openConnection() method, which returns the new URLConnection to its caller. If the String representation of the URL doesn't look like a standard HTTP URL, you should also override the parseURL() and toExternalForm() methods.

Finally, you may need to create a class that implements the URLStreamHandlerFactory interface. The URLStreamHandlerFactory helps the application find the right protocol handler for each type of URL. The URLStreamHandlerFactory interface has a single method, createURLStreamHandler(), that returns a URLStreamHandler object. This method must find the appropriate subclass of URLStreamHandler given only the protocol (e.g., finger or HTTP); that is, it must understand whatever package and class naming conventions you use for your stream handlers. Since URLStreamHandlerFactory is an interface, you can place the createURLStreamHandler() method in any convenient class, perhaps the main class of your application.

By default, Sun's Java implementation looks for URLStreamHandler classes named sun.net.www.protocol.*name*.Handler, where *name* is replaced by the name of the protocol; for example, http or news. If you follow the same naming scheme, you don't need to provide your own stream handler factory. That may make testing easier, and it will also allow applications like HotJava to find your new protocol handlers. Applications you distribute should set a URLStreamHandlerFactory, rather than relying on the user to install your class files within Sun's package hierarchy. The factory can tell an application to look for URLStreamHandler classes in any place that's convenient: on a web site, in the same directory as the application, or somewhere in the user's CLASSPATH.

When you've written and compiled each of these classes, you're ready to write an application that uses your new protocol handler. To allow your application to find the new protocol handler, pass the implementation of URLStreamHandlerFactory to the static method setURLStreamHandlerFactory() from java.net.URL:

```
URL.setURLStreamHandlerFactory(new myURLStreamHandlerFactory());
```

You can only call this method once in the lifetime of an application. If you call it a second time, it will throw a SecurityException. Therefore, programs that run inside other applications (for example, applets that run within browsers or applet viewers) cannot install their own URLStreamHandlerFactory(); they must use the factory installed by the parent application. In the future, better standards may be established for locating protocol handlers for unknown protocols. In the meantime, protocol handlers are primarily of use to standalone applications and HotJava, which can load protocol handlers, if they follow Sun's naming conventions and are installed on a local disk. Netscape Navigator and Internet Explorer don't load protocol handlers dynamically; you're limited to the protocols they provide.

To summarize, here's the sequence of events:

1. The main application attempts to construct a URL with a java.net.URL() constructor.

2. The constructor uses the arguments it's passed to determine the protocol part of the URL, e.g. http.

3. The URL() constructor tries to find a URLStreamHandler for the given protocol. If the protocol has been used before, the URLStreamHandler object is retrieved from a cache. Otherwise, if a URLStreamHandlerFactory has been set, the protocol string is passed to the factory's createURLStreamHandler() method. If the protocol hasn't been seen before and there's no URLStreamHandlerFactory, the constructor attempts to instantiate a URLStreamHandler object of the class sun.net.www.*protocol.protocol*.Handler. If the right URLStreamHandler object can be created it is and is returned to the constructor. If it can't be created, a MalformedURLException is thrown.

4. The main application calls the URL object's openConnection() method.

5. The URL object asks the URLStreamHandler to return an opened URLConnection object appropriate for this URL. If there's any problem, an IOException is thrown. Otherwise, a URLConnection object is returned.

6. The methods of the URLConnection class are used to interact with the remote resource.

Instead of calling openConnection() in step 4, the main program can call URL.getContent() or URL.getInputStream(). In this case, the URLStreamHandler still instantiates a URLConnection object of the appropriate class. However instead of returning the URLConnection object itself, the URLStreamHandler returns URLConnection.getContent() or URLConnection.getInputStream().

You can modify this chain of events by creating new subclasses of URLConnection and URLStreamHandler that understand new protocols.

Writing a URLStreamHandler

The abstract URLStreamHandler class is a superclass for classes that handle specific protocols like HTTP. You rarely call the methods of the URLStreamHandler class directly; they are called by other methods in the URL and URLConnection classes. By overriding the URLStreamHandler methods in your own subclass, you allow the URL class to handle new protocols. Therefore, I have taken a different approach in discussing the methods of URLStreamHandler. We'll focus on overriding the methods of URLStreamHandler, rather than on calling the methods.

The Constructor

You do not create URLStreamHandler objects directly. Instead, when you construct a URL with a protocol that hasn't been seen before, Java asks the application's URLStreamHandlerFactory to create the appropriate URLStreamHandler subclass for the protocol.

public URLStreamHandler()

The constructor for URLStreamHandler has no arguments. Because URLStreamHandler is an abstract class, its constructor is never called directly; it is only called from the constructors of subclasses.

Methods for Parsing URLs

The first responsibility of a URLStreamHandler is to split a string representation of a URL into its component parts, and use those parts to set the various fields of the

URL object. The parseURL() method splits the URL into parts, possibly using setURL() to assign values to the URL's fields (although there are other ways to accomplish this that may be more convenient). It is very difficult to imagine a situation in which you would call parseURL() directly; instead, you override it to change the behavior of the URL class.

protected void parseURL(URL u, String s, int start, int limit)

This method parses a string s into a URL u. It takes the substring of s beginning with the character at start, and continues until it reaches the character at limit, or the String is used up. The first character of the String is character 0. The task of parseURL() is to set the URL u's protocol, host, port, file, and ref fields. It can assume that any parts of the String that are before start and after limit have already been parsed, or can be ignored. In most cases, the protocol portion of the URL (everything before the first colon) will have already been parsed, and start will point to the first character after the colon. For example, if s is http://www.ora.com/, start is 5. The caller may also use the start and limit arguments to strip leading and trailing white space from s.

The parseURL() method Java supplies assumes that the URL looks more or less like an HTTP URL, that is:

```
protocol://www.host.com:port/file#ref
```

This works for FTP and gopher URLs. It does not work for mailto or news URLs, and may not be appropriate for any new URL types you define. If your protocol handler uses URLs that fit this form, you don't have to override parseURL() at all; the method inherited from URLStreamHandler will work just fine. If your URLs are completely different, you must supply a parseURL() method that parses the URL completely. However, there's often a middle ground that can make your task easier. If your URL looks somewhat like a standard URL, you can implement a parseURL() method that handles the nonstandard portion of your URL, and then calls super.parseURL() to do the rest of the work, setting the start and limit arguments to indicate the portion of the URL that you didn't parse.

For example, a mailto: URL looks like mailto:elharo@sunsite.unc.edu. First, you need to figure out how to map this into the URL class's protocol, host, port, file, and ref fields. The protocol is clearly mailto. Everything after the @ can be the host. The hard question is what to do with the username. Since a mailto URL really doesn't have a file portion, we will use the URL class's file field to hold the username. The port and the ref can be set to empty strings, or null. The following parseURL() method implements this scheme. A StringTokenizer is used to split the URL into three parts. This method is a little short on error checking; a more capable parseURL() method should be careful in case the string has the wrong syntax.

```
protected void parseURL(URL u, String spec, int start, int limit) {

    StringTokenizer st = new StringTokenizer(spec.substring(start), ":@", false);
    String protocol = st.nextToken(); // should be mailto
    String file = st.nextToken();   // really the username
    String host = st.nextToken();
    String ref = null;
    int port = 25;

    setURL(u, protocol, host, port, file, ref);

}
```

Rather than borrowing an unused field from the URL object, it's possibly a better idea to store protocol specific parts of the URL, like the username, in fields of your URLStreamHandler subclass. The disadvantage of this approach is that such fields can only be seen by your own code; in this example, you couldn't use URL.getFile() to retrieve the username. Here's a version of parseURL() that stores the username in a field of the Handler subclass:

```
String username;

protected void parseURL(URL u, String spec, int start, int limit) {

    StringTokenizer st = new StringTokenizer(spec.substring(start), ":@", false);
    String protocol = st.nextToken(); // should be mailto
    username = st.nextToken();
    String host = st.nextToken();
    String file = null;
    String ref = null;
    int port = 25;

    setURL(u, protocol, host, port, file, ref);

}
```

protected String toExternalForm(URL u)

This method puts the pieces of the URL u—that is, its protocol, host, port, file, and ref fields—back together in a String. If you override parseURL(), you should also override toExternalForm(). Here's a toExternalForm() method for a mailto URL; it assumes that the username has been stored in the URL's host field:

```
protected String toExternalForm(URL u) {

    return "mailto:" + u.getFile() + "@" + u.getHost();

}
```

Since `toExternalForm()` is protected, you probably won't call this method directly. However, it is called by the public `toExternalForm()` and `toString()` methods of the URL class, so any change you make here is reflected when you convert URL objects to strings.

protected void setURL(URL u, String protocol, String host, int port, String file, String ref)

This method sets the `protocol`, `host`, `port`, `file`, and `ref` fields of the URL u to the given values. This method is used by `parseURL()` to set these fields to the values it has found by parsing the URL. You might need to call this method if you subclass `URLStreamHandler` with a class that is not in the `java.net` package, and override `parseURL()`. (If your class is in the `java.net` package, it can access these fields directly.)

A Method for Connecting

The second responsibility of a `URLStreamHandler` is to create a `URLConnection` object appropriate to the URL. This is done by the `openConnection()` method.

protected abstract URLConnection openConnection(URL u)
throws IOException

This method must be overridden in each subclass of `URLConnectionStreamHandler`. It takes a single argument u, the URL to connect to. It returns a closed `URLConnection`, directed at the resource u points to. Each subclass of `URLStreamHandler` should know how to find the right subclass of `URLConnection` for the protocol it handles.

`openConnection()` is protected, so you usually do not call it directly; it is called by the `openConnection()` method of a URL object. The URL u passed as an argument is the URL that needs a connection. You override this method in your subclasses to handle a specific protocol. Your subclass's `openConnection()` method is usually extremely simple; in most cases, it just calls the constructor for the appropriate subclass of `URLConnection`. For example, a `mailto` `URLStreamHandler` might have an `openConnection()` method that looks like this:

```
protected URLConnection openConnection(URL u) throws IOException {
  return new mailtoURLConnection(u);
}
```

Example 11–1 demonstrates a complete `URLStreamHandler` for `mailto` URLs; the name of the class is `Handler`, following Sun's naming conventions. It assumes the existence of a `mailtoURLConnection` class.

Example 11–1: A mailto URLStreamHandler

```
import java.net.*;
import java.io.*;
import java.util.*;

public class Handler extends java.net.URLStreamHandler {

  protected URLConnection openConnection(URL u) throws IOException {
    return new mailtoURLConnection(u);
  }

  protected void parseURL(URL u, String spec, int start, int limit) {

    StringTokenizer st = new StringTokenizer(spec.substring(start), ":@", false);
    String protocol = st.nextToken(); // should be mailto
    String file = st.nextToken();  // really the username
    String host = st.nextToken();
    String ref = null;
    int port = 25;

    setURL(u, protocol, host, port, file, ref);
  }

  protected String toExternalForm(URL u) {

    return "mailto:" + u.getFile() + "@" + u.getHost();;

  }

}
```

Writing a Protocol Handler

To demonstrate a complete protocol handler, let's write one for the chargen protocol, defined in RFC864. chargen is a very simple protocol that was designed for testing clients. The server listens for connections on port 19. When a client connects, the server sends an endless stream of characters until the client disconnects. Any input from the client is ignored. The RFC does not specify the character sequence to send, but recommends that the server use a recognizable pattern. One common pattern is rotating, 72-character lines of the 95 printing ASCII characters, like this:

```
!"#$%&'()*+,-./0123456789:;<=>?@ABCDEFGHIJKLMNOPQRSTUVWXYZ[\]^_`abcdefgh
"#$%&'()*+,-./0123456789:;<=>?@ABCDEFGHIJKLMNOPQRSTUVWXYZ[\]^_`abcdefghi
#$%&'()*+,-./0123456789:;<=>?@ABCDEFGHIJKLMNOPQRSTUVWXYZ[\]^_`abcdefghij
$%&'()*+,-./0123456789:;<=>?@ABCDEFGHIJKLMNOPQRSTUVWXYZ[\]^_`abcdefghijk
%&'()*+,-./0123456789:;<=>?@ABCDEFGHIJKLMNOPQRSTUVWXYZ[\]^_`abcdefghijkl
&'()*+,-./0123456789:;<=>?@ABCDEFGHIJKLMNOPQRSTUVWXYZ[\]^_`abcdefghijklm
'()*+,-./0123456789:;<=>?@ABCDEFGHIJKLMNOPQRSTUVWXYZ[\]^_`abcdefghijklmn
()*+,-./0123456789:;<=>?@ABCDEFGHIJKLMNOPQRSTUVWXYZ[\]^_`abcdefghijklmno
```

Since there's no standard for the format of a chargen URL, we will start by creating one. Ideally, this should look as much like an HTTP URL as possible. Therefore, we will implement a chargen URL like this:

```
chargen://hostname:port
```

Second, we need to determine the content type returned by the chargen protocol's getContentType() method. New protocols like HTTP use MIME headers to indicate the content type; in these cases, you do not need to override the default getContentType() method provided by the URLConnection class. However, since most protocols outdate MIME, you often need to specify the MIME type explicitly or use the static methods, URLConnection.guessContentTypeFromName(String name) and URLConnection.guessContentTypeFromStream(InputStream is), to make an educated guess. For this example, you don't need anything so complicated. A chargen server returns ASCII text, so the getContentType() method should return the string text/plain. The text/plain MIME type has the advantage that Java already understands it. In the next chapter, you'll learn how to write content handlers that let Java understand additional MIME types.

Example 11–2 is a chargenURLConnection class that subclasses URLConnection. This class overrides the getContentType() and getInputStream() methods of URLConnection, and implements connect(). It also has a constructor that builds a new URLConnection from a URL.

Example 11–2: The chargenURLConnection class

```java
package sun.net.www.protocol.chargen;

import java.net.*;
import java.io.*;

public class chargenURLConnection extends URLConnection {

  Socket theConnection = null;
  public final static int defaultPort = 19;

  public chargenURLConnection(URL u) {
    super(u);
  }

  public synchronized InputStream getInputStream() throws IOException {

    if (!connected) {
      connect();
    }
    return theConnection.getInputStream();

  }

  public String getContentType() {
```

Example 11–2: The chargenURLConnection class (continued)

```
    "return text/plain;
  }

  public synchronized void connect() throws IOException {

    int port;

    if (!connected) {
      port = url.getPort();
      if ( port < 0) {
        port = defaultPort;
      }
      theConnection = new Socket(url.getHost(), port);
      connected = true;
    }


  }

}
```

This class has two fields. theConnection is a Socket between the client and the server. Both the getInputStream() method and the connect() method need access to this field, so it can't be a local variable. The second field is defaultPort, a final static int, that contains the chargen protocol's default port; this port is used if the URL does not specify the port explicitly.

The class's constructor holds no surprises. It just calls the superclass's constructor with the same argument, the URL u. The connect() method opens a connection to the specified server on the specified port (or, if no port is specified, then to the default chargen port, 19); and, assuming the connection is successfully opened, sets the boolean variable connected to true. Recall from Chapter 10 that connected is a protected field in java.net.URLConnection that is inherited by this subclass. The Socket that connect() opens is stored in the field theConnection for later use by getInputStream(). The connect() method is synchronized to avoid a possible race condition on the connected variable.

The getContentType() method returns a String containing a MIME type for the data. This is used by the getContent() method of java.net.URLConnection to select the appropriate content handler. The data returned by a chargen server is always ASCII text, so this getContentType() method returns text/plain. The get-InputStream() method returns an InputStream from the Socket that connect created. If the connection has not already been established when getInputStream() is called, the method calls connect() itself.

Once you have a URLConnection, you need a subclass of URLStreamHandler that knows how to handle a chargen server. This class needs an openConnection() method that builds a new chargenURLConnection from a URL. Since you defined the chargen URL so that it is similar to an HTTP URL, you don't need to implement a parseURL() method. Example 11–3 is a stream handler for the chargen protocol. For the moment, you're going to use Sun's convention for naming protocol handlers, so call this class Handler and then place it in the package sun.net.www.protocol.chargen. This restriction will be removed in the next section when we discuss stream handler factories.

Example 11–3: The chargen Handler class

```
package sun.net.www.protocol.chargen;

import java.net.*;
import java.io.*;

public class Handler extends URLStreamHandler {

  protected URLConnection openConnection(URL u) throws IOException {
    return new chargenURLConnection(u);
  }

}
```

Compile Example 11–2 and Example 11–3 in a directory in your CLASSPATH. Two files are created: *Handler.class* and *chargenURLConnection.class.* Some Java development environments, such as the JDK for the Mac, may write the *.class* files inside a hierarchy of directories called *sun/net/www/protocol/chargen.* In other environments, such as Solaris, you'll need to create these directories in your CLASSPATH and move the *.class* files there yourself.

You can use the *URLRequestor.class* file from Example 5–14 to test this protocol handler. Run it, and ask for a URL of a site running a chargen server such as *sunsite.unc.edu.* Figure 11–1 shows the result.

Instead of using a standalone application, you can test the protocol handler with HotJava if you make sure the classes are in HotJava's CLASSPATH, and you set HotJava's network security preferences to "unrestricted."

Factories for URLStreamHandlers

Adding files to the sun packages, like we did in the last section, is not a very convenient way to install new protocol handlers. The proper way to install a new protocol handler is to implement the createURLStreamHandler() method of the URLStreamHandlerFactory interface.

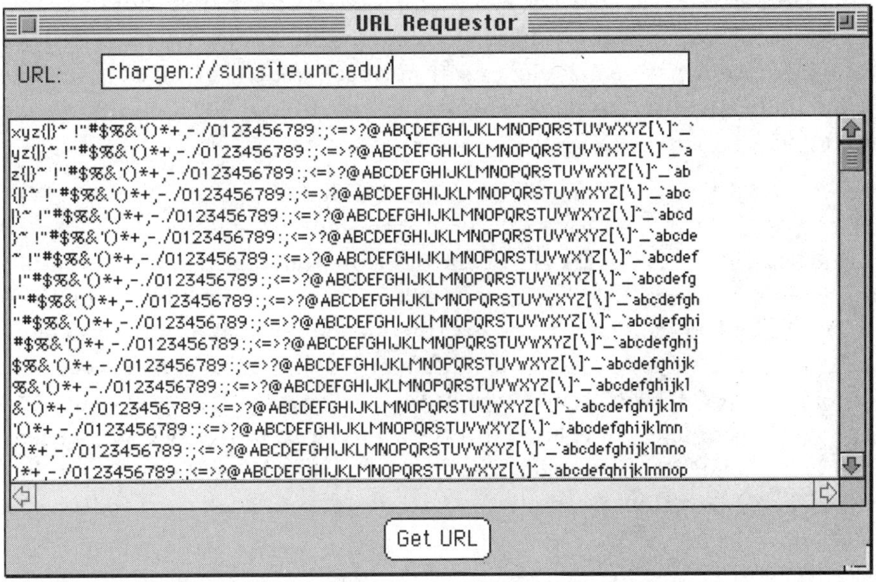

Figure 11–1: The URLRequestor applet using the chargen protocol handler

Only applications are allowed to install a new URLStreamHandlerFactory. Applets that run in the applet viewer or Netscape must use the URLStreamHandlerFactory that is provided. An attempt to set a different one throws a SecurityException. The default URLStreamHandlerFactory just looks for handlers in the file *sun.net.www*.protocol.*Handler.class* where "protocol" is replaced by the protocol specified in the URL—for example, http or ftp.

Installing a URLStreamHandler

public abstract URLStreamHandler
createURLStreamHandler(String protocol)

The createURLStreamHandler() method of the URLStreamHandlerFactory() interface loads the appropriate protocol handler for the specified protocol. To use this method, write a class that implements the URLStreamHandlerFactory interface and include a createURLStreamHandler() method in that class. This method needs to know how to find the protocol handler for a given protocol. This is no more complicated than knowing the names and packages of the custom protocols you've implemented. A class may be created especially for this purpose; or, more commonly, you can add this method to your application.

If no URLStreamHandlerFactory has been set, Java looks for a class with the name sun.net.www.*protocol*.Handler, where *protocol* is the protocol name. If your application does not have a handlers for a protocol, your createURLStreamHandler() method should return null. This signals Java to look for a handler in the default location.

In order to install the stream handler factory, you should pass an instance of the class that implements the URLStreamHandlerFactory interface to the static method URL.setURLStreamHandlerFactory() at the start of your program. For example, suppose you want to search for protocol handlers first in the directory from which the applet was loaded (the codebase), and then in the normal locations. Remove the package statements from Example 11–2 and Example 11–3, since you're no longer going to put the chargen classes in the sun package hierarchy. The URL-StreamHandler class may conceivably live in a directory with other stream handlers, so we'll rename it chargenURLStreamHandler, which is more descriptive than its original name, Handler. Example 11–4 is the revised URLStreamHandler subclass.

Example 11–4: The chargenURLStreamHandler

```
import java.net.*;
import java.io.*;

public class chargenURLStreamHandler extends URLStreamHandler {

  protected URLConnection openConnection(URL u) throws IOException {
    return new chargenURLConnection(u);
  }

}
```

Next, declare that your application implements URLStreamHandlerFactory, and add this createURLStreamHandler method:

```
    public URLStreamHandler createURLStreamHandler(String protocol) {

        if (protocol.equalsIgnoreCase("chargen")) {
          return new chargenURLStreamHandler();
        }
        else {
          return null;
        }

    }
```

This method begins by using the equalsIgnoreCase() method from java.lang.String to test whether the protocol is chargen. According to the URL specification, it shouldn't make a difference whether you ask for *CHAR-GEN://sunsite.unc.edu* or *chargen://sunsite.unc.edu*. Therefore, we use a method that ignores case for the comparison, rather than the more familiar equals() method; the latter is case-sensitive, and thus would consider chargen and CHARGEN to be different strings.

If the protocol is chargen, then createURLStreamHandler() creates a new chargenURLStreamHandler, and returns it; otherwise, the method returns null, which tells the URL class to look for a URLStreamHandler in the standard locations. The .*class* file for the chargenURLStreamHandler is just like any other user-defined class. If this method is in an applet, then the chargenURLStreamHandler.class is returned across the network from the same place the applet came from.

Example 11–5 is a program that uses the chargen protocol handler to display chargen data. The program is structured so that it can run standalone (as an application) or in a browser (as an applet). The main() method builds a frame for the applet, instantiates the applet, and puts it inside the frame. The init() method puts a TextArea in the applet and connects to the chargen server on *sunsite.unc.edu*. The applet itself implements the createURLStreamHandler() method just discussed, and its init() method calls setURLStreamHandlerFactory() with an argument of this (i.e., the applet itself). The run() method reads data from the URLConnection and adds it to the text in the TextArea.

Since the AppletSecurityManager does not allow setURLStreamHandlerFactory to be called, a SecurityException is thrown if you put this applet on a web page and look at it with the AppletViewer 1.0.x or Netscape 3.0 or earlier. Therefore, for the present, this program can only be run as an application from the command line, though it is ready to be run as an applet when the browsers catch up. The chargenURLConnection and chargenURLStreamHandler classes must be recompiled after the package statements are removed. Then they should be placed in the same directory as the applet itself. Figure 11–2 shows the applet in action.

Example 11–5: A chargen applet

```
import java.applet.Applet;
import java.net.*;
import java.awt.*;
import java.io.*;

public class chargenApplet extends Applet
    implements URLStreamHandlerFactory, Runnable {

  TextArea theText;
  URL theServer;
  DataInputStream dis = null;

public static void main(String[] args) {
```

Example 11–5: A chargen applet (continued)

```
    Frame f = new Frame("chargen applet");
    f.resize(300, 300);
    f.move(50, 50);
    chargenApplet cg = new chargenApplet();

    f.add("Center", cg);
    cg.init();
    f.show();
    cg.start();

  }

  public void init() {

    URL.setURLStreamHandlerFactory(this);
    setLayout(new BorderLayout());
    theText = new TextArea();
    add("Center", theText);
    String s = "chargen://sunsite.unc.edu/";
    try {
      theServer = new URL(s);
      dis = new DataInputStream(theServer.openStream());
    }
    catch (MalformedURLException e) {
      theText.setText("Error: Could not handle URL " + s);
    }
    catch (IOException e) {
      theText.setText("Error: Could not open connection to " + s);
      theText.appendText("There may not be a chargen server running" +
        "on this host or network connections may be disallowed.");
    }
    Thread t = new Thread(this);
    t.start();

  }

public URLStreamHandler createURLStreamHandler(String protocol) {

    if (protocol.equalsIgnoreCase("chargen")) {
      return new chargenURLStreamHandler();
    }
    else {
      return null;
    }

  }

public void run() {

    try {
      String theLine;
      if (dis != null) {
```

Example 11–5: A chargen applet (continued)

```
        while ((theLine = dis.readLine()) != null) {
          theText.appendText(theLine + "\r");
        }
      }
    }
    catch (IOException e) {
    }
  }
}
```

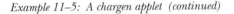

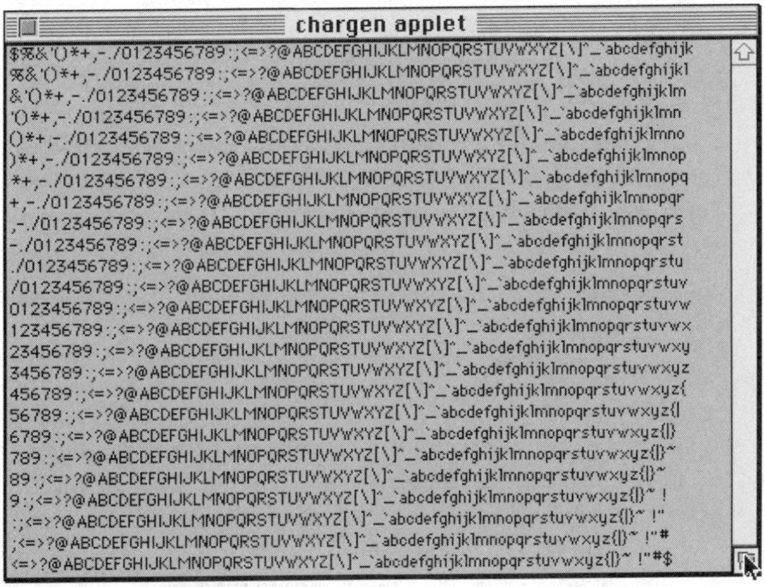

Figure 11–2: The chargen applet

More Protocol Handler Examples and Techniques

Now that you've seen how to write one protocol handler, it's not at all difficult to write more. Remember the five basic steps of creating a new protocol handler:

1. Design a URL for the protocol, if a standard URL for that protocol doesn't already exist. The URL specification only defines eight kinds of URLs; for anything else, you need to define your own. Try to make your new URL as similar to an HTTP URL as possible.

2. Decide what MIME type should be returned by the protocol handler's getContentType() method. The text/plain content type is often appropriate for legacy protocols. Another option is to convert the incoming data to HTML inside getInputStream() and return text/html. Binary data often uses one of the many application types. In some cases, you may be able to use the guessContentTypeFromName() or guessContentTypeFromStream() methods to guess the right MIME type. If you're creating a new protocol, seriously consider using MIME to specify content types, even if you think the protocol will only handle one kind of data. If you ever extend the protocol to handle other content types, you will be glad you decided to use MIME typing.

3. Create a subclass of URLConnection that understands this protocol. It should implement the connect() method, and may override the getContentType(), getOutputStream() and getInputStream() methods of URLConnection. It also needs a constructor that builds a new URLConnection from your URL.

4. Create a subclass of URLStreamHandler with an openConnection() method that knows how to return a new instance of your subclass of URLConnection. If your URL does not look like an HTTP URL, override parseURL() and toExternalForm().

5. Implement the URLStreamHandlerFactory interface and the createStreamHandler() method in a convenient class.

daytime

We'll finish the chapter by developing one more complete protocol handler, this one for the daytime protocol. For a daytime protocol handler, let's say that the URL should look like *daytime://sunsite.unc.edu*. Allow for nonstandard port assignments in the same way as with HTTP: follow the hostname with a colon and the port (*daytime://sunsite.unc.edu:2082*). Finally, allow a terminating slash, and ignore everything following the slash. For example, *daytime://sunsite.unc.edu/index.html* is equivalent to *daytime://sunsite.unc.edu*. This is similar enough to an HTTP URL that you'll be able to use the default toExternalForm() and parseURL() methods.

Although the content returned by the daytime protocol is really text/plain, this protocol handler is going to reformat the data into an HTML page. Then it can return a content type of text/html, and let the web browser display it more dramatically. To do this, it reads all the data from the connection, parses it, reformats it into a String, and then returns a StringBufferInputStream that contains the reformatted data. This is a neat trick for protocols like daytime that return a very limited amount of data, and generally do so rather quickly.

Example 11–6 is a daytimeURLConnection class that subclasses URLConnection. This
class overrides the getContentType() and getInputStream() methods of URLConnection and implements connect(). It also has a constructor that builds a new
URLConnection from a URL.

Example 11–6: The daytimeURLConnection class

```java
import java.net.*;
import java.io.*;

public class daytimeURLConnection extends URLConnection {

  Socket theConnection = null;
  public final static int defaultPort = 13;

  public daytimeURLConnection (URL u) {
    super(u);
  }

  public synchronized InputStream getInputStream() throws IOException {

    if (!connected) {
      connect();
    }
    DataInputStream dis = new DataInputStream(theConnection.getInputStream());
    String time = dis.readLine();
    String html = "<html><head><title>The Time at " +
      url.getHost() + "</title></head><body><h1>" +
      time + "</h1></body></html>";

    return new StringBufferInputStream(html);
  }

  public String getContentType() {
    return "text/html";
  }

  public Object getContent() {
    return getInputStream();
  }

  public synchronized void connect() throws IOException {

    int port;

    if (!connected) {
      port = url.getPort();
      if ( port < 0) {
        port = defaultPort;
      }
      theConnection = new Socket(url.getHost(), port);
      connected = true;
    }
```

Example 11–6: The daytimeURLConnection class (continued)

```
  }
}
```

This class has two fields. The first is theConnection, which is a Socket between the client and the server. The second field is defaultPort, a final static int variable, that holds the default port for the daytime protocol (port 13), and is used if the URL doesn't specify the port explicitly.

The constructor has no surprises. It just calls the superclass's constructor with the same argument, the URL u. The connect() method opens a connection to the specified server on the specified port (or, if no port is specified, to the default daytime port); if the connection is opened successfully, connect() sets the boolean variable connected to true. Recall from Chapter 10 that connected is a protected field in java.net.URLConnection that is inherited by this subclass. The Socket that's opened by this method is stored in the field theConnection for later use by getInputStream().

The getContentType() method returns a String containing a MIME type for the data. This method is called by the getContent() method of java.net.URL-Connection to select the appropriate content handler. The getInputStream() method reformats the text into HTML, so the getContentType() method returns text/html.

The getInputStream() method returns the InputStream that it gets from the Socket connecting the client to the server. If the Socket is not connected when this method is called, then the method calls connect() to establish the connection. The time is read from the connection, and embedded within the String HTML. This String is used to create a new StringBufferInputStream.

Next, you need a subclass of URLStreamHandler that knows how to handle a daytime server. This class needs an openConnection() method that builds a new daytimeURLConnection from a URL. Since the daytime URL has been made similar to an HTTP URL, we don't need to override parseURL(); once we have written openConnection(), we're done. Example 11–7 shows the daytime protocol's URLStreamHandler.

Example 11–7: The daytimeURLStreamHandler class

```
import java.net.*;
import java.io.*;

public class daytimeURLStreamHandler extends URLStreamHandler {

  protected URLConnection openConnection(URL u) throws IOException {
    return new daytimeURLConnection(u);
  }
```

Example 11–7: The daytimeURLStreamHandler class (continued)

```
}
```

Finally, you need a URLStreamHandlerFactory to instantiate this class. It would be simple enough to add an additional if block to the createURLStreamHandler method of Example 11–7 to recognize the daytime protocol. However, if you're going to be adding lots of protocols, it makes sense to establish a common way of naming and finding them. Example 11–8 looks for protocols named *nameURLConnection* where *name* is the name of the protocol. This way, a new protocol can be added at runtime without modifying and recompiling the URLStreamHandlerFactory.

Example 11–8: A Protocol Tester that can be extended with new classes at runtime

```
import java.io.*;
import java.net.*;

public class ProtocolTester implements URLStreamHandlerFactory {

  String theURL;

  public static void main (String[] args) {

    if (args.length == 1) {
      ProtocolTester pt = new ProtocolTester(args[0]);
      URL.setURLStreamHandlerFactory(pt);
      pt.test();
    }
    else {
      System.err.println("Usage: java ProtocolTester url");
    }

  }

  public ProtocolTester(String s) {

    theURL = s;

  }

public void test() {

  String theLine;

  try {
    URL u = new URL(theURL);
    DataInputStream dis = new DataInputStream(u.openStream());
    while ((theLine = dis.readLine()) != null) {
      System.out.println(theLine);
    }
  }
```

Example 11–8: A Protocol Tester that can be extended with new classes at runtime (continued)

```
  catch (IOException e) {
    System.err.println(e);
  }

}


public URLStreamHandler createURLStreamHandler(String protocol) {

  protocol = protocol.toLowerCase();
  try {
    Class ph = Class.forName(protocol + "URLStreamHandler");
    Object o = ph.newInstance();
    return (URLStreamHandler) o;
  }
  catch (Exception e) {
    return null;
  }

}

}
```

The most significant thing about the ProtocolTester is its createURLStreamHandler() method. Unlike the previous version of this method, which had the names of all our protocol handlers built in at compile time, this method builds a class name by appending the string URLStreamHandler to the argument s. It then uses the forName() and newInstance() methods of java.lang.Class to create an instance of the new stream handler. If it succeeds, createURLStreamHandler() casts the new Object to URLStreamHandler and returns the result. If forName() or newInstance() fails, they will throw exceptions. In this case, createURLStreamHandler() catches the exception and returns null, and the default locations are searched for a matching protocol handler.

12

Content Handlers

What Is a Content Handler?

Content handlers are one of the ideas that got developers excited about Java in the first place. At the time HotJava was created, Netscape, NCSA, Spyglass, and a few other players were fighting a battle over who would control the standards for web browsing. One of the battlegrounds was the ability of different browsers to handle various kinds of files. The first browsers only understood HTML. The next generation understood HTML and GIF. JPEG support was soon added. The intensity of this battle meant that new versions of browsers were released every couple of weeks. Netscape made the first attempt to break this infinite loop by introducing plug-ins in Navigator 2.0. Plug-ins are platform-dependent browser extenders written in C that add the ability to view new content types like Acrobat PDF and VRML. However, plug-ins have their drawbacks. Each new content type requires the user to download and install a new plug-in, if indeed the right plug-in is even available for the user's platform. To keep up, users had to use huge amounts of bandwidth just to download new browsers and plug-ins, each of which would fix a few bugs and add a few new features.

The Java team saw a way around this. Their idea was to use Java to download only the parts of the program that had to be updated rather than the entire browser. Furthermore, when the user encountered a web page that used a new content type, the browser could automatically download the code that was needed to view that content type. The user doesn't have to stop, FTP a plug-in, quit the browser, install the plug-in, restart the browser, and reload the page. (Netscape has announced plans to make plug-ins automatically downloadable, when needed, perhaps in Navigator 4.0. Plug-ins will still need to be written in C for each platform, though; and automatically downloaded plug-ins written in C will introduce a security hole big enough to walk a herd of elephants through.)

A content handler is a subclass of `java.net.ContentHandler`. This class knows how to take an `InputStream` and a MIME type, and turn the data coming from the `InputStream` into a Java object of an appropriate type. Thus, a content handler allows a browser or applet to understand new kinds of data. Since Java lowers the bar for writing code below what's needed to write a browser or a Netscape plug-in, many different websites can write custom handlers, rather than having to rely on the overworked browser manufacturers.

Java can already download classes from the Internet. Thus, there isn't much magic to getting it to download a class that can understand a new content type. A content handler is just a *.class* file like any other. The magic is all inside the web browser, which knows when and where to request a *.class* file to view a new content type. Of course some browsers are more magical than others. Netscape 3.0 and Internet Explorer 3.0 do not support automatically downloadable content handlers. Automatically downloadable content handlers should, however, be available in future versions of HotJava including those running on network computers.

Specifically, a content handler reads data from a `URLConnection`, and constructs an object from the data appropriate for the content type. Each subclass of `ContentHandler` handles a specific MIME type and subtype, like `text/plain` or `image/gif`. Thus an `image/gif` content handler returns a `URLImageSource` object (a class that implements the `ImageProducer` interface), while a `text/plain` content handler returns a `String`. A database content handler might return a database or a record object (which the programmer would have to define, since there's no such class built into Java).

Content handlers are intimately tied to protocol handlers. In the last chapter, the `getContent()` method of the `URLConnection` class returned an `InputStream` that fed the data from the server to the client. This works for simple protocols that only return ASCII text, like `finger`, `whois`, and `daytime`. However, returning an input stream doesn't work well for protocols like FTP, gopher, and HTTP that can return many different content types, many of which can't be understood as a stream of ASCII text. For protocols like these, `getContent()` needs to check the MIME type, and then use the `createContentHandler()` method of the application's `ContentHandlerFactory` to produce a matching content handler. Once a `ContentHandler` exists, the `getContent()` method of `URLConnection` calls the `ContentHandler`'s `getContent()` method, which creates the Java object to be returned. Outside of the `getContent()` method of a `URLConnection`, you rarely, if ever, call any `ContentHandler` method. Applications should never call the methods of a `ContentHandler` directly. Instead, they should use the `getContent()` method of the `URL` or `URLConnection`.

An object that implements the ContentHandlerFactory interface is responsible for choosing the right ContentHandler to go with a MIME type. This interface can be implemented by any convenient class. A ContentHandlerFactory is installed in a program by the static URLConnection.setContentHandlerFactory() method. Only one ContentHandlerFactory may be chosen during the lifetime of an application. When a program starts running, there is no ContentHandlerFactory (the ContentHandlerFactory is null). When there is no factory, Java looks for content handler classes with the name sun.net.www.content.*type*.*subtype*, where *type* is the MIME type of the content, and *subtype* is the MIME subtype. These conventions are also used to search for a content handler when the createContentHandler() method returns null.

To summarize, here's the sequence of events:

1. A URL is created that points at some Internet resource.

2. The URL's getContent() method is called to return an object representing the contents of the resource.

3. If the connection to the URL isn't already open, it is opened.

4. The getContent() method of the URLConnection is called.

5. URLConnection.getContent() calls URLConnection.getContentHandler() to find a content handler for the MIME type and subtype.

6. getContentHandler() checks to see if it already has a handler for this type in its cache. If it does, that handler is returned to URLConnection.getContent(). Thus, browsers won't download content handlers for common types, like text/html, every time the user goes to a new web page.

7. If there wasn't an appropriate ContentHandler in the cache and the ContentHandlerFactory isn't null, getContentHandler() calls the ContentHandlerFactory's createContentHandler() method to instantiate a new ContentHandler. If this is successful, the ContentHandler object is returned to URLConnection.getContent().

8. If the ContentHandlerFactory is null or createContentHandler() fails to instantiate a new ContentHandler, Java looks for a content handler class named sun.net.www.content.*type*.*subtype*, where *type* is the MIME type of the content, and *subtype* is the MIME subtype. If a content handler is found, it is returned; otherwise createContentHandler() returns null.

9. At this point, there is a ContentHandler object (which may be null) in URLConnection.getContent(). This ContentHandler's getContent() method is now called. This method returns an object appropriate for the content type. If the ContentHandler is null, an IOException is thrown.

10. Either the returned object or the exception is passed up the call chain, eventually reaching the method that invoked URL.getContent().

You can affect this chain of events in three ways: Firstly, by constructing a URL u and calling u.getContent(); second, by creating a new ContentHandler subclass that getContent() can use; thirdly, by installing a ContentHandlerFactory with URLConnection.setContentHandlerFactory(), and changing the way the application looks for content handlers.

NOTE   Netscape and Internet Explorer versions 3.0 and earlier do not support content handlers. Programs in this chapter require HotJava or the JDK to run.

The ContentHandler Class

A subclass of ContentHandler should override the getContent() method to return an object that's the Java equivalent of the content. This method can be quite simple or quite complex, depending almost entirely on the complexity of the content type you're trying to parse. A text/plain content handler is quite simple; a text/rtf content handler would be very complex.

Currently, the biggest problem with the content handler mechanism is that it is often unclear what type of object a content handler should return. The problem is understanding what kinds of content a browser is able to display. Most current content handlers for text-like content seem to return some subclass of InputStream. Content handlers for images return ImageProducer objects. Perhaps in the future, content handlers will return objects of arbitrary types, but also implement an interface that provides instructions for rendering the content in a two-dimensional rectangle in the browser. Or there may be a standard that defines what Java objects are equivalent to different types of content. For now, the most portable solution seems to be using an applet to show the content so you control both the format of the content and its display.

The Constructor

public ContentHandler()

The ContentHandler class doesn't supply a constructor; it uses the default (no arguments) constructor provided by the system. Since ContentHandler is an abstract class, you never call its constructor explicitly.

The getContent Method

public abstract Object getContent(URLConnection uc)
throws IOException

You only call this method from inside the getContent() method of a URLConnection object. It is overridden in a subclass that is specific to the type of content being handled. getContent() should use the URLConnection's InputStream to create an object.

The getContent() method of a content handler does not get the full InputStream that the URLConnection has access to. The InputStream that a content handler sees should only include the content's raw data. Any MIME headers or other protocol-specific headers that come from the server should be stripped by the URLConnection before it passes the stream to the ContentHandler. A ContentHandler is only responsible for content, not any header that may be present. The URLConnection should have already performed any necessary handshaking with the server, and interpreted any headers it sends.

To see how content handlers work, let's create a ContentHandler that handles the text/tab-separated-values content type. You aren't concerned with how you get the tab-separated values. That's for a protocol handler to deal with. All a ContentHandler needs to know is the MIME type and format of the data.

Tab-separated values are produced by many database and spreadsheet programs. A tab-separated file may look something like this:

```
JPE Associates    341 Lafayette St.Suite 1025      Nowhere NY      10012
O'Reilly & Associates     103 Morris Str.  Suite A Sebastopol     CA  95472
```

In database parlance, each line is a *record*, and the data before each tab is a *field*. It is usually (though not necessarily) true that each field has the same meaning in each record. In the above example, the first field is the company name.

The first question to ask is: what kind of Java object should you convert the tab-separated-values to? The simplest and most general way to store each record is as an array of Strings. Successive records can be collected in a Vector. However, in many applications you have a great deal more knowledge about the exact format and meaning of the data than you do here. The more you know about the data you're dealing with, the better ContentHandler you can write. For example, if you know that the data you're downloading represents addresses, you could define a class like this:

```
public class address {

   String name;
   String street;
```

```
        String suite;
        String state;
        String city;
        String zip;


    }
```

This class would also have appropriate constructors and other methods to represent each record. In the example, you don't know anything about the data in advance, or how many records you'll have to store. Therefore, you will take the most general approach, and convert each record into an array of Strings, using a Vector to store each array until there are no more records. The getContent() method can return the Vector of records. Example 12–1 shows the code for this ContentHandler.

Example 12–1: A ContentHandler for text/tab-separated-values

```
import java.net.*;
import java.io.*;
import java.util.*;

public class tabSeparatedValueHandler extends ContentHandler {

  public Object getContent(URLConnection uc) {

    String theLine;
    Vector v = new Vector();

    try {
      DataInputStream dis = new DataInputStream(uc.getInputStream());
      while ((theLine = dis.readLine()) != null) {
        String[] linearray = lineToArray(theLine);
        v.addElement(linearray);
      }
    }
    catch (IOException e) {
    }

    return v;

  }

  private String[] lineToArray(String line)  {

    StringTokenizer st = new StringTokenizer(line, "\t");
    int numFields = st.countTokens();
    String[] fields = new String[numFields];
    for (int i = 0; i < numFields; i++) {
      fields[i] = st.nextToken();
    }
```

Example 12–1: A ContentHandler for text/tab-separated-values (continued)

```
    return fields;

  }

}
```

Example 12–1 has two methods. The private method `lineToArray()` is a simple utility that converts a tab-separated string into an array of strings with a `StringTok-enizer()`. This method is for the private use of this subclass, and is not required by the `ContentHandler` interface. The more complicated the content you're trying to parse, the more such methods your class will need. The `lineToArray()` method begins by creating a `StringTokenizer` from the `String` line with the single delimiter (`\t`, a tab). The `numFields` variable is set to the number of tokens in the `String` with `st.countTokens()`. An array is created for the fields with the length `numFields`. Then a `for` loop fills the array with the tokens. Finally, `lineToArray()` returns this array.

The `getContent()` method starts by instantiating a `Vector`. Then it gets the `Input-Stream` from the `URLConnection` uc, and chains this to a `DataInputStream`, so it can read it one line at a time in a `while` loop. Each line is fed to the `lineToArray()` method, which splits it into an array of `Strings`. This `Strings` array is then added to the `Vector`. When no lines are left, the loop exits, and the `Vector` is returned.

Factories for ContentHandlers

Now that you've written your first `ContentHandler`, let's see how to use it in a program. Files of MIME type `text/tab-separated-values` can be served by gopher servers, HTTP servers, FTP servers, and more. Let's assume you're retrieving a tab-separated-values file from an HTTP server. The file name should end with the *.tsv* extension so that the server knows it's a `text/tab-separated-values` file. (Not all servers are configured to support this out of the box. Consult your server documentation to see how to set up MIME-type mapping for your server.)

NOTE   It's not unusual for MIME types to contain characters that are illegal in Java identifiers. For example, `application/octet-stream` has a hyphen. If either the MIME type or sub-type contains any non-alphanumeric characters, these are replaced by the underscore (`_`). For example, using Sun's naming conventions, the content handler for the MIME type `application/octet-stream` would be `sun.net.www.content.application.octet_stream`.

First, your application or browser needs to know how to find your ContentHandler. A ContentHandlerFactory defines the rules for where ContentHandler classes are stored. Create a class that implements ContentHandlerFactory, and give this class a createContentHandler() method that knows how to instantiate your ContentHandler. The createContentHandler() method should return null if it can't find a ContentHandler appropriate for a MIME type; null signals Java to look for ContentHandler classes in the default locations. When your application starts, call the URLConnection's setContentHandlerFactory() method to set the ContentHandlerFactory. This method may only be called once in the lifetime of an application.

The createContentHandler Method

public abstract ContentHandler createContentHandler(String mimetype)

Just as the createURLStreamHandler() method of the URLStreamHandlerFactory interface was responsible for finding and loading the appropriate protocol handler, the createContentHandler() method of the ContentHandlerFactory interface is responsible for finding and loading the appropriate ContentHandler given a MIME type. This method should only be called by the getContent() method of a URLConnection object. For example, the following factory adds the text/tab-separated-values content handler of the last section:

```
public ContentHandler createContentHandler(String mimeType) {

  if (mimeType.equals("text/tab-separated-values") {
    return new tabSeparatedValueHandler();
  }
  else {
    return null;
  }

}
```

Example 12–2 is a class that downloads and prints a text/tab-separated-values file using the ContentHandler in Example 12–1.

Example 12–2: The tab-separated-values ContentTester class

```
import java.io.*;
import java.net.*;
import java.util.*;

public class tsvContentTester implements ContentHandlerFactory {

  String theURL;

  public static void main (String[] args) {
```

Example 12–2: The tab-separated-values ContentTester class (continued)

```
    if (args.length == 1) {
      tsvContentTester ct = new tsvContentTester(args[0]);
      URLConnection.setContentHandlerFactory(ct);
      ct.test();
    }
    else {
      System.err.println("Usage: java tsvContentTester url");
    }

  }

  public tsvContentTester(String s) {

    theURL = s;

  }

  public void test() {



    try {
      URL u = new URL(theURL);
      Vector v = (Vector) u.getContent();
      for (Enumeration e = v.elements() ; e.hasMoreElements() ;) {
        String[] sa = (String[]) e.nextElement();
        for (int i = 0; i < sa.length; i++) {
          System.out.print(sa[i] + "\t");
        }
        System.out.println();
      }
    }
    catch (IOException e) {
      System.err.println(e);
    }

  }

public ContentHandler createContentHandler(String type) {

    if (type.equalsIgnoreCase("text/tab-separated-values")) {
      return new tabSeparatedValueHandler();
    }
    else {
      return null;
    }

  }

}
```

If you have trouble getting this content handler to work, make sure the server that the *.tsv* file is downloaded from returns the proper MIME type, text/tab-separated-values. You can test this by connecting to port 80 of the web server with *telnet*, and requesting the file manually:

```
% telnet localhost 80
Trying 127.0.0.1...
Connected to localhost.
Escape character is '^]'.
GET /javafaq/index.tsv HTTP/1.0

HTTP/1.0 200 OK
Date: Thu, 22 Aug 1996 20:24:40 GMT
Server: Apache/1.0.5
Content-type: text/tab-separated-values
Content-length: 127
Last-modified: Thu, 22 Aug 1996 20:24:20 GMT

JPE Associates   341 Lafayette Str.     Suite 1025   Nowhere      NY     10012
O'Reilly & Associates    103 Morris Str. Suite A Sebastopol      CA     95472
Connection closed by foreign host.
%
```

You're looking for a line that says Content-type: text/tab-separated-values. If you see a content type of text/plain, application/octet-stream, or some other value, the server is misconfigured.

Some More Content Handlers

application/x-time

The Time protocol sends the content as a 32-bit signed binary number that represents the number of seconds since midnight, January 1, 1900. The following simple content handler converts this into a java.util.Date object. First, it converts the signed 32-bit integer into a Java int using the readInt() method of DataInputStream.[*] Next, this integer is converted to the number of milliseconds since January 1, 1970 by subtracting the number of seconds between 1900 and 1970. The resulting value is used to construct a Date object that getContent() returns to the caller.

---

[*] It's fortuitous that this works. The people who designed Java, and the people who designed the time protocol, were both used to 32-bit, big-endian UNIX machines, so they thought of ints in the same way. If Java's designers had been accustomed to 16-bit ints or little-endian architectures, this example would be considerably more complex.

Example 12–3: A Time content handler

```
import java.net.*;
import java.io.*;
import java.util.*;

public class timeContentHandler extends ContentHandler {

  public Object getContent(URLConnection uc) {

    Date now = null;

    try {
      DataInputStream dis = new DataInputStream(uc.getInputStream());
      int theTime = dis.readInt();
      // 86400 seconds a day
      // midnight January 1970 = 2,208,988,800 seconds since midnight January 1, 1900
      long secondsSince1970 = theTime - 2208988800L;
      long millisecondsSince1970 = secondsSince1970 * 1000L;
      now = new Date(millisecondsSince1970);
    }
    catch (IOException e) {
    }

    return now;
  }
}
```

A Content Handler for an Image Format: *image/x-fits*

The Flexible Image Transport System (FITS) format is in common use among astronomers. FITS files are greyscale, bitmapped images with headers that determine the bit depth of the picture, the width and the height of the picture, and the number of pictures in the file. Although FITS files commonly contain several images (typically pictures of the same thing taken at different times), in this example we only look at the first image in a file.[*]

There are a few key things you need to know to process FITS files. First, FITS files are broken up into blocks of exactly 2880 bytes. If there isn't enough data to fill a block, it is padded with spaces at the end. Each FITS file has two parts, the header and the primary data unit. The header occupies an integral number of blocks, as does the primary data unit. If the FITS file contains extensions, there may be additional data after the primary data unit; but you ignore that here. Any extensions that are present will not change the image contained in the primary data unit.

---

* For more details about the FITS format and how to handle FITS files see *The Encyclopedia of Graphics File Formats* by James D. Murray and William VanRyper, 2nd ed., from O'Reilly & Associates (pp. 392–400).

The header begins in the first block of the FITS file. It may occupy one or more blocks; the last block may be padded with spaces at the end. The header is ASCII text. Each line of the header is exactly 80 bytes wide. The first eight characters of each header line contain a keyword, followed by an equal sign (character 9), followed by a space (10). The keyword is padded on the right with spaces to make it eight characters long. Columns 11 through 30 contain a value; the value may be right-justified, and padded on the left with spaces if necessary. The value may be an integer, a floating-point number, a T or an F signifying the boolean values true and false, or a string delimited with single quotation marks. A comment may appear in columns 31 through 80; comments are separated from the value of a field by a slash (/). Example 12–4 is a simple header taken from a FITS image produced by K. S. Balasubramaniam at the Vacuum Tower Telescope at the National Solar Observatory in Sunspot, New Mexico (*http://www.sunspot.noao.edu/*).

Example 12–4: A simple FITS header

```
SIMPLE  =                    T /
BITPIX  =                   16 /
NAXIS   =                    2 /
NAXIS1  =                  242 /
NAXIS2  =                  252 /
DATE    = '19 Aug 1996'       /
TELESC  = 'NSO/SP - VTT'      /
IMAGE   = 'Continuum'         /
COORDS  = 'N29.1W34.2'        /
OBSTIME = '13:59:00 UT'       /
END
```

Every FITS file must begin with keyword SIMPLE. This keyword always has the value T; if this isn't the case, the file is not valid. The second line of a FITS file always has the keyword BITPIX, which tells you how the data is stored. There are five possible values for BITPIX, four of which correspond exactly to Java primitive datatypes. The most common value of BITPIX is 16, meaning that there are 16 bits per pixel, equivalent to a Java short. A BITPIX of 32 is a Java int. A BITPIX of –32 means that each pixel is represented by a 32-bit floating-point number (equivalent to a Java float); a BITPIX of –64 is equivalent to a Java double. A BITPIX of 8 means that 8 bits are used to represent each pixel; this is similar to a Java byte, except that FITS uses unsigned bytes ranging from 0 to 255; Java's byte datatype is signed, taking values that range from –128 to 127.

The remaining keywords in a FITS file may appear in any order. They are *not* necessarily in the order shown here. In our FITS content handler, we first read all the keywords into a Hashtable and then extract the ones we want by name.

The NAXIS header tells you how many axes or dimensions there are to the primary data array. An NAXIS value of one means you have a one-dimensional image. A NAXIS value of two means you have a standard two-dimensional rectangular image. A NAXIS value of three is called a *data cube*, and generally means the file contains a series of pictures of the same object taken at different moments in time. In other words, time is the third dimension. On rare occasions, the third dimension can represent depth; i.e., the file contains a true three-dimensional image. An NAXIS of four means you have a sequence of three-dimensional pictures taken at different moments in time. Higher values of NAXIS, while theoretically possible, are rarely seen in practice. The example is only going to look at the first two-dimensional image in a file.

The NAXISn headers (where n is an integer ranging from 1 to NAXIS) tell you the length of the image in pixels along that dimension. Thus in this example, NAXIS1 is 242, so you know the image is 242 pixels wide. NAXIS2 is 252, so this image is 252 pixels high. Since FITS images are normally pictures of astronomical bodies like the sun, it doesn't really matter if you reverse width and height. All FITS images contain the SIMPLE, BITPIX, END, and NAXIS keywords, plus a series of NAXISn keywords. These keywords all provide information that is essential to displaying the image.

The next five keywords are specific to this file, and may not be present in other FITS files. They give meaning to the image, though they are not needed to display it. The DATE keyword says this image was taken on August 19, 1996. The TELESC keyword says this image was taken by the Vacuum Tower Telescope (VTT) at the National Solar Observatory (NSO) on Sacramento Peak (SP). The Image keyword tells you that this is a picture of the white light continuum; images taken through spectrographs might only look at a particular wavelength in the spectrum. The COORDS keyword gives the latitude and longitude of the telescope. Finally, the OBSTIME keyword says this image was taken at 1:59 P.M. Universal Time (essentially Greenwich Mean Time). There are many more optional headers that don't appear in this example. Like the five discussed here, the remaining keywords may help someone interpret an image, but don't provide information needed to display it.

The keyword END terminates the header. Following the END keyword, the header is padded with spaces so that it fills a 2880-byte block. A header may take up more than one 2880-byte block, but it must always be padded to an integral number of blocks.

The image data follows the header. How the image is stored depends on the value of BITPIX, as explained above. Fortunately, these datatypes are stored in formats (big-endian, two's complement) that can be read directly with a DataInputStream. The exact meaning of each number in the image data is completely file-dependent. More often than not, it's the number of electrons that were collected in a specific time interval by a particular pixel in a charge-coupled detector (CCD); in older FITS files, the numbers could represent the value read from photographic film by a densitometer. However, the unifying theme is that larger numbers represent brighter light. To interpret these numbers as a greyscale image, you map the smallest value in the data to pure black, the largest value in the data to pure white, and scale all intermediate values appropriately. A general-purpose FITS reader cannot interpret the numbers as anything else except abstract brightness levels. Otherwise, differences tend to get washed out. For example, a dark spot on the Sun tends to be about 4000° K. That is dark compared to the normal solar surface temperature of 6000° K, but considerably brighter than anything you're likely to see on the surface of the Earth.

Example 12–5 is a FITS content hander. FITS files should be served with the MIME type image/x-fits. This is almost certainly not included in your server's default MIME types mappings, so make sure to add a mapping between files that end in *.fit* or *.fits* and the MIME type image/x-fits.

Example 12–5: An x-fits content handler

```
import java.net.*;
import java.io.*;
import java.awt.image.*;
import java.util.Hashtable;
import java.util.Enumeration;

public class fitsContentHandler extends ContentHandler {

  public Object getContent(URLConnection uc) {

    int width = -1;
    int height = -1;
    int bitpix = 16;
    int[] theData = null;
    int naxis = 2;
    Hashtable header = null;

    try {
      DataInputStream dis = new DataInputStream(uc.getInputStream());
      header = readHeader(dis);

      bitpix = getIntFromHeader("BITPIX  ", -1, header);
      if (bitpix  <= 0) return null;
      naxis = getIntFromHeader("NAXIS   ", -1, header);
      if (naxis  < 1) return null;
      width = getIntFromHeader("NAXIS1  ", -1, header);
      if (width  <= 0) return null;
```

Example 12–5: An x-fits content handler (continued)

```
    if (naxis == 1) height = 1;
    else height = getIntFromHeader("NAXIS2  ", -1, header);
    if (height  <= 0) return null;

    if (bitpix == 16) {
        short[] theInput =  new short[height * width];
        for (int i = 0; i < theInput.length; i++) {
          theInput[i] = dis.readShort();
        }
        theData = scaleArray(theInput);
    }
  else if (bitpix == 32) {
    int[] theInput =  new int[height * width];
    for (int i = 0; i < theInput.length; i++) {
      theInput[i] = dis.readInt();
    }
    theData = scaleArray(theInput);
  }
  else if (bitpix == 64) {
    long[] theInput =  new long[height * width];
    for (int i = 0; i < theInput.length; i++) {
      theInput[i] = dis.readLong();
    }
   theData = scaleArray(theInput);
  }
  else if (bitpix == -32) {
    float[] theInput =  new float[height * width];
    for (int i = 0; i < theInput.length; i++) {
      theInput[i] = dis.readFloat();
    }
    theData = scaleArray(theInput);
  }
  else if (bitpix == -64) {
    double[] theInput =  new double[height * width];
    for (int i = 0; i < theInput.length; i++) {
      theInput[i] = dis.readDouble();
    }
    theData = scaleArray(theInput);
  }
  else {
    System.err.println("Invalid BITPIX");
    return null;
  }// end if-else-if

} // end try
catch (IOException e) {

}

  return new MemoryImageSource(width,  height,  theData,  0,  width);

} // end getContent
```

Example 12–5: An x-fits content handler (continued)

```java
Hashtable readHeader(DataInputStream dis) throws IOException {

  int blocksize = 2880;
  int fieldsize = 80;
  String key, value;
  int linesRead = 0;

  byte[] buffer = new byte[fieldsize];

  Hashtable h = new Hashtable();
  while (true) {
    dis.readFully(buffer);
    key = new String(buffer, 0, 0, 8);
    linesRead++;
    if (key.substring(0, 3).equals("END")) break;
    if (buffer[8] != '=' || buffer[9] != ' ') continue;
    value = new String(buffer, 0, 10, 20);
    h.put(key, value);
  }
  int linesLeftToRead = (blocksize - ((linesRead * fieldsize) % blocksize))/fieldsize;
  for (int i = 0; i < linesLeftToRead; i++) dis.readFully(buffer);

  return h;

}


int getIntFromHeader(String name, int Default, Hashtable header) {

    String s = "";
    int result = Default;

    try {
      s = (String) header.get(name);
    }
    catch (NullPointerException e) {
      return Default;
    }
    try {
      result = Integer.parseInt(s.trim());
    }
    catch (NumberFormatException e) {
      System.err.println(e);
      System.err.println(s);
      return Default;
    }

    return result;

}


int[] scaleArray(short[] theInput) {
```

Example 12–5: An x-fits content handler (continued)

```
    int theData[] = new int[theInput.length];
    int max = 0;
    int min = 0;
    for (int i = 0; i < theInput.length; i++) {
      if (theInput[i] > max) max = theInput[i];
      if (theInput[i] < min) min = theInput[i];
    }
    long r = max - min;
    double a = 255.0/r;
    double b = -a * min;
    int opaque = 255;
    for (int i = 0; i < theData.length; i++) {
      int temp = (int) (theInput[i] * a + b);
      theData[i] =  (opaque << 24)  | (temp << 16)  | (temp << 8) | temp;
    }
    return theData;


  }


  int[] scaleArray(int[] theInput) {

    int theData[] = new int[theInput.length];
    int max = 0;
    int min = 0;
    for (int i = 0; i < theInput.length; i++) {
      if (theInput[i] > max) max = theInput[i];
      if (theInput[i] < min) min = theInput[i];
    }
    long r = max - min;
    double a = 255.0/r;
    double b = -a * min;
    int opaque = 255;
    for (int i = 0; i < theData.length; i++) {
      int temp = (int) (theInput[i] * a + b);
      theData[i] =  (opaque << 24)  | (temp << 16)  | (temp << 8) | temp;
    }
    return theData;


  }


  int[] scaleArray(long[] theInput) {

    int theData[] = new int[theInput.length];
    long max = 0;
    long min = 0;
    for (int i = 0; i < theInput.length; i++) {
      if (theInput[i] > max) max = theInput[i];
      if (theInput[i] < min) min = theInput[i];
    }
    long r = max - min;
    double a = 255.0/r;
    double b = -a * min;
```

Example 12–5: An x-fits content handler (continued)

```
    int opaque = 255;
    for (int i = 0; i < theData.length; i++) {
      int temp = (int) (theInput[i] * a + b);
      theData[i] =  (opaque << 24)  | (temp << 16)  | (temp << 8) | temp;
    }
    return theData;


  }


  int[] scaleArray(double[] theInput) {

    int theData[] = new int[theInput.length];
    double max = 0;
    double min = 0;
    for (int i = 0; i < theInput.length; i++) {
      if (theInput[i] > max) max = theInput[i];
      if (theInput[i] < min) min = theInput[i];
    }
    double r = max - min;
    double a = 255.0/r;
    double b = -a * min;
    int opaque = 255;
    for (int i = 0; i < theData.length; i++) {
      int temp = (int) (theInput[i] * a + b);
      theData[i] =  (opaque << 24)  | (temp << 16)  | (temp << 8) | temp;
    }
    return theData;


  }


  int[] scaleArray(float[] theInput) {

    int theData[] = new int[theInput.length];
    float max = 0;
    float min = 0;
    for (int i = 0; i < theInput.length; i++) {
      if (theInput[i] > max) max = theInput[i];
      if (theInput[i] < min) min = theInput[i];
    }
    double r = max - min;
    double a = 255.0/r;
    double b = -a * min;
    int opaque = 255;
    for (int i = 0; i < theData.length; i++) {
      int temp = (int) (theInput[i] * a + b);
      theData[i] =  (opaque << 24)  | (temp << 16)  | (temp << 8) | temp;
    }
    return theData;
  }
}
```

The key method of the fitsContentHandler class is getContent(); it is the one method that the ContentHandler class requires us to implement. The other methods in this class are all utilities, and could reasonably be made private. getContent() is called by a URLConnection, which passes a reference to itself in the argument uc. The getContent() method reads data from that URLConnection, and uses it to construct an object that implements the ImageProducer interface. To simplify the task of creating an ImageProducer, you create an array of image data, and use a MemoryImageSource object, which implements the ImageProducer interface, to convert that array into an image. getContent() returns this MemoryImageSource.

MemoryImageSource has several constructors. The one used here requires you to provide the width and height of the image, an array of integer values containing the RGB data for each pixel, the offset of the start of that data in the array, and the number of pixels per line in the array:

```
public MemoryImageSource(int width, int height, int pixels[], int offset,
                         int scanlines);
```

The width, height, and pixel data can be read from the header of the FITS image. Since you are creating a new array to hold the pixel data, the offset is 0, and the scanlines are the width of the image.

The content handler has a utility method called readHeader(), which reads the image header from uc's InputStream. This method returns a Hashtable containing the keywords and their values as Strings. Comments are thrown away. readHeader() reads 80 bytes at a time, since that's the length of each field. The first eight bytes are transformed into the String key. If there is no key, the line is a comment, and is ignored. If there is a key, the eleventh through thirtieth bytes are stored in a String called value. The key-value pair is stored in the Hashtable, h. This continues until the END keyword is spotted. At this point you break out of the loop, and read as many lines as necessary to finish the block. (Recall that the header is padded with spaces to make an integral multiple of 2880.) Finally, readHeader() returns the Hashtable h.

After the header has been read into the Hashtable h, the InputStream is now pointing at the first byte of data. However, before you're ready to read the data, you must extract the height, width, and bits per pixel of the primary data unit from the header. These are all integer values, so to simplify the code you use the getIntFromHeader(String name, int Default, Hashtable header) method. This method takes as arguments the name of the header whose value you want (e.g., BITPIX), a default value for that header, and the Hashtable that contains the header. The argument name Default is capitalized to avoid confusion with the Java keyword default. This method retrieves the value associated with the string name from the Hashtable, and casts the result to a String object, s—you know this cast is safe because you only put String data into the Hashtable. This String is then converted to an int using Integer.parseInt(s.trim()); you then return the resulting int. If an exception is thrown, getIntFromHeader() returns the Default argument instead. In this content handler, you use an impossible flag value (–1) as the Default to indicate that getIntFromHeader() failed.

getContent() uses getIntFromHeader() to retrieve four crucial values from the header: NAXIS, NAXIS1, NAXIS2, and BITPIX. NAXIS is the number of dimensions in the primary data array; if it is greater than or equal to two, you read the width and height from NAXIS1 and NAXIS2. If there are more than two dimensions, you still read a single two-dimensional frame from the data. A more advanced FITS content handler might read subsequent frames, and include them below the original image, or display the sequence of images as an animation. If NAXIS is one, the width is read from NAXIS1, and the height is set to one.[*] If NAXIS is less than one, there's no image data at all, so you return null.

Now you are ready to read the image data. The data can be stored in one of five formats, depending on the value of BITPIX: unsigned bytes, shorts, ints, floats, or doubles. This is where the lack of parameterized types and templates in Java makes coding painful: you need to repeat the algorithm for reading data five times, for each of the five possible datatypes. In each case, first read the data from the stream into an array of the appropriate type called theInput. Then pass this array to the scaleArray() method, which returns a new array, theData. scaleArray() is an overloaded method that reads the data in theInput, and copies the data into the int array theData, while scaling the data to fall between 0 and 255; there is a different version of scaleArray() for each of the five datatypes you might need to handle. Thus, no matter what format the data starts in, it becomes an int array with values between zero and 255. You now need to convert this data into greyscale RGB values. The standard 32-bit RGB color model allows 256 different shades of grey ranging from pure black to pure white; eight bits are used to represent opacity, usually called "alpha." To get a particular shade of grey, the red, green, and blue bytes of an RGB triple should all be set to the same value, and the alpha value should be 255 (fully opaque). Thinking of these as four-byte values, you need colors like 255.127.127.127 (medium grey) or 255.255.255.255 (pure white). This is produced by the lines:

```
int temp = (int) (theInput[i] * a + b);
theData[i] = (opaque << 24) | (temp << 16) | (temp << 8) | temp;
```

---

[*] A FITS file with NAXIS one would typically be produced from observations that used a one-dimensional CCD.

Once it has converted every pixel in theInput[] into a 32-bit color value and stored the result in theData[], scaleArray() returns theData. The only thing left for getContent() to do is feed this array, along with the header values previously retrieved, into the MemoryImageSource constructor, and return the result.

Example 12–6 is a simple program that tests this content handler by loading and displaying a FITS image from a URL. It implements the ContentHandlerFactory interface, and therefore uses itself as a ContentHandlerFactory.

Example 12–6: The FITS Viewer

```java
import java.awt.*;
import java.awt.image.*;
import java.net.*;
import java.io.*;

public class fits extends Frame implements ContentHandlerFactory {

  URL u;
  Image theImage;
  String name;
  ContentHandler fc;

  public static void main(String[] args) {

    String name;
    if (args.length == 0) name = "test.fit";
    else name = args[0] + ".fits";

    fits f = new fits(name);
    URLConnection.setContentHandlerFactory(f);
    f.resize(252, 252);
    f.fc = new fitsContentHandler();
    f.init();
    f.show();

  }

  public ContentHandler createContentHandler(String mimetype) {

    if (mimetype.equalsIgnoreCase("image/x-fits")) return fc;
    return null;

  }

  public fits(String s) {

    super(s);
    name = s;

  }

  public void init() {
```

Example 12–6: The FITS Viewer (continued)

```
  try {

    u = new URL("http://sunsite.unc.edu/javafaq/" + name);

    ImageProducer ip = (ImageProducer) u.getContent();
    if (ip == null)  {
      System.err.println("Content handler returned null");
    }
    else {
      theImage = createImage(ip);
    }

  }
  catch (MalformedURLException e) {
    System.err.println(e);
  }
  catch (IOException e) {
    System.err.println(e);
  }
  catch (NullPointerException e) {
    System.err.println(e);
    e.printStackTrace();
  }

  }

public void paint(Graphics g) {

    g.drawImage(theImage, 0, 0, this);

  }

}
```

This FITS content handler has one glaring problem. You have to completely load the image before the method returns. Since FITS images are quite literally astronomical in size, loading the image can take a significant amount of time. It would be better to create a new class for FITS images that implements the ImageProducer interface, and that streams the data asynchronously. The ImageConsumer that eventually displays the image can use the methods of ImageProducer to determine when the height and width are available, when a new scanline has been read, when the image is completely loaded or errored out, and so on. getContent() would spawn a separate thread to feed the data into the ImageProducer, and would return almost immediately. However, a FITS ImageProducer would not be able to take significant advantage of progressive loading, because the file format doesn't define unambiguously what each data value means; before you can generate RGB pixels, you must read all of the data, and find the minimum and maximum values.

13

Multicast Sockets

What Is a Multicast Socket?

All the sockets and datagrams you've seen in the previous chapters have been *unicast* sockets; they provided point-to-point communication. That is, unicast sockets create a connection with two well-defined endpoints. There is one sender and one receiver; and, although they may switch roles, at any given time, it is easy to tell which is which. However, although point-to-point communications serve many, if not most, needs (people have engaged in one-on-one conversations for millenia), there are many situations in which you need a different model. In a public meeting, you have a one-to-many conversation: people may come and go as they please, but the speaker (who changes from time to time) addresses a group rather than an individual. Television and radio stations broadcast data from one location to every point that can be reached by their signal. Video conferencing sends a feed of audio and video to a select group of people. Usenet news is posted at one site, and distributed around the world to tens of thousands of people. DNS router updates travel from the site announcing a change to many other routers.

The TCP/IP protocols support broadcasting, but the use of broadcasts is strictly limited. Protocols only require broadcasts when there is no alternative, and routers limit broadcasts to the local network or subnetwork, preventing broadcasts from reaching the Internet at large. Even a few limited broadcasts would bring the Internet to its knees. Broadcasting high-bandwidth data like audio, video, or even text and still images is out of the question. However, there's a middle ground between point-to-point communications and broadcasts to the whole world. There's no reason to send a video feed to hosts that aren't interested in it; we need a technology that lets us send data to the hosts that want it, without bothering the rest of the world. One way to do this would be to use many unicast streams. If one thousand clients want to listen to a RealAudio broadcast, the data would be sent one thousand times. This is inefficient since it duplicates data needlessly, but it's orders of magnitude more efficient than broadcasting the data to every host on the Internet. Still, if the number of interested clients is large enough, you will eventually run out of bandwidth or CPU power—probably sooner rather than later.

Another approach to the problem is to create static *connection trees*. This is the solution used by Usenet news and some conferencing systems (notably CU-SeeMe). Data is fed from the originating site to other servers, which replicate it to still other servers, which eventually replicate it to clients. Each client connects to the nearest server. This is more efficient than sending everything to all interested clients via multiple unicasts, but the scheme is kludgy, and beginning to show its age. New sites need to find a place to hook into the tree manually; the tree does not necessarily reflect the best possible topology at any one time. Servers still need to maintain many point-to-point connections to their clients and send the same data to each one. It would be better to allow the routers in the Internet to determine dynamically the best possible routes for transmitting distributed information, and to replicate data only when absolutely necessary.

This is where *multicasting* comes in. Multicasting sends data from one host to many different hosts, but not to everyone; the data only goes to clients that have expressed an interest in the data by joining a particular multicast group. In a way, this is like a public meeting. People can come and go as they please, leaving when the discussion no longer interests them. Before they arrive, and after they have left, they don't need to process the information at all: it just doesn't reach them. On the Internet, we implement a "public meeting" using a multicast socket that sends a single data stream to a location (or a group of locations) close to the parties declaring an interest in the data. In the best case, we only have to duplicate the data when it reaches the local network serving the interested clients; the data stream only crosses the Internet once. More realistically, we will have to send several identical data streams across the Internet; but, by carefully choosing the points where the streams are duplicated, we minimize the load on the network. The good news is that we aren't responsible for choosing these points, or even for sending duplicate streams; that is handled by the Internet's routers.

For example, if you're multicasting video in New York, and twenty people attached to one LAN are watching you in Los Angeles, your show will only be sent to that LAN once. If fifty more people are watching in San Francisco, the data stream will be duplicated somewhere (let's say Fresno), and sent to the two cities. If a hundred more people are watching in Houston, another data stream will be sent there (perhaps from St. Louis); see Figure 13–1. The data has only made two cross-country trips—not the 170 trips required by point-to-point connections, or the millions of trips required by a true broadcast. Multicasting is halfway between the point-to-point communication common to the Internet, and the broadcast model of television—but it's more efficient than either. When a packet is multicast, it is addressed to a multicast group, and sent to each host belonging to the group. It does not go to a single host (as in unicasting), nor does it go to every host (as in broadcasting). Either would be too inefficient.

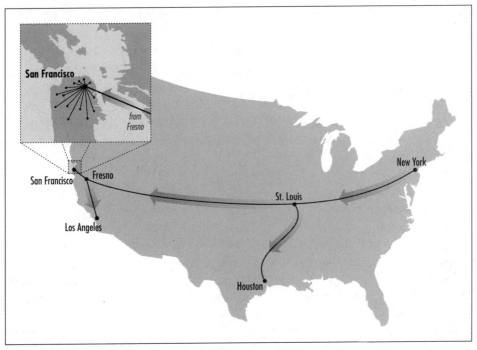

Figure 13–1: Multicast between New York, San Francisco, and Los Angeles

When people start talking about multicasting, audio and video are the first applications that come to mind; however, they are the tip of the iceberg. Other possibilities include multiplayer games, distributed file systems, massively parallel computing, multiperson conferencing, database replication, and more. You could send Usenet news more efficiently via multicasting. You can use multicasting to implement name services and directory services that don't require the client to know a server's address in advance; to look up a name, you could multicast your request to some well-known address, and wait until you receive a response from the nearest server.

Multicasting should also make it easier to implement various kinds of caching for the Internet, important if the Net's population continues to grow faster than available bandwidth. Martin Hamilton has proposed using multicasting to build a distributed server system for the World Wide Web.[*] For example, a high-traffic web server could be split across multiple machines, all sharing a single hostname that is mapped to a multicast address. Suppose one machine chunks out HTML files, another handles images, and a third processes CGI requests. When a client makes a request to the multicast address, that request is sent to each of the three servers. When each server receives the request, it looks to see whether the client wants an HTML file, an image, or CGI processing. If the server can handle the request, it responds. Otherwise, the server ignores the request, and lets the other servers process it. It is easy to imagine more complex divisions of labor between distributed servers.

Multicasting on the Internet

Multicasting has been designed to fit into the Internet as seamlessly as possible. Most of the work is done by routers, and should be transparent to application programmers. An application simply sends datagram packets to a multicast address, which isn't fundamentally different from any other IP address. The routers make sure that the packet is delivered to all the hosts in the multicast group. The biggest problem is that multicast routers are not yet ubiquitous; therefore, you need to know enough about them to find out whether multicasting is supported on your network. As far as the application itself, you need to pay attention to an additional header field in the datagrams called the Time-To-Live (TTL) value. The TTL is the maximum number of routers the datagram is allowed to cross; when it reaches the maximum, it is discarded. When multicasting, you use the TTL as an *ad hoc* way to limit how far a packet can travel. For example, you don't want packets for a friendly on-campus game of Dogfight reaching routers on the other side of the world. At present, you can't limit your packets to the local campus, but you can give them a low TTL to prevent them from straying too far afield. Figure 13–2 shows how TTL limits a packet's spread. A packet starting at the source with a TTL of 5 reaches the entire campus, plus a few local Internet sites, but it dies before it gets very far off campus.

Multicast addresses and groups

A multicast address is the address of a group of hosts called a multicast group. We'll talk about the address first. Multicast addresses are IP addresses in the range 224.0.0.0 to 239.255.255.255. All the addresses in this range have the binary digits

---

[*] Martin Hamilton, "Multicast Approaches to World-Wide Web Caching," *http://gizmo.lut.ac.uk/ ˜martin/wwwcac/wwwcac.html*, 1995.

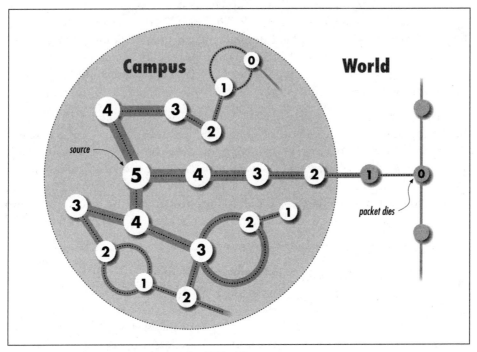

Figure 13–2: Coverage of a package with a TTL of 5

1110 as their first four bits. They are called Class D addresses to distinguish them from the more common Class A, B, and C addresses.* Like any IP address, a multicast address can have a hostname; for example, the multicast address 224.0.1.1 (the address of the Network Time Protocol Distributed Service) is assigned the name *NTP.MCAST.NET*.

A multicast group is a set of Internet hosts that share a multicast address. Any data sent to the multicast address is relayed to all the members of the group. Membership in a multicast group is open; hosts can enter or leave the group at any time. Groups can be either permanent or transient. Permanent groups have assigned addresses that remain constant, whether or not there are any members in the group. However, most multicast groups are transient, and exist only as long as they have members. Java currently does not have classes that allow you to create new multicast groups; you can only join existing ones. This is a significant weakness, and should be corrected in the future.

A number of multicast addresses have been set aside for special purposes. *ALL-SYSTEMS.MCAST.NET*, 224.0.0.1, is a multicast group that includes all systems

---

* Addresses starting with 11110 are now called Class E addresses; currently, they're unused, and reserved for future experimentation.

supporting multicasting on the local subnet. This group is commonly used for local testing, as is *experiment.mcast.net*, 224.0.1.20. (There is no multicast address that sends data to all hosts on the Internet.) All addresses beginning with 224 (i.e., addresses from 224.0.0.0 to 224.0.0.255) are reserved for routing protocols and other low-level activities, such as gateway discovery and group membership reporting. Multicast routers never forward datagrams with destinations in this range.

The IANA (Internet Asssigned Number Authority) is responsible for handing out permanent multicast addresses as needed; so far, about eighty have been assigned. Table 13–1 lists a few of these permanent addresses. The complete list is available from *ftp://ftp.isi.edu/in-notes/iana/assignments/multicast-addresses*. The remaining 248 million Class D addresses are used on a temporary basis by anyone who needs them. Multicast routers (*mrouters* for short) are responsible for making sure two different systems don't try to use the same Class D address at the same time.

Table 13–1: Common Permanent Multicast Addresses

Domain Name	IP Address	Purpose
BASE-ADDRESS.MCAST.NET	224.0.0.0	The reserved base address. This is never assigned to any multicast group.
ALL-SYSTEMS.MCAST.NET	224.0.0.1	All systems on the local subnet.
ALL-ROUTERS.MCAST.NET	224.0.0.2	All routers on the local subnet.
DVMRP.MCAST.NET	224.0.0.4	All Distance Vector Multicast Routing Protocol routers on this subnet. An early version of the DVMRP protocol is documented in RFC1075; the current version has changed substantially.
MOBILE-AGENTS.MCAST.NET	224.0.0.11	Mobile-Agents on the local subnet.
DHCP-AGENTS.MCAST.NET	224.0.0.12	This multicast group allows a client to locate a DHCP (Dynamic Host Configuration Protocol) server or relay agent on the local subnet.
PIM-ROUTERS.MCAST.NET	224.0.0.13	All Protocol Independent Multicasting routers on this subnet.

Table 13–1: Common Permanent Multicast Addresses (continued)

Domain Name	IP Address	Purpose
RSVP-ENCAPSULATION.MCAST.NET	224.0.0.14	RSVP-ENCAPSULATION on this subnet. RSVP stands for Resource reSerVation setup Protocol, an effort to allow people to reserve a guaranteed amount of Internet bandwidth in advance for an event.
NTP.MCAST.NET	224.0.1.1	The Network Time Protocol.
SGI-DOG.MCAST.NET	224.0.1.2	Silicon Graphics Dogfight game.
NSS.MCAST.NET	224.0.1.6	The Name Service Server.
AUDIONEWS.MCAST.NET	224.0.1.7	Audio news multicast.
SUB-NIS.MCAST.NET	224.0.1.8	Sun's NIS+ Information Service.
MTP.MCAST.NET	224.0.1.9	The Multicast Transport Protocol.
IETF-1-LOW-AUDIO.MCAST.NET	224.0.1.10	Channel 1 of low-quality audio from IETF meetings.
IETF-1- AUDIO.MCAST.NET	224.0.1.11	Channel 1 of high-quality audio from IETF meetings.
IETF-1-VIDEO.MCAST.NET	224.0.1.12	Channel 1 of video from IETF meetings.
IETF-2-LOW-AUDIO.MCAST.NET	224.0.1.13	Channel 2 of low-quality audio from IETF meetings.
IETF-2-AUDIO.MCAST.NET	224.0.1.14	Channel 2 of high-quality audio from IETF meetings.
IETF-2-VIDEO.MCAST.NET	224.0.1.15	Channel 2 of video from IETF meetings.
MUSIC-SERVICE.MCAST.NET	224.0.1.16	MUSIC-SERVICE.
SEANET-TELEMETRY.MCAST.NET	224.0.1.17	Telemetry data for the SeaNet Project's attempt to extend the Internet to vessels at sea. See *http://dubhe.cc.nps.navy.mil/ ˜seanet/*.
SEANET-IMAGE.MCAST.NET	224.0.1.18	SeaNet images.

Table 13–1: Common Permanent Multicast Addresses (continued)

Domain Name	IP Address	Purpose
MLOADD.MCAST.NET	224.0.1.19	MLOADD measures the traffic load through one or more network interfaces over a number of seconds. Multicasting is used to communicate between the different interfaces being measured.
EXPERIMENT.MCAST.NET	224.0.1.20	Experiments that do not go beyond the local subnet.
XINGTV.MCAST.NET	224.0.1.23	XING Technology's Streamworks TV multicast.
MICROSOFT.MCAST.NET	224.0.1.24	This group is used by WINS (Windows Internet Name Service) servers to locate one another.
NBC-PRO.MCAST.NET	224.0.1.25	NBC Professional news: round-the-clock live video coverage of news that affects the financial markets and other business news. See *http://www.desktop.nbc.com/pro/pro.html.*
NBC-PFN.MCAST.NET	224.0.1.26	The NBC Private Financial Network, a stock market-oriented video feed covering primarily corporate news conferences, announcements, shareholder meetings, CEO interviews, and other news closely related to the stock market. See *http://www.desktop.nbc.com/pfn/pfn.html.*
MTRACE.MCAST.NET	224.0.1.32	A multicast version of traceroute.

Table 13–1: Common Permanent Multicast Addresses (continued)

Domain Name	IP Address	Purpose
	224.0.6.000- 224.0.6.127	This block of multicast addresses is used by the ISIS project, an effort to build distributed systems software that is high-performance, parallel, and robust, despite both hardware and software crashes. See *http://www.stratus.com/ISIS/www.html*.
	224.0.9.000- 224.0.9.255	This block of multicast addresses is used by the Internet Railroad project, an effort to build a 45 megabit per second Internet backbone for governmental data that circles the globe. See *http://amsterdam.park.org/About/InternetRailroad/index.text.html*.
	224.2.0.0- 224.2.255.255	The MBONE. These addresses are reserved for multimedia conference calls, i.e., audio, video, whiteboard, and shared Mosaic conferencing between many people.
	224.2.2.2	Port 4000 on this address is used to broadcast the currently available MBONE programming. You can look at this with the X window utility *sd*.

Although the original IP multicast RFC dates back to 1985, practical IP multicasting is still new enough and uncommon enough that permanent multicast addresses are assigned manually by the IANA. Manual assignment will certainly break down as IP multicasting becomes more popular. Some automated system for the assignment and allocation of multicast addresses is probably inevitable.

The MBONE (or Multicast Backbone on the Internet) is the range of Class D addresses beginning with 224.2.*.* that are used for audio and video broadcasts over the Internet. (This range may soon be expanded by allocating the addresses between 239.0.0.0 and 239.255.255.255 for administratively scoped* MBONE broadcasts.) The word MBONE is also used to mean the portion of the Internet that understands how to route class D addressed packets.

Clients and servers

When a host wants to send data to a multicast group, it puts that data in multicast datagrams, which are nothing more than UDP datagrams addressed to a multicast group. Most multicast data is either audio, video, or both. These sorts of data tend to be relatively large, and relatively robust against data loss. If a few pixels or even a whole frame of video is lost in transit, the signal isn't blurred beyond recognizability. Therefore, multicast data is sent via UDP, which, though unreliable, can be as much as three times faster than data sent via connection-oriented TCP.[†] If you're developing a multicast application that can't tolerate data loss, it's your responsibility to determine whether data was damaged in transit, and how to handle the missing data. For example, if you are building a distributed cache system, you might simply decide to leave any files that don't arrive intact out of the cache.

Earlier, I said that from an application programmer's standpoint, the primary difference between multicasting and using regular UDP sockets is that you have to worry about the Time-To-Live (TTL) value. This is a single byte in the IP header that takes values from 0 to 255; it is interpreted roughly as the number of routers that a packet can pass through before it is discarded. Each time the packet passes through a router, its TTL field is decremented by at least one; some routers may decrement the TTL by two or more. When the TTL reaches 0, the packet is discarded. The TTL field was originally designed to prevent routing loops by guaranteeing that all packets would eventually be discarded; it prevents misconfigured routers from sending packets back and forth to each other indefinitely. In IP multi-casting, the TTL is used to limit the multicast geographically. For example, a TTL value of 16 limits the packet to the local area, generally one organization, or perhaps an organization and its immediate upstream and downstream neighbors. A TTL of 127, however, sends the packet around the world. Intermediate values are also possible. By default, multicast packets use a TTL of 1, which specifies that the packet goes no further than the local subnet. (As you can see, using TTL to limit a packet's range leaves a lot to be desired; administrative scope, which is still

---

* Administrative scope, in contrast to TTL scope, uses different ranges of multicast addresses to constrain multicast traffic to a particular region or group of routers. For example, the IP addresses between 239.178.0 and 239.178.255 might be an administrative scope for the state of New York. Data addressed to one of those addresses would not be forwarded outside of New York. This system is still in the developmental stage as I write. The idea is to allow the possible group membership to be established in advance without relying on less-than-reliable TTL values.

† If you think about it, multicast over TCP would be next to impossible. TCP requires hosts to acknowledge that they have received packets; handling acknowledgments in a multicast situation would be a nightmare.

under development, addresses these problems.) Packets addressed to a multicast group between 224.0.0.0 and 224.0.0.255 are never forwarded beyond the local subnet, regardless of the TTL values used.

Once the data has been stuffed into one or more datagrams, the sending host launches the datagrams onto the Internet. This is just like sending regular (unicast) UDP data. The sending host begins by transmitting a multicast datagram to the local network. This packet immediately reaches all members of the multicast group in the same subnet. If the time-to-live field of the packet is greater than 1, any multicast routers on the local network forward the packet to any other networks with members of the destination group. When the packet arrives at one of the final destinations, the multicast router on the foreign network transmits the packet to each host it serves that is a member of the multicast group. If necessary, it also retransmits the packet to the next routers in the path between the current router, and all its eventual destinations.

When data arrives at a host in a multicast group, the host receives it as it receives any other UDP datagram—even though the packet's destination address doesn't match the receiving host. The host recognizes that the datagram is intended for it because it belongs to the multicast group the datagram is addressed to, much as most of us accept mail addressed to Occupant, even though none of us are named Mr. Occupant. The receiving host must be listening on the proper port, and be ready to process the datagram when it arrives.

Routers and routing

Figure 13–3 shows one of the simplest possible multicast configurations: a single server sending the same data to four clients served by the same router. A multicast socket sends one stream of data over the Internet to the clients' router; the router duplicates the stream, and sends it to each of the clients. Without multicast sockets, the server would have to send four separate but identical streams of data to the router, which would route each stream to a client. Using the same stream to send the same data to multiple clients significantly reduces the bandwidth required on the Internet backbone. This moves video and audio broadcasting on the Internet from something completely impossible to something that is marginally possible, as long as too many people don't try it at the same time. (Widespread use of broadcasting on the Internet still has to wait for faster communications technologies.) Furthermore, some local network technologies may let the router multicast the data to its clients, reducing the bandwidth required on the LAN.

Of course, real world routes can be much more complex, involving multiple hierarchies of redundant routers. However, the goal of multicast sockets is simple: no matter how complex the network, the same data should never be sent more than once over any given network segment. Fortunately, you don't need to worry about routing issues. Just create a MulticastSocket, have the socket join a multicast group, and stuff the address of the multicast group in the DatagramPacket you want to send. The routers and the MulticastSocket class take care of the rest.

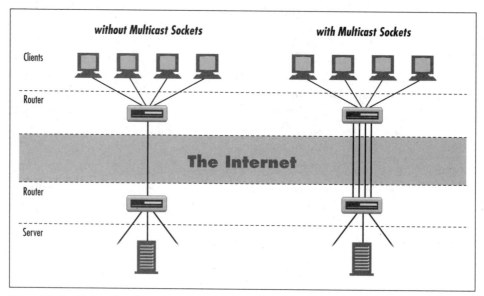

Figure 13–3: With and without multicast sockets

The biggest restriction on multicasting is the availability of special multicast routers (mrouters). Mrouters are reconfigured Internet routers or workstations that support the IP multicast extensions. In 1997, it is still possible to find hosts between which no multicast route exists (i.e., there is no route between the hosts that travels exclusively over mrouters). This situation is being remedied rapidly, especially in the United States. However, it is often the case that a more efficient route would be possible if more multicast routers were available.

Before you can use multicasting, you must be using an operating system, hardware platform, and network router that provide multicast support. Most major UNIX variants support multicasting in 1996. The notable exceptions are SunOS 4.1.x and Digital Ultrix,[*] which require special patches to the kernel for multicasting. Multicasting is supported in the built-in TCP stack of Microsoft Windows 95 and NT. On Macs, multicasting is supported by OpenTransport but not by MacTCP.

---

[*] Although these systems are popular, they are both obsolete, and have been replaced by Solaris and Digital UNIX, respectively.

To send and receive multicast data beyond the local subnet, you need a multicast router. Check with your network administrator to see if your routers support multicasting. Furthermore, to receive from, or send to, the MBONE, your ISP needs to connect you to it.

Working with Multicast Sockets

Enough theory. In Java, you multicast data using a MulticastSocket, an instance of sun.net.MulticastSocket in Java 1.0 and java.net.MulticastSocket in Java 1.1. The MulticastSocket class is a subclass of java.net.DatagramSocket. As you would expect, its behavior is very similar; you create DatagramPackets that you send and receive with the socket. Therefore, I won't repeat the basics; this discussion assumes that you already know how to work with datagrams. However, if you're jumping around in this book rather than reading it cover to cover, now might be a good time to go back and read Chapter 9, *UDP Datagrams and Sockets*.

NOTE   This discussion is based on the sun.net.MulticastSocket class in Java 1.0.2. In release 1.1, this class was moved into the java.net package.

To receive data that is being multicast from a remote site, you first create a MulticastSocket with the MulticastSocket() constructor. Next, you need to join a multicast group; to do so, you use the MulticastSocket's joinGroup() method. This signals the routers in the path between you and the server to start sending data your way, and tells the local host that it should pass you IP packets addressed to the multicast group.

Once you've joined the multicast group, you receive UDP data just as you would with a DatagramSocket. That is, you create a DatagramPacket with a byte array that serves as a buffer for data, and enter a loop in which you receive the data. To receive data, call the receive() method from the DatagramSocket class, which we explored in Chapter 9. When you no longer want to receive data, you leave the multicast group by calling your MulticastSocket's leaveGroup() method. You can then close the socket with the close() method of java.net.DatagramSocket.

Sending data to a multicast address is similar to sending UDP data to a unicast address. You do not need to join a multicast group to send data to it. You create a new DatagramPacket, stuff the data and the address of the multicast group into the packet, and pass it to the send() method. The one difference is that you must explicitly specify the packet's Time-To-Live (TTL).

The Constructors

The constructors are simple. Each one calls the equivalent constructor in the superclass, java.net.DatagramSocket.

public MulticastSocket() throws SocketException

This constructor creates a socket that is bound to an anonymous port (i.e., an unused port assigned by the system). It is useful for clients (i.e., programs that initiate a data transfer), because they don't need to use a well known port; the recipient replies to the port contained in the packet. If you need to know the port number, you can find it out with the getLocalPort() method inherited from java.net.DatagramSocket. This constructor throws a SocketException if the Socket can't be created.

Example 13–1: Multicast constructor

```
import sun.net.*;
import java.net.*;

public class MulticastConstructor {

  public static void main(String[] args) {

    try {
      MulticastSocket ms = new MulticastSocket();
      System.out.println(ms);
    }
    catch (SocketException se) {
      System.err.println(se);
    }

  }

}
```

Note that in the first line, we import the package sun.net. In Java 1.1, Multicast-Socket is in the java.net package, and this line is unnecessary.

public MulticastSocket(int port) throws SocketException

This constructor creates a socket that receives datagrams on a well-known port. The port argument specifies the port on which this socket listens for datagrams. As with DatagramSockets, you need to be root on a UNIX system to create a Multi-castSocket on a port numbered between 1 and 1023.

This constructor throws a SocketException if the Socket can't be created. A SocketException occurs if you don't have sufficient privileges to bind to the port (remember that on UNIX, you must be root to bind to ports 1 through 1023), or that the port you're trying to connect to is already occupied. Note that a Multi-castSocket cannot occupy a port already occupied by a DatagramSocket, and vice versa.

Example 13–2: Multicast constructor on a port

```
import sun.net.*;
import java.net.*;

public class MulticastPortConstructor {

  public static void main(String[] args) {

    try {
      MulticastSocket ms = new MulticastSocket(2048);
      System.out.println(ms);
    }
    catch (SocketException se) {
      System.err.println(se);
    }

  }

}
```

Communicating with a Multicast Group

Once a MulticastSocket exists, there are four key operations it can perform. These are:

1. Join a multicast group

2. Send data to the members of the group

3. Receive data from the group

4. Leave the multicast group

The MulticastSocket class has methods for operations 1, 2, and 4. No new method is required to receive data. The receive() method of the superclass, java.net.DatagramSocket, is all you need for receiving. You can perform these operations in any order, but you must join a group before you can receive data from it (or, for that matter, leave it). You do not need to join a group to send data to it, and sending and receiving of data may be freely interwoven.

public void joinGroup(InetAddress mcastaddr) throws SocketException

To receive data from a MulticastSocket, you must first join a multicast group. To join a group, pass an InetAddress object for the multicast group to the joinGroup() method. If you successfully join the group, you'll receive any datagrams intended for that group.

NOTE	There is no technical reason one MulticastSocket can't join multiple multicast groups. Information about membership in multicast groups is stored in multicast routers, not in the object. However, belonging to more than one would be very confusing since you'd have no easy way to sort out the data coming from different multicast groups.

Once you've joined a multicast group, you receive datagrams exactly as you received unicast datagrams in Chapter 10, *The URLConnection Class.* That is, you set up a DatagramPacket as a buffer, and pass it into this socket's receive() method (inherited from java.net.DatagramSocket).

If the address you try to join is not a multicast address (not between 224.0.0.0 to 239.255.255.255), the joinGroup() method throws a SocketException. (In Java 1.1, this exception will change to an IOException.)

public void leaveGroup(InetAddress mcastaddr) throws SocketException

The leaveGroup() method signals that you no longer want to receive datagrams from this multicast group. You send a signal to the appropriate multicast router telling it stop sending you datagrams. If the address you try to leave is not a multicast address (not between 224.0.0.0 to 239.255.255.255), the method throws a SocketException. (In Java 1.1, this exception has changed to an IOException.) However, no exception occurs if you leave a multicast group you never joined.

public synchronized void send(DatagramPacket dp, byte ttl) throws IOException, SocketException

Sending data with a MulticastSocket is similar to sending data with a Datagram-Socket. Stuff your data into a DatagramPacket object dp, and send it off. The data is sent to every host that belongs to the multicast group to which your packet is addressed.

As I've said, the Time-To-Live (TTL) field was designed to prevent routing loops. All IP packets, unicast or multicast, UDP or TCP, contain this header field. A packet's TTL is decremented by at least one (possibly two or more) by every router that handles it; when the TTL reaches 0, the packet is discarded, even if it hasn't reached its destination. The default value used for the TTL field for regular UDP datagrams is 255, the maximum. When multicasting, TTL values are used to control how far a packet travels. Therefore, when you call send(), you should specify an appropriate TTL value; the MulticastSocket class overrides send() with a method that takes a ttl argument. However, there is no precise way to map TTLs to geographical distance. Generally, the further away a site is, the more routers a packet has to pass through before reaching it. Therefore, packets with small TTL values won't travel as far as packets with large TTL values. Table 13–2 gives some ideas about how to set TTL values.

Table 13–2: Estimated TTL Values for Datagrams Originating in the Continental U.S.

If you want your multicast to reach these destinations	Use this TTL value
The local host	0
The local subnet	1
The local campus, that is the same side of the nearest Internet router, but on possibly different LANs	16
High-bandwidth sites in the United States, generally those fairly close to the backbone	32
The United States	48
North America	64
High-bandwidth sites worldwide	128
All sites worldwide	255

public void setInterface(InetAddress interface) throws SocketException (Java 1.1 only)

On a multihomed host, the setInterface() method chooses the network interface to be used for multicast sending and receiving. setInterface() throws a SocketException if the InetAddress you give it is not the address of a network interface on the local machine. It is unclear why choosing the network interface is immutably set in the constructor for unicast Socket objects, but is variable and set with a separate method for MulticastSocket objects. To be safe, you should set the interface immediately after constructing a MulticastSocket, and not change it thereafter. Here's how you might use setInterface():

```
MulticastSocket ms;
InetAddress ia;
try {
  ia = new InetAddress("sunsite.unc.edu");
  ms = new MulticastSocket(2048);
  ms.setInterface(ia);
  System.out.println(ms);
}
catch (UnknownHostException ue) {
  System.err.println(ue);
}
```

```
     catch (SocketException se) {
       System.err.println(se);
     }
```

It's possible that the mechanism for selecting a network interface on a multi-homed host may change to be more similar to the Socket class in the final release of Java 1.1.

public InetAddress getInterface() throws SocketException

If you need to know the address of the interface you're using, you can call get-Interface(). It isn't clear why this method would throw an exception; in any case, you must be prepared for it. For example:

```
     try {
       ms = new MulticastSocket(2048);
       ia = ms.getInterface();
     }
     catch (SocketException se) {
       System.err.println(ue);
     }
```

Two Simple Examples

Most multicast servers are indiscriminate about who they will talk to. Therefore, it's easy to join a group, and watch the data that's being sent to it. Example 13–3 is a MulticastSniffer that reads the name of a multicast group from the command line, constructs an InetAddress from that hostname, then creates a Multicast-Socket that attempts to join the multicast group at that hostname. If the attempt succeeds, we receive datagrams from the socket, and print their contents on System.out. This program is primarily useful to verify that you are receiving multicast data at a particular host. Most multicast data is binary, and won't be intelligible when printed as ASCII.

NOTE   MulticastSockets are broken in Java 1.0.2. They work in Java 1.0 and Java 1.1.

Example 13–3: MulticastSniffer

```
     import sun.net.*;
     import java.net.*;
     import java.io.*;

     public class MulticastSniffer {

       public static void main(String[] args) {
```

Example 13–3: MulticastSniffer (continued)

```
        InetAddress ia = null;
        byte[] buffer = new byte[65509];
        DatagramPacket dp = new DatagramPacket(buffer, buffer.length);
        int port = 0;

        // read the address from the command line
        try {
          try {
            ia = InetAddress.getByName(args[0]);
          }
          catch (UnknownHostException e)  {
            ia = InetAddressFactory.newInetAddress(args[0]);
          }
          port = Integer.parseInt(args[1]);
        } // end try
        catch (Exception e) {
          System.err.println(e);
          System.err.println("Usage: java MulticastSniffer MulticastAddress port");
          System.exit(1);
        }

        try {
          MulticastSocket ms = new MulticastSocket(port);
          ms.joinGroup(ia);
          while (true) {
            ms.receive(dp);
            String s = new String(dp.getData(), 0, 0, dp.getLength());
            System.out.println(s);
          }
        }
        catch (SocketException se) {
          System.err.println(se);
        }
        catch (IOException ie) {
          System.err.println(ie);
        }

      }

    }
```

The program begins by setting up a byte array and `DatagramPacket` to be used as a buffer for incoming data. Next, it reads the name of the multicast group from the first command-line argument, and tries to create an `InetAddress` from it. Many domain name servers can't resolve Class D IP addresses that aren't permanently attached to hostnames. In this case, the `InetAddress` constructor throws an `UnknownHostException` if you try to listen to an address DNS doesn't already know about. This exception is caught; the `InetAddressFactory.newInetAddress()`

method from Chapter 4, *Processing Internet Addresses* is used to build an `InetAddress` from a numeric IP address string like "224.2.2.2.". If for some reason you don't want to install this class, modify the `MulticastSniffer` to exit if you get an `UnknownHostException`. It will still be useful for multicast groups whose names are known to DNS.

Once we know the `InetAddress`, we create a new `MulticastSocket` `ms` on the specified port. This socket joins the multicast group at the specified `InetAddress`. Then it enters a loop where it waits for packets to arrive. As each packet arrives, the program reads its data, converts the data to a `String`, and prints it on `System.out`. Finally, when the user interrupts the program or an exception is thrown, the socket leaves the group and closes itself.

Example 13–4 is a `MulticastSender` that sends data to a multicast group. It is fairly simple, though there is one twist that is worth noting. Although the `Multicast-Socket` knows what multicast group it's sending to, you still need to store the IP address of the multicast group in the `DatagramPacket`. Again, we use the `InetAddressFactory` from Chapter 4 to create an `InetAddress` object from a numeric IP address string if your local domain server doesn't understand multicast addresses.[*]

Example 13–4: MulticastSender

```
import java.net.*;
import java.io.*;
import sun.net.*;

public class MulticastSender {

  public static void main(String[] args) {

    InetAddress ia = null;
    int port = 0;
    String characters = "Here's some multicast data\n";
    byte[] data = new byte[characters.length()];

    // read the address from the command line
    try {
      try {
        ia = InetAddress.getByName(args[0]);
      }
      catch (UnknownHostException e)  {
        ia = InetAddressFactory.newInetAddress(args[0]);
      }
      port = Integer.parseInt(args[1]);
    }
    catch (Exception e)  {
```

---

[*] `InetAddress` Factory addresses a bug in the `InetAddress` class that was fixed in Java 1.1. If you have Java 1.1, you can rewrite this program so that it doesn't need the factory.

Example 13–4: MulticastSender (continued)

```
            System.err.println(e);
            System.err.println("Usage: java MulticastSender MulticastAddress port");
            System.exit(1);
        }

        characters.getBytes(0, characters.length(), data, 0);
        DatagramPacket dp = new DatagramPacket(data, data.length, ia, port);

        try {
          MulticastSocket ms = new MulticastSocket();
          ms.joinGroup(ia);
          for (int i = 1; i < 10; i++) {
            ms.send(dp, (byte) 1);
          }
          ms.leaveGroup(ia);
          ms.close();
        }
        catch (SocketException se) {
          System.err.println(se);
        }
        catch (IOException ie) {
          System.err.println(ie);
        }
    }
}
```

Example 13–4 reads the address of a multicast group, and a port number from the command line. It then stuffs the String "Here's some multicast data" into the byte array data using the getBytes() method of java.lang.String, and places this byte array in the DatagramPacket dp. Next, it constructs the MulticastSocket ms, and this joins the group ia. Once it has joined, ms sends the datagram packet dp to the group ia ten times. The TTL value is set to one to make sure this data doesn't go beyond the local subnet. Having sent the data, ms leaves the group, and closes itself.

Run Example 13–3 on one machine in your local subnet. Listen to the group ALL-SYSTEMS.MCAST.NET on port 4000 like this:

```
% java MulticastSniffer ALL-SYSTEMS.MCAST.NET 4000
```

Then send data to that group by running Example 13–4 on another machine in your local subnet. You can also run it in a different window on the same machine, though that's not as exciting. However, you must start running the MulticastSniffer before you start running the MulticastSender. Send to the group *ALL-SYSTEMS.MCAST.NET* on port 4000 like this:

```
% java MulticastSender ALL-SYSTEMS.MCAST.NET 4000
```

Back on the first machine you should see this output:

```
Here's some multicast data
Here's some multicast data
Here's some multicast data
Here's some multicast data
Here's some multicast data
Here's some multicast data
Here's some multicast data
Here's some multicast data
Here's some multicast data
```

For this to work, you must have a multicast router on your local subnet. If you can receive MBONE feeds, there is such a router. Otherwise, ask your network administrator to make sure.

14

Remote Method Invocation

What Is Remote Method Invocation?

Historically, networking has been concerned with two fundamental applications. The first application is moving files and data between hosts, and is handled by FTP, SMTP (email), HTTP, NFS, and many other protocols. The second application is allowing one host to run programs on another host. This is the traditional province of telnet, rlogin, remote procedure calls (RPC), and a lot of database middleware; you can also think of CGI as a means to get a server to run a program for a client. Except for the sections on CGI, most of this book has implicitly concerned itself with file and data transfer. This chapter and the next discuss ways to run programs on a server. In this chapter, we will discuss remote method invocation (RMI), a facility that allows Java programs to call certain methods on a remote server. RMI doesn't require either the client or the server to run an HTTP server; in fact, one way to look at RMI is as a mechanism for defining custom protocols and servers with minimal effort.

The RMI interface (Java 1.1, though alpha and beta releases appeared significantly earlier) lets Java objects on different hosts communicate with each other. A remote object lives on a server. Each remote object implements a remote interface that specifies which of its methods can be invoked by clients. Clients can invoke the methods of the remote object almost exactly as they invoke local methods. For example, a client can ask a database object on a server to sum up a series of records and return the result. This is more efficient than downloading all the records and summing them locally. Java-compatible web servers can implement remote methods that allow clients to ask for a complete index of the public files on the site. This could dramatically reduce the time a server spends filling requests from web spiders like Lycos and Altavista. Indeed, Excite already uses a non-Java-based version of this idea.

From the programmer's perspective, remote objects and methods work just like the local objects and methods you're accustomed to. All the implementation details are hidden. You just import one package, look up the remote object in a registry (which takes one line of code), and make sure you catch RemoteExceptions when you call the object's methods. From that point on, you can use a remote object almost as freely and easily as you use an object running on your own system.

More formally, a *remote object* is an object whose methods may be called by a different Java virtual machine than the one where the object itself lives, generally one running on a different computer. Each remote object implements one or more *remote interfaces* that declare which methods of the remote object the foreign system can invoke. RMI is the facility that enables a Java program running on one machine, say *www.ora.com*, to invoke a method in an object on a completely different machine, say *sunsite.unc.edu*.

For example, suppose an object on *sunsite.unc.edu* has a query method that looks up information in a local database. The query method would be exported in a remote interface. The client on *www.ora.com* would look up the object in sunsite's registry, then call the query method, just like it would call a query method in an object on *www.ora.com*. The object that queries the database runs on the server, but it accepts arguments from and returns results to the client on *www.ora.com*. This is simpler than designing and implementing a new socket-based protocol for communication between the database server and its client. The details of making the connections between the hosts and transferring the data is hidden in the RMI classes.

Security

The prospect of remote clients invoking methods in your host's objects raises a lot of security issues. *Super.secret.cia.gov* probably doesn't want *spy.kremlin.ussr* to be able to call readFile() methods on its machine. Java is uniquely suited to solving these problems. Just as an applet host can limit the activities of an applet, a host that allows RMI can limit what the remote clients can do.

The activities that a remote object can perform are limited in much the same way as an applet's activity is limited. A SecurityManager object checks all operations to make sure they're allowed by the server. Custom security managers can be defined for specific applications. Public key authentication can be used to verify a user's identity, and allow different users different levels of access to a remote object. For example, the general public may be allowed to query a database, but not update it; users from inside a company might be allowed to query and update the database.

RPC

Remote Procedure Calls (RPC) is an older technology Sun developed that does much the same thing as RMI. RPC is language- and processor-independent; RMI is processor-independent by nature, but limited to programs written in Java. RPC will eventually be made available in Java, although it wasn't at the time this book was written.

To get the cross-platform portability that Java provides, RPC requires a lot more overhead than RMI. RPC has to convert arguments between architectures, so that each computer can use its native datatypes. For example, integers have to be converted between big-endian and little-endian implementations. Furthermore, RPC can only send primitive datatypes, while RMI can send objects.

In short, RMI is the best solution for communication between Java programs on different hosts. However, if you need to connect with programs written in other languages, you should investigate RPC, or look into CORBA.

Where Does Object Serialization Fit In?

When an object is passed to or returned from a Java method, what's really transferred is a reference to the object. In current implementations of Java, references are handles (doubly indirected pointers) to the location of the object in the memory of the virtual machine. Passing objects between two machines thus raises some problems. The remote machine can't read what's in the memory of the local machine. A reference that's valid on one machine isn't meaningful on the other.

There are two ways around this problem. You can pass a special remote reference to the object (a reference that points to the memory in the remote machine), or you can pass a copy of the object. When the local machine passes a remote object to the remote machine, it passes a remote reference. The object has never really left the remote machine. However, when the local machine passes one of its own objects to the remote machine, it makes a copy of the object and sends the copy. The copy of the object moves from the local machine to the remote machine.

To copy an object, you need a way to convert the object into a stream of bytes. This is more difficult than it appears at first glance because objects can include other objects as fields; these fields also need to be copied when the object is copied. Object serialization is a scheme that converts objects into a byte stream that is passed around to other machines; these rebuild the original object from the bytes. These bytes can also be written to disk, and read back from disk at a later time, allowing you to save the state of a program (or even an individual object).

For security reasons, Java places some limitations on which objects can be serialized. All Java primitive types and remote objects can be serialized, but non-remote Java objects can only be serialized if they implement the java.io.Serializable interface. Basic Java types that implement java.io.Serializable in Java 1.1 include Strings and AWT Components. Container classes like Hashtable are serializable if all the objects they contain are serializable. Furthermore, subclasses of a serializable class are also serializable. For example, java.lang.Integer and java.lang.Float are serializable because the class they extend, java.lang.Number, is serializable. Table 14–1 summarizes which classes may be serialized.

Table 14–1: Serializable and Non-Serializable Classes

Serializable	Not Serializable
java.lang.Character	Threads
java.lang.Boolean	InputStreams
java.lang.String	OutputStreams
java.lang.Throwable	Peer classes
java.lang.Number	JDBC ResultSet
java.lang.StringBuffer	Most of the sun classes
java.util.Hashtable	
java.util.Random	
java.util.Vector	
java.util.Date	
java.util.BitSet	
java.io.File	
java.net.InetAddress	
java.net.URL[a]	
java.awt.BorderLayout	
java.awt.Color	
java.awt.Dimension	
java.awt.Event	
java.awt.Font	
java.awt.Polygon	
java.awt.CardLayout	
java.awt.FontMetrics	
java.awt.Image	
java.awt.Window	
java.awt.FlowLayout	
java.awt.GridLayout	
java.awt.Point	

Table 14–1: Serializable and Non-Serializable Classes (continued)

Serializable	Not Serializable
`java.awt.Rectangle`	
`java.awt.MenuComponent`	
`java.awt.Insets`	
`java.awt.CheckboxGroup`	
`java.awt.MediaTracker`	
`java.awt.GridBagLayout`	
`java.awt.GridBagConstraints`	
`java.awt.Cursor`	
`java.rmi.server.RemoteObject`	

[a] Only in Java 1.1 and later, not in the pre-beta version of RMI.

CORBA and Friends

RMI isn't the final word in distributed computing. Its biggest limitation is that you can only call methods written in Java. What if you already have an application written in some other language like C++, and you want to communicate with it? You could use RPC, which I mentioned earlier, but RPC isn't well adapted for object-oriented programming. The most general solution for distributed objects is CORBA, the Common Object Request Broker Architecture. CORBA lets objects written in different languages communicate with each other. Java hooks into CORBA through the Java Interface Definition Language (IDL), and JOE, the Java Object Environment. This goes beyond the scope of this book; to start learning about these topics, see:

Java-IDL
> *http://splash.javasoft.com/JavaIDL/pages/index.html*

Information Resources for CORBA
> *http://www.acl.lanl.gov/CORBA/*

The Object Management Group
> *http://www.omg.org/*

The CORBA FAQ list
> *http://www.cerfnet.com/~mpcline/Corba-FAQ/*

Under the Hood

The last two sections skimmed over a lot of details. Fortunately, Java hides most of the details from you. However, it never hurts to understand how things really work. The fundamental difference between remote objects and local objects is that remote objects reside in a different virtual machine. Normally, object arguments are passed to methods, and object values are returned from methods by referring to something in a particular virtual machine. This is called *passing a reference*. However, this method doesn't work when the invoking method and the invoked method aren't in the same virtual machine; for example, object 243 in one virtual machine has nothing to do with object 243 in a different virtual machine. In fact, different virtual machines may implement references in completely different and incompatible ways.

Therefore, three different mechanisms are used to pass arguments to and return results from remote methods, depending on the type of data being passed. Primitive types (int, boolean, double, etc.) are passed by value, just as in local Java method invocation. References to remote objects (that is, objects that implement the Remote interface) are passed as a *remote reference* that allows the recipient to invoke methods on the remote object. This is similar to the way local object references are passed to local Java methods. Objects that do not implement the Remote interface are passed by value; that is, complete copies are passed, using object serialization. Objects that do not allow themselves to be serialized cannot be passed to remote methods. Remote objects run on the server but can be called by objects running on the client. Non-remote, serializable objects run on the client system.

To ensure compatibility with existing Java programs and implementations, and to make the process as transparent to the programmer as possible, communication between a remote object client and a server is implemented in a series of layers as shown in Figure 14–1.

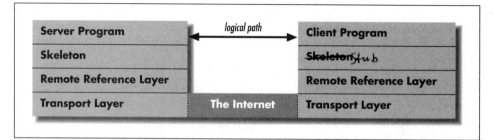

Figure 14–1: The RMI layer model

To the programmer, the client appears to talk directly to the server. In reality, the client program talks only to a stub. The stub passes the conversation along to the remote reference layer, which talks to the transport layer. The transport layer on the client passes the data across the Internet to the transport layer on the server. The server's transport layer then communicates with the server's remote reference layer, which talks to a piece of server software called the skeleton. The skeleton communicates with the server itself. In the other direction (server-to-client), this flow is simply reversed. Logically, data flows horizontally (client-to-server and back), but the actual flow of data is vertical.

This approach may seem overly complex, but remember that most of the time you don't need to think about it, any more than you need to think about how a telephone translates your voice into a series of electrical impulses that are translated back to sound at the other end of the phone call. You just call methods and return values. However, there are two situations in which you should be aware of the way data flows between the client and the server. First, we haven't discussed how a client finds a server, or where the stub comes from. A client finds an appropriate server by using a registry, which has a method called `lookup()`. When you call `lookup()`, it finds the stub that's needed for the object you want, and downloads it. (This is one situation in which Java's extreme portability comes into play. The stub doesn't need to be compiled into the client; it can be downloaded at runtime, regardless of the server platform.) Second, you need to be aware of how the client and server communicate in situations when the difference between passing an object by reference and by value becomes significant.

A client invokes a remote method by using a stub. The stub is a special object that implements the remote interfaces of the remote object; this means that the stub has methods matching the signatures of all the methods the remote object exports. In effect, the client thinks it is calling a method in the remote object, but it is really calling an equivalent method in the stub. Stubs are used in the client's virtual machine in place of the real objects and methods that live on the server; you may find it helpful to think of the stub as the remote object's surrogate on the client. When the stub is invoked, it passes the invocation into the remote reference layer.

The remote reference layer carries out a specific remote reference protocol that is independent of the specific client stubs and server skeletons. The remote reference layer is responsible for understanding what a particular remote reference means. Sometimes the remote reference refers to multiple virtual machines on multiple hosts. In other situations, the reference may refer to a single virtual machine on the local host, or a virtual machine on a remote host. In essence, the remote reference layer translates the local reference to the stub into a remote reference to the object on the server, whatever the syntax or semantics of the remote reference may be. Then it passes the data to the transport layer.

The transport layer handles the actual movement of data across the Internet. It provides connection setup, connection management, and tracking and dispatching of remote objects. On the server side, the transport layer listens for incoming connections or data. When it receives an invocation, it forwards the invocation to the remote reference layer on the server. The remote reference layer converts the remote references sent by the client into references for the local virtual machine. Then it passes the request to the skeleton. The skeleton reads the arguments, and passes the data to the server program, which makes the actual method call. If the method call returns a value, that value is sent down through the skeleton, remote reference, and transport layers on the server side, across the Internet, and then up through the transport, remote reference, and stub layers on the client side.

Implementation

Most of the methods you need for working with remote objects are in four packages: `java.rmi`, `java.rmi.server`, `java.rmi.registry`, and `java.rmi.dgc`. The `java.rmi` package defines the classes, interfaces, and exceptions that will be seen on the client side. You need these when you're writing programs that access remote objects but are not themselves remote objects. The `java.rmi.server` package defines the classes, interfaces, and exceptions that will be visible on the server side. You use these classes when you are writing a remote object that will be called by clients. The `java.rmi.registry` package defines the classes, interfaces, and exceptions that are used to locate and name remote objects. The `java.rmi.dgc` package handles distributed garbage collection. These packages are part of the core of Java 1.1, so you can assume that they are present in all later releases.

NOTE   I'm writing this late in 1996, based on early access releases. The final
              API is not scheduled to be completed until early 1997. It's almost
              certain some of this will change. Please check the web site at
              http://sunsite.unc.edu/javafaq/ for updates.

In this chapter and Sun's documentation, the server side is always considered to be "remote" and the client is always considered "local." This can be confusing, particularly when you're writing a remote object. When writing a remote object, you're probably thinking from the viewpoint of the server, so that the client appears to be remote.

The Server Side

To create a new remote object, you first define an interface that extends the java.rmi.Remote interface. The Remote interface does not have any methods of its own; its sole purpose is to tag remote objects so they can be identified as such. One definition of a remote object is an instance of a class that implements the Remote interface, or any interface that extends Remote.

Your subclass of Remote determines which methods of the remote object you're creating may be called by clients. A remote object may have many public methods, but only those declared in a remote interface can be invoked remotely. The other public methods may only be invoked from within the virtual machine where the object lives. Each method in your sub-interface must declare that it throws Remote-Exception. java.rmi.RemoteException is the superclass for most of the exceptions that can be thrown when RMI is used. Many of these are related to the behavior of external systems and networks, and are thus beyond your control.

Example 14–1 is a simple interface for a "Hello World" remote object. This interface has a single method, sayHello(), which returns a String and throws Remote-Exception. A more complex remote object could have many methods.

Example 14–1: The Hello interface

```
import java.rmi.*;

public interface Hello extends Remote {

  public String sayHello() throws java.rmi.RemoteException;

}
```

After defining a remote interface, define a class that implements your remote interface. This class should extend java.rmi.UnicastRemoteObject, either directly or indirectly (i.e., by extending another class that extends UnicastRemoteObject). Without going much into the details, UnicastRemoteObject provides a number of methods that make remote method invocation work; if your remote object merely extends the Object class, you will have to write a lot more code yourself. In particular, your class will need methods to marshal and unmarshal remote references to the object. (Marshaling is the process that converts arguments and return values into a stream of bytes that can be sent over the network. Unmarshaling is the reverse: the conversion of a stream of bytes into a group of arguments or a return value.) It's possible that there will be other kinds of remote objects in the future (the idea of multicast remote objects is intriguing), but for now, UnicastRemoteObject is your only choice.

Example 14–2, the HelloImpl class, implements the remote interface Hello and extends UnicastRemoteObject. This class has a constructor, a main() method, and a sayHello() method. Only the sayHello() method will be available to the client because it's the only method defined by the Hello interface. The other two methods, main() and HelloImpl(), are used on the server side, but not available to the client.

Example 14–2: The HelloImpl class

```
import java.rmi.*;
import java.rmi.server.*;
import java.net.*;

public class HelloImpl extends UnicastRemoteObject implements Hello {

  public HelloImpl() throws RemoteException {
    super();
  }

  public String sayHello() throws RemoteException {
    return "Hello, World!";
  }

  public static void main(String args[]) {

    try {
      HelloImpl h = new HelloImpl();
      Naming.rebind("hello", h);
      System.out.println("Hello Server ready.");
    }
     catch (RemoteException re) {
      System.out.println("Exception in HelloImpl.main: " + re);
    }
    catch (MalformedURLException e) {
      System.out.println("MalformedURLException in HelloImpl.main: " + e);
    }

  }

}
```

The HelloImpl() constructor calls the default superclass constructor. Normally, you wouldn't bother to write a constructor this simple. However, when writing a remote object, it's necessary because you must declare that the constructor can throw a RemoteException.

The sayHello() method is trivial. It merely returns the String "Hello, world!" to clients that invoke this remote object. Although this is a remote method, there's nothing different about the method itself. This is a very simple case, but even vastly more complex remote methods are not different than their local counterparts. The only difference—that a remote method is declared in a remote interface and a local method is not—is completely external to the method itself.

The `main()` method starts the remote server process running. It can be invoked from the command line, by an HTTP server, or by some other process. It begins by entering a `try-catch` block that catches `RemoteException`. Since the `main()` method is `static`, an instance of `HelloImpl` has not yet been created when this method runs. Therefore, we construct a new `HelloImpl` object and bind that object to the name "hello" in the `Naming` registry.* A registry keeps track of the available objects on an RMI server and the names by which they can be requested. When a new remote object is created, the object adds itself and its name to the registry with the `bind()` or `rebind()` method. Clients can then ask for that object by name, or get a list of all the remote objects that are available. After registering itself, the server prints a message on `System.out` signaling that it is ready to begin accepting remote invocations. If something goes wrong, the `catch` block prints a simple error message.

This completes the code you need to write. However, before your server can begin accepting invocations, you must generate the stubs and skeletons your program requires. We have already discussed what the stubs and skeletons do; we know that the stub contains the information in the `Remote` interface (in this example, an object with a `sayHello()` method), and that a skeleton is similar, but on the server side. Fortunately, we don't have to write them ourselves; they can be generated automatically from the remote object's Java source code, using a utility called *rmic*. To generate the stubs and skeletons for the `HelloImpl` remote object, run *rmic* on the *.class* file. For example:

```
% rmic HelloImpl
% ls Hel*
Hello.class           HelloImpl.class          HelloImpl_Skel.class
Hello.java            HelloImpl.java           HelloImpl_Stub.class
```

rmic reads the *.class* file of a remote object, and produces *.class* files for the stubs and skeletons needed for the remote object. The command-line argument to *rmic* is the package-qualified class name (e.g., `java.rmi.examples.chat`, not just `chat`) of the remote object class. If the class doesn't fall in your CLASSPATH, you can specify the location with the *-classpath* command-line argument. For example, the following command searches for *HelloImpl.class* in the directory *test/classes*:

```
% rmic -classpath test/classes HelloImpl
```

---

* `java.rmi.Naming` is a simple registry provided by Sun; other registries may become available later.

The compiled *.class* files are placed in the current directory unless the –d option is specified. For example, to put the *.class* files in the directory *test/classes* (relative to the current directory), type:

```
% rmic HelloImpl -d -classpath test/classes
```

Finally, you're ready to start your server. Since the server expects to talk to the Naming registry, you must first start the registry like this:

```
% rmiregistry &
```

On Windows you start it from a DOS prompt like this:

```
C:> start rmiregistry
```

Make sure you run it in the background, if possible. The registry tries to listen to port 1099 by default. If it fails, especially if it does so with a message like "java.net.SocketException: Address already in use," some other program is using port 1099, possibly (though not necessarily) another registry service. You can run the registry on a different port by appending a port number like this:

```
% rmiregistry 2048 &
```

If you use a different port, you'll need to include that port in URLs that refer to this registry service.

Next, you launch the server like this:

```
% java HelloImpl &
Hello Server ready.
%
```

Now your server and registry are ready to accept remote method calls. In the next section, we develop a client that communicates with this server.

The Client Side

Before a client can call a remote method, it needs to retrieve a remote reference to the remote object. A program retrieves a remote reference by asking a registry on the server for a remote object. It asks by calling the registry's lookup(String url) method. The exact naming scheme depends on the registry you use; the Naming class that is implemented in java.rmi provides a URL-based scheme for locating objects. As you can see in the following example, these URLs have been designed so that they are similar to HTTP URLs. The string rmi is used to indicate the protocol, and means that the URL references a remote object. The URL's file field specifies the remote object's name. The fields for the hostname and the port number are unchanged.

```
Object o1 = Naming.lookup("rmi://sunsite.unc.edu/hello");
Object o2 = Naming.lookup("rmi://sunsite.unc.edu:2048/hello");
```

Like objects stored in Hashtables, Vectors, and other data structures that store objects of different classes, the object that is retrieved from a registry loses its type information. Therefore, before using the object, you must cast it to the remote interface that the remote object implements (not to the actual class, which is hidden from clients):

```
Hello h = (Hello) Naming.lookup("hello");
```

Once the object has been retrieved and its type restored, the client can call the object's remote methods exactly as it would call methods in a local object:

```
String message = h.sayHello();
```

Example 14–3 is a simple client for the Hello interface of the last section.

Example 14–3: The Hello client

```java
import java.rmi.*;

public class HelloClient {

  public static void main(String args[]) {

    System.setSecurityManager(new RMISecurityManager());

    try {

      Hello h = (Hello) Naming.lookup("hello");

      String message = h.sayHello();
      System.out.println("HelloClient: " + message);
    }
    catch (Exception e) {
      System.out.println("Exception in main: " + e);
    }
  }
}
```

The main() method of this class begins by setting the SecurityManager to a new RMISecurityManager, just as the server did. The try-catch block that follows is the meat of the method. It retrieves the remote object from the server and casts the object to the Hello interface. The lookup() method used here assumes the registry, the server, and the client are all on the same host. To look up a remote object on a remote host, pass an rmi URL to the lookup() method. For example:

```
Hello h = (Hello) Naming.lookup("rmi://sunsite.unc.edu/hello");
```

Once the object is retrieved, the client calls the sayHello() method. The result is stored in the String message, and then printed on System.out.

Remote methods that pass arguments are no more complicated. Just pass the arguments in the usual fashion. Figure 14–2 shows how the client talks to the registry and the server.

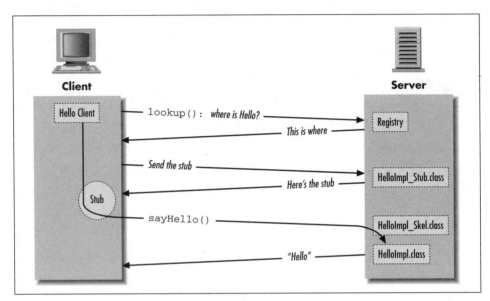

Figure 14–2: Client talking to registry

The java.rmi Package

The java.rmi package contains the classes that are seen by clients (objects that invoke remote methods). Both clients and servers should import java.rmi. While servers need a lot more infrastructure than what's present in this package, java.rmi is all that's needed by clients. This package contains one interface, two classes, and a handful of exceptions.

The Remote Interface

The Remote interface tags objects as being remote objects. It doesn't declare any methods; remote objects usually implement a subclass of Remote that does declare some methods. The methods declared in the interface are the methods that can be invoked remotely.

Example 14–4 is a database interface that declares a single method, SQLQuery(), accepts a String, and returns an array of Strings. A class that implements this interface would include the code to send a SQL query to a database, and return the result as an array of Strings.

Example 14–4: A database interface

```
import java.rmi.*;
import java.rmi.server.*;

public interface SQL extends Remote {

  public String[] SQLQuery(String query) throws java.rmi.RemoteException;

}
```

An SQLImpl class that implemented the SQL interface would probably have more methods, some of which might be public. However, only the SQLQuery() method can be invoked by a client.

Because the Remote interface is not a class, a single object can implement multiple Remote interfaces. In this case, any method declared in any Remote interface can be invoked by a client. However, there's a catch. Your remote object may implement three remote interfaces—but, on the client, you can only cast the object to one interface at a time. Therefore, it's a good idea to package all the interfaces your object implements into a single interface, and to work with that composite interface, rather than to write a remote object that implements several interfaces.

The Naming Class

The java.rmi.Naming class is a registry that maps URLs like *rmi://sunsite.unc.edu/ myRemoteObject* to particular remote objects. You can think of a registry as a DNS for remote objects. Each entry in the registry has a name and an object reference. Clients give the name (via a URL) and get back a reference to the remote object.

Naming is the only registry included with RMI at this time; others may be included in the future, or may be provided by other vendors. The biggest deficiency of Naming is that it requires the client to know the server where the remote object lives; you might also complain that Naming implements a flat (i.e., non-hierarchical) name space.

As we've seen, an RMI URL looks exactly like an HTTP URL, except that the protocol field is rmi instead of http, and the port is more often specified than not. For example:

    rmi://sunsite.unc.edu:2001/myRemoteObject

The file part of the URL is an arbitrary name the server has bound to a particular remote object, not a file name.

The Naming class has five public methods: bind(), to bind a name to a specific remote object; list(), to list all the names bound in the registry; lookup(), to find a specific remote object given its URL; rebind(), to bind a name to a different remote object; and unbind(), to remove a name from the registry. Let's look at these methods in turn.

public static Remote lookup(String url) throws RemoteException, NotBoundException, AccessException, UnknownHostException

A client uses the lookup() method to retrieve a Remote interface associated with the file portion of the name; so given *rmi://sunsite.unc.edu:2001/myRemoteObject*, it would return the object named myRemoteObject from *sunsite.unc.edu*.

This method throws a NotBoundException if the name has not been bound to an object. An AccessException is thrown if the client is not allowed to connect to this registry (e.g., *Super.secret.cia.gov* might have disallowed connections from *kgb.gov.ussr*). If the host in the URL can't be located, the method throws Unknown-HostException.

public static void bind(String url, Remote ro)
throws RemoteException, AlreadyBoundException, AccessException,
UnknownHostException

A server uses the bind() method to link a name like *myRemoteObject* to a remote object. If the binding is successful, clients can retrieve the remote object from the registry using a URL like *rmi://sunsite.unc.edu:2001/myRemoteObject*.

Many things can go wrong with the binding process. bind() throws an Unknown-HostException if the host cannot be located. If the client is not allowed to bind objects in this registry, an AccessException is thrown. (Remote clients are usually not allowed to add objects to a registry.) If the URL is already bound to a local object, bind() throws an AlreadyBoundException. Finally, if the registry can't be contacted (e.g., the connection times out), bind() throws a RemoteException.

public static void unbind(String url) throws RemoteException, NotBoundException, AccessException, UnknownHostException

The unbind() method removes the object with the given URL from the registry. It is the opposite of the bind() method. What bind() has bound, unbind() unbinds. unbind() throws a NotBoundException if the URL is not bound to an object in the first place. Otherwise, this method can throw the same exceptions as bind().

public static void rebind(String url, Remote obj)
throws RemoteException, AccessException, UnknownHostException

The rebind() method is just like the bind() method, except that it binds the URL to the object, even if the URL is already bound. If the URL is already bound to an object, the old binding is lost. Thus, this method cannot throw an AlreadyBound-Exception. It can still throw RemoteExceptions, AccessExceptions, and Unknown-HostExceptions, with the same meanings they have when thrown by bind().

public static String[] list(String url) throws RemoteException,
AccessException, UnknownHostException

The list() method returns all the URLs that are currently bound as an array of strings. The url argument is the URL of the Naming registry to query. Only the protocol, host, and port are used. The file part of the URL is ignored.

The RMISecurityManager Class

A client loads stubs from a potentially untrustworthy server; in this sense, the relationship between a client and a stub is sort of like the relationship between a browser and an applet. Although a stub is only supposed to marshal arguments, unmarshal return values, and send them across the network, from the standpoint of the virtual machine, a stub is just another class with methods that can do just about anything. Stubs produced by *rmic* shouldn't misbehave, but there's no reason someone couldn't handcraft a stub that would do all sorts of nasty things, like reading files or erasing data. The Java virtual machine does not allow stub classes to be loaded across the network unless there's some SecurityManager object in place. (Like other classes, stub classes can always be loaded from the local CLASS-PATH.) For applets, the standard AppletSecurityManager fills this need.

Applications can use the RMISecurityManager class to protect themselves from miscreant stubs. This simple security manager (a subclass of java.lang.SecurityManager) disables everything except class definition and access. In other words, it only allows the minimum functionality for accessing remote objects, passing arguments to a remote method, and returning values from a remote method. If no security manager is set, stub classes will only be loaded from the local files in the CLASSPATH. This guarantees that stubs and classes are only loaded from the network if there is a security manager in place to watch over them.

public RMISecurityManager()

RMISecurityManager has a single constructor that takes no arguments. To set the security manager, use the static System.setSecurityManager() method. Most often you create a new SecurityManager directly inside this method:

```
System.setSecurityManager(new RMISecurityManager());
```

public Object getSecurityContext()

The getSecurityContext() method determines the environment for certain operations. A RMISecurityManager allows more operations by a class loaded from a local host than from a network host. Eventually (though not as of this writing), public key signatures will be used to grant different classes different trust levels.

Checking operations

There are 23 methods that check various operations to see whether they're allowed. All of these methods are public, synchronized, and void, except for checkTopLevelWindow(), which returns a boolean. Each one throws a StubSecurityException if the action is forbidden; if the action is allowed, the method just returns. These methods only check actions performed by stubs, not by other classes in the application. Since only one SecurityManager can be installed in an application, you may have to replace this class with a class of your own, if you want to check both actions performed by stubs, and actions performed by other classes like applets.

Table 14–2 lists the methods of the RMISecurityManager, what they check for, and the circumstances that will allow the operation. It is unlikely that you will need to call these methods yourself. However, you need to know these methods to understand what a stub can and cannot do.

Table 14–2: RMISecurityManager Permissions

Method	Checks For	If Stub Is Local	If Stub Is Remote
checkCreateClassLoader()	Can a stub create a ClassLoader?	No	No
checkAccess(Thread t) checkAccess(ThreadGroup g)	Can a stub manipulate threads outside the Stub's own thread group?	No	No

Table 14–2: RMISecurityManager Permissions (continued)

Method	Checks For	If Stub Is Local	If Stub Is Remote
checkExit(int status)	Can a stub force the virtual machine to exit? (Can it call System.exit()?)	No	No
checkExec(String cmd)	Can a stub execute system processes? (Can it call System.exec()?)	No	No
checkLink(String lib)	Can a stub link to dynamic libraries?	No	No
checkPropertiesAccess()	Can a stub read the properties of the local machine?	No	No
checkPropertyAccess (String key)	Can a stub check a specific property?	No	No
checkRead(String file) checkRead(String file, URL base) checkRead(String file, Object context) checkRead(FileDescriptor fd)	Can a stub read a file?	No	No
checkWrite(String file) checkWrite(FileDescriptor fd)	Can a stub write to a file?	No	No
checkListen(int port)	Can a stub listen for connections on a port?	No[a]	No
checkAccept(String host, int port)	Can a stub accept connections on a port?	No[a]	No
checkConnect(String host, int port) checkConnect(String host, int port, Object context) checkConnect(String fromHost, String toHost)	Can a stub open a connection to this host on this port?	Yes	Yes, if the host is the one from which the stub was downloaded; otherwise, no.
checkTopLevelWindow (Object window)	Can the stub create a new window?	No	No

Table 14–2: RMISecurityManager Permissions (continued)

Method	Checks For	If Stub Is Local	If Stub Is Remote
checkPackageAccess (String pkg)	Can a stub access the specified package?	No (May be user-adjustable in the future)	No (May be user-adjustable in the future)
checkPackageDefinition (String pkg)	Can a stub define classes in the specified package?	No (May be user-adjustable in the future)	No (May be user-adjustable in the future)
checkSetFactory()	Can a stub set a network factory?	No	No

^a This may be allowed in a future release.

Remote Exceptions

The java.rmi package defines seventeen exceptions (Table 14–3). All except RemoteException extend java.rmi.RemoteException; java.rmi.RemoteException extends java.lang.Exception. Thus none is a runtime exception, and all must be caught by a catch block or declared in a throws clause.

With remote method calls, there's a huge amount that's not under your control: for example, the state of the network, and other necessary services like DNS. Therefore, any remote method can fail: there's no guarantee that the network won't be down when the method is called. Consequently, all remote methods must be declared to throw the generic RemoteException, and you should wrap all calls to remote methods in a try-catch block. When you just want to get a program working, it's simplest to catch RemoteException:

```
try {
  // call remote methods
}
catch (RemoteException e) {
  System.err.println(e);
}
```

More robust programs should try to catch more specific exceptions and respond accordingly.

Table 14–3: Remote Exceptions

Exception	Meaning
`java.rmi.RemoteException`	The generic superclass for all exceptions having to do with remote methods.
`java.rmi.AlreadyBoundException`	The URL is already bound to another object.
`java.rmi.NotBoundException`	The URL is not bound to an object. This might be thrown when you try to reference an object whose URL was rebound out from under it.
`java.rmi.StubNotFoundException`	The stub for a class could not be found. The stub file may be in the wrong directory on the server. There could be a name space collision between the class that the stub substitutes for and some other class. The client could have requested the wrong URL.
`java.rmi.RMISecurityException`	An object tried to do something that is prohibited by the stub's `SecurityManager`.
`java.rmi.NoSuchObjectException`	The object reference is invalid or obsolete. This might occur if the remote host becomes unreachable while the program is running, perhaps because of network congestion, system crash, or some other malfunction.
`java.rmi.UnknownHostException`	The host cannot be found. This is very similar to the exception `java.net.UnknownHostException`.
`java.rmi.ServerRuntimeException`	An unchecked, uncaught runtime exception occurred on the server, such as `ArrayIndexOutOfBoundsException`.
`java.rmi.UnexpectedException`	Something unforeseen happened. This is a catch-all that should occur only in bizarre situations.
`java.rmi.AccessException`	A client tried to do something that only local objects are allowed to do.
`java.rmi.ConnectException`	The server refused the connection.
`java.rmi.ConnectIOException`	An I/O error occurred while trying to make the connection between the local and the remote host.
`java.rmi.MarshalException`	An I/O error occurred while attempting to marshal (serialize) arguments to a remote method. This exception could be caused by a corrupted I/O stream, and making the remote method call again may be successful.

Table 14–3: Remote Exceptions (continued)

Exception	Meaning
java.rmi.UnmarshalException	An I/O error occurred while attempting to unmarshal (deserialize) the value returned by a remote method. This exception could be caused by a corrupted I/O stream, and making the remote method call again may be successful.
java.rmi.ServerError	An Error (that is a subclass of java.lang.Error) was thrown while the remote method was executing.
java.rmi.ServerException	A RemoteException was thrown while the remote method was executing.

The java.rmi.registry Package

How does a client that needs a remote object locate that object on a distant server? More precisely, how does it get a remote reference to the object? Clients find out what remote objects are available by querying the server's *registry*. A registry advertises the availability of the server's remote objects. Clients query the registry to find out what remote objects are available, and to get remote references to those objects. You've already seen one registry: the java.rmi.Naming class. This class implements the java.rmi.registry.Registry interface; all public methods of java.rmi.Naming are public methods of java.rmi.registry.Registry.

The Registry and RegistryHandler interfaces and the LocateRegistry class allow clients to retrieve remote objects on a server by name. A RegistryImpl is a subclass of RemoteObject, which links names to particular RemoteObject objects. Clients use the methods of the LocateRegistry class to retrieve the RegistryImpl for a specific host and port.

The Registry Interface

The java.rmi.registry.Registry interface has five public methods: bind(), to bind a name to a specific remote object; list(), to list all the names bound in the registry; lookup(), to find a specific remote object given its URL; rebind(), to bind a name to a different remote object; and unbind(), to remove a name from the registry. All of these behave exactly as previously described in the java.rmi.Naming class, which implements this interface. Other classes that implement this interface may use a different scheme for mapping names to particular objects, but the methods still have the same meaning and signatures.

As well as these five methods, the Naming interface also has one public final static int field, REGISTRY_PORT, the default port on which the registry listens. This is currently 1099.

The RegistryHandler Interface

The java.rmi.registry.RegistryHandler interface is the bridge between the public interface provided by java.rmi.registry.Registry and the detailed private implementation. You only need to concern yourself with this interface if you're writing your own registry. It is unnecessary if you're merely relying on the Naming class or some other pre-written registry.

This interface declares two methods: registryImpl(int port), which constructs and exports a Registry object on the specified port, and registryStub(String host, int port), which returns a stub object you can use to communicate with the registry running on the specified host at the specified port. The signatures of these methods are:

```
public abstract Registry registryStub(String host, int port)
        throws RemoteException, UnknownHostException
public abstract Registry registryImpl(int port) throws RemoteException
```

As usual, each of these can throw a RemoteException.

The LocateRegistry Class

The java.rmi.Registry.LocateRegistry class lets the client find the registry in the first place. This is achieved with four polymorphic versions the static getRegistry() method.

```
public static Registry getRegistry() throws RemoteException
public static Registry getRegistry(int port) throws RemoteException
public static Registry getRegistry(String host)
        throws RemoteException, UnknownHostException
public static Registry getRegistry(String host, int port)
        throws RemoteException, UnknownHostException
```

Each of these methods returns a Registry object that can be used to get remote objects by name. LocateRegistry.getRegistry() returns the Registry running on the local host on the default port, 1099. LocateRegistry.getRegistry(int port) returns the Registry running on the local host on the specified port. LocateRegistry.getRegistry(String host) returns the Registry for the specified host on the default port, 1099. Finally LocateRegistry.getRegistry(String host, int port) returns the Registry for the specified host on the specified port. If the host String is null, getRegistry() uses the local host; if the port argument is negative, it uses the default port.

Each of these methods can throw an arbitrary RemoteException. Furthermore, the two methods that request a Registry from a specific host also throw UnknownHostException if the host can't be found.

For example, a remote object that wanted to make itself available to clients would do this:

```
Registry r = LocateRegistry.getRegistry();
r.bind("My Name", this);
```

A remote client that wished to invoke this remote object might then say:

```
Registry r = LocateRegistry.getRegistry("thehost.site.com");
TheRemoteObjectInterface tro = (TheRemoteObjectInterface) r.lookup("MyName");
tro.invokeRemoteMethod();
```

The final method in the LocateRegistry class is createRegistry(int port). This creates a registry and starts it listening on the specified port. As usual, it can throw a RemoteException. Its signature is:

```
public static Registry createRegistry(int port) throws RemoteException
```

The java.rmi.server Package

The java.rmi.server package is the most complex of all the RMI packages; it contains the scaffolding for building remote objects, and thus is used by objects whose methods will be invoked by clients. The package defines six exceptions, seven interfaces, and ten classes. Fortunately, you only need to be familiar with a few of these to write remote objects. The important classes are the RemoteObject class, which is the basis for all remote objects; the RemoteServer class, which extends RemoteObject; and the UnicastRemoteObject class, which extends RemoteServer. Any remote objects you write will probably extend UnicastRemoteObject. Clients that call remote methods but are not themselves remote objects don't use these classes, and therefore don't need to import java.rmi.server.

The RemoteObject Class

Technically, a remote object is not an instance of the RemoteObject class, but rather an instance of any class that implements a Remote interface. However, in practice you will find that most remote objects will be instances of a subclass of java.rmi.server.RemoteObject. The RemoteObject class is essentially a special version of java.lang.Object for remote objects. It provides toString(), hashCode(), clone(), and equals() methods that make sense for remote objects. If you create a remote object that does not extend RemoteObject, you need to override these methods yourself.

The equals() method compares the remote object references of two RemoteObjects and returns true if they point to the same remote object. As with the equals() method in the Object class, you may want to override this method to provide a more meaningful definition of equality.

The toString() method returns a String that describes the remote object. Currently, toString() returns the hostname and port from which the remote object came, and a reference number for the object. Future RMI implementations will probably return more detailed information. You should override this method in your class if you convert your objects to strings for more than debugging purposes.

The hashCode() method maps a presumably unique int to each unique object; this integer may be used as a key in a Hashtable. It returns the same value for all remote references that refer to the same remote object. Thus, if a client has several remote references to the same object on the server, or multiple clients have references to that object, they should all have the same hash code.

RemoteObject does not implement the java.lang.Cloneable interface. However, the RemoteObject class has a clone() method, so subclasses can implement Cloneable if they need to.

The RemoteServer Class

The RemoteServer class extends RemoteObject; it is an abstract superclass for server implementations like UnicastRemoteObject. As of this writing, UnicastRemoteObject is the only subclass of RemoteServer included in the default package. You can add others (for example, a UDP or multicast remote server) by writing your own subclass of RemoteServer.

Constructors

There are two constructors for this class:

```
protected RemoteServer()
protected RemoteServer(RemoteRef r)
```

You won't instantiate this class yourself. Instead, you will instantiate its subclass, UnicastRemoteObject, or create your own subclass. When you do, you will call one of these protected constructors from the first line of your subclass's constructor.

Getting information about the client

The RemoteServer class has two methods you can use to locate the client with whom you're communicating:

```
public static String getClientHost() throws ServerNotActiveException
public int getClientPort() throws ServerNotActiveException
```

getClientHost() returns a String containing the hostname of the client that invoked the method currently running; getClientPort() returns an int containing the port of the client that invoked the method currently running. Both methods throw a ServerNotActiveException if the current thread is not running a remote method.

Logging

For debugging purposes, it is sometimes useful to see the calls that are being made to your remote object, and the object's responses. You can get a log for your RemoteServer by passing an OutputStream object to the setLog() method.

```
public static void setLog(OutputStream os)
```

Passing null for os turns off logging. For example, to see all the calls on System.err (which sends the log to the Java console), you would write:

```
RemoteServer.setLog(System.err);
```

If you want to add extra information to the log, in addition to that provided by the RemoteServer class, you can retrieve the log's PrintStream with the getLog() method:

```
public static PrintStream getLog()
```

Once you have the print stream, you can write on it to add your own comments to the log. For example:

```
PrintStream p = RemoteServer.getLog();
p.println("There were " + n + " total calls to the remote object.");
```

The UnicastRemoteObject Class

The UnicastRemoteObject class is a subclass of RemoteServer. To create a remote object, you usually extend UnicastRemoteObject in your own subclass, and declare that your subclass implements some subclass of the java.rmi.Remote interface. The methods of the Remote interface provide functionality specific to the class, while the methods of UnicastRemoteObject handle general remote object tasks such as marshaling and unmarshaling arguments and return values. All of this happens behind the scenes. As an application programmer, you don't need to worry about it.

A UnicastRemoteObject runs on a single host, uses TCP sockets to communicate, and has remote references that do not remain valid across server restarts. While this is a good general purpose framework for remote objects, it is worth noting that you can implement other kinds of remote objects. For example, you may want a remote object that uses UDP, or one that remains valid if the server is restarted, or even one that distributes the load across multiple servers. To create remote objects with these properties, you would extend RemoteServer directly, and implement the abstract methods of that class. However, if you don't need anything so esoteric, you will find it much easier to subclass UnicastRemoteObject.

The UnicastRemoteObject class has one constructor, UnicastRemoteObject() (the default), which creates a UnicastRemoteObject on an anonymous port chosen at runtime.[*] For example:

```
urs1 = new UnicastRemoteObject();
```

When you write a subclass of UnicastRemoteObject, you call this constructor, either explicitly or implicitly, in the first line of each constructor of your subclass. This constructor can throw a RemoteException if the remote object can't be created.

The UnicastRemoteObject class has two other public methods, clone() and exportObj(). Although these are public, they are primarily for the use of the Registry and other parts of the RMI infrastructure. You rarely need to call them directly. The clone() method simply creates a clone of the remote object. The static UnicastRemoteObject.exportObj(Remote ro) method is called by the runtime environment to start a particular remote object listening for invocations.

Exceptions

The java.rmi.server package defines six new exceptions. The exceptions and their meanings are listed in Table 14–4. All of these listings except java.rmi.server.ServerNotActiveException extend, directly or indirectly, java.rmi.RemoteException. You must catch or declare them all in a throws clause.

Table 14–4: java.rmi.server Exceptions

Exception	Meaning
ExportException	You're trying to export a remote object on a port that's already in use.
SocketSecurityException	This subclass of ExportException is thrown when the SecurityManager prevents a remote object from being exported on the requested port.

---

[*] By the way, this is an example of an obscure situation I mentioned in Chapter 8, *Sockets for Servers*, and Chapter 9, *UDP Datagrams and Sockets*. The server is listening on an anonymous port. Normally, this would be next to useless, because it would be impossible for clients to locate the server. In this case, clients locate servers by using a registry that keeps track of the available servers, and the ports to which they are listening.

Table 14–4: java.rmi.server Exceptions (continued)

Exception	Meaning
ServerNotActiveException	An attempt was made to invoke a method in a remote object that wasn't running.
SkeletonNotFoundException	The server is unable to load the skeleton it needs to respond to a remote method invocation. This can mean several things: the skeleton class file may not be anywhere in the codebase; the skeleton is in the codebase, but has a name conflict with another class; the URL given may be incorrect; or the skeleton may be of the wrong class.
SkeletonMismatchException	The skeleton and the stub for a class don't match. This is unusual, but may happen if different versions of the source code are used to make the stub and the skeleton.
ServerCloneException	An attempt to clone a remote object on the server failed.

The Java Server
API and Servlets

What Is the Java Server API?

The Java Server API is a set of classes, a framework if you will, for the development of IP servers, especially http servers. The Server API is a standard *extension* to Java, which means that it is not included in the base Java release. If you want to use it in a program, you need to download and install the necessary classes from Sun.[*] You should not use the server API in an applet. There are many interesting aspects of the Server API, but the most interesting is a concept called *servlets*; that's what we will focus on in this chapter. It is possible to use the Server classes as a general purpose toolkit for building servers, but that's beyond the bounds of this book.

Servlets are Java programs that make servers extensible. Much as you can load applets into a web browser, you can load servlets into a running server to extend its capabilities. Like applets, the byte codes for a servlet can be read from the local file system or from the network. In the future, it will even be possible for clients to upload servlets to a server to be run there, just as today clients download and run applets from a server. A servlet can return data to the client as a new web page, as data inside a web page, or through a custom protocol spoken by both. However, servlets themselves are faceless; they do not have a graphical interface or output stream to which they can send output. They rely on the web client to provide these services.

Servlets provide yet another way for a web server to generate dynamic data. Normally, a web server receives a URL requesting a certain page. The server maps this

---

[*] Assuming Sun doesn't reorganize its web site before this book hits the shelves, you can get the necessary packages from *http://www.javasoft.com/jeeves/*. You can probably also get them via ftp from *ftp://ftp.javasoft.com/pub/*. However, the filenames will almost certainly change by the time you have this book. Look for something with the word "jeeves" in the filename.

URL to a file, reads the file from the local disk, and sends the data to the client. In this situation, the data is static; it doesn't change until the server administrator changes the file. However a servlet can generate new data for each request because it is a program. Thus it can deliver changing information such as a time of day or a stock price.

Of course, that's nothing really new; CGI programs can also dynamically generate data to send to a client. How does a servlet differ from a CGI program? Why should you consider writing servlets, rather than sticking with CGI? Those are good questions. CGI has been around for awhile, and it's well understood. It's easy to write a web page that invokes a CGI program, and easy to write a program that sends data back to the browser. Furthermore, virtually all web servers understand CGI; currently, Jeeves (a demonstration server that Sun supplies with the Server distribution) is the only server that can handle servlets, though there are more to come. From that standpoint, it's clearly not time to forget your CGI skills; the most I can hope to do is convince you that servlets are worth investigating, and may be important in the future. Servlets are interesting precisely because they are more than just CGI programs written in Java; servlets can do many things that CGI programs cannot:

1. A servlet can continue to run in the background after it has finished processing a request so that it's ready to process the next request without incurring additional startup costs. On an active server, the overhead of starting CGI programs is significant. Furthermore, a servlet can use threads to process simultaneous requests efficiently. A servlet can even pass data between multiple connections. For example, a servlet can act as a multiplayer game server that listens for input from multiple clients, and then broadcasts that data to all connected clients.

2. A servlet can communicate interactively with an applet on the client. A CGI program receives a request from a client, and then sends a response; at that point the connection is closed. The client cannot send another request to the CGI program in response to the data it received. In constrast, a servlet-applet pair can carry on a conversation, making many data transfers between the client and the server. They can even implement a new protocol if necessary. This is much more efficient than multiple calls to the same CGI program, and much easier to code than a CGI program that stores some form of state on the server or in the URL.

3. Servlets can originate on the client. Like applets, servlets run in a secure environment, so the server does not need to worry about hostile servlets. For example, a client can upload a custom servlet that searches a web site for

information. With local access to the files, the search can take place much more quickly than it would if the client had to download each file on the web site. Web spiders and indexers like Lycos can become far more efficient, and use far less Internet bandwidth, since only the results of a site index need to be transmitted, not every page on the web site.

4. Servlets are a step towards agents. A servlet can be uploaded to different servers, performing the same action on each server in turn. Until now, all agent technologies shared several severe limitations. First, hosts had to trust the agents. Using Java's security features, a web server can execute a servlet without worrying that it may crash the system or open a security hole. Second, agents could only run on certain platforms; Java's portability means that servlets don't care what kind of system they run on. The possibilities for intelligent agents are almost limitless, including shopping agents that search for the best prices, clipping service agents that continuously comb the net for information, system management servlets that update mirror sites with copies of changed files, servlets that back up data to a central host, and more. However, servlets are not yet true agents because they must be explicitly invoked and moved by something other than themselves; that may change in the future.

Granted, there are some extensions to CGI that address some of its deficiencies. However, should the servlet model succeed, servlets will almost certainly remain more flexible and versatile than CGI scripts.

There are several ways a client can ask a server to run a servlet. The first way is that a server can map certain URLs to predefined servlet locations. For example, a web server can be configured to know that if the client requests the file at *http://sunsite.unc.edu/javafaq/index.html,* the web server should run a servlet that dynamically generates the page. In Jeeves these mappings are stored in the *rules.config* file and are accessible through the administrative interface. This is deliberately similar to the implementation of CGI on many systems. Second, a user can, in addition, request a servlet by using its own URL; for example, *http://sunsite.unc.edu/javafaq/servlets/index.class.* Finally, the <servlet> tag can be inserted in an HTML file; this is an example of server-parsed-HTML (SHTML). When the file is requested, the server parses the <servlet> tag, runs the servlet, and replaces the tag with the servlet's output before sending the file to the client. In the future, there will undoubtedly be more ways for servlets to interact with the server and its clients, but these are the only ones revealed to date.

Jeeves

Jeeves is an HTTP server from Sun designed to showcase the power of servlets. Jeeves uses servlets to perform all operations, including basic file service and server administration. Several standard servlets are started when the server initializes: the `FileServlet` serves static documents; the `InvokerServlet` launches servlets requested by the client via a URL; the `SSInclude` servlet handles servlets embedded in HTML files as server-side includes; the `CgiServlet` launches CGI programs; the `Admin` servlet lets the webmaster administer the server; and the `ImagemapServlet` processes image map selections. All of these servlets run until the server dies.

- The `FileServlet` responds to normal HTTP requests for files, caching frequently requested files. It recognizes files that contain server-side includes, and passes them to the `SSInclude` servlet. The `SSInclude` servlet parses the HTML file, replaces the server-side include tags with the actual data, and sends the data to the client.

- The `InvokerServlet` class invokes servlets requested by the client by name, *http://sunsite.unc.edu/javafaq/servlets/myServlet.class*, for example. In Jeeves 1.0A1 only servlets that reside on the same host as the server may be invoked; future versions of Jeeves will be able to run servlets from remote hosts (subject to more stringent security mangers).

- The `CgiServlet` executes CGI programs and sends their results back to the client. Jeeves can run any CGI program that conforms to the CGI 1.1 interface. These programs can be written in C, Perl, C++, Java, or any other language you would use to write a CGI on the host platform.

- The `Admin` servlet provides a graphical interface for administering Jeeves through a web browser.

- The `ImagemapServlet` handles server-side image maps. The image map format is an extension of the standard NCSA format. A server-side image map is included in an HTML file like this:

```
<A HREF="http://www.ora.com/myMapFile.map"><IMG SRC="map.gif" ISMAP></A>
```

Text-only browsers, such as Lynx, are presented with a menu of links when the user selects an image map. You can add a double-quoted string to the end of each line in the image map file; this string is used to create the menu. For example, *myMapFile.map* might contain:

```
base http://www.ora.com/
rect http://www.macfaq.com 227,0 340,65 "The Well Connected Mac"
rect http://sunsite.unc.edu 114,0 227,65 "Cafe Au Lait"
rect /index.html 1,0 114,65 "O'Reilly & Associates"
```

The base directive defines the base URL for any relative URLs in the mapfile. This is normally a full URL like *http://www.ora.com/*. There are two special values for base: the keyword map sets the base URL to the URL of the map image; the keyword referrer sets the base URL to the URL of the page that contains the image map.

Currently, Jeeves is the only HTTP server that can handle servlets, but more are expected. Jigsaw, the W3C reference server, implements a similar idea called *resource objects*. Since Jigsaw is written in Java, it is likely that these two interfaces will be merged together at some point. For more information about Jigsaw, see *http://www.w3.org/pub/WWW/Jigsaw/*.

Writing Servlets

A servlet is a programmer-defined class that is designed to implement the java.servlet.Servlet interface. The easiest way to implement this particular interface is to extend one of these two classes: java.servlet.http.HttpServlet or java.servlet.GenericServlet. HttpServlet is for classes that expect to be run by an HTTP server and have access to the usual MIME headers of an HTTP request. GenericServlet is for servlets that do not need the special features provided by an HTTP server; they may be run by any servlet-compatible server.

NOTE   This section is based on the alpha 2 pre-release of Jeeves. The server
                API is not scheduled to be complete until 1997. It's almost certain
                some of this will change. Please check the web site at
                http://sunsite.unc.edu/javafaq/ for updates.

A server communicates with servlets by invoking the methods of the java.servlet.Servlet interface: init(), service(), and destroy(). The server calls init() to initialize a servlet; it calls destroy() to unload a servlet; and it calls service() to ask the servlet to process a request. The request is passed to the service() method as an object that implements the ServletRequest interface. The servlet responds by invoking methods of a ServletResponse object, which is also passed into the service() method. The sequence of events is:

1. The server loads the byte codes for the requested servlet.

2. The server instantiates the servlet object.

3. The server calls the servlet's init() method.

4. The server constructs a request object that implements the ServletRequest interface from the data provided in the client request.

5. The server constructs a response object that implements the ServletResponse interface.

6. The server invokes the servlet's service(request, vresponse) method.

7. The service method processes the request, calling methods in the response argument to send information back to the client.

8. While there are more client requests, go to step 4.

9. When the server no longer needs the servlet, it invokes the servlet's destroy() method.

The HttpServlet and GenericServlet classes provide init() and destroy() methods that are suitable for many servlets. A servlet overrides at least one method from java.servlet.Servlet, service(), with the signature:

```
public void service(ServletRequest request,
                    ServletResponse response) throws Exception
```

HttpServlet subclasses also override a polymorphic version of service() that provides more information about the MIME headers:

```
public void service(HttpServletRequest request,
                    HttpServletResponse response) throws Exception
```

The service() method has two arguments, request and response. The request object represents a request made to the web server. It implements the ServletRequest or the HttpServletRequest interface, which has methods to read the request. (HttpServletRequest is a sub-interface of ServletRequest.) Likewise, the response object represents the server's response to this request; it implements the ServletResponse (or HTTPServletResponse) interface, which provides methods for responding to the request. service doesn't have a return value; it does everything necessary to respond to a request by calling methods in its ServletResponse object.

Example 15–1 is a simple servlet that says hello to the client:

Example 15–1: The Hello World servlet

```
import java.servlet.*;
import java.io.*;

public class HelloWorldServlet extends GenericServlet {

  static String helloString = "Hello, world\r\n";

  public void service(ServletRequest request, ServletResponse response) {

    response.setContentLength(helloString.length());
    response.setContentType("text/plain");
    try {
```

Example 15–1: The Hello World servlet (continued)

```
        PrintStream rs = new PrintStream(response.getOutputStream());
        rs.print(helloString);
    }
    catch (IOException e) {
    }

    }

}
```

Example 15–1 begins by importing the necessary packages, *java.servlet* and *java.io*. Line 4 declares that the HelloWorldServlet class is public, and extends java.servlet.GenericServlet. Line 6 puts the data to be returned in a static String called helloString; a more complex servlet would calculate this data on the fly. Line 8 begins the service() method. This servlet doesn't care what the request is; it doesn't try to read any information from the request argument. It generates its response using the response object: it calls setContentLength() to provide a value (the length of helloString) for the response's Content-length header; likewise, it calls setContentType() to set the response's Content-type header to text/plain. Then service() retrieves an OutputStream for this response, and chains it to a PrintStream; in turn, the PrintStream is used to send the data to the client.

After writing the servlet, you need to compile it. There are no tricks here. However, you need to make sure that the servlet package is in your CLASSPATH first, probably by adding *<Jeeves-directory>/lib/classes.zip* to the end of your CLASSPATH (where *Jeeves-directory* represents the directory where Jeeves is installed).

After compiling the servlet, you need to make it available to the server. As of JeevesA2, this is unnecessarily complex; the procedure will probably be simplified in the future. First edit the *servlet.properties* file in the *admin* directory to map the servlet name to a class. The *.class* file must be in the server's CLASSPATH—a good place for it would be the *servlets* directory. In this example, to associate the class HelloWorldServlet with the name hello, add this line to *servlet.properties*:

```
    hello.code=HelloWorldServlet
```

Next, edit the *rules.properties* file in the *admin* directory. This file maps URLs on your server to servlet names. Continuing with the example above, to map the URL *http://<host>/hello.txt* to the servlet named hello, add this line to *rules.properties*:

```
    /hello.txt=hello
```

Restart the server to force it to reload its properties files. Then the servlet should also be available at the following two URLs: *http://<host:port>/hello.txt* and *http://<host:port>/servlet/hello*.

Using Servlets with Server-Side Includes

Servlets can also be embedded in an HTML page using the server-side include mechanism; in this case, the servlet only produces a part of the HTML that is sent to the client. For example, a servlet could return live data, like the current time, the number of hits to a page, or the stock price of the company serving the page at a given moment. The rest of the page could display logos, headers, footers, setup backgrounds, and provide other information that doesn't change. To embed a servlet in an HTML file as a server-side include, use the <servlet> tag:

```
<servlet name="MyServlet" code="MyServlet" NAME_1="VALUE_1" ... NAME_N="VALUE_N">
<PARAM NAME="param_1" value="value_1">
...
<PARAM NAME="param_n" value="value_n">
</servlet>
```

The server attempts to invoke a servlet with the name given by the NAME attribute of the servlet tag. If a servlet with this name can't be found, or if there isn't a NAME attribute, then the server tries to load the servlet with the byte code file given by the CODE attribute. If the server successfully loads the servlet from the CODE attribute, and there was also a valid NAME attribute, the server keeps the servlet loaded and bound to that name; the next time this servlet is requested, it will not need to be reloaded. If there is no NAME attribute, the server reloads the servlet each time it is requested. This can be useful when you're first writing a servlet, and need to keep loading changed versions. However, production servlets should always have names. Omitting the NAME attribute can be useful when you're developing a servlet, and frequently want the server to load an updated version. However, for the sake of efficiency, production servlets should always have names.

The <SERVLET> tag may contain any number of name-value pairs.[*] These pairs are passed to the servlet as *init parameters* to the servlet. They can be retrieved using two methods of the GenericServlet class: getInitParameter(String name) and getInitParameters(). getInitParameter() takes the name of the init parameter with the value you want as an argument, and returns that value as a String. getInitParameters() returns all the init parameters given in the <SERVLET> tag in a Hashtable. The names of the attributes in the <SERVLET> tag are the keys of the Hashtable, and the values of the attributes in the <SERVLET> tag are the values in the Hashtable.

There may also be any number of <PARAM> tags between the <SERVLET> and </SERVLET> tags. The name-value pairs in these tags are passed to the servlet as

---

[*] As it now stands, the <SERVLET> tag does not conform to the HTML standard in the same way as the <APP> tag used in the alpha release of Java: there is no limit to the number of parameters that the <SERVLET> tag can contain. This may not be an issue, since the <SERVLET> tag is always replaced before it is seen by the client.

parameters. They are accessible through the getParameter() and getParameters() methods of the ServletRequest interface. getParameter() requests the value of a <PARAM> tag by name, and returns the value of that <PARAM> as a String. getParameters() returns all the parameters given in <PARAM> tags in a Hashtable. The NAME attributes of the <PARAM> tags are the keys of the Hashtable, and the VALUE attributes of the <PARAM> tags are the values in the Hashtable.

NOTE   It is important to remember that *init parameters* and *parameters* are two different things. Init parameters are attributes of the <SERVLET> tag, while parameters are attributes of the <PARAM> tags. Init parameters are available to the servlet as soon as it is loaded, and from any of its methods, whereas parameters passed in <PARAM> tags are only available when you have a ServletRequest object, generally in the service() method.

This is an unnecessary and potentially confusing dichotomy. Although this is the way parameters work in Jeeves A2, I would not be surprised if initialization parameters were removed completely in a future release.

You use the response argument's OutputStream to return HTML that will be embedded in the web page before it is returned to the client.

Example 15–2 is a simple counter servlet that tells the reader how many times a page has been accessed since the servlet started running. This servlet does not need to process an InputStream or read any parameters; it just increments and returns an int that tells the reader how many times the page has been accessed since the servlet was first invoked. The servlet can be used either as an independent servlet, or as a server-side include; when used as a server-side include, its output (the counter) is inserted into the HTML file sent to the client.

Example 15–2: The Counter servlet

```
import java.servlet.*;
import java.io.*;
import java.util.Hashtable;
import java.util.Date;

/**
 * Counter Servlet
 *
 * This simple servlet uses server-side includes
 * to embed a hit counter in a page.
 * @author Elliotte Rusty Harold
 * @version 1.2, 3/22/97
 */
public class CounterServlet extends GenericServlet {
```

Example 15–2: The Counter servlet (continued)

```
static int count = 0;
static Date start = new Date();

public void service(ServletRequest request, ServletResponse response)
  throws ServletException, IOException {

  int temp;

  response.setContentType("text/plain");
  PrintStream ps = new PrintStream(response.getOutputStream());
  synchronized (this) {
    temp = count++;
  }
  ps.println("This servlet has been accessed " + temp + " times since "
    + start );

  }

}
```

To include this access counter on a web page, just add the tag `<servlet name="CounterServlet">` to the page in the appropriate place:

```
<html>
<head>
<title>Server Side Include Example</title>
</head>

<body>
<H1>Server Side Include Example</H1>

This page has been accessed <servlet name="CounterServlet" code="CounterServlet">
</servlet>.

</body>
</html>
```

Now let's look at the code. There are two static fields: count, an int, and start, a Date. count holds the number of times this servlet has been invoked; start holds the time when the servlet was first constructed.

Incrementing a value isn't a big deal, but there is one trick in this servlet that's worth noting. By their nature, web servers are heavily multithreaded. It is likely that multiple copies of this servlet will execute in different threads simultaneously. The busier a server is, the larger a problem this becomes. It is therefore extremely important for servlets to pay attention to synchronization issues. If you only use local variables, synchronization won't be a problem. In this servlet, you must synchronize access to the counter field. The Date variable, start, is read-only after the servlet is first constructed, so access to it does not need to be synchronized.

The java.servlet Package

The java.servlet package contains three classes (GenericServlet, Servlet-InputStream, and ServletOutputStream), five interfaces (Servlet, ServletResponse, ServletRequest, ServletContext, and ServletStub), and one exception (ServletException). The ServletInputStream and ServletOutputStream classes, although public, are primarily for the use of the other servlet classes, so we won't discuss them here. You can do all the input and output you need with the familiar DataInputStream, DataOutputStream, and PrintStream classes.

The Servlet interface has three public methods: init(), service(), and destroy(). Each user-defined servlet implements java.servlet.Servlet, possibly extends java.servlet.GenericServlet, and overrides at least the service() method. The first time a servlet is loaded, the server reads the byte codes from disk or the network, converts them into a class using a ClassLoader, instantiates the servlet, and calls the servlet's init() method.

To request action from a servlet, the server calls the servlet's service() method. Two arguments are passed into the service() method. The first is a ServletRequest object, which implements the ServletRequest interface. The second is a ServletResponse object, which implements the ServletResponse interface. The client's request is passed into the servlet through the ServletRequest object, and the response to the client is built in the ServletResponse object. Once the server has handed the client request to the servlet, the server does not further concern itself with that client. Communicating with the client is entirely the servlet's responsibility.

Servlets may find themselves running on many different servers. The ServletContext interface lets a servlet query its environment to find out what capabilities are available to it. Finally, the ServletStub interface is used to create a servlet loader. You don't use it if you're just writing servlets; it is only important if you're writing a server that supports servlets.

ServletRequest

The ServletRequest interface is an abstract representation of the request a client makes to a server; it contains methods to request the values of different environment variables. If you're writing a server, then you will need to add methods to your class to set these values so that servlets can read them. Servlets never need to set values in a ServletRequest object; they only need to read them.

public abstract String getProtocol()

This method returns the protocol and protocol version used to submit the request: "HTTP/1.0" or "HTTP/1.1" for the two current versions of HTTP, and the empty String ("") for HTTP versions prior to 1.0. For example:

```
String version = request.getProtocol();
if (version == null) version = "HTTP/0.9";
```

public abstract int getContentLength()

Some requests, notably forms that are POSTed, have some content beyond the simple request. If so, the client is also supposed to send along a Content-length header. Assuming it does, this method returns that length. If there is no Content-length header (as would be the case for a GET request), or if the value of that header cannot be parsed, getContentLength() returns –1. For example:

```
int cl = request.getContentLength();
```

public abstract String getContentType()

If the request includes data, the client is supposed to send a MIME Content-type header; for example:

```
Content-type: text/plain
```

or

```
Content-type: text/html
```

Assuming it does, this method returns that content type as a string. If there is no Content-type header (as would be the case for a GET request), getContentType() returns null. For example:

```
String ct = request.getContentType();
```

public abstract String getServerName()

getServerName() returns the host name of the server as it appears in the host part of the requested URL. This method lets you distinguish the name used to access a server with many names (for instance, a large web server farm). For example:

```
String here = request.getServerName();
```

public abstract int getServerPort()

This method returns the port on which the request was received. For example:

```
int port = request.getServerPort();
```

public abstract String getRemoteAddr()

This method returns a `String` containing the numeric IP address of the client that sent the request. For example:

```
InetAddress ia = InetAddress.getByName(request.getRemoteAddr());
```

public abstract String getRemoteHost()

This method returns a `String` containing the hostname of the client that sent the request. For example:

```
InetAddress ia = InetAddress.getByName(request.getRemoteHost());
```

public abstract InputStream getInputStream()

This method returns an `InputStream` that can be used to read data sent along with a POST or PUT request after the MIME header is complete. For example:

```
DataInputStream dis = new DataInputStream(request.getInputStream());
String theData = "";
while ((String s = dis.readLine()) != null) {
  theData += s;
}
```

public abstract String getParameter(String name)

This method returns the `String` value of the `<PARAM>` tag whose `NAME` attribute is name. This method behaves almost exactly like the `getParameter()` method of applets. For example, suppose you have this `<SERVLET>` tag:

```
<SERVLET NAME="MyServlet" CODE="MyServlet">
<PARAM NAME="time" VALUE="300">
<PARAM NAME="weight" VALUE="600">
</SERVLET>
```

Then you might get the value of the second `<PARAM>` tag like this:

```
String weightString = request.getParameter("weight");
int weight = Integer.parseInt(weightString);
```

public abstract Hashtable getParameters()

This method returns a `Hashtable` containing all the parameters passed to this request in <PARAM> tags. The values of the `NAME` attributes of the <PARAM> tags form the keys of the `Hashtable`. The values of the `VALUE` attributes of the <PARAM> tags are the values in the `Hashtable`. Using this method and the `keys()` method of the `Hashtable` class, you can read all the parameters passed to the servlet, even if you don't know their names at compile-time. For example:

```
Hashtable params = request.getParameters();
Enumeration e = params.keys();
for (Enumeration e = params.keys(); e.hasMoreElements();) {
  String s = (String) e.NextElement();
  // process each parameter
}
```

ServletResponse

The second argument to the `service()` method of a servlet is an object, typically named `response`, that implements the `ServletResponse` interface. You use the `ServletResponse` interface to build a response to a client request. Usually, you give a MIME type, specify the content length, and follow that with the actual data, which is written on an output stream you get from the `response` object. The `ServletResponse` interface includes methods to do all these things.

public abstract void setContentLength(int length)

The `setContentLength()` method places a Content-length MIME header in the response. The `length` argument is the length of the document body, not including the length of the MIME header. In most cases, you will calculate this dynamically. For example:

```
String html = "<html><body><h1>Thanks!</h1></body></html>";
response.setContentLength(html.length());
```

public abstract void setContentType(String MIMEtype)

The `setContentType()` method places a Content-type MIME header in the response. The `MIMEtype` argument is a `String` that contains a MIME type, like text/html or image/gif. For example:

```
response.setContentType("text/html");
```

public abstract OutputStream getOutputStream()

Once you've written the headers to the client, you're ready to write the actual data. The `getOutputStream()` method returns an `OutputStream` that you can use to write data into the response. For example:

```
String html = "<html><body><h1>Thanks!</h1></body></html>";
OutputStream os = response.getOutputStream();
PrintStream ps = new PrintStream(os);
ps.println(html);
os.close();
```

Writing on the output stream automatically sends any headers you have built to the client. (If you have been watching the development of the Server API, you may remember a writeHeaders() method from earlier versions; this no longer exists.)

GenericServlet

java.servlet.GenericServlet is a convenient superclass for implementations of the java.servlet.Servlet interface. It contains default methods for init() and destroy(). If you use this class as a basis for your servlets, you only need to override service() and getServletInfo().

public GenericServlet()

The GenericServlet class has a single constructor that takes no arguments and throws no exceptions. Should you need to use this constructor, you call it just like any other:

```
GenericServlet s = new GenericServlet();
```

However, this constructor is rarely used. In most cases, only subclasses of Generic-Servlet are instantiated, not the GenericServlet class itself; those are instantiated by the server, not by your own code.

public String getInitParameter(String name)

This method requests a specific initialization parameter of a servlet by name. If the parameter cannot be found, the method returns null. This method returns the String value of the attribute of the <SERVLET> tag with the given name. For example, suppose you have this <SERVLET> tag:

```
<SERVLET NAME="MyServlet" CODE="MyServlet" time="300" weight="600">
</SERVLET>
```

Then you might get the value of the second init parameter like this:

```
String weightString = getInitParameter("weight");
int weight = Integer.parseInt(weightString);
```

public Hashtable getInitParameters()

This method returns a Hashtable containing all the init parameters within the <SERVLET> tag. The names of the attributes are the keys of the Hashtable; the values of the attributes are the values in the Hashtable. Using this method and the

keys () method of the Hashtable class, you can read all the init parameters passed
to the servlet, even if you don't know their names at compile-time. For example:

```
Hashtable params = getInitParameters();
Enumeration e = params.keys();
for (Enumeration e = params.keys(); e.hasMoreElements();) {
  String s = (String) e.NextElement();
  // process each parameter
}
```

public void log(String msg)

The log() method writes the specified message string in the server's event log file.
In Jeeves, the log file is shared by all servlets; it is called *JeevesA1/logs/event-log*,
where *JeevesA1* is the directory in which Jeeves is installed.

public String getServletInfo()

Your servlet subclass should override this method with a method that returns a
String containing your name, the version of the servlet, and copyright information. For example:

```
public String getServletInfo() {
  return "Super Servlet (c) 1996 Elliotte Rusty Harold (elharo@sunsite.unc.edu)";
}
```

public void init()

The ServletContext calls init() when it first loads the servlet. Use it as you use
the init() method of an applet: to set up variables, and perform any initialization
tasks that apply to all requests. Servlets do not have the equivalent of an applet's
start() method.

public void service(ServletRequest request, ServletResponse response) throws Exception

The service() method is where a servlet does most of its work. Given a request
(that is, an object that implements the ServletRequest interface and looks a lot
like an HTTP request to a web server), this method evaluates the request and produces a response. The various methods of the ServletRequest and ServletResponse interface are used to parse the request and format the response.

Since one instance of a servlet may be called upon to process many different
requests, you should make the service() method as fast and compact as possible
so it does not become a bottleneck. If processing a request will take a significant
amount of time, you should consider starting a separate thread to handle each
request.

public void destroy()

This method destroys the servlet and frees any resources the servlet has allocated. Override this method in your servlet subclass if you have any specific cleanup functions to perform when the servlet is destroyed. For example, the CounterServlet (above) might write the current value of count into a file. This value could then be read by init() when the servlet was next created, letting the servlet count the total number of hits on the page, rather than the number of hits since the server was initialized. For most servlets, the default destroy() method is just fine.

public final void setStub(ServletStub stub)

The system that loads and runs the servlet calls this method to set the Servlet-Stub. The ServletStub provides the implementation specific methods get-ServletContext() and getInitParameter(). You do not call this method if you're writing servlets, only if you're writing a server.

public ServletContext getServletContext()

This method returns the servlet context, an object that implements the Servlet-Context interface. The servlet context lets a servlet get information about, and control of the environment of the server it is running.

ServletContext

The ServletContext interface allows a servlet to get information about the server on which it is running. This is important since different servers may have different capabilities. It also provides the servlet with a standard interface to common server functions that should be provided by all servers that support the Java Server API. To access its context, a servlet calls its getServletContext() method.

public abstract Servlet getServlet(String name)

The getServlet() method requests a servlet by name. It is the responsibility of the ServletContext (generally some part of the server) to find and load the requested servlet. It is unclear at this time how the name will map to *.class* files on a disk or on the network. This method is also similar to the getApplet() method of java.applet.AppletContext. getServlet() returns null if the servlet cannot be found.

public abstract Enumeration getServlets()

This method returns an Enumeration of the servlets to which this ServletContext currently has access. For example, to list all the servlets, you might write:

```
ServletContext sc =  getServletContext();
for (Enumeration e = sc.getServlets(); e.hasMoreElements;) {
  System.out.println((Servlet) e.nextElement());
}
```

This is similar to the getApplets() method of java.applet.AppletContext.

public abstract void log(Servlet s, String message)

This method writes an arbitrary string message to the log of the servlet s. For example:

```
ServletContext sc =  getServletContext();
Servlet s = new Servlet();
sc.log(s, "Kilroy was here");
```

Each message is prefixed with the servlet's class name and a colon. Otherwise, the logfile has no particular format. In Jeeves, the log file is shared between different servlets and the ServletContext; it is named *<Jeeves-dir>/logs/event-log*, where *<Jeeves-dir>*is the directory in which Jeeves is installed.

public abstract String getServerInfo()

This method returns a String that includes the name and version of the server. For example:

```
ServletContext sc =  getServletContext();
System.out.println(sc.getServerInfo());
```

public abstract String getRealPath(String path)

This method takes the virtual path that appears in a URL (for example, */˜elharo/books/jdr.html*), and returns an absolute path to the file that can be used on the host system (for example, */home/users/elharo/books/jdr.html*). Not all strings map to file names on the local filesystem. If the translation fails (for example, if you request sc.getRealPath("There's no such file")), getRealPath() returns null.

public abstract String getMimeType(String Filename)

The getMimeType() method returns a String containing the MIME type of the specified file, such as "text/html" or "image/gif". The MIME type returned is based on the filename, not the contents of the file.

ServletStub

The ServletStub interface is used by a servlet loader, which is part of a server. Therefore, you only need to concern yourself with this interface if you're writing a server; it isn't important if you're writing servlets.

public abstract ServletContext getServletContext()

This method returns an object that implements the ServletContext interface. If you are writing a server, you will define an object that implements ServletContext, and implement this method to return that object. You do not call this method directly; instead, you call the getServletContext() method of the servlet class, which calls this method.

public abstract String getInitParameter(String name)

This method requests one of the servlet's initialization parameters by name. If the parameter cannot be found, getInitParameter() returns null. You do not call this method directly. Instead, you call the getInitParameter() method of the Servlet class, which calls this method.

public abstract Hashtable getInitParameters()

This method returns a Hashtable containing all the servlet's initialization parameters. This allows you to retrieve and respond to initialization parameters you don't necessarily know about when the servlet is written. You do not call getInitParameters() directly. Instead, you call the getInitParameters() method of the Servlet class, which calls this method.

The java.servlet.http Package

The java.servlet.http package contains classes and interfaces to write servlets that run only on HTTP servers. HTTP clients (web browsers) provide much more information in each request than clients speaking other protocols (for example, the MIME types that the browser can accept). If your servlet will only run on a web server, you might as well take advantage of this added information.

The java.servlet.http package has two interfaces and three classes: HttpServletRequest is a sub-interface of java.servlet.ServletRequest that represents a request from a web browser to an HTTP server; HttpServletResponse is a subinterface of java.servlet.ServletResponse that represents a response from a web server to a web browser; HttpServlet is a subclass of GenericServlet for use with HTTP requests and responses; FormServlet is a subclass of HttpServlet especially for processing form input; finally, the HttpUtils class provides some utility methods for servlets that work with HTTP.

HttpServletRequest

The HttpServletRequest interface provides an abstract representation of the request a web client makes to a web server. This request has three parts. There's the request itself, a single line that looks like:

```
GET /index.html HTTP/1.0
```

The request is followed by a MIME header that looks like this:

```
Accept: text/html
Accept: text/plain
User-Agent: Lynx/2.4 libwww/2.1.4
```

Finally, there's a series of environment variables including the port, the server name, the remote host, and the authentication type. The HttpServletRequest interface contains methods to request arbitrary MIME headers, to get the values of different environment variables, and to get the parts of the request URI. There are no methods to create a new header; that is relegated to the HttpServletResponse interface you'll see in the next section. If you're writing a server, you will need to add additional methods to your class to set these values in the first place. Adding methods to set variables in an HttpServletRequest isn't necessary (or appropriate) if you are writing servlets.

Don't forget that an HttpServletRequest object has access to the methods of the ServletRequest interface, in addition to the methods described here. This includes crucial methods like getProtocol() and getInputStream(), which we won't repeat.

public abstract String getMethod()

This method returns the HTTP method by which the request was made (not a Java object method). The result can be "GET", "HEAD", "POST", "PUT", or a custom method. For example:

```
String method = request.getMethod();
```

public abstract String getRequestURI()

In theory, the getRequestURI() method returns the full Universal Resource Identifier (URI) of the requested resource. In practice, URIs aren't well-defined at the current time, so getRequestURI() returns the relative URL of the requested resource instead. For example:

```
String uri = request.getRequestURI();
```

public abstract String getServletPath()

This method returns the path portion of the requested URI. For example, if the URI is *http://sunsite.unc.edu/javafaq/servlets/myServlet.class*, then getServletPath() returns the string "/servlets/myServlet.class". Any query string or extra path information is omitted.

public abstract String getPathInfo()

This method returns the extra path information. This has the same semantics as the CGI/1.1 PATH_INFO environment variable. For example, if the URI for the servlet is *http://sunsite.unc.edu/javafaq/servlets/myServlet.class* but the URI requested *http://sunsite.unc.edu/javafaq/servlets/myServlet.class/username/elharo/password/secret*, the extra path information is "username/elharo/password/secret". If no extra path information is present, getPathInfo() returns null.

public abstract String getPathTranslated()

This method returns the extra path information, translated to a real path on the server's file system relative to the server's document root. This has the same semantics as the CGI/1.1 PATH_TRANSLATED environment variable. For example, if the URI for the servlet is *http://sunsite.unc.edu/javafaq/servlets/myServlet.class*, the document root for the web server is */var/docroot*, and the URI requested is *http://sunsite.unc.edu/javafaq/servlets/myServlet.class/users/elharo/*, the translated path information is "/var/docroot/users/elharo". If no extra path information is present, then getPathTranslated() returns null.

public abstract String getQueryString()

This method returns the query string part of the URL, if there is one. The query string consists of anything in the URL that falls after a question mark (?). Query strings are used to pass arguments to CGI programs and servlets. If the URL is *http://sunsite.unc.edu/javafaq/servlets/myServlet.class?username=elharo:password=secret*, for example, getQueryString() returns "username=elharo:password=secret". If no query string is present, getQueryString() returns null.

public abstract String getQueryParameter(String name)

This method allows you to request a specific parameter from the query string by name. The result returned is a String. If the value of the parameter is numeric, you need to convert it to a numeric datatype yourself. For example, if the URL is *http://sunsite.unc.edu/javafaq/servlets/myServlet.class?username=elharo:password=secret*, getQueryParameter("username") returns "elharo". If the parameter is not found in the query string, getQueryParameter() returns null.

Example 15–3 is a servlet that says "hello" to the client by name. The name is passed to the servlet in the URI's query string. A link to a servlet might look like:

```
<a href="/servlet/myServlet?firstname=David">Say Hello</a>
```

The query string is everything after the question mark: i.e., "firstname=David". Instead of being hard-coded, the first name could be read from a form that uses the GET method. For example:

```
<FORM METHOD=GET ACTION="/servlet/myServlet">
Please enter your name: <Input NAME="firstname" size=40>
<Input TYPE="submit" VALUE="Say Hello">
</FORM>
```

The HttpServletRequest method getQueryParameter() retrieves the value of a named item in the query string. Here we retrieve the value of the firstname field.

Example 15–3: The Hello Name servlet

```
import java.servlet.*;
import java.servlet.http.*;
import java.io.*;

public class HelloNameServlet extends HttpServlet {

public void service(ServletRequest request, ServletResponse response) {

  service((HttpServletRequest) request, (HttpServletResponse) response);

}

public void service(HttpServletRequest request, HttpServletResponse response) {

    String msg = "<HTML><BODY>";
    String name = request.getParameter("firstname");
    if (name != null) {
      msg += "Hello " + name;
    }
    else {
      msg += "Hello whoever you are.";
    }
    msg += "</BODY></HTML>";

    response.setContentLength(msg.length());
    response.setContentType("text/html");
    try {
      PrintStream rs = new PrintStream(response.getOutputStream());
      rs.print(msg);
    }
    catch (IOException e); {
    }
  }
}
```

public abstract Hashtable getQueryParameters()

This method returns the query string part of the URL as a Hashtable. Each key in the Hashtable is the name of a field in the query string; the values in the Hashtable are the values from the query string. For example, to print out all the query parameters, you would write:

```
if (request.getMethod().equals("GET")) {
  Hashtable qs = request.getQueryParameters();
  Enumeration names = qs.keys();
  while (names.hasMoreElements()) {
    Object key = names.nextElement();
    System.out.println(key + ": " + qs.get(key));
  }
}
```

public abstract String getHeader(String name)

The getHeader() method returns the value of an arbitrary named header field. If the named header can't be found, the method returns null. If there is more than one header with the given name in the request, you can't predict the one that will be returned. For example, the code below retrieves the name of the user agent (browser) used to make the request:

```
String agent = request.getHeader("User-Agent");
```

Note that the colon (:) from the MIME header should not be included.

public abstract int getIntHeader(String name, int default)

The getIntHeader() method reads headers with integer values, like "Content-length." The value returned is the value of the requested header. If the header can't be found or parsed, the method returns the value you passed in as the default argument. For example, the line below returns the content length; if the header is missing or garbled, it returns –1.

```
int cl = request.getIntHeader("Content-length", -1);
```

public abstract long getDateHeader(String name, long default)

The getDate() method reads headers with date values like "Last-Modified" or "Expiration." The value it returns should be interpreted as the number of seconds since midnight, GMT, January 1, 1970; you can convert it to a Date using java.util.Date. The second argument is a default value that the method returns if the date can't be found. For example, the code below reads the value of the If-modified-since header, and converts it to a Date object:

```
long ims = request.getDateHeader("If-modified-since");
Date d = new Date(ims * 1000);
```

public abstract String getHeaderName(int n)

The getHeaderName() method returns the name of the nth MIME header. It can be used in conjunction with the getHeader() method to iterate through all the headers in the request, even if you don't know what headers are present in advance. If there are fewer than n fields, null is returned. The first header is number 0.

public abstract String getHeader(int n)

The getHeader() method returns the String value of the nth MIME header. It can be used in conjunction with the getHeaderName() method to iterate through all the headers in the request, even if you don't know what headers are present in advance. If there are fewer than n fields, null is returned. The first header is number 0. For example:

```
int counter = 0;
String name;
while ((name = request.getHeaderName(counter)) != null) {
    System.out.println(name + ": " + request.getHeader(counter));
    counter++;
}
```

public abstract String getRemoteUser()

On rare occasions, a web browser sends a username in the MIME header. If it does, this method returns the username. getRemoteUser() returns null if the username is not sent (which is almost always the case). For example:

```
String username = request.getRemoteUser();
```

public abstract String getAuthType()

If the request used authentication, getAuthType() returns the authentication scheme of the request. If no authentication scheme was used, the method returns null. For example:

```
if (request.getAuthtype() == null) {
    System.err.println("Insecure Link");
}
```

HttpServletResponse

The second argument to the service() method of an HttpServlet is an object, typically named response, that implements the HttpServletResponse interface. You use the HttpServletResponse interface to build a response to a client request. To build a response, you must create a MIME header, include an HTTP status code, and follow that with the actual data.

HttpServletResponse extends java.servlet.ServletResponse. Therefore, you can use the methods of the ServletResponse interface, such as the getOutput-Stream() method.

HTTP response codes

The HttpServletResponse interface defines a number of mnemonic constants (public final static int fields) for the common HTTP response codes. They are listed in Table 15–1, along with their common meanings. You include one of these in the header of your response by passing it to response.setStatus().

Table 15–1: Server Response Codes

Mnemonic Constant	Code	Default Message	Meaning
SC_OK	200	OK	The most common response code. If the request used GET or POST, the requested data is contained in the response along with the usual headers. If the request used HEAD, only the header information is included.
SC_CREATED	201	Created	The server has created a data file at the URL specified in the body of the response. The web browser should now attempt to load that URL. This code is sent only in response to POST requests.

Table 15–1: Server Response Codes (continued)

Mnemonic Constant	Code	Default Message	Meaning
SC_ACCEPTED	202	Accepted	This rather uncommon response indicates that a request (generally from POST) is being processed, but the processing is not yet complete, and no response can be returned. However, the server should return an HTML page that explains the situation to the user, provides an estimate of when the request is likely to be completed, and, ideally, has a link to a status monitor of some kind.
SC_NO_CONTENT	204	No Content	The server has successfully processed the request but has no information to send back to the client. This is normally the result of a poorly written form-processing CGI that accepts data, but does not return a response to the user.
SC_MOVED_PERMANENTLY	301	Moved Permanently	The page has moved to a new URL. The web browser should automatically load the page at this URL, and update any bookmarks that point to the old URL.
SC_MOVED_TEMPORARILY	302	Moved Temporarily	This unusual response code indicates that a page is at a new URL temporarily, but its location will change again in the foreseeable future, and therefore bookmarks should not be updated.

Table 15–1: Server Response Codes (continued)

Mnemonic Constant	Code	Default Message	Meaning
SC_NOT_MODIFIED	304	Not Modified	The client has performed a GET request but used the If-modified-since header to indicate that it only wants the document if it has been recently updated. This status code is returned if the document has not been updated. In this case the web browser should load the document from its cache.
SC_BAD_REQUEST	400	Bad Request	The client request to the server used improper syntax. This is rather unusual, but may become more common as more people start writing custom clients and servers.
SC_UNAUTHORIZED	401	Unauthorized	Authorization, generally username and password controlled, is required to access this page. Either a username and password have not yet been presented or the username and password are invalid.
SC_FORBIDDEN	403	Forbidden	The server understood the request, but is deliberately refusing to process it. Authorization will not help. This might be used when access to a certain page is denied to a certain range of IP addresses.
SC_NOT_FOUND	404	Not Found	This most common error response indicates that the server cannot find the requested page. It may indicate a bad link, a page that has moved with no forwarding address, a mistyped URL, or something similar.

Table 15–1: Server Response Codes (continued)

Mnemonic Constant	Code	Default Message	Meaning
SC_INTERNAL_SERVER_ ERROR	500	Internal Server Error	An unexpected condition occurred that the server does not know how to handle.
SC_NOT_IMPLEMENTED	501	Not Implemented	The server does not have a feature that is needed to fulfill this request. A server that cannot handle POST requests might send this response to a client that tried to POST form data to it.
SC_BAD_GATEWAY	502	Bad Gateway	This code is only applicable to servers that act as proxies or gateways. It indicates that the proxy received an invalid response from a server it was connecting to in an effort to fulfill the request.
SC_SERVICE_UNAVAILABLE	503	Service Unavailable	The server is temporarily unable to handle the request, perhaps due to overloading or maintenance.

public abstract void setStatus(int code)

This version of the setStatus() method sets the status code for an HTTP response. Along with the numeric code, it includes the default message corresponding to that code. The code passed into the method should be one of the mnemonic constants from Table 15–1. For example:

```
response.setStatus(ServletResponse.SC_OK);
```

public abstract void setStatus(int code, String msg)

This version of the setStatus() method sets the status code for an HTTP response. Along with the numeric code, it includes a message supplied by the programmer. The code argument passed into the method should be one of the mnemonic constants from Table 15–1. For example:

```
response.setStatus(ServletResponse.SC_OK, "Here you go.");
```

public abstract void setContentLength(int length)

The setContentLength() method places a Content-length MIME header in the response. The length argument is the length of the document body, not including the length of the MIME header. In most situations, you calculate the content length dynamically. For example:

```
String html = "<html><body><h1>Thanks!</h1></body></html>";
response.setContentLength(html.length());
```

public abstract void setContentType(String MIMEtype)

The setContentType() method places a Content-type MIME header in the response. The MIMEtype argument is a String that contains a MIME type such as "text/html" or "image/gif". For example:

```
response.setContentType("text/html");
```

public abstract void setHeader(String name, String value)

This method sets an arbitrary header field. The name of the header field is passed in through the name argument, and the value of that field is passed in the value argument. For example, the code below creates a Set-Cookie header with the value "Username=elharo":

```
response.setHeader("Set-Cookie", "Username=elharo");
```

For more cookie specification details, see the document located at *http://www.netscape.com/news-ref/std/cookie_spec.html.*

public abstract void setIntHeader(String name, int value)

setIntHeader() sets an arbitrary header field with an integer value. The name of the header field is passed in through the name argument, and the value of that field is passed in the value argument. The method handles the conversion of the int to a String. For example:

```
String html = "<html><body><h1>Thanks!</h1></body></html>";
response.setIntHeader("Content-length", html.length());
```

public abstract void setDateHeader(String name, long date)

setDateHeader() sets an arbitrary header field with a date value. The name of the header field is passed in through the name argument, and the value of that field is passed in the date argument. The method handles the conversion of the long to a String. It is assumed that date represents the time in seconds since midnight,

January 1, 1970, GMT. For example, to prevent a document from being cached by setting the expiration date to the current time (not a bad idea for servlets that generate responses dynamically), try:

```
Date now = new Date();
response.setDateHeader("Expiration", now.getTime() * 1000);
```

public abstract void sendError(int code) throws IOException

The `writeErrorResponse()` method sets the status code for an HTTP response, then sends the response to the client. This variant includes the default message for that code. The code passed into the method should be one of the mnemonic constants from Table 15–1 with a value of 400 or higher. For example:

```
try {
  response.sendError(ServletResponse.SC_FORBIDDEN);
}
catch (IOException e) {
}
```

An `IOException` is thrown if an I/O error occurs.

public abstract void sendError(int code, String message) throws IOException

The `writeErrorResponse()` method sets the status code for an HTTP response, then sends the response to the client. This variant includes a message supplied by the programmer with the code. The code passed into the method should be a mnemonic constant from Table 15–1 with a value of 400 or higher. An `IOException` is thrown if an I/O error occurs. For example:

```
try {
  response.sendError(ServletResponse.SC_FORBIDDEN,
                     "You're not getting that, no way, no how");
}
catch (IOException e) {
}
```

public abstract void sendRedirect(String url) throws IOException

This method sends a response to the client that redirects it to the specified URL. Most modern browsers will seamlessly load the specified URL, though a few older ones may require the user to click on a link manually. An `IOException` is thrown if an I/O error occurs. For example:

```
try {
  response.sendRedirect("http://www.ora.com/");
}
catch (IOException e) {
}
```

HttpUtils

As of late 1996, the `HttpUtils` class contains a single useful method, `parse-Query()`. More are likely to be added in the future.

The `parseQuery()` method has this signature:

```
public static Hashtable parseQueryString(String q)
```

The string passed to this method should be a typical CGI query string, like "username=elharo:password=secret". This string will be parsed into a `Hashtable` of name-value pairs: the names are used as keys in the `Hashtable`.

If the string `q` is not a properly formatted query string, `parseQueryString()` throws an `IllegalArgumentException`.

A Form Echoing Servlet

You can handle quite complex data in a servlet. Example 15–4 is a servlet that parses an arbitrary form request that used either GET or POST. It echoes the data back in an HTML page. Of course, a real form servlet would do something useful with this data; but even as-is, this servlet is useful for testing forms.

Example 15–4: A form servlet

```
import java.servlet.*;
import java.servlet.http.*;
import java.io.*;
import java.util.*;

public class EchoFormServlet extends HttpServlet {

  public void service(HttpServletRequest request, HttpServletResponse response) {

    String msg = "<HTML><HEAD><TITLE>\r\n";

    msg += "Form Response</TITLE></HEAD><BODY><H1>Form Response</H1>\r\n";

    // get the request
    msg += "Method: " + request.getMethod() + "<br>\r\n";
    msg += "URI: " + request.getRequestURI() + "<br>\r\n";
    msg += "Protocol: " + request.getProtocol() + "<br>\r\n";
    msg += "Path Info: " + request.getPathInfo() + "<br>\r\n";

    // get MIME header name-value pairs
    Enumeration e = request.getHeaderNames();
    while (e.hasMoreElements()) {
      String header = (String) e.nextElement();
      msg += header + ": " + request.getHeader(header) + "<br>\r\n";
    }
    msg += "<P>";
```

Example 15–4: A form servlet (continued)

```
// read the form data
String qs = "";
if (request.getMethod().equals("GET")) {
  qs = request.getQueryString();
}
else if (request.getMethod().equals("POST")) {
  try {
    DataInputStream dis = new DataInputStream(request.getInputStream());
    String s;
    while ((s = dis.readLine()) != null) {
      qs += s + "\r\n";
    }
  }
  catch (IOException ie) {
  }
}
else {
  msg += "I can't handle the " + request.getMethod() + " method.<br>";
}

// split the form data into pieces
// For the moment no URL decoding is done
if (qs != null) {
  StringTokenizer st = new StringTokenizer(qs, "&");
  while (st.hasMoreTokens()) {
    String temp = st.nextToken();
    String name = temp.substring(0, temp.indexOf('='));
    String value = temp.substring(temp.indexOf('=') + 1, temp.length());
    msg += name + ": " + value + "<br>\r\n";
  }
}

// Finish the HTML
msg += "</BODY></HTML>\r\n";

// send the output to the client
response.setContentLength(msg.length());
response.setContentType("text/html");
try {
  DataOutputStream rs = new DataOutputStream(response.getOutputStream());
  rs.writeBytes("\r\n" + msg);
}
catch (IOException ie) {
}

}

}
```

This servlet uses several `ServletRequest` methods to get information about the request the client made. `getMethod()` returns the method used to submit the request (POST or GET). `getRequestURI()` returns the URI which was requested, that is, the file part of the URI, generally something like */servlets/myServlet.class*. `getProtocol()` returns the protocol part of the URI, normally HTTP. `getPathInfo()` returns any extra path info. The `getHeaderName(int n)` method returns the name of the nth header. By passing this name to the `getHeader(String header_name)` method, you can retrieve the value of the nth header. With these two methods, you loop through all the headers in the request. Each name-value pair in the header is appended to the string variable, `msg`, for eventual display to the client.

NOTE　　JeevesA1 has trouble handling POST requests. Therefore, this servlet has only been successfully tested with GET. Future versions of Jeeves should be able to handle POST and even PUT.

Finally, we read the input from the form. If the request method is GET, this data is stored in the query string retrieved by `request.getQueryString()`. Most GET requests do not have query strings, so you have to be careful in case `getQueryString()` returns `null`. If the request method is POST, the data is presented as an `InputStream` by `request.getInputStream()`. A `StringTokenizer` splits the request into name-value pairs. The next five statements read tokens and add them to `msg`, completing the HTML response. Once the entire page has been built, we call `response.setContentLength(msg.length())` to get the length of the page,and `response.setContentType("text/html")` to put a Content-type header in the response's MIME header. To send the headers and the actual HTML file, we get an output stream from the `ServletResponse`, chain that to a `DataOutputStream`, and write the stream `msg` on it. The headers are sent automatically as soon as we write on the output stream. Note that we add an extra `\r\n` pair before `msg` to make sure the headers are terminated properly.

Index

Symbols

& (ampersand) in query strings, 97
= (equal sign) in query strings, 97
% (percent sign) in encoded URLs, 94
# in URLs, 35
" (quotation marks) in tags, 37
/ (slash) for document root, 36

Numbers

128-bit addresses, 57

A

ABORT constant (ImageObserver), 121
ABORTED constant (MediaTracker), 130
absolute URLs, 36, 82
   getting from virtual paths, 392
Accept keyword (HTTP), 39
accept( ), 189–191
   SO_TIMEOUT option and, 193
addImage( ), 124
addresses (see IP addresses)
Admin servlet, 378
agents, intelligent, 9–11, 377
ALLBITS constant (ImageObserver), 120–121
allowUserInteraction field, 257
ampersand (&) in query strings, 97
analog-to-digital conversion, 15
anchors, named, 35, 85, 93

animation player (example application), 139
API, Java Server, 375–379
Applet class, downloading data with, 109–117
Applet Host security level, 54
<APPLET> tags (HTML), 51
AppleTalk, 13
AppletContext class, 110–111, 131–133
applets, 51–55, 109, 375
   downloading (example), 274
   URLs for, 110
   (see also servlets)
AppletStub class, 110
application/ content types, 45–48, 264
   application/octet-stream, 52
   application/x-time, 312
   application/x-www-form-urlencoded, 95, 276
application layer, 14, 17
application servers, 25
applications, 51
   client-server model, 25
   consumer, 7, 10
   future, 7–8
   search, 8
   (see also applets)
audio/ content types, 46, 48, 265
   (see also sounds)
AudioClip object, 115–117
authentication, 398

About the Author

Elliotte Rusty Harold is a noted writer and programmer, both on and off the Internet. He started by writing FAQ lists for the Macintosh newsgroups on Usenet, and has since branched out into books, web sites, and newsletters. He's currently fascinated by Java, which is beginning to consume his life. His Cafe Au Lait web site at *http://sunsite.unc.edu/javafaq/* is a frequently visited Java site.

Elliotte resides in New York City with his wife Beth and cat Possum. When not writing about Java, he enjoys genealogy, mathematics, and quantum mechanics, and has been known to try to incorporate these subjects into his computer books (when he can slip them past his editors). So far he hasn't been able to, but he suspects that a short, last-minute biography might not be inspected as closely as the rest of a manuscript. His previous book is *Java Developer's Resource* from Prentice Hall.

Colophon

Our look is the result of reader comments, our own experimentation, and feedback from distribution channels. Distinctive covers complement our distinctive approach to technical topics, breathing personality and life into potentially dry subjects.

The inside layout was designed by Nancy Priest. Text was set in SGML by Ellen Siever and Erik Ray. The heading font is Bodoni BT; the text font is New Baskerville. The illustrations that appear in the book were created in Macromedia Freehand 5.0 by Chris Reilley.

More Titles from O'Reilly

Java

Java in a Nutshell, DELUXE EDITION

By David Flanagan, et al.
1st Edition June 1997
628 pages, includes CD-ROM & book
ISBN 1-56592-304-9

Java in a Nutshell, Deluxe Edition, brings together on CD-ROM five volumes for Java developers and programmers, linking related info across books. Exploring Java, 2nd Edition, covers Java basics. Java Language Reference, 2nd Edition, Java Fundamental Classes Reference, and Java AWT Reference provide a definitive set of documentation on the Java language and the Java 1.1 core API. Java in a Nutshell, 2nd Edition, our bestselling quick reference, is included both on the CD-ROM and in a companion desktop edition. This deluxe library is an indispensable resource for anyone doing serious programming with Java 1.1.

Java Cryptography

By Jonathan B. Knudsen
1st Edition May 1998
362 pages, ISBN 1-56592-402-9

Java Cryptography teaches you how to write secure programs using Java's cryptographic tools. It includes thorough discussions of the java.security package and the Java Cryptography Extensions (JCE), showing you how to use security providers and even implement your own provider. It discusses authentication, key management, public and private key encryption, and includes a secure talk application that encrypts all data sent over the network. If you work with sensitive data, you'll find this book indispensable.

Java in a Nutshell, Second Edition

By David Flanagan
2nd Edition May 1997
628 pages, ISBN 1-56592-262-X

This second edition of the bestselling Java book describes all the classes in the Java 1.1 API, with the exception of the still-evolving Enterprise APIs. And it still has all the great features that have made this the Java book most often recommended on the Internet: practical real-world examples and compact reference information. It's the only quick reference you'll need.

Java Security

By Scott Oaks
1st Edition May 1998
474 pages, ISBN 1-56592-403-7

This essential Java 1.2 book covers Java's security mechanisms and teaches you how to work with them. It discusses class loaders, security managers, access lists, digital signatures, and authentication and shows how to use these to create and enforce your own security policy.

Java Virtual Machine

By Jon Meyer & Troy Downing
1st Edition March 1997
452 pages, includes diskette
ISBN 1-56592-194-1

This book is a comprehensive programming guide for the Java Virtual Machine (JVM). It gives readers a strong overview and reference of the JVM so that they may create their own implementations of the JVM or write their own compilers that create Java object code. A Java assembler is provided with the book, so the examples can all be compiled and executed.

Java Swing

By Robert Eckstein, Marc Loy & Dave Wood
1st Edition September 1998
1252 pages, ISBN 1-56592-455-X

The Swing classes eliminate Java's biggest weakness: its relatively primitive user interface toolkit. Java Swing helps you to take full advantage of the Swing classes, providing detailed descriptions of every class and interface in the key Swing packages. It shows you how to use all of the new components, allowing you to build state-of-the-art user interfaces and giving you the context you need to understand what you're doing. It's more than documentation; Java Swing helps you develop code quickly and effectively.

O'REILLY®

TO ORDER: **800-998-9938** • *order@oreilly.com* • *http://www.oreilly.com/*
OUR PRODUCTS ARE AVAILABLE AT A BOOKSTORE OR SOFTWARE STORE NEAR YOU.
FOR INFORMATION: **800-998-9938** • **707-829-0515** • *info@oreilly.com*

Java

Java Examples in a Nutshell

By David Flanagan
1st Edition September 1997
414 pages, ISBN 1-56592-371-5

From the author of *Java in a Nutshell*, this companion book is chock full of practical real-world programming examples to help novice Java programmers and experts alike explore what's possible with Java 1.1. If you learn best by example, this is the book for you.

Java Threads, Second Edition

By Scott Oaks and Henry Wong
2nd Edition January 1999
336 pages, ISBN 1-56592-418-5

Revised and expanded to cover Java 2, *Java Threads, 2nd Edition*, shows you how to take full advantage of Java's thread facilities: where to use threads to increase efficiency, how to use them effectively, and how to avoid common mistakes. It thoroughly covers the Thread and ThreadGroup classes, the Runnable interface, and the language's synchronized operator. The book pays special attention to threading issues with Swing, as well as problems like deadlock, race condition, and starvation to help you write code without hidden bugs.

Java Language Reference, Second Edition

By Mark Grand
2nd Edition July 1997
492 pages, ISBN 1-56592-326-X

This book helps you understand the subtle nuances of Java—from the definition of data types to the syntax of expressions and control structures—so you can ensure your programs run exactly as expected. The second edition covers the new language features that have been added in Java 1.1, such as inner classes, class literals, and instance initializers.

Java Fundamental Classes Reference

By Mark Grand & Jonathan Knudsen
1st Edition May 1997
1114 pages, ISBN 1-56592-241-7

The *Java Fundamental Classes Reference* provides complete reference documentation on the core Java 1.1 classes that comprise the *java.lang, java.io, java.net, java.util, java.text, java.math, java.lang.reflect,* and *java.util.zip* packages. Part of O'Reilly's Java documentation series, this edition describes Version 1.1 of the Java Development Kit. It includes easy-to-use reference material and provides lots of sample code to help you learn by example.

Java Servlet Programming

By Jason Hunter with William Crawford
1st Edition November 1998
528 pages, ISBN 1-56592-391-X

Java servlets offer a fast, powerful, portable replacement for CGI scripts. *Java Servlet Programming* covers everything you need to know to write effective servlets. Topics include: serving dynamic Web content, maintaining state information, session tracking, database connectivity using JDBC, and applet-servlet communication.

Java Distributed Computing

By Jim Farley
1st Edition January 1998
384 pages, ISBN 1-56592-206-9

Java Distributed Computing offers a general introduction to distributed computing, meaning programs that run on two or more systems. It focuses primarily on how to structure and write distributed applications and, therefore, discusses issues like designing protocols, security, working with databases, and dealing with low bandwidth situations.

O'REILLY®

TO ORDER: **800-998-9938** • **order@oreilly.com** • **http://www.oreilly.com/**
OUR PRODUCTS ARE AVAILABLE AT A BOOKSTORE OR SOFTWARE STORE NEAR YOU.
FOR INFORMATION: **800-998-9938** • **707-829-0515** • **info@oreilly.com**

How to stay in touch with O'Reilly

1. Visit Our Award-Winning Web Site

http://www.oreilly.com/

★ "Top 100 Sites on the Web" —*PC Magazine*
★ "Top 5% Web sites" —*Point Communications*
★ "3-Star site" —*The McKinley Group*

Our web site contains a library of comprehensive product information (including book excerpts and tables of contents), downloadable software, background articles, interviews with technology leaders, links to relevant sites, book cover art, and more. File us in your Bookmarks or Hotlist!

2. Join Our Email Mailing Lists

New Product Releases

To receive automatic email with brief descriptions of all new O'Reilly products as they are released, send email to:
listproc@online.oreilly.com
Put the following information in the first line of your message (*not* in the Subject field):
subscribe oreilly-news

O'Reilly Events

If you'd also like us to send information about trade show events, special promotions, and other O'Reilly events, send email to:
listproc@online.oreilly.com
Put the following information in the first line of your message (*not* in the Subject field):
subscribe oreilly-events

3. Get Examples from Our Books via FTP

There are two ways to access an archive of example files from our books:

Regular FTP

- ftp to:
  ftp.oreilly.com
  (login: anonymous
  password: your email address)
- Point your web browser to:
  ftp://ftp.oreilly.com/

FTPMAIL

- Send an email message to:
  ftpmail@online.oreilly.com
  (Write "help" in the message body)

4. Contact Us via Email

order@oreilly.com
To place a book or software order online. Good for North American and international customers.

subscriptions@oreilly.com
To place an order for any of our newsletters or periodicals.

books@oreilly.com
General questions about any of our books.

software@oreilly.com
For general questions and product information about our software. Check out O'Reilly Software Online at **http://software.oreilly.com/** for software and technical support information. Registered O'Reilly software users send your questions to: **website-support@oreilly.com**

cs@oreilly.com
For answers to problems regarding your order or our products.

booktech@oreilly.com
For book content technical questions or corrections.

proposals@oreilly.com
To submit new book or software proposals to our editors and product managers.

international@oreilly.com
For information about our international distributors or translation queries. For a list of our distributors outside of North America check out:
http://www.oreilly.com/www/order/country.html

O'Reilly & Associates, Inc.
101 Morris Street, Sebastopol, CA 95472 USA
TEL 707-829-0515 or 800-998-9938
(6am to 5pm PST)
FAX 707-829-0104

O'REILLY®

TO ORDER: **800-998-9938** • **order@oreilly.com** • **http://www.oreilly.com/**
OUR PRODUCTS ARE AVAILABLE AT A BOOKSTORE OR SOFTWARE STORE NEAR YOU.
FOR INFORMATION: **800-998-9938** • **707-829-0515** • **info@oreilly.com**

Titles from O'Reilly

WEB

Advanced Perl Programming
Apache: The Definitive Guide,
  2nd Edition
ASP in a Nutshell
Building Your Own Web Conferences
Building Your Own Website™
CGI Programming with Perl
Designing with JavaScript
Dynamic HTML:
  The Definitive Reference
Frontier: The Definitive Guide
HTML: The Definitive Guide,
  3rd Edition
Information Architecture
  for the World Wide Web
JavaScript Pocket Reference
JavaScript: The Definitive Guide,
  3rd Edition
Learning VB Script
Photoshop for the Web
WebMaster in a Nutshell
WebMaster in a Nutshell,
  Deluxe Edition
Web Design in a Nutshell
Web Navigation:
  Designing the User Experience
Web Performance Tuning
Web Security & Commerce
Writing Apache Modules

PERL

Learning Perl, 2nd Edition
Learning Perl for Win32 Systems
Learning Perl/TK
Mastering Algorithms with Perl
Mastering Regular Expressions
Perl5 Pocket Reference, 2nd Edition
Perl Cookbook
Perl in a Nutshell
Perl Resource Kit—UNIX Edition
Perl Resource Kit—Win32 Edition
Perl/TK Pocket Reference
Programming Perl, 2nd Edition
Web Client Programming with Perl

GRAPHICS & MULTIMEDIA

Director in a Nutshell
Encyclopedia of Graphics
  File Formats, 2nd Edition
Lingo in a Nutshell
Photoshop in a Nutshell
QuarkXPress in a Nutshell

USING THE INTERNET

AOL in a Nutshell
Internet in a Nutshell
Smileys
The Whole Internet for Windows95
The Whole Internet:
  The Next Generation
The Whole Internet
  User's Guide & Catalog

JAVA SERIES

Database Programming with
  JDBC and Java
Developing Java Beans
Exploring Java, 2nd Edition
Java AWT Reference
Java Cryptography
Java Distributed Computing
Java Examples in a Nutshell
Java Foundation Classes in a Nutshell
Java Fundamental Classes Reference
Java in a Nutshell, 2nd Edition
Java in a Nutshell, Deluxe Edition
Java I/O
Java Language Reference, 2nd Edition
Java Media Players
Java Native Methods
Java Network Programming
Java Security
Java Servlet Programming
Java Swing
Java Threads
Java Virtual Machine

UNIX

Exploring Expect
GNU Emacs Pocket Reference
Learning GNU Emacs, 2nd Edition
Learning the bash Shell, 2nd Edition
Learning the Korn Shell
Learning the UNIX Operating System,
  4th Edition
Learning the vi Editor, 6th Edition
Linux in a Nutshell
Linux Multimedia Guide
Running Linux, 2nd Edition
SCO UNIX in a Nutshell
sed & awk, 2nd Edition
Tcl/Tk in a Nutshell
Tcl/Tk Pocket Reference
Tcl/Tk Tools
The UNIX CD Bookshelf
UNIX in a Nutshell, System V Edition
UNIX Power Tools, 2nd Edition
Using csh & tcsh
Using Samba
vi Editor Pocket Reference
What You Need To Know:
  When You Can't Find Your
  UNIX System Administrator
Writing GNU Emacs Extensions

SONGLINE GUIDES

NetLaw   NetResearch
NetLearning   NetSuccess
NetLessons   NetTravel

SOFTWARE

Building Your Own WebSite™
Building Your Own Web Conference
WebBoard™ 3.0
WebSite Professional™ 2.0
PolyForm™

SYSTEM ADMINISTRATION

Building Internet Firewalls
Computer Security Basics
Cracking DES
DNS and BIND, 3rd Edition
DNS on WindowsNT
Essential System Administration
Essential WindowsNT
  System Administration
Getting Connected:
  The Internet at 56K and Up
Linux Network Administrator's Guide
Managing IP Networks with
  Cisco Routers
Managing Mailing Lists
Managing NFS and NIS
Managing the WindowsNT Registry
Managing Usenet
MCSE: The Core Exams in a Nutshell
MCSE: The Electives in a Nutshell
Networking Personal Computers
  with TCP/IP
Oracle Performance Tuning,
  2nd Edition
Practical UNIX & Internet Security,
  2nd Edition
PGP: Pretty Good Privacy
Protecting Networks with SATAN
sendmail, 2nd Edition
sendmail Desktop Reference
System Performance Tuning
TCP/IP Network Administration,
  2nd Edition
termcap & terminfo
The Networking CD Bookshelf
Using & Managing PPP
Virtual Private Networks
WindowsNT Backup & Restore
WindowsNT Desktop Reference
WindowsNT Event Logging
WindowsNT in a Nutshell
WindowsNT Server 4.0 for
  Netware Administrators
WindowsNT SNMP
WindowsNT TCP/IP Administration
WindowsNT User Administration
Zero Administration for Windows

X WINDOW

Vol. 1: Xlib Programming Manual
Vol. 2: Xlib Reference Manual
Vol. 3M: X Window System
  User's Guide, Motif Edition
Vol. 4M: X Toolkit Intrinsics
  Programming Manual,
  Motif Edition
Vol. 5: X Toolkit Intrinsics
  Reference Manual
Vol. 6A: Motif Programming Manual
Vol. 6B: Motif Reference Manual
Vol. 8 : X Window System
  Administrator's Guide

PROGRAMMING

Access Database Design and
  Programming
Advanced Oracle PL/SQL
  Programming with Packages
Applying RCS and SCCS
BE Developer's Guide
BE Advanced Topics
C++: The Core Language
Checking C Programs with lint
Developing Windows Error Messages
Developing Visual Basic Add-ins
Guide to Writing DCE Applications
High Performance Computing,
  2nd Edition
Inside the Windows 95 File System
Inside the Windows 95 Registry
lex & yacc, 2nd Edition
Linux Device Drivers
Managing Projects with make
Oracle8 Design Tips
Oracle Built-in Packages
Oracle Design
Oracle PL/SQL Programming,
  2nd Edition
Oracle Scripts
Oracle Security
Palm Programming:
  The Developer's Guide
Porting UNIX Software
POSIX Programmer's Guide
POSIX.4: Programming
  for the Real World
Power Programming with RPC
Practical C Programming, 3rd Edition
Practical C++ Programming
Programming Python
Programming with curses
Programming with GNU Software
Pthreads Programming
Python Pocket Reference
Software Portability with imake,
  2nd Edition
UML in a Nutshell
Understanding DCE
UNIX Systems Programming for SVR4
VB/VBA in a Nutshell: The Languages
Win32 Multithreaded Programming
Windows NT File System Internals
Year 2000 in a Nutshell

USING WINDOWS

Excel97 Annoyances
Office97 Annoyances
Outlook Annoyances
Windows Annoyances
Windows98 Annoyances
Windows95 in a Nutshell
Windows98 in a Nutshell
Word97 Annoyances

OTHER TITLES

PalmPilot: The Ultimate Guide

TO ORDER: **800-998-9938** • **order@oreilly.com** • **http://www.oreilly.com/**
OUR PRODUCTS ARE AVAILABLE AT A BOOKSTORE OR SOFTWARE STORE NEAR YOU.
FOR INFORMATION: **800-998-9938** • **707-829-0515** • **info@oreilly.com**

International Distributors

UK, EUROPE, MIDDLE EAST AND AFRICA (EXCEPT FRANCE, GERMANY, AUSTRIA, SWITZERLAND, LUXEMBOURG, LIECHTENSTEIN, AND EASTERN EUROPE)

INQUIRIES
O'Reilly UK Limited
4 Castle Street
Farnham
Surrey, GU9 7HS
United Kingdom
Telephone: 44-1252-711776
Fax: 44-1252-734211
Email: josette@oreilly.com

ORDERS
Wiley Distribution Services Ltd.
1 Oldlands Way
Bognor Regis
West Sussex PO22 9SA
United Kingdom
Telephone: 44-1243-779777
Fax: 44-1243-820250
Email: cs-books@wiley.co.uk

FRANCE

ORDERS
GEODIF
61, Bd Saint-Germain
75240 Paris Cedex 05, France
Tel: 33-1-44-41-46-16 (French books)
Tel: 33-1-44-41-11-87 (English books)
Fax: 33-1-44-41-11-44
Email: distribution@eyrolles.com

INQUIRIES
Éditions O'Reilly
18 rue Séguier
75006 Paris, France
Tel: 33-1-40-51-52-30
Fax: 33-1-40-51-52-31
Email: france@editions-oreilly.fr

GERMANY, SWITZERLAND, AUSTRIA, EASTERN EUROPE, LUXEMBOURG, AND LIECHTENSTEIN

INQUIRIES & ORDERS
O'Reilly Verlag
Balthasarstr. 81
D-50670 Köln
Germany
Telephone: 49-221-973160-91
Fax: 49-221-973160-8
Email: anfragen@oreilly.de (inquiries)
Email: order@oreilly.de (orders)

CANADA (FRENCH LANGUAGE BOOKS)
Les Éditions Flammarion ltée
375, Avenue Laurier Ouest
Montréal (Québec) H2V 2K3
Tel: 00-1-514-277-8807
Fax: 00-1-514-278-2085
Email: info@flammarion.qc.ca

HONG KONG
City Discount Subscription Service, Ltd.
Unit D, 3rd Floor, Yan's Tower
27 Wong Chuk Hang Road
Aberdeen, Hong Kong
Tel: 852-2580-3539
Fax: 852-2580-6463
Email: citydis@ppn.com.hk

KOREA
Hanbit Media, Inc.
Sonyoung Bldg. 202
Yeksam-dong 736-36
Kangnam-ku
Seoul, Korea
Tel: 822-554-9610
Fax: 822-556-0363
Email: hant93@chollian.dacom.co.kr

PHILIPPINES
Mutual Books, Inc.
429-D Shaw Boulevard
Mandaluyong City, Metro
Manila, Philippines
Tel: 632-725-7538
Fax: 632-721-3056
Email: mbikikog@mnl.sequel.net

TAIWAN
O'Reilly Taiwan
No. 3, Lane 131
Hang-Chow South Road
Section 1, Taipei, Taiwan
Tel: 886-2-23968990
Fax: 886-2-23968916
Email: benh@oreilly.com

CHINA
O'Reilly Beijing
Room 2410
160, FuXingMenNeiDaJie
XiCheng District
Beijing, China PR 100031
Tel: 86-10-86631006
Fax: 86-10-86631007
Email: frederic@oreilly.com

INDIA
Computer Bookshop (India) Pvt. Ltd.
190 Dr. D.N. Road, Fort
Bombay 400 001 India
Tel: 91-22-207-0989
Fax: 91-22-262-3551
Email: cbsbom@giasbm01.vsnl.net.in

JAPAN
O'Reilly Japan, Inc.
Kiyoshige Building 2F
12-Bancho, Sanei-cho
Shinjuku-ku
Tokyo 160-0008 Japan
Tel: 81-3-3356-5227
Fax: 81-3-3356-5261
Email: japan@oreilly.com

ALL OTHER ASIAN COUNTRIES
O'Reilly & Associates, Inc.
101 Morris Street
Sebastopol, CA 95472 USA
Tel: 707-829-0515
Fax: 707-829-0104
Email: order@oreilly.com

AUSTRALIA
WoodsLane Pty., Ltd.
7/5 Vuko Place
Warriewood NSW 2102
Australia
Tel: 61-2-9970-5111
Fax: 61-2-9970-5002
Email: info@woodslane.com.au

NEW ZEALAND
Woodslane New Zealand, Ltd.
21 Cooks Street (P.O. Box 575)
Waganui, New Zealand
Tel: 64-6-347-6543
Fax: 64-6-345-4840
Email: info@woodslane.com.au

LATIN AMERICA
McGraw-Hill Interamericana
Editores, S.A. de C.V.
Cedro No. 512
Col. Atlampa
06450, Mexico, D.F.
Tel: 52-5-547-6777
Fax: 52-5-547-3336
Email: mcgraw-hill@infosel.net.mx

O'REILLY®

TO ORDER: **800-998-9938** • order@oreilly.com • http://www.oreilly.com/
OUR PRODUCTS ARE AVAILABLE AT A BOOKSTORE OR SOFTWARE STORE NEAR YOU.
FOR INFORMATION: **800-998-9938** • **707-829-0515** • info@oreilly.com